THEOLOGY AS CONVERSATION

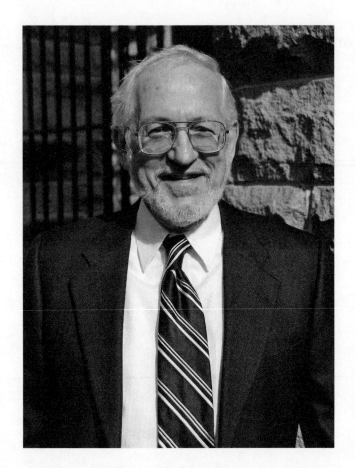

Daniel L. Migliore

Theology as Conversation

The Significance of Dialogue in Historical and Contemporary Theology

A Festschrift for
Daniel L. Migliore

Edited by

Bruce L. McCormack *&* Kimlyn J. Bender

William B. Eerdmans Publishing Company
Grand Rapids, Michigan / Cambridge, U.K.

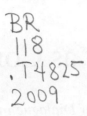

Published 2009 by
Wm. B. Eerdmans Publishing Co.
2140 Oak Industrial Drive N.E., Grand Rapids, Michigan 49505 /
P.O. Box 163, Cambridge CB3 9PU U.K.

Printed in the United States of America

15 14 13 12 11 10 09   7 6 5 4 3 2 1

Library of Congress Cataloging-in-Publication Data

Theology as conversation: the significance of dialogue in historical
and contemporary theology: a festschrift for Daniel L. Migliore /
edited by Bruce L. McCormack & Kimlyn J. Bender.

    p.   cm.

    Includes bibliographical references.

    ISBN 978-0-8028-4859-8 (cloth: alk. paper)

    1. Theology — Methodology. 2. Dialogue — Religious aspects —
Christianity. 3. Barth, Karl, 1886-1968. I. Migliore, Daniel L., 1935-
II. McCormack, Bruce L. III. Bender, Kimlyn J., 1969-

BR118.T4825 2009
230 — dc22

                       2009004110

www.eerdmans.com

Contents

FOREWORD   ix
  Kimlyn J. Bender and Bruce L. McCormack

ENGAGEMENTS WITH THE THEOLOGY OF KARL BARTH

Christ and Canon, Theology and History:
The Barth-Harnack Dialogue Revisited   3
  Kimlyn J. Bender

Argue Theologically with One Another:
Karl Barth's Argument with Emil Brunner   30
  Gerhard Sauter

God *Is* His Decision: The Jüngel-Gollwitzer "Debate" Revisited   48
  Bruce L. McCormack

The Time That Remains: Hans-Georg Geyer in the Intellectual
Debate about a Central Question in the Twentieth Century   67
  Gerrit Neven

Contents

Echoes of Barth in Jon Sobrino's Critique of Natural Theology:
A Dialogue in the Context of Post-Colonial Theology   82

  Matthew D. Lundberg

"Beautiful Playing": Moltmann, Barth, and the
Work of the Christian   101

  Cynthia L. Rigby

CONVERSATIONS WITH TRADITIONAL THEOLOGICAL TOPICS

"Inspired Heterodoxy"? The Freedom of Theological Inquiry
and the Well-Being of the Church   119

  Dawn DeVries

What Is the Meaning of Revelation? H. Richard Niebuhr,
Modernism, and Nicene Christianity   142

  George Hunsinger

Interpretatio in bonem partem: Jürgen Moltmann
on the Immanent Trinity   159

  Thomas R. Thompson

God's Body or Beloved Other? Sallie McFague and
Jürgen Moltmann on God and Creation   179

  David J. Bryant

In Search of a Non-Violent Atonement Theory:
Are Abelard and Girard a Help, or a Problem?   194

  Gregory Anderson Love

The People of God in Christian Theology   215

  Katherine Sonderegger

Will All Be Saved, or Only a Few?
A Dialogue between Faith and Grace   235

  Jürgen Moltmann

Wholly Called, Holy Callings: Questioning the
Secular/Sacred Distinctions in Vocation   241
  Stephen L. Stell

Theological Identity: A Dance of Loyalty   259
  Kathleen D. Billman

Luther's Ghost – Ein gluehender Backofen voller Liebe   273
  George Newlands

THEOLOGY IN DIALOGUE WITH SOCIETY AND CULTURE

Which Forms and Themes Should Christian Theology
Uphold in Dialogue with Secular Culture?   297
  Michael Welker

Faith in the Public Square   313
  David Fergusson

Reading for Preaching: The Preacher in Conversation
with Storytellers, Biographers, Poets, and Journalists   327
  Cornelius Plantinga Jr.

Charles Hodge as a Public Theologian   341
  John Stewart

CONTRIBUTORS   361

Foreword

When Daniel L. Migliore retires in May 2009, he will be bringing the curtain down on a forty-seven-year teaching ministry at Princeton Theological Seminary. An era is coming to an end in the life of the Seminary, and it is important that we mark the occasion in a festive way.

Dan Migliore first came to Princeton Seminary in 1956 on a Danforth Graduate Fellowship for study in the Master of Divinity program. Three years later, he graduated first in his class and moved across the street to begin his Ph.D. work in the Graduate School of Princeton University. His original intention upon his arrival at the University was to write a dissertation on the humanity of God in Karl Barth's theology, under the direction of Professor Arthur McGill. However, the original plan underwent an abrupt change in 1962 when President James McCord asked the young Migliore whether he might not be willing to teach New Testament theology at the Seminary. And so it came about that Dan's first post was that of an instructor in New Testament. In order better to prepare himself for this teaching responsibility, he changed his dissertation topic to "The Problem of the Historical Jesus in Karl Barth's Theology." He graduated in 1964 and was ordained to the ministry of word and sacrament in the Presbyterian Church (USA) in that same year.

Dan's first three years on the Faculty at Princeton were spent teaching exegetical courses on the Gospels of Mark and Matthew, Current Issues in New Testament Interpretation, The History of the Search for the Historical Jesus, and Law and Gospel in the Pauline Epistles. It was at that point, however, that President McCord came to the realization that Dan's heart really belonged to the systematic enterprise. And so he arranged for Dan to spend a post-doctoral year in Germany. Dan had already read Moltmann's *Theology of Hope* (1964) and been deeply impacted by it. The temptation was great to go to Bonn, where Moltmann was teaching at that time. In the end, however, he decided to go to Tübingen. There he was able to hear not only Gerhard Ebeling and Ernst Käsemann but also Hans Küng (in the Catholic faculty). Vatican II was then in session, and Küng made frequent trips to Rome to gather intelligence on what was happening, which he then duly reported to his graduate seminar. Dan also travelled a good deal and was able to hear and meet Moltmann in Bonn, Wolfhart Pannenberg in Mainz, and Eberhard Jüngel (whose "paraphrase" of Barth's doctrine of the Trinity Dan read with great excitement) during Jüngel's visit to Tübingen that year.

In 1966, Dan returned to Princeton Seminary to begin work as an Assistant Professor of Systematic Theology. Though his interests have ranged widely over the years that followed, the center of gravity in his teaching program has always lain in the theology of Karl Barth. Not only did he teach a regular survey course on Barth's theology for Masters of Divinity students; he also devoted his Ph.D. seminar to various volumes of the *Church Dogmatics*. One of the striking features of Dan's seminar lay in the fact that it was never the same. He wanted always to demonstrate Barth's ongoing relevance by bringing the great man's theology into conversation with current movements and figures. And bringing Barth into conversation with others always meant adopting an appropriately critical attitude. It lay far from Dan to promote the kind of "sterile Barthian scholasticism" of which Eberhard Jüngel once rightly complained — one which sought to erect a "Great Wall of China" around the *Church Dogmatics* in order to dwell securely within those walls for the remainder of one's life.[1] To this end, Dan always included a large number of critics of Barth in his required reading list, and he often brought in guests — some of whom were greatly appreciative of Barth, some more critical. Among them were Jürgen Moltmann, Alasdair Heron, Helmut Gollwitzer, Gustavo Gutiérrez, Gerhard Sauter, Michael Welker, T. F. Torrance, and Robert Jenson. In this way, Dan's seminars were greatly enriched by conversations with some of the leading theologians of the day.

But in addition to dogmatic theology, there is a second *focus* to the ellipse that has been and is Dan's theological existence, viz. politics and political the-

---

1. Eberhard Jüngel, "Unterbrechung des Weltlebens: Eberhard Jüngel über 'Gottes Sein ist im Werden' (1965)," in *Werkbesichtigung Geisteswissenschaften: Fünfundzwanzig Bücher von ihren Autoren gelesen,* ed. Henning Ritter (Frankfurt am Main: Insel Verlag, 1990), 135.

ology. Dan's theology and his approach to teaching were greatly influenced by
the events of the 1960s. In 1966, he served as a delegate to the Christian Peace
Conference (Christian-Marxist Dialogue) that met in Basel, Switzerland. He
was very active during this period in "Clergy and Laity Opposed to the War in
Vietnam." The political engagement which he believed to be a necessary element in any serious theological reflection found initial expression in his 1980
book, *Called to Freedom*.[2] His most recent work, *The Power of God and the
Gods of Power* also gives expression to this basic conviction.[3] The impact of
these two foci of Dan's theological existence — dogmatics and politics — also
makes itself felt in what is arguably the finest introductory dogmatics available to beginning English-language students of theology today, his *Faith
Seeking Understanding* (first printed in 1991 with a second revised edition appearing in 2004).[4] What makes this work so remarkable is Dan's ability to
combine attention to the core commitments in traditional (Reformed) dogmatic theology with an appreciative listening to other voices — to feminist,
womanist, black, Latino/Latina theologies — and to bring them into a wholly
positive synthesis which honors the pain and suffering of those who have
raised the necessary protest against harmful uses of Christian doctrines. The
same level of pastoral sensitivity is also to be found in a work co-authored
with Kathleen Billman (one of our contributors) in 1999: *Rachel's Cry: Prayer
of Lament and Rebirth of Hope*, a work which proved a godsend to many
working pastors in the aftermath of 9/11.[5]

Dan Migliore is a respected scholar who has just finished a year as President of the American Theological Society. He is a member of the Princeton-
Kampen Barth Consultation, which, since 1998, has met bi-annually in either
Princeton or the Netherlands, and a member of the Center of Theological Inquiry (in Princeton). But he is also a master teacher. He is one of those rare
individuals possessed of the ability to present a survey of the thinking of a
great many theologians centered upon perennial problems or themes of current interest — with no loss of substance. He is a devoted churchman who
has served both on the presbyterial and the national levels — most recently as

2. Daniel L. Migliore, *Called to Freedom: Liberation Theology and the Future of Christian Doctrine* (Philadelphia: Westminster Press, 1980).
3. Daniel L. Migliore, *The Power of God and the Gods of Power* (Louisville: Westminster/John Knox Press, 2008).
4. Daniel L. Migliore, *Faith Seeking Understanding: An Introduction to Christian Theology*, 2nd ed. (Grand Rapids, MI: Wm. B. Eerdmans Publishing Co., 2004).
5. Kathleen D. Billman and Daniel L. Migliore, *Rachel's Cry: Prayer of Lament and Rebirth of Hope* (Cleveland: United Church Press, 1999).

a member of the General Assembly Task Force on the Doctrine of the Trinity. He is a man of great personal integrity, always a bridge-builder and reconciler among colleagues, an elder statesman whose wisdom is valued by all. Finally, he (with his wife Margaret) are people of hospitality. Dr. Bender and his wife fondly remember the gracious invitation by Dan and Margaret to a celebratory dinner at a restaurant the evening of Dr. Bender's dissertation defense.

What better theme for a collection of essays published in honor of this man and his ministry than the theme of "Theology as Conversation"! Our initial appeal for contributions was sent out to a carefully chosen group of twenty scholars. Several were scholars with a very strong international reputation, giving the reader a sense of the breadth of Dan's friendships and impact. Several were members of the Princeton-Kampen Barth Consultation. And fully eight were former doctoral students who now serve variously as a president of a seminary and as seminary, university, and college professors). Contributors were told they could write a historically inclined essay on a dialogue or debate which had actually taken place — one which had helped to shape the theological reflection of the time in which it occurred. Or they could create a "dialogue" (of the kind Dan loved to imagine) between two or more figures which had *not* taken place but which the contributors wished had. Or they could take a more thematic approach, creating a dialogue between religions or between theology and a pressing social or political issue or movement. What we were looking for is the kind of creative/synthetic thinking that breaks up a long-standing impasse and contributes to moving a stalled conversation forward or that creates conditions needed for new conversations to get off the ground. The results are now before you as readers. Not one person we asked declined the invitation they received! Everyone we wrote was eager to participate.

We would like above all to thank Mr. Bill Eerdmans for his willingness to publish this collective testimony to the influence of his old friend. A special word of thanks goes to Dr. Keith Johnson, who devoted hours to copy-editing contributions from scholars from several nations. Most of all, we want to thank Dan himself — and his wife, Margaret! — for their selfless service to Princeton Theological Seminary, to the Presbyterian Church (USA), and to the many churches scattered throughout the world whose existence has been impacted by these remarkable people. We will miss you, but you will most certainly not be forgotten.

KIMLYN J. BENDER
BRUCE L. MCCORMACK

ENGAGEMENTS WITH THE
THEOLOGY OF KARL BARTH

Christ and Canon, Theology and History: The Barth-Harnack Dialogue Revisited

Kimlyn J. Bender

We live in an age in which the boundaries of the canon are questioned within the academy and the reverberation of these questions are felt within the church.[1] In order to comment on these developments, I wish to revisit the exchange between Adolf von Harnack and Karl Barth of the early twentieth century that is most often discussed regarding matters of exegesis and hermeneutics, but which I will examine with an eye toward the question of the biblical canon.[2] This conversation sheds light not only upon issues regarding the content and interpretation of Scripture, but also upon its form and parameters in historical and theological conversation.

The Harnack-Barth Correspondence of 1923

During Barth's time, there was no historian with the credentials or the achievements of Adolf von Harnack. Harnack's erudition was and remains

---

1. For two recent examples of such questioning, see Bart D. Ehrman, *Lost Christianities: The Battles for Scripture and the Faiths We Never Knew* (Oxford/New York: Oxford University Press, 2003); and Robert W. Funk, "The Once and Future New Testament," in *The Canon Debate*, ed. Lee Martin McDonald and James A. Sanders (Peabody: Hendrickson Publishers, 2002), 541-557.

2. For Barth's early view of the canon, see Kimlyn J. Bender, "Scripture and Canon in Karl Barth's Early Theology," in *From Biblical Criticism to Biblical Faith: Essays in Honor of Lee Martin McDonald,* ed. William H. Brackney and Craig A. Evans (Macon: Mercer University Press, 2007), 164-198. The present essay draws upon this article.

famous, and in spite of critical evaluations of his work that have appeared with the passing of time, he continues to stand as a giant of historical studies.[3] In a similar manner, no theologian of the twentieth century was as influential as Karl Barth in restoring Scripture to the center of the theological enterprise.[4] In 1923, following tensions brought about by Barth's criticisms and renunciation of the liberal inheritance he had received from his former teachers such as Harnack, what had been for the most part private tension became public debate as Harnack critically questioned the dialectical movement, and thus Barth, in the pages of the *Christlichen Welt,* and Barth returned the favor in what became a spirited and extended exchange.[5]

This published conversation ranged widely in the number of issues addressed, but no small part of the debate concerned the matter of Scripture and how it should be approached and understood. Harnack's position on Scripture was shaped by and influential in shaping the liberal school of historical-critical exegesis, and in the opening salvo Harnack's primary criticism of the dialectical theologians is that they have abandoned scientific and historical exegesis for a naïve biblicism. As he states in his first of fifteen questions:

> Is the religion of the Bible, or are the revelations in the Bible, something so unequivocal that in reference to faith, worship, and life it is permissible to speak simply of the "Bible"? But if they are not, can the determining of the content of the gospel be left entirely to subjective "experience," or to the "experiences" of the individual, or are not historical knowledge and critical reflection necessary here?[6]

3. For an introduction into Harnack's life and work, see *Adolf von Harnack: Liberal Theology at Its Height,* ed. Martin Rumscheidt (London: Collins, 1989), as well as G. Wayne Glick, *The Reality of Christianity: A Study of Adolf von Harnack as Historian and Theologian* (New York: Harper & Row, 1967).

4. Richard Burnett, *Karl Barth's Theological Exegesis: The Hermeneutical Principles of the* Römerbrief *Period* (Grand Rapids/Cambridge: Eerdmans, 2004), 9; see also 23.

5. This exchange between Barth and Harnack may be found in: Karl Barth, *Offene Briefe 1909-1935,* ed. Diether Koch (Zürich: Theologischer Verlag Zürich, 2001), 55-88. An English translation (ET) is found in: *The Beginnings of Dialectical Theology,* ed. James M. Robinson, trans. Louis De Grazia and Keith R. Crim (Richmond: John Knox Press, 1968), 165-187. For perceptive commentary on this debate, see H. Martin Rumscheidt, *Revelation and Theology: An Analysis of the Barth-Harnack Correspondence of 1925* (Cambridge: Cambridge University Press, 1972); also, George Hunsinger, *Disruptive Grace: Studies in the Theology of Karl Barth* (Grand Rapids: Eerdmans, 2000), 319-337.

6. Karl Barth, *Offene Briefe 1909-1935,* 62; ET 166.

For Harnack, the content of the Bible is only rightly determined and understood by means of "historical knowledge and critical reflection."[7] The need for such historical knowledge and critical reflection *(geschichtliches Wissen und kritisches Nachdenken)* is hammered home by Harnack over and again in his questions. In the dialectical school, Harnack believed that he was witnessing a flight from history and science into the dangers of fanaticism and a resurgent gnosticism. Such a flight threatened the heart of Christian faith itself. If Christ stands at the "center of the gospel," Harnack asked, then "how can the basis for a reliable and common knowledge of this person be gained other than through critical historical study, lest we exchange the real Christ for one we have imagined? But how else can this study be accomplished than by scientific theology?"[8]

Barth responded to Harnack's fifteen questions one by one, and his answers demonstrate how far he had moved during his Safenwil pastorate from the position of his former teacher and the liberal tradition.[9] Upon his joyful discovery of "a new world within the Bible" during that period, Barth had turned to a redoubled study of Scripture and an attempt to understand its character.[10] Barth's new outlook is readily evident in his answers to Harnack's questions.

In response to Harnack's charge that the diversity of the Bible makes

7. Ibid., 60; ET 165.

8. Ibid., 62; ET 166.

9. The story of Barth's break with liberalism has been often told — see Eberhard Busch, *Karl Barth: His Life from Letters and Autobiographical Texts,* trans. John Bowden (Grand Rapids: Eerdmans, 1994), chapters two and three; Eberhard Busch, *The Great Passion: An Introduction to Karl Barth's Theology,* trans. Geoffrey W. Bromiley (Grand Rapids/Cambridge: Eerdmans, 2004), section one, chapters one and two; Gary Dorrien, *The Barthian Revolt in Modern Theology* (Louisville: Westminster John Knox, 2000), chapters one and two; Eberhard Jüngel, *Karl Barth: A Theological Legacy,* trans. Garrett E. Paul (Westminster, 1986), chapters one and two; Bruce L. McCormack, *Karl Barth's Critically Realistic Dialectical Theology: Its Genesis and Development 1909-1936* (Oxford: Clarendon Press, 1995), chapters one and two; and John Webster, *Karl Barth* (London/New York: Continuum, 2000), chapters one and two.

10. See Barth, "Die neue Welt in der Bibel," in *Das Wort Gottes und die Theologie* (München: Chr. Kaiser Verlag, 1929), 18-32. English translation [ET]: "The Strange New World Within the Bible," in *The Word of God and the Word of Man,* trans. Douglas Horton (Gloucester: Peter Smith, 1978), 28-50. Barth would extend these themes in his 1920 essay "Biblische Fragen, Einsichten und Ausblicke" in *Das Wort Gottes und die Theologie,* 70-98; ET: "Biblical Questions, Insights, and Vistas," in *The Word of God and the Word of Man,* 51-96. Burnett writes: "To read the Bible in a way that is 'sachlicher, inhaltlicher, wesentlicher,' that is, 'more in accordance with its subject matter, content, and substance,' represents Karl Barth's most important hermeneutical principle" (*Karl Barth's Theological Exegesis,* 65; cf. 95).

"historical knowledge and critical reflection" necessary to understand its content in the midst of its heterogeneity, Barth unflinchingly responded by saying: "Beyond the 'religion' and the 'revelations' of the Bible, the *one revelation of God* should be taken into consideration as the theme of theology."[11] For Barth, the unity of the Bible's content is not a message distilled by means of critical science, and is certainly not the reductionistic moralism that Harnack espoused, but is instead grounded in the *Deus dixit,* so that theology is scientific insofar as it remembers that "its object had *previously* been the subject, and must become this again and again."[12] What becomes clear in Barth's responses to Harnack is Barth's insistence that it is not historical knowledge and critical reflection, but the power of the Spirit and the corresponding faith it establishes, that provides the true understanding of the content of Scripture, which is God's own Self-revelation in Christ.[13] Historical criticism may play a part in preparation for the task of theology, which is to communicate the "word of Christ," but it is nonetheless a divine act rather than a human achievement that is the basis for a proper understanding of Scripture. The center of Scripture, therefore, is none other than the One to whom it testifies, and this One can only properly be known for who he truly is by an acknowledgement of his Lordship, which is a true recognition of the unique objectivity of revelation that supersedes claims of a scientific method and its own abstract objectivity. As Barth writes:

> The reliability and common nature of the knowledge of the person of Jesus Christ as the midpoint of the gospel can be no other than that of a *faith* awakened by God. Critical historical study signifies the deserved and necessary end of the "bases" of this knowledge, which are not really bases, because they were not laid by God himself. He who still does not know (and we all still do not know it) that we no longer know Christ according to the flesh may let himself be told this by critical biblical science; the more radically he is terrified the better it is for him and for the subject matter. And this may well be the service which "historical knowledge" can render to the real task of theology.[14]

Harnack was not appeased by these answers. In an open letter to Barth that was published following their appearance in print, Harnack stated that

11. Barth, *Offene Briefe 1909-1935,* 62; ET 167.
12. Ibid., 62; ET 167.
13. Ibid., 63; ET 167.
14. Ibid., 66-67; ET 170.

he found Barth's position flummoxing. Where Barth saw scientific theology as a recent development, Harnack asserted that it was the only means forward for "mastering an object through knowledge." By sacrificing this means, Barth was guilty of transforming the professor's chair into a pulpit and confusing the scientific task of theology with that of spiritual edification.[15] Furthermore, reiterating his initial criticisms once again, Harnack maintained that Barth was losing his grip on history for an ahistorical faith that would in the end prove to be nothing more than pure subjectivism. In response to Barth's prior statement that we do not know Christ "according to the flesh," Harnack trenchantly asked: "Thus we no longer know the Jesus Christ of the Gospels, the historical Jesus Christ? How am I to understand that? On the basis of the theory of the exclusive inner word? Or on the basis of one of the many other subjective theories?"[16] The only way forward if true knowledge is the goal is that of historical science; the alternative to science and reason is not faith but occultism.[17] Barth's disdain for historical science would in the end be evidenced in an absolute division of the Christ of faith from the Jesus of history. Without historical science to place parameters upon our claims of this Christ and give true knowledge of the historical person of Jesus, such a faith as that of Barth's would at best give rise to unchecked speculative fantasy and at worst to a theological dictatorship that "seeks to torture the consciences of others with its own experience."[18] For Barth's theology to gain ascendancy over that of historical science would lead to nothing less, Harnack concluded, than the handing over of the gospel to revival preachers who are unhindered in their idiosyncratic understandings of the Bible.

Barth responded to this open letter with one of his own. Though initially somewhat more conciliatory in tone in this letter than in his prior answers, Barth's response displayed an unwillingness to back down in the face of Harnack's charges. Three themes of relevance for our investigation emerge: the identity of the Jesus of history with the Christ of faith; the unity of Scripture in light of this identity; and the need for an ordered unity between what Barth deems the wider task of theology (with regard to discerning the identity of Christ and the unity of Scripture) and historical science itself. In Barth's response the question of unity becomes a prominent theme.

15. Ibid., 68; ET 171.
16. Ibid., 69, ET 172.
17. Ibid., 71; ET 174.
18. Ibid., 71-72; ET 174.

Where Harnack was most inclined to draw simple distinctions, such as that between the task of preaching and that of historical science, and to note simple unities, such as that between revelation and history, as well as that between the accomplishments of religion and culture, Barth's dialectical position intimated complex unities of ordered relations between permanently distinct realities even while at other times falling into simple disjunctions that his later theology eventually would move beyond. The unity of revelation and history in the person of Jesus Christ without their confusion; the unity of Scripture among its undeniable diversity of voices, such that divine Word and human word are united yet distinct; and the unity and ordered relation of theology and historical science in which the latter is taken up into the service of the former were all important, if inadequately developed, themes in Barth's response.

First, Barth turned the accusation that he had bifurcated the Jesus of history and the Christ of faith back against Harnack himself. Barth rejected Harnack's distinction between the confessed Christ of the church and the historical person of Jesus as discerned by the professional academy, a distinction that played no small part in Harnack's entire historiography and sharp inviolable division between professor's lectern and pastor's pulpit. For Barth, the Jesus of Nazareth known by historical science fails to display Jesus' true identity if abstracted from the confession of him as the Risen Lord:

> The historical reality of Christ (as reality of revelation, or of the "central point of the gospel") is not the "historical Jesus," whom an all too zealous historical research had wanted to lay hold of while bypassing those warnings erected in the sources themselves (only to come upon a banality which is now and will continue to be vainly proclaimed as something precious), of course not, as you said, an "imagined" Christ, but rather the *Risen One,* or let us say — holding back because of our little faith — the Christ witnessed to as risen. *That* is the "evangelical, the historic Jesus Christ," and otherwise, that is, apart from this testimony to him, apart from the revelation which must here be believed, "we know him no longer."[19]

The recognition of this Jesus as the Risen Lord, which is his true identity, cannot be gleaned by historical study alone but is a gift of the Spirit and a confession of faith. This is the content of the scriptural witness: "The witness relates that the word became *flesh,* God himself became human, histori-

19. Ibid., 79; ET 180.

cal *reality,* and that this occurred in the *person of Jesus Christ.*"[20] Jesus of Nazareth *is* the Christ and Lord of history, and therefore any historical reconstruction of his earthly life that ignores his Lordship can at best be an abstraction. What Barth insisted upon was that there was no "Jesus of history" that was more true, more real, than the risen Jesus Christ the Gospels attested, and that there was no accessibility to this Jesus behind the text but only within and through it.

This reality of God's revelation in Christ is the true identity of Jesus' historical existence, such that the Jesus of history and the Christ of faith cannot be divided or played against one another. This unity itself is then mirrored in the fact that this revelation of God in Christ is the center of Scripture, and the unity of this God with his revelation entails that Scripture itself possesses a unity in the midst of its diversity. Because the God who speaks through Scripture is one and is to be identified with the One who has been revealed in Jesus, Barth maintains that the entire Scripture (as Old and New Testaments) is a unified whole, for Scripture is a witness to this one God. The writings of Scripture are not the products of detached observers of various religious phenomena, nor of subjective recorders of their own idiosyncratic religious experiences, but of diverse witnesses to an objective revelation, and thus are better understood as testimonies to a single revelation to be accepted by faith than as religious sources understood by means of historical science. It is the central reality of God's revelation in Christ that lies at the heart of Scripture and provides its unity, even while Barth himself at this point could remain quite ambivalent about the parameters of the canon itself.[21]

Therefore, Scripture cannot be rightly understood if considered solely as a repository of various historical, cultural, and literary materials from antiquity (while it is certainly that, too), but is only truly understood if seen as a united witness to a single Lord. Scripture possesses a unity that transcends its real and undeniable diversity not because we can discern within it or synthesize from it an overarching idea or concept, such as Harnack's own "simple gospel," but because of the unity and singularity of the one Lord to whom it witnesses and who speaks through it. It is the unity of this Lord for Barth that grounds the unity of Scripture and makes it a unified witness.[22]

20. Ibid., 78; ET 179.
21. As Barth states: "This witness, which can never be analyzed enough by historical criticism, but which will not for that reason cease being *this* witness, is what I term in its totality the 'Scripture.' In this the question of the delimitation of 'Scripture' in reference to other writings seems to me to be a secondary one . . ." (ibid., 77; ET 178-179).
22. Burnett, *Karl Barth's Theological Exegesis,* 77.

What is clear in Barth's debate with Harnack is Harnack's uneasiness with Barth's readiness to speak of the Bible as a *unity*, and Barth's own undaunted insistence that this unity is at the heart of Scripture's identity, and his own uneasiness in turn with Harnack's historicism, positivism, reductionism, and scientism that prioritized method over subject matter *(Sache)* and content *(Inhalt)* and whittled Scripture down to a central core.[23]

Finally, the unity of God's revelation in Christ, witnessed in the unity of Scripture's content, entails that the reality and recognition of this revelation and this unity are the requirements for, rather than the conclusions reached from, a valid interpretation of Scripture, such that the content, or object, of Scripture must shape the method by which we approach it. With regard to Harnack's overarching theme of the need for historical science as the proper method for determining knowledge of the gospel of Jesus, Barth reasserted that for modern theological schools "the concept of an authoritative *object* [*Gegenstand*] has become foreign and monstrous because of the sheer authoritativeness of *method* [*Methode*]."[24] If the true content of Scripture is nothing less than God's own Self-giving, then this can never be grasped from our side as an accomplishment, but only given as a gift by God's own Spirit, for "it cannot be proper to reverse this order and make out of 'thus saith the Lord' a 'thus heareth man.'"[25] A theology which took such divine disclosure as its starting point, a theology which Barth remarked was that of Luther and Calvin, was to be embraced not in slavish imitation of revered Reformers, nor as a mindless repristination of theology past that ignored the recent accomplishments of historical science, but as a way of rightfully acknowledging the proper objectivity of theology itself.

Therefore, the unity of revelation of the one Lord of Scripture, and the unity of Scripture itself, entails that there be a unity, albeit an ordered one, between theology and historical science. Against a priority given to historical science, Barth states that historical criticism itself must be taken up into the larger aim of theology, which is nothing less than putting forth the reality of God's revelation in thought and speech for understanding in the present. As Barth wrote to Harnack, "it is really not specifically a question of removing from theological study the critical historical method of biblical and historical research developed in recent centuries, but of a meaningful way of incorporating it into theology and of sharpening the questions which result from

23. Barth, *Offene Briefe 1909-1935*, 59-60, 62-63; 77; ET 165, 167; 178-179.
24. Ibid., 74; ET 176.
25. Ibid., 76; ET 178.

it."²⁶ For Barth, a correct understanding of Scripture can therefore only be a theological one that incorporates the historical into itself.²⁷

A proper examination of Scripture must therefore squarely face the question of the *truth* of the message of Scripture and cannot simply rest content with objective description of past events, thought forms, and literary conventions. Indeed, long before it became *avant-garde* to decry the myth of pure objectivity, Barth called into question the very notion of impartiality in exegesis devoid of all presuppositions.²⁸ For Barth, Harnack's historicism is therefore not so much objective as self-deceived. To understand Scripture rightly entails that one read it as a participant in its truth, or at least as one open to such participation, and not with a cool and passive affectation and detachment.²⁹ This different approach to the task of reading Scripture lies at the heart of Barth's disagreement with Harnack, for whom such participation, when incorporated within the historical task, entailed a loss of scientific objectivity and responsibility. Barth's commitment to a different kind of objectivity and responsibility is also, in large part, what lies behind his insistence in the preface to the third edition of the Romans commentary that we must think not so much *about* Paul but *after* and *with* Paul towards the subject matter with which he himself was concerned, what Barth so famously coined as *Nachdenken* and *Mitdenken*. Barth elaborated this point in debate with Harnack:

> What I must defend myself against is not historical criticism, but rather the matter-of-course way in which one, still today, *empties* theology's task: Instead of that which our predecessors called *"the Word"* (the correlation of "Scripture" and "Spirit") one has placed this and that which have been dug up by historical criticism *beyond* the "Scripture" and *apart from* the "Spirit," which one calls the "simple gospel [*schlichte Evangelium*]," a gospel that can be called "word of God" only as a figure of speech, because it is in fact at best a human impression thereof.³⁰

---

26. Ibid., 74-75; ET 176.
27. "Strictly speaking, for Barth, there was no such thing as a genuine theological understanding of the Bible apart from a historical understanding, just as apart from a theological understanding there was nothing but the most trivial, banal sort of historical understanding of the Bible" (Burnett, *Karl Barth's Theological Exegesis*, 85).
28. See Barth, *The Göttingen Dogmatics: Instruction in the Christian Religion*, Vol. 1, ed. Hannelotte Reiffen, trans. Geoffrey W. Bromiley (Grand Rapids: Eerdmans, 1991), 257-260. Hereafter cited as *GD*.
29. Barth, *GD*, 254-255; see also Burnett, *Karl Barth's Theological Exegesis*, 95-100, 111, 125-127, 192-197.
30. Barth, *Offene Briefe 1909-1935*, 75; ET 177.

Therefore, if Scripture's content can only be truly understood theologically, and if this content is a unity, then there can be no dichotomy of method between "scientific" and "edifying" exegesis. Barth insisted that the object of investigation must determine the method, rather than a single scientific method superimposed upon the object, and he rejected the common view of his day regarding the uniformity of a single scientific method (so fundamental to Harnack) with its attendant reductionism, historicism, and scientism.[31] In response to Harnack's charge that he had replaced the professor's lectern with a pulpit, Barth maintains that there cannot be different truths for each:

> The *theme* of the theologian . . . which he *investigates* in history, and which he must strive to express in a manner relevant to his own situation, cannot be a second truth distinct from the truth which he is obliged to present as a preacher. . . . I cannot see . . . how the subsequent abstract separation of "scholarly" [*gelehrten*] and "edifying" [*erbaulichen*] thinking and speaking can be based on the nature of the subject matter [*Sache*].[32]

Consequently, while there are real and practical differences between the *purposes* of critical theology and preaching, there is no difference in terms of their subject matter. Indeed, to posit two different subjects for each would

31. Hunsinger, *Disruptive Grace*, 331-333. Burnett states that scientific objectivity "had come to mean something different to Barth than it did to the majority of his contemporaries. They understood scientific objectivity in terms of impartiality and unprejudiced observation; he understood it in terms of being faithful to the object of investigation. To be scientific to him meant fidelity to the object" (*Karl Barth's Theological Exegesis*, 97). It should also be noted that contrary to much opinion past and present, Barth was not a well-intentioned but naïve exegete who failed to understand the complexities of critical interpretation, but one who had in fact been thoroughly introduced and inducted into the historical-critical method of his day through his studies in Berne and later in Berlin. He had himself studied under Adolf Jülicher and Johannes Weiss at Marburg. Barth produced various studies examining both biblical and historical topics in light of the critical method of his day during his student years, including a paper in 1905 examining the Capernaum centurion pericopes of Matthew 8:5-13 and Luke 7:1-10, and one on the Lord's Prayer in the Gospels in 1906 — see Karl Barth, *Vorträge und kleinere Arbeiten 1905-1909* (Zürich: Theologischer Verlag Zürich, 1992), 46-60 and 126-147. Most important for this early period in Barth's studies are the extensive paper Barth wrote in Berlin for Harnack himself on Acts, "Die Missionsthätigkeit des Paulus nach der Darstellung der Apostelgeschichte" (1907), and his Tübingen qualifying dissertation, "Die Vorstellung vom Descensus Christi ad inferos in der kirchlichen Literatur bis Origines" (1908) — see ibid., 148-243 and 244-312.

32. Barth, *Offene Briefe 1909-1935*, 75-76; ET 177.

imply that the "Jesus of history" and the "Christ of faith" were in fact two different realities.[33] Barth single-mindedly refused any such dichotomy and bifurcation. As noted earlier, because Jesus of Nazareth is Christ the Lord, there can be no absolute separation of historical and theological claims or methods. Jesus Christ must be known for who he is — any purely "historical" reconstruction that fails to see him in this light can only be an abstraction that fails to address his true identity.[34]

Historical science thus has a two-fold purpose from Barth's perspective. Negatively, it witnesses to its own inability to move beyond historical reconstruction to confession, and thus betrays its own limitations. For Barth, this negative function contributes by witnessing to the reality that a true understanding of the gospel can only come as a gift from the side of God's activity rather than human scholarly effort.[35] What is less clear in this exchange, however, is what exactly Barth takes to be historical science's positive and preparatory function, which he can allude to and affirms but he never fully explains.[36]

The public debate in the *Christlichen Welt* came to an end with Harnack's brief postscript in response to Barth's lengthy letter, in which he once again reiterated the sharp division between historical critical science and that of theology's witnessing to revelation. The boundaries between these were irrevocable for Harnack.[37] Concluding the correspondence, he again stressed the diversity of the biblical texts and the irreducibly human character of them, such that to speak of an objective and united "revelation" is futile when accompanied by a conviction that the "influence of human speech, hearing, perception, and understanding can be eliminated."[38] Harnack's response to Barth's adamancy regarding the unity of Scripture was a reitera-

---

33. Ibid., 78-80; ET 179-180.

34. T. F. Torrance rightly states that while Barth has no interest in a construct and adheres to the historical Jesus, he holds that "the attempt to find a 'Jesus' apart from his Gospel, a Jesus apart from the concrete act of God in him, a 'Jesus' that can be constructed out of the historical records by means of criteria derived from secular sources alone, is a failure to understand the New Testament. The real, objective, historical Jesus is the Jesus Christ who cannot be separated from his self-revelation or from his Gospel, for that Revelation and Gospel are part of the one historical Jesus Christ who is to be understood out of himself, and in accordance with his own being and nature" (Torrance, *Karl Barth: An Introduction to His Early Theology* [London: SCM Press, 1962], 208). See also Barth, *GD*, 91.

35. Barth, *Offene Briefe 1909-1935*, 80; ET 180.

36. For a discussion of Barth's later articulation of the positive role of historical criticism, see Burnett, *Karl Barth's Theological Exegesis*, 230-240.

37. Barth, *Offene Briefe 1909-1935*, 87-88; ET 186.

38. Ibid., 88; ET 186.

tion of the priority of Scripture's diversity only partly overcome by means of critical science. As we shall see, when such diversity was intractable, Harnack's solution was to abridge the canon itself and dissolve the very notion of canonical authority.[39]

The Question of the Canon

In the present essay, it is impossible to evaluate and adjudicate between the rival viewpoints of Harnack and Barth with the attention their positions deserve, nor is it my intention here to attempt as much. I more modestly want to address the question of Scripture and canon in light of three themes that have emerged above, namely, the center of Scripture as canon, the unity of Scripture as canon, and the relationship of theological and historical understandings of the canon with an eye toward how such matters might inform the church's response to challenges to its canon in the present.[40] I will take these themes in reverse order.

The conversation between Harnack and Barth is indeed a particular instance of a more general one affecting church and academy regarding the relationship of a theological and historical understanding of the biblical canon and its bearing upon our understanding of revelation, faith, and the person of Jesus Christ. In light of the positions of Barth and Harnack outlined above, I want to propose a number of theses, not as definitive or exhaustive, but in order to provoke further thought and in the spirit of dialogue that defines this volume. They are not meant so much to settle questions as to help sharpen the ones we might ask when we consider the canon as a central reality of Christian faith and life, and thus, of the church.

> *Thesis 1: Questions about the canon are ultimately theological in nature and penultimately historical, for the definition of the canon finally rests in the acknowledgement of it as testimony and norm rather than as source and cultural artifact.*

39. See Glick, *The Reality of Christianity,* 245, 247; cf. 242-255.

40. Scripture and canon are not, necessarily, coterminous in meaning. It is possible to distinguish between the authority attributed to scriptural books in the early church apart from the later definitive lists of such texts. For a brief discussion of this matter within the context of current studies of the history of the Jewish and Christian canons, see McDonald and Sanders, "Introduction," in *The Canon Debate,* 8-15; and Harry S. Gamble, "The New Testament Canon: Recent Research and the Status Quaestionis," in ibid., 267-294.

While the content and development of both Scripture and the canon are worthy objects of historical investigation, the question of the *truth* of Scripture's content and the *reality* underlying its development are matters of confession that lie beyond the reach of what biblical criticism can establish. The ultimate question to be asked of both particular books within the canon, as well as of the canon itself, is not the precise determination of their development, much of which seems, even after the excellent historical investigations of the recent past, lost to history, but the question of its subject matter which is nothing less than the God to whom the canon witnesses, and the contemporary confession of faith in this God. This confession is the sole proper response of the church in light of ascertaining Scripture's true content within its particular boundaries, echoed in Barth's later statement that "the fixing of the Canon is the basic act of church confession."[41] It is the question of truth rather than historical development that is primary, for to take the Scriptures in their objectivity is to treat them not only as ancient sources of historical, cultural, and religious interest but as testimonies that demand a verdict. For this reason, the ultimate significance of the canon hangs upon ongoing recognition rather than past establishment.

At the same time, this theological definition of the canon cannot ignore questions of historical development nor be indifferent to them. How such historical findings are to be incorporated into a broader theological understanding of the canon is an unavoidable and perennial question and one scarcely settled by Barth and Harnack in their exchange. Barth was certainly justified to reaffirm the theological center of Scripture that hinged upon the work of the Spirit against Harnack's reductive positivism, yet Barth's indifference at the time to matters of Scripture's periphery and its form could not be sustained.[42] Questions of the latter are impacted by historical realities and investigation, and in this, Harnack poses a valid question to Barth's side.

As but one example, while the exact genetic history of canonical development may ultimately be unanswerable, we are still left with the canonical question that arises from the historical fact that the canon of the Old Testament of the patristic period and the following medieval world of the West

41. Barth, *Church Dogmatics* 1/2, trans. G. T. Thompson and Harold Knight, ed. G. W. Bromiley and T. F. Torrance (Edinburgh: T&T Clark, 1956), 597; Barth had made a related observation earlier in his lectures collected in *The Theology of the Reformed Confessions, 1923*, trans. Darrell L. Guder and Judith J. Guder (Louisville/London: Westminster John Knox, 2002). He there says that "the express or silent confirmation of the biblical canon may perhaps be called the fundamental act of Reformed confessing" (50).

42. See Bender, "Scripture and Canon," 180-191.

Kimlyn J. Bender

(against the recommendations of Jerome, who drew the distinction between canonical and what he termed apocryphal writings), was not what later came to be determined as the Hebrew Bible, but was in fact the Septuagint with its more inclusive listing of books.[43] Should the contemporary church side with Jerome or Augustine on this issue, and thus respectively with Luther or with Trent? To put the question perhaps more pointedly — should we side in solidarity with Judaism in determining the canon, or with the ancient church? Both arguments for historical continuity with Judaism and for the catholicity of the churches and their respective Scriptures had their proponents in the early church with regard to the question of the canon. While most Protestants, following the Reformers, side with the former, and most Catholics with the latter, no straightforward answer is provided by an acknowledgement of Scripture's theological nature and Christological center. For instance, Brevard Childs firmly attests to the theological nature of Scripture when he states that the canon is predicated upon its witness to Christ: "The scriptures of the Old and New Testament were authoritative in so far as they pointed to God's redemptive intervention for the world in Jesus Christ."[44] But such a firm and unqualified Christological affirmation does not entail that Childs finds the peripheral questions of the canon's boundaries and determination (in light of the aforementioned historical develop-

43. For the role of the Old Testament apocrypha in the New Testament and patristic period, see Daniel J. Harrington, S.J., "The Old Testament Apocrypha in the Early Church and Today," in *The Canon Debate*, 196-210; and Martin Hengel, *The Septuagint as Christian Scripture: Its Prehistory and the Problem of Its Canon*, trans. Mark E. Biddle (Grand Rapids: Baker Academic, 2002). As noted, historical criticism itself can only draw provisional judgments due to off-setting evidence regarding the boundaries of Jewish Scripture during the New Testament era, for while the New Testament never directly quotes from the Apocrypha (though some do dispute this), it is deeply stamped by its use of the Septuagint. Harrington concludes: "The historical evidence is not adequate to justify the conclusion that the apocrypha were always part of the Christian Old Testament. Neither does it prove that they were never part of the Christian canon" (205-206). See also Hengel, who argues that in terms of the limited number of books cited within the New Testament, one would actually expect a *smaller* Old Testament canon in Christianity, though in terms of actual reference (such as Jude's use of *Enoch*) one sees a more fluid and inclusive approach to texts as authorities (110-112). That the church eventually accepted the apocryphal books in the West, and eventually in the East, is for Hengel ultimately explained by Luther's own assessment, namely, that such writings were useful, if secondary (122-127). It might also be noted that the Apocrypha was included in the Geneva Bible until its 1559 edition, as well as in the first edition of the King James Bible.

44. Brevard Childs, *Biblical Theology of the Old and New Testaments: Theological Reflection on the Christian Bible* (Minneapolis: Fortress, 1993), 64.

ments) easily answered, for such an affirmation does not finally resolve the question regarding the choice for a narrower or more inclusive canon, but indeed exacerbates it and rightly makes the question of the canon not a past accomplishment discerned by historical science but a matter of present-day and perennial confession.[45] Thus this question of history continues to have contemporary theological significance for the Christian churches insofar as the canons of the churches inherited from the past are not conterminous in form.[46]

Therefore, while the ultimate definition of the canon must be theological and Christological in nature, the questions of its composition and parameters are not straightforwardly answered by such a definition. If one states that the guiding criterion for the determination of the contents of the canon is that which testifies to Christ, one must remember that Luther's adoption of precisely such a principle led him negatively to judge, though not ultimately exclude, such books as James and Jude that are broadly accepted books of the New Testament canon.[47] Moreover, such a principle could also be appealed to as a justification to expand the canon, or at least

45. Childs does not despair in such indetermination, but rather concludes: "Perhaps the basic theological issue at stake can be best formulated in terms of the church's ongoing *search* for the Christian Bible. The church struggles with the task of continually discerning the truth of God being revealed in scripture and at the same time she stands within a fully human, ecclesiastical tradition which remains the trident of the Word. The hearing of God's Word is repeatedly confirmed by the Holy Spirit through its resonance with the church's Christological rule-of-faith. At the same time the church confesses the inadequacy of its reception while rejoicing over the sheer wonder of the divine accommodation to limited human capacity" (67). Childs's own discussion of the strengths and weaknesses of the Protestant and Catholic canonical decisions is extremely insightful — see 66-68.

46. James Sanders states: "Relevance or adaptability has always been the primary trait of a canon, early and late. When one speaks of canon, in fact, one has to ask which canon of which community is meant, whether in antiquity or today. The Protestant canon is the smallest and the Ethiopian Orthodox canon the largest. While canons differ, all believing communities agree that their canon is relevant to their ongoing life. The concept of canon cannot be limited to a final stage in the history of the formation of a Bible, as it has been until recently. It must, on the contrary, be understood as part of the history of transmission of the text. Even the issue of its closure must be so understood" ("The Issue of Closure in the Canonical Process," in *The Canon Debate*, 259). However much one might object to Sanders's central criterion of relevance or adaptability as an understanding of the canon *kata sarka* (and one can), the questions of canonical boundaries and diversity among the Christian churches that he points to remain.

47. Harrington, "The Old Testament Apocrypha in the Early Church and Today," 204-205.

imply such an expansion. In antiquity, Tertullian could defend the authority
of pseudepigraphal *Enoch* by stating that it is to be accepted as authoritative
precisely because it was rejected by the Jews who "just as they also rejected
other things which proclaim Christ (sicut et caetera fere quae Christum
sonant)" also reject it and other works as well.[48] Such a radically expansive
view of the Old Testament canon was opposed by Augustine, and, of course,
Jerome, though they differed on other canonical questions.[49] Yet even today
a Christological principle can be used not to narrow the canon but to com-
mend that the Apocryphal books be included within all Christian canons.[50]
Barth himself would later defend their exclusion but admit that such a decision by the Protestant church can only be provisional rather than final because it is based upon human rather than divine authority.[51] Like Childs,
Barth sees the determination of the canon as a current ecclesial confession of
an imperfectly discerned eschatological reality.

It is not surprising in light of the historical messiness of canonical development and contested boundaries that Barth in his mature reflections on the
canon appealed not only to its theological center in revelation, but also to the
historical judgment of the church, in determining its parameters even while
refusing the latter any final authority on the question. The latter did not super-
sede the superiority of the former. For Barth, the revelation of God which
comes through Scripture is the ultimate basis and criterion for the canon itself,
and the freedom of God in this address overrules even historic usage and the
past decisions of councils regarding canonical lists, such that the canon does

48. Tertullian continues: "Nor is it remarkable if they have not received other scriptures
which speak of him, just as they would not receive him when he spoke openly." Quoted in
William Adler, "The Pseudepigrapha in the Early Church," in *The Canon Debate*, 224. Even
here, however, matters are more complicated, for Tertullian may be arguing not for a revision of the Old Testament canon so much as for a justification and defense of his own use
and reliance upon *Enoch,* though this book and *4 Esdras* did obtain canonical status in the
Ethiopian Orthodox Church, and the latter is also included in the Vulgate. See Adler, 227.

49. Adler, "The Pseudepigrapha in the Early Church," 224.

50. See Harrington, "The Old Testament Apocrypha in the Early Church and Today,"
206. He argues that such texts help us take Jesus' identity in Judaism seriously. What is unclear, however, is where such canonical expansion will end, for he lists Josephus and Philo,
the Dead Sea scrolls, and the Old Testament Pseudepigrapha as doing the same thing, yet it
is quite doubtful he would want to see these included in the canon itself. Here, again, we may
simply be witnessing an inability to distinguish *apostolic* texts from simply illuminating historical ones. Hengel, however, entertains a more radical thought: "Does the church still need
a clearly demarcated, strictly closed Old Testament canon, since the New Testament is, after
all, the 'conclusion', the goal and the fulfillment of the Old? . . ." (125-126).

51. Barth, *CD* 1/2, 598.

and must remain open in principle. Yet the church's long-standing recognition of these past ecclesial decisions, itself predicated upon recognition of the Spirit's speaking through these particular books, ensures that the canon is effectively closed in practice, even if with regard to the Old Testament it is closed differently between the Catholic and Protestant (and Eastern) churches.[52]

Barth's emphasis in the *Church Dogmatics* upon the relative authority of the early church's acceptance of these books, later ratified in ecclesial decisions regarding the canon, once again demonstrates the inalienable, if not determinative, place of historiography in the church's contemporary task of confession, though in Barth's case, and this is quite important, one that respects the past decisions of the church perhaps more than the viewpoints of individual historians and even the findings of contemporary biblical scholarship. In face of those who today might challenge particular books of the canon due to their pseudepigraphal origins, or, more seriously, by questioning whether God's revelation is indeed heard in them in the present (or ever was), Barth gives precedence not to the contemporary discernment of individuals, but to a measured reservation and corresponding preservation of such books in light of the church's judgment of having heard God's Word in them in the past.[53] So while the canon does remain open in principle, for the Spirit is not bound, it is closed in practice, and Barth seems quite skeptical regarding the possibility of future revisions to the canon the church has received, for it has been through these books that the church has heard the voice of God in the past and can hope to again in the future in light of God's faithfulness. Such divine faithfulness over time entails that it is the long-standing decision and practice of the church continually reaffirmed through history, rather than of an individual or individuals in the transitory present, which truly matters.

However much Barth rebelled against the liberalism of Harnack in the early years of his professional life, it was in the years of the *Church Dogmatics*, and precisely as a theologian of the *church*, that he most testifies to his overcoming of its *individualism*, which, along with historical relativism, he discerned to be hallmark of modern theology's identity, and did so even before his break with liberalism.[54] It is the church, rather than the academy, that con-

52. Ibid., 597-603; see also 473-537. Barth writes: "When we adopt the Canon of the Church we do not say that the Church itself, but that the revelation which underlies and controls the Church, attests these witnesses and not others as the witnesses of revelation and therefore as canonical for the Church" (474).

53. Ibid., 597-601.

54. Barth, "Moderne Theologie und Reichsgottesarbeit" (1909) in *Vorträge und kleinere Arbeiten 1905-1909*, 342-344; cf. 341-347; see also Busch, *Karl Barth*, 50-52.

fesses the Word of God in the canon, and therefore the final arbiter of the canon's parameters remains the church itself, though whether the church of today (in its manifold forms) should rethink the decisions of the church of the past in light of the historical and critical knowledge of the canon possessed in the present remains a question the church must answer, and can only answer, by a reaffirmation of what it understands the canon to be. It must at least remember in its considerations that "there is no more dangerous subjectivism than that which is based on the arrogance of a false objectivity,"[55] and thus take care not to fall into the hubris of chronological snobbery. There is good reason to believe, however, that the "canon will stand for long enough yet against the 'it seems to me' of some agitators."[56]

> *Thesis 2: An acknowledgement of the canon is ultimately an acknowledgement of its unity and only penultimately one of its diversity, for to speak of Scripture as canon entails more than speaking of it as a collection of texts.*

Questions of unity with regard to the canon can be addressed from two perspectives: the functional and pragmatic unity that a canon of texts serves in shaping a communal tradition over time, or the question of the intrinsic unity of the canon itself. While the first is an essential outcome of the concept of canon, the second is determinative for the definition of canon itself. When unity in the second sense is not recognized, then questions of pragmatic usefulness come to the fore and eventually lead to problematic reevaluations of the received canon and dissolution of its authority.

As noted above, the question of the unity of Scripture was a central element in the correspondence between Barth and Harnack. Harnack's reticence to speak of Scripture as a unity was shaped by his own particular conviction that whatsoever unity existed was to be discerned and derived by means of historical science. For Harnack, such is the particular achievement made possible by a true scientific objectivity. Yet it was such objectivity itself that time has revealed to be a chimera, for the presuppositions of Harnack's scientism ruled out a serious consideration of the unity of the canon and in fact denied the validity of the question. Thus supposed objectivity could readily give way to pragmatism and axiology.[57]

---

55. Barth, *CD* 1/2, 553.

56. Barth, *GD*, 247.

57. Glick, *The Reality of Christianity*, 14; for the presuppositions behind Harnack's supposed objectivity, and his implicit utilitarianism with regard to the question of Scripture in

It is not difficult to determine that Harnack was struck much more by the diversity of the canon than by its unity and saw Barth's appeal to a unity grounded in a unified revelation as both naïve and unscientific. Harnack saw not so much a unity but an essence in Scripture, defined as a spiritual-moral norm, and the criterion for this norm was not simply read out of the New Testament, but read into it, not so much a canon within the canon as a canon outside of it.[58] Moreover, whatever failed to fit this norm was considered the husk of the kernel and thus expendable. Nowhere is this more evident than in Harnack's rejection of the Old Testament.[59] When the emphasis is placed upon the irreconcilable diversity of Scripture, it should not be surprising that unity is not discovered within it but imposed upon it, and imposed by means of subtraction, a subtraction itself determined by an external principle, and one that ultimately dissolves canonicity into canonical essence.[60] Objective scientific rigor thus bows to pragmatic cultural apologetics.[61]

In his own later reflections on the canon, Barth went a very different direction, emphasizing the unity of Scripture and the inalienable canonical status of the Old Testament. Such was due to a number of factors, but no doubt the central one was that Barth saw Scripture as the witness to a single Lord and saw Scripture as a testimony to a united revelation, and thus through the single lens of Christology, whereas Harnack approached Scripture through multiple lenses, most notably those of a spiritual moralism that was predicated upon a Kantian universal rationalism modified in light of Schleiermacher, as well as through a modern Lutheran law and gospel di-

---

mediating religion and culture, see ibid., 3-15, 65-67, 68-84, 94-95, 105-111, 117-118, 158-161, 161-176, 202, 213-215, 230, 240, et al.

58. I borrow this latter phrase from James D. G. Dunn, "Has the Canon a Continuing Function?" in *The Canon Debate*, 569.

59. "The rejection of the Old Testament during the second century A.D. would have been a mistake, which the great Church rightly refused to make. Its retention in the sixteenth century was a fate from which the Reformation was not yet able to extricate itself. Its conservation as a canonical document for Protestantism since the nineteenth century is the consequence of a religious and ecclesiastical paralysis" (Harnack, *Marcion, das Evangelium vom fremden Gott* [Leipzig: J. C. Hinrichs Verlag, 1924], 217; quoted in Rumscheidt, *Revelation and Theology*, 98).

60. Glick, *The Reality of Christianity*, 249.

61. As Glick perceptively asks: "Was the Old Testament adjudged noncanonical by Harnack simply because he did not believe it contributed to the needs of his time? Does this not mean, then, that the central category of interpretation must always be 'worthfulness'?" (13).

chotomy (both via and modified by Ritchl).[62] When these lenses focused, they focused together upon an essential message which Harnack deemed the "simple gospel."[63] This gospel, when once understood, Harnack believed, entailed that the Old Testament had to be discarded in Marcionite fashion not only because of this gospel's opposition to law (in spite of its own moralism), but also because of the Old Testament's intractable parochialism, or, put differently, because of the scandal of its particularity.[64] In the end, Barth was perhaps more true to history if for no other reason than that he refused to divide in *any* way the person of Jesus from the content of his message and just as resolutely refused to separate him from his context in Judaism. Thus he was more true to the *particularity* of Jesus and accepted the scandal rather than attempting to overcome it. Barth's primary concern was not the gospel's relevance but its truth, and he had little or no interest in serving as a mediating theologian or in such apologetic tasks, whereas Harnack, like Schleiermacher, saw the mediation between Christian faith and culture as a — if not *the* — central task of a theologian.[65] Such mediation entailed a jettisoning of particularity for universal or contemporary concerns.

What we must consider, then, is that a recognition of Scripture's unity as a canon is dependent upon the acceptance of revelation's scandal of particularity. A rejection of the latter always leads to a reductive program, moral or otherwise. It has often led to a jettisoning of the Old Testament. Harnack has been criticized for such, but he was not the first to question the place of the Old Testament in the Christian canon, and he will not be the last. Once again, such an acknowledgement does not alleviate questions regarding the boundaries of the canon, and historical considerations cannot be ignored

---

62. Ibid., 77-78; cf. 161-176, 240.

63. Perhaps most famously put forward in Harnack's *What Is Christianity?* trans. Thomas B. Saunders (New York: Harper & Brothers, 1957). For Harnack, the gospel can be summarized in three propositions: *"Firstly, the kingdom of God and its coming; Secondly, God the Father and the infinite value of the human soul; Thirdly, the higher righteousness and the commandment of love"* (51). The kingdom is thus supernatural, purely religious, and the most important experience a person can have (62). The gospel itself is an ethical message of love for humanity (70).

64. Harnack's definitive study of Marcion is *Marcion, das Evangelium vom fremden Gott.* For Harnack, Marcion achieved what Paul intimated and what Luther attempted but ultimately could not accomplish, namely, definitively to overcome the law with the gospel. See Glick's discussion, 117-120. He later writes that "it becomes quite evident that for all his emphasis on historical event, Harnack is really quite contemptuous of historical particularity" (253).

65. Glick, *The Reality of Christianity,* 83-84.

when such questions are considered. Indeed, Barth's own disdain for apologetics (inherited from Herrmann) may be unhelpfully extended to exclude valid historical arguments that need to be made today, such as that against recent appeals even by some within the churches for an inclusion of the *Gospel of Thomas* within the canon because of its early date and supposed authenticity, when in reality, it is demonstrably late and typically gnostic in its rejection of the scandal of Jesus' particularity and its indifference to his rootedness in first-century Palestine (thus akin to other late gnostic gospels and their modern-day proponents).[66] As Barth had to admit in his other famous debate of 1923, that with Paul Tillich, the *particularity* of God's revelation entails a particular *history*.[67] This fact entails that historiographical concerns and biblical criticism are integral for Christian faith, even while they also need to be taken up into larger theological frameworks, and can indeed serve them in no small way by correcting these frameworks themselves.[68]

66. See the groundbreaking work of Nicholas Perrin, *Thomas: The Other Gospel* (Louisville: Westminster John Knox, 2007); as well as his *Thomas and Tatian* (Atlanta: Society of Biblical Literature, 2002); an accessible evaluation of *Thomas* is provided by Craig A. Evans, *Fabricating Jesus* (Downers Grove: InterVarsity Press, 2006), 52-77; for the decontextualizing of Jesus from Judaism among some prominent members of the Jesus Seminar, see Philip Jenkins, *Hidden Gospels: How the Search for Jesus Lost Its Way* (Oxford/New York: Oxford University Press, 2001), 99-100; et al. For the importance of historical study to correct such misperceptions and domestications, see Dunn, "Has the Canon a Continuing Function?" 574-575.

67. This published debate is found within *The Beginnings of Dialectical Theology*, 133-158. While Barth was facing an entrenched historicism in Harnack, in Tillich he faced a true flight from history altogether into the transcendence of the "unconditioned" (147-148). Whereas Barth against Harnack asserted the distinctiveness of revelation from history, such that the former could not simply be subsumed into the latter and be directly ascertained by means of historical criticism, against Tillich Barth now had to assert that revelation and history were not to be torn asunder and that God has bound himself to a particular history in his Self-revelation. As Barth writes, "Christ is *the* salvation history, the salvation history *itself*," whereas for Tillich, Christ is "the presentation of a salvation history which more or less occurs always and everywhere with completely symbolic power" (150). The decisive difference between Tillich and himself, Barth concluded, was a difference of Christology. Both Barth and Tillich opposed the idolatry of the "man-god," but where they parted company was on the reality of the "God-man." For Barth, the pride of humanity that must be opposed in the former should not be used to negate the freedom and love of God in choosing to be the latter, and who does so in a history which is "*the* site of *the* salvation history" (151).

68. For a strong and provocative defense of the need for biblical criticism against its contemporary detractors, see John Barton, *The Nature of Biblical Criticism* (Louisville/London: Westminster John Knox, 2007); also Dunn, "Has the Canon a Continuing Function?"

> *Thesis 3: Judgments about the canon are ultimately Christological judg-ments, for the central question of the canon pertains to its center rather than its periphery and constituent membership, as important as these are.*

The question of the canon is to be addressed from its center, rather than its periphery, and when this is done, it is not cynicism and skepticism, but a deep impression of its overarching narrative unity, that has impressed itself upon the church. However contentious such a claim might be from the standpoint of an exacting historiography, it is nonetheless true that for Christian faith it is the center, rather than the periphery, its content rather than its boundaries, which is the primary question of the canon. When this is kept in mind, the matter of discerning boundaries itself gains in clarity, both with respect to the Old Testament and New Testament canons.

First, while the exact scope of the Old Testament canon was and remains a question for the church, the Old Testament itself was not questioned as Scripture but central to the church's very definition of it. The contested nature of the Old Testament canon mentioned earlier should not distract from the larger affirmation to be made regarding the ongoing normativity of the First Testament along with that of the Second in the church's history.[69] That the early church retained the Old Testament and saw the New Testament as a commentary upon it, rather than a replacement for it, entails a very particular understanding of the God the church confessed and the Christ it worshipped.[70] And it is undeniable that Barth came to see the Old Testament more in terms of the first, and Harnack in terms of the second.[71] Furthermore, Barth's increasing appreciation for classical Chalcedonian Christology, and Harnack's disavowal of it (along with a rejection of the resurrection), could only stem

---

574-575. With regard to the question of the canon, Jenkins writes: "Contrary to recent claims, the more access we have to ancient 'alternative gospels,' the more we must respect the choices made by the early church in forming its canon" (106).

69. Childs, *Biblical Theology*, 66.

70. As Glick perceptively notes regarding Harnack's understanding of the history of dogma: "The fact that the Church from the beginning laid claim to the Old Testament, interpreting it, to be sure, in most unusual ways, is of crucial importance here. For whatever the mode of interpretation, it was still to this content that it was applied. And the indisputable fact that the New Testament, when written by the Church, placed itself within the framework of Jewish thought ("the God of Abraham, Isaac, and Jacob," "God spoke of old to our fathers by the prophets"), is certainly presumptive evidence that the situation from which the dogma developed was by no means as 'Hellenic' as Harnack assumes" (173).

71. For Barth's mature reflections on the Old Testament within the Christian canon, see *CD* 1/2, 70-101.

from and in turn entail hermeneutical and canonical judgments. Barth would emphasize Jesus as the Risen Messiah of Israel, the *fulfillment* of the promises to Abraham, whereas Harnack, in true nineteenth-century fashion, saw him primarily as the *founding personality* of a new faith, even while acknowledging the usefulness of the Old Testament for the early church, if not for today. So while it is true that both Harnack and Barth can rightly be deemed Christo-centric theologians, their Christologies differed dramatically, and such Christologies inescapably had canonical implications.[72]

One implication directly affects the question of canonical unity. Indeed, another way to say that Barth focused upon the unity of Scripture is to say that Barth saw all of Scripture as ultimately about Christ. The same could not be said of Harnack. Where Barth saw Scripture as grounded in a particular revelation in Christ, foreshadowed in the Old and attested in the New, Harnack was enamored by a universal message that could be extracted ultimately from both. One must be fair to Harnack here, for he resolutely refused to dispense with the person of Jesus in favor of his message and would not give up on the uniqueness of Jesus against the later objections of the *Religionsgeschichtliche Schule*.[73] Nevertheless, he was inclined to separate Jesus from his own history. Barth could not follow this path, because in his view, to divide the Testaments is tantamount to committing a Christological heresy.[74] His emphasis upon the unity of revelation entailed that he emphasize the unity of the testaments. The canon of Scripture was thus not the source of a message but a testimony to a Lord and a testimony throughout. Barth never would refrain from treating the Old Testament as extended infancy narratives, and this has been and remains perhaps one of the most controversial aspects of his understanding of the canon.

Barth's Christological understanding of the canon is, nevertheless, in

---

72. For Harnack's Christology, see the selections in *Adolf von Harnack: Liberal Theology at Its Height*, 63-77; cf. 155-166, 303-312; also the summary in Glick, *The Reality of Christianity*, 181-215. It was in view of the nineteenth century's view of Jesus, culminating in Ritchl and Harnack, that Barth surprisingly claimed in his first dogmatic cycle that theology must be less Christocentric (*GD*, 90-91). The end result for Barth was of course not a theology less Christocentric but a radically different theology and Christology altogether.

73. Harnack thus attempted to preserve the uniqueness of Jesus against those like D. F. Strauss and Ernst Troeltsch who insisted upon a more consistent historicism, though Troeltsch himself would later attempt to find a way to preserve the "absoluteness of Christianity."

74. "Whether we like it or not, the Christ of the New Testament is the Christ of the Old Testament, the Christ of Israel. The man who will not accept this merely shows that in fact he has already substituted another Christ for the Christ of the New Testament" (Barth, *CD* 1/2, 488-489).

line with that of the historic church. While Barth's approach to the Old Testament has been challenged on various fronts for its failure to take the Old Testament on its own terms, it is very difficult to see the Old Testament and New Testament as *one* canon if not by means of Christ hidden in the Old and revealed in the New. It is no doubt more difficult to see this unity with a dialectic of law and gospel as the primary hermeneutic, and perhaps impossible for a reductive moralism. Certainly it became impossible for Harnack in light of his "simple gospel." We should not expect it to be any less difficult for contemporary moral programs with their own axiological judgments and mediating agendas that call for canonical revision. As but one example, consider the lament of Robert Funk: "To retain the traditional New Testament and understand it as a canon is to condemn it to progressive irrelevance with each passing century."[75] His answer? — "My own solution to the problem is to issue a revised canon, a new New Testament, by both shrinking and expanding the texts to be included."[76] Let us make no mistake — Funk's argument is not just canonical, it is Christological, again hidden behind the veil of (dubious) scientific respectability. He asks: "Shall we continue to affirm the picture of Jesus provided by the four canonical gospels, or shall we heed the findings of historical research?"[77] We have heard this before.

In his time, Harnack (as well as Jülicher) judged Barth to be a Marcionite, yet it was Harnack the scientific historian, not Barth the pneumatic exegete, who ultimately tipped his hand in this direction. On the question of the canon, Barth's position seems to coincide with what historical investigation has itself discovered, i.e., that Jesus Christ was the early church's canon, and the Old and New Testament became the canon of the church as a witness to him.[78] It remains the canon of the church today for the same reason.

75. Funk, "The Once and Future New Testament," 544.

76. Ibid., 549, 542. The Old Testament does not make out so well in Funk's proposal, either.

77. Ibid., 541. It should not be surprising that Funk is enamored only with the diversity of Scripture and sees historical criticism as entirely undermining any sense of its unity (542-544).

78. Lee McDonald argues that "during the formative years of the early church Jesus was the church's primary canon par excellence and . . . the biblical tradition (the OT scriptures) gave witness to that canon" (*The Formation of the Christian Biblical Canon, Revised and Expanded Edition* [Peabody: Hendrickson, 1995], 95; see also 153, 189). The larger point here made is in no way negated even should we adopt a more narrow definition of "canon" as a closed list of sacred books — see Eugene Ulrich, "The Notion and Definition of Canon," in *The Canon Debate,* 34-35. For a judgment similar to that of McDonald, see Dunn, "Has the Canon a Continuing Function?" 560-562, as well as William R. Farmer, "Reflections on Jesus

Moreover, Barth's position on Scripture makes his own theology more amenable to later judgments of biblical criticism than Harnack's and with reference to two in particular. The first is that New Testament studies have not been kind to Harnack's reductive moralism, for if there is one thing that contemporary biblical scholarship has grown increasingly to affirm in the past century, it is the Jewishness of Jesus and his place in the context of rabbinic Judaism and the eschatology of his day, no matter how contested the precise nature of this relationship may be among New Testament scholars.[79] Harnack's isolation of Jesus from his Jewish environment is nothing less than a subtle gnosticism, and there is no more subtle form of gnosticism than an ahistorical moralism.[80] Barth averted this temptation. Yet in his struggle to wrestle with how the New Covenant not only completes but supersedes the Old one, Harnack rightly wrestled with a question that Barth was simply less interested to answer, yet one the church must perennially face in the challenge of relating old and new wineskins.

Second, the increasing appreciation in biblical studies for the intertextuality of the Bible affirms the deeply-woven unity of the New Testament with the Old, further demonstrating the problems with Harnack's canonical judgment. It is precisely an appreciation for the unity of the subject

---

and the New Testament Canon," in *The Canon Debate*, 322-323. Dunn judges that "the canon of the New Testament still has a continuing function in that *the New Testament in all its diversity still bears consistent testimony to the unifying center*. Its unity canonizes Jesus-the-man-now-exalted as the canon within the canon" (561).

79. And this is the consensus of biblical scholars who are more akin to the presuppositions of Harnack, treating the Jesus of history as a person behind the Gospels, as well as to those who may be more sympathetic to the presuppositions of Barth. For an example of the former, see E. P. Sanders, *The Historical Figure of Jesus* (London: Penguin/Allen Lane, 1993), esp. 78-97 and 169-188. For the latter, see N. T. Wright, *Jesus and the Victory of God* (Minneapolis: Fortress, 1996), esp. 91-98. Wright concludes that in light of the Third Quest, what is emerging is a position in which Jesus can neither be separated from the Judaism of his day nor simply be subsumed into it so that his critique of it disappears (98).

80. As Harnack writes: "Since Christianity is the only true religion and is not a national religion, but belongs to all mankind and pertains to our inmost life, it follows that it can have no special alliance with the Jewish people, or with their peculiar cult. The Jewish people of today, at least, stand in no favored relationship with the God whom Jesus has revealed; whether they formerly did is doubtful; this, however, is certain, that God has cast them off, and that the whole Divine revelation, so far as there was any revelation prior to Christ . . . had as its end the calling of a 'new nation' and the spreading of the revelation of God through his Son" (*Outlines of the History of Dogma*, trans. Edwin K. Mitchell [Boston: Beacon Press, 1957], 42). Such a quote reveals that a rejection of the scandal of the gospel is the flip side of gnosticism, and indeed recent history has not judged Harnack's position lightly.

matter that is mirrored in an appreciation for the contemporaneity of the Old in the New in the light of Christ, for, as Robert Wall presciently notes: "The intertextual character of Scripture — the constant repetition of one text alluding to or citing an earlier text — reflects the simultaneity of its subject matter."[81]

In the end, the irony of the Barth and Harnack debate is that it was the scientific historian who strove for objectivity who was the most unknowingly captive to passing presuppositions of his own time and its intrinsic gnosticism, and it was the openly confessional position of the theologian accused of gnosticism that has proved more rooted in history and able to weather the changes of time in biblical studies. If Barth indeed had a fault in this regard, it was in his too ready acceptance of the findings of radical biblical criticism, failing to question not only its presuppositions but also its findings. This was in no small part due to Barth's own liberal inheritance from Herrmann and his early ambivalence toward history, as well as to a dialectic of contradiction that had in time to be taken up and overcome in a richer dialectic of correspondence. Nevertheless, from the very first, and evident in his debate with Harnack, it is his hermeneutics of trust and canonical richness, rather than suspicion and canonical reductionism, which continues to intrigue many.

Epilogue

Readers of this paper will no doubt note the treacherous and tenuous dialogue between theology and biblical studies within it. Practitioners of both may find fault with such egregious discipline-crossing. Yet (without excusing any shortcomings of content), no apology from my side will be forthcoming.

One of the greatly unfortunate realities of contemporary Christian scholarship is the parting of the ways of biblical studies and systematic theology (although there are some recent attempts to bring them back into vibrant dialogue with one another). Yet if both of these are to be *Christian*, and thus servants of the church, and not simply professional avocations of a

---

81. Robert W. Wall, "The Significance of a Canonical Perspective of the Church's Scripture," in *The Canon Debate*, 531. Later he writes: "The current reductionism of interpreting the Old Testament or New Testament in isolation from the other, thereby undermining the New Testament's relationship to the 'Hebrew Bible,' is subverted by the New Testament's appeal to and exegesis of the Old Testament" (537).

guild, such a division can only be ad hoc, provisional, and practical, not systematic, permanent, and principled.

It is perhaps a little known fact that Daniel Migliore began his long and august tenure as a theologian at Princeton Seminary not in the theology faculty but in that of biblical studies as an instructor of New Testament, later joining the theology faculty. I doubt that this cross-over could happen in today's highly specialized and compartmentalized academic environment, and that is, in my estimation, a shame.[82]

82. I would like to thank Kathleen Painter and Jennifer Knutson for help during the research of this article, as well as the institutional support provided to me by the University of Sioux Falls.

Argue Theologically with One Another: Karl Barth's Argument with Emil Brunner

Gerhard Sauter

Translated by John Flett

A family anecdote to begin with: Several weeks ago, two of our grandchildren visited us. We selected for the table prayer what we thought would be a version suitable for children: "Each animal has its food,/Each little flower drinks from you,/And you did not forget us today,/Dear God, we thank you!" The younger one, three and a half years old, did not at all agree with this: "That is not right! One must always begin with God!" (Here I encountered the phenomenon of an *anima naturaliter Barthiana,* a naturally Barthian soul, of which the question of "religious socialization" has, as far as I know, not yet been sufficiently investigated.) My wife and I suggested that he might prefer the prayer we had planned for the conclusion of the meal: "Dear God, we thank you for the good meal." The small one, however, was not yet content. "One must always begin with God — but one must continue talking with God!" Thus, we began with the second prayer and added the first. Does not this small scene contain *in nuce* the controversy between Karl Barth and Emil Brunner, possibly even offering a tiny beginning for clarifying the problems raised at that time?

I. The Barth-Brunner Controversy as Theological Paradigm

Why is it worthwhile to revisit the argument Brunner and Barth had with one another in the first half of the 1930s? It is essentially found in Brunner's 1929 essay "Die andere Aufgabe der Theologie"[1] — material that Barth re-

1. Emil Brunner, "Die andere Aufgabe der Theologie," *Zwischen den Zeiten* 7 (1929):

jected in *Church Dogmatics* I/1[2] — the 1932 essay "Die Frage nach dem 'Anknüpfungspunkt' als Problem der Theologie,"[3] and finally in Brunner's programmatic 1934 *Natur und Gnade*,[4] which was followed by Barth's rejoinder *Nein!*[5] What Barth and Brunner had appeared to share in a more or less friendly, if not a somewhat distant, exchange of opinions, proved itself to be extremely fragile. This was so much the case from Barth's perspective that he even looked upon past agreements as misunderstandings. What had been simmering between them for many years now exploded into a battle about the fundamentals.[6] As this debate became associated with the struggle for theological guidance for the Protestant Church in National Socialist Germany, the confrontation gained a trailblazing significance which extended far beyond the simple termination of an alliance of interest or a working association. This dispute, now conducted in a highly personal way, signaled an axiomatic turning point for theology and the church.

I will limit myself to summarizing the main points. Since the beginning of the thirties, Barth had accused Brunner several times of deviating from the theological line that he, Barth, had adopted. Since direct personal communication had failed, Brunner resolved to challenge Barth to a public discussion. Brunner's desire was to recover a proper understanding of natural theology, one that had otherwise been lost in modern theology and that had been turned into an unnatural appeal to human nearness to God. According to Brunner's view, "natural theology" may and ought to count upon the *humanum*: humans

---

225-276, later reprinted in Emil Brunner, *Ein offenes Wort: Vorträge und Aufsätze 1917-1962*, ed. Rudolf Wehrli, 2 vols. (Zürich: TVZ, 1981), vol. 1: 171-193.

2. *CD* I/1, 26-29, 238f. See further, Eberhard Busch, ed., *Karl Barth–Emil Brunner: Briefwechsel 1916-1966*, Karl Barth Gesamtausgabe (Zürich: TVZ, 2000), 174-183, 200-205, 207f., 210-212, 214; Caren Algner, ed., *Karl Barth — Eduard Thurneysen: Briefwechsel Band III, 1930-1935*, Karl Barth Gesamtausgabe (Zürich: TVZ, 2000), 55, 64, 304, 324.

3. Emil Brunner, "Die Frage nach dem 'Anknüpfungspunkt' als Problem der Theologie," *Zwischen den Zeiten* 10 (1932): 505-532; later reprinted in Brunner, *Ein offenes Wort*, vol. 1, 239-267.

4. Emil Brunner, *Natur und Gnade: Zum Gespräch mit Karl Barth* (Tübingen: J. C. B. Mohr, 1934), with a second edition published in 1935. The following quotes are from the first edition. This was later reprinted in Brunner, *Ein offenes Wort*, vol. 1, 333-375.

5. Karl Barth, *Nein! Antwort an Emil Brunner*, Theologische Existenz heute, Heft 14 (München: Chr. Kaiser, 1934).

6. Beginning with Brunner's total rejection of Schleiermacher, in Emil Brunner, *Die Mystik und das Wort: Der Gegensatz zwischen moderner Religionsauffassung und christlichem Glauben dargestellt an der Theologie Schleiermachers* (Tübingen: J. C. B. Mohr, 1924); and Barth's criticisms of this work, later published in Holger Finze, ed., *Karl Barth: Vorträge und kleinere Arbeiten 1922-1925*, Karl Barth Gesamtausgabe (Zürich: TVZ, 1990), 401-425.

can be addressed, without exception, as God's creatures because they are capable of communication and are responsible. To be sure, the human as a sinner is a "person violating one's personhood" *(widerpersönliche Person)*. Nevertheless, as Brunner put it, the "formal" image of God persists. It should be distinguished "categorically" from the "material" image of God, which by virtue of the justification of the sinner by grace alone is created anew: "that which is truly personal," the "being in love."[7] If responsibility for the proclamation of the free grace of God is theology's first task — in affirming this Brunner sees himself in complete unity with Barth — then Brunner wants to stress that this proclamation encounters *creaturely* existence. To that extent, proclamation is not conditionless but stands in a critical dialectical relationship with the relative orderedness of *created* life. Comprehending this relationship is "the other task of theology." What God retains in his faithfulness to his creation can and must be taken seriously in the dialogue with one's contemporaries. This happens "eristically" in that they open themselves to the fact that their insights and cultural contexts of action need correction, and thereby become receptive to God's gracious act. This "other task" must be pursued as complementary to the primary commission. Brunner regarded this as not only culpably neglected but also as actually excluded in principle by Barth.

Barth responded to this offer of an "agree to disagree" reconciliation of interests with a curt "no" and, in doing so, he ended the discussion.[8] If Brunner thought that they could continue on the path they so far had taken together, and perhaps that he should even move beyond Barth's position, then Barth regarded this as a fatal backward step which must terminate in a dead end. He thought Brunner's distinction between a formal and material *imago Dei* was completely wrong because it sidelined the decisive question: *why* and *how* can the image of God be perceived at all? Barth accused Brunner of wanting to gain theological knowledge by the devious means of utilizing philosophical insights; this same criticism had already been directed against Brunner's foundation for theological ethics.[9] Barth's irritation with countless obscurities in Brunner's thought process, and his displeasure about Brunner's goals, intensified into the explicit suspicion that Brunner had crossed over to Barth's theological opponents, even to the point of being a German Christian in disguise.[10]

7. Brunner, *Natur und Gnade,* 11.

8. See, for example, Thurneysen's observation of Barth's "personal policy" in a letter to Barth, September 12, 1933 (in *Barth-Thurneysen: Briefwechsel Bd III,* 493).

9. Emil Brunner, *Das Gebot und die Ordnungen: Entwurf einer protestantisch-theologischen Ethik* (Tübingen: J. C. B. Mohr, 1932).

10. See, for example, Barth's margin notes in his personal copy of Brunner's *Das Gebot*

Thus far the outlines of the controversy in which Barth stamped Brunner as an exponent of a theologically erroneous trend. Later on, Barth would react against this very trend. Indeed, this front line as Barth then drew it on the ordinance map of theology remains decisive in making a basic decision for or against the reception of Barth's theology even today. In this sense, Barth's rebuke of Brunner did not fail in its intention. However, we must ask: have the problems as they were then raised been sufficiently clarified, perhaps even brought to a solution, or do they remain unresolved, perhaps as questions directed to both sides? At the conclusion of his "No!" against Brunner, Barth prophesies the appearance of a mediating theology for which Brunner, at least, prepared the way, and certainly did not avert. It bears the marks of the antichrist, appearing confoundingly similar to Christian theology, but on closer inspection is of a completely different spirit. This is a dangerous suspicion which can lead to character assassination. But, apart from Brunner, and in light of subsequent developments, could Barth have been right with this Cassandra cry?

For a new consideration of the controversy during those turbulent thirties, and perhaps also for a revision of the received history of its impact, I will first cite four motives, the content of which I will then outline.

First, the *historical and biographic background* of the argument has been enlightened by the exchange of letters between Barth and Eduard Thurneysen from the years 1930 to 1935 which was published in the year 2000 and which splendidly supplements Barth's correspondence with Brunner.[11] The editor of this third volume of the Barth-Thurneysen correspondence, Caren Algner, in her dissertation evaluated some insufficiently known perspectives, such as Barth's self-critical reflection on his interaction with Brunner. This can enrich our understanding of the relevant texts.[12]

Second, Barth believed that Brunner, in the necessary *clarifications* of the emerging *Church struggle,* had stabbed him in the back and supported the position of the German Christians certainly in fact and at least indirectly. With this Barth ascribed to theological differences, including their diverse ways of framing the task, a politically decisive quality — "political" in terms of their structure, not in the sense of the daily political process — that is, by

---

und die Ordnungen; as noted by Caren Algner, *Kirchliche Dogmatik im Vollzug: Karl Barths Kampf um die Kirche im Spiegel von seiner und Charlotte von Kirschbaums Korrespondenz mit Eduard Thurneysen 1930-1935* (Neukirchen-Vluyn, 2004), 22ff.

11. See footnote 2.
12. See footnote 10.

setting up a strategy which permits only a yes or no. Key terms like "select," "one must decide," "no compromises," etc., play a decisive role: what matters is gaining clarity by demarcation. Placing suspicion on "natural theology" epitomized this strategy, a fundamental and comprehensive suspicion to which Brunner should also fall victim. Barth formed an extremely complex and extensive "concept of dispute" *(Streitbegriff)* by taking up this designation and using it to evaluate the rightness of theological decisions. This concept of disputation, which almost became for Barth and his supporters a red flag, permits no distinction between a right and wrong *theologia naturalis* or between its correct use and its abuse. In 2001, Christoph Kock published a dissertation on this "concept of dispute," one which investigates the after-effects of that problematic situation up to the contemporary discussion of fundamental theology.[13]

Third, "natural theology" signifies, in Barth's view, a fundamentally wrong track that emerges very early in modernity and which characterizes *neo-Protestantism.* This designation for one epoch of German Protestant theology and church history becomes a polemically charged description of those years, even if one can demonstrate that the term was already formerly in existence.[14] Barth is persuaded that this pathway back into neo-Protestantism — in his view, a relapse into the errors of the intellectual history of eighteenth and nineteenth centuries, if not in traces of the seventeenth century — has a profoundly negative effect upon the Protestant profile in contrast to *Catholicism.* In the background music of a "pact with natural theology,"[15] he hears the "Thomist song of the siren,"[16] the Thomist dictum *"gratia non tollit naturam sed perficit,"* which destroys the Protestant church. The neo-Protestantism appears crypto-Catholic to Barth because it has relapsed into synergism and a *theologia gloriae.* Did Thomas really think this way, and is Barth's criticism germane to his thought? Eugene Rogers, who teaches at the University of Virginia in Charlottesville, contests such an idea in his study on Thomas Aquinas and Karl Barth.[17] This work, however, treats Barth's *Kurze*

13. Christoph Kock, *Natürliche Theologie: Ein evangelischer Streitbegriff* (Neukirchen-Vluyn, 2001).

14. See ibid., 39-41.

15. From a letter from Barth to Paul Althaus (1933), cited by Hinrich Stoevesandt in his new edition of Barth's *Theologische Existenz heute!*, Theologische Existenz heute, Neue Folge 219 (München: Chr. Kaiser, 1984), 156.

16. Ibid.

17. Eugene F. Rogers, *Thomas Aquinas and Karl Barth: Sacred Doctrine and the Natural Knowledge of God* (Notre Dame, IN: University of Notre Dame, 1995).

Erklärung des Römerbriefes (1956)[18] and the *Church Dogmatics* rather than his argument with natural theology à la Brunner.

Fourth, in *English-language theology,* and in particular in Anglicanism, Barth's rejection of natural theology was not widely understood, let alone accepted, at the time. It appeared to be nothing other than a bloody continental battle, a Teutonic duel with a Swiss hue. In England and the United States, at first Brunner was more enthusiastically received than Barth, partly because his theology was easier to translate than Barth's — and not only linguistically. Thus, it seemed incomprehensible that his support for natural theology might make one susceptible to the error of National Socialism.

How does the Barth-Brunner controversy appear nowadays among English-speaking theologians? John W. Hart, an American Presbyterian minister, examines this in his Oxford dissertation.[19] This does not only investigate all the details of the prehistory of Barth's rejection of Brunner. He regards its theological content as totally illuminating and has no objections to the consequences drawn. This could indicate that the constellation of the period, partly diagnosed and partly caused by Barth, was not only conditioned by time and context. Rather, it becomes clear that this constellation bequeaths an abiding and basic theological problem. The about-face which Barth himself advocated at that time and which he demanded uncompromisingly from others is not a finished issue. In contemporary German Protestant theology, this seems to be either broadly denied or remains undiscussed. Perhaps elsewhere the situation is much too critical, or it is seen too clearly for one to be content with such historicizing.[20] Supporting this, in 2001, Stanley Hauerwas — at the Gifford Lectures of all places, which were established for the promotion of a natural theology of English origin! — regarded Barth's sublimation of natural theology as the decisive theological turn of the twentieth century. In modification of the metaphor, "God

18. Karl Barth, *A Shorter Commentary on Romans by Karl Barth,* trans. Maico M. Michielin and D. H. Van Daalen (Aldershot: Ashgate, 2007).

19. John W. Hart, *Karl Barth vs. Emil Brunner: The Formation and Dissolution of a Theological Alliance, 1916-1936* (New York: Peter Lang, 2001).

20. To that extent, much has fundamentally changed since the overview given by Richard H. Roberts on the occasion of Barth's 100th birthday, in R. H. Roberts, "Die Aufnahme der Theologie Karl Barths im angelsächsischen Bereich: Geschichte — Typologie — Ausblick," *Evangelische Theologie* 46 (1986): 369-393. The approach to Barth reception which draws primarily on the sociology of religion, as preferred by Roberts, in my opinion plays only an ancillary role today. In addition, there has been since then a blossoming of intensive interpretations of Barth's work, undertaken in the USA and in England.

scattered seeds in the world," Hauerwas understands Barth's new christological grounding of natural theology likewise in terms of a seed, but regards
it as something completely different from a seed of discord and thus sows it
himself anew.[21]

II. The Historical Background

Caren Algner has demonstrated how much Barth's entreaty for clarification
is not derived only from the thought process which he gained through his
engagement with Anselm's argument for the existence of God in his
Proslogion.[22] He, in addition, increasingly struggled, from January 1933 on —
and thus prior to Hitler's seizure of power — for a truly Protestant church
capable of taking its stand beyond and above church-political and socio-
political partisanship. It can only be truly Protestant to the extent that it is
driven by a genuinely *spiritual crisis.* This crisis can only be resolved through
a strict, faithful and obedient listening to the biblically proclaimed will of
God.[23] That Barth labels his third attempt at the elaboration of church doctrine *Church Dogmatics* is something that he understands more and more
against this background, that is, as a vehement *question about the truth of the
church,* and not (merely) as an indication of proximity to churchly life. Only
if the church lets itself be called to its "task" can it address the "context." By
this Barth means — drawing on advice he gave to Thurneysen regarding an
actual controversy in Swiss church politics, and in allusion to Brunner:
"'The other task . . .'? No, just the *one* task all the more!"[24]

I cannot resist, in this connection, quoting a comparison made between
Brunner's "Other Task of Theology" and the daily paper. Barth writes to
Thurneysen in January 1933, suggesting that "the reading of the newspaper is
certainly a recommendable thing, but perhaps not the placing of the newspaper to the left of the Bible" as a representative voice of the world's goings

21. Stanley Hauerwas, *With the Grain of the Universe: The Church's Witness and Natural Theology* (Grand Rapids: Brazos Press, 2001).

22. Karl Barth, *Fides quaerens intellectum: Anselms Beweis der Existenz Gottes,* ed. Eberhard Jüngel and Ingolf U. Dalferth, Karl Barth Gesamtausgabe (Zürich: TVZ, [1931] 1981).

23. See the letter from Barth to Thurneysen, January 30-31, 1933 (in *Barth-Thurneysen: Briefwechsel Bd III,* 346-354), 351; and Barth to Thurneysen, February 10, 1933 (ibid., 357-364), 361.

24. Ibid., 361.

on.[25] As is well known, Barth had otherwise occasionally recommended putting the Bible and the newspaper next to each other, and this recommendation is only too gladly repeated. But he had articulated early and clearly how this was to be interpreted — what he does not ever reveal is which newspaper the theologian ought to select, and whether it should be placed to the right or the left of the Bible! That question may yet offer sufficient material for many dissertations.

Already in *CD* I/1, Barth issues extremely harsh words concerning Brunner spending his time on opinions related to the area of culture, and, in doing so, departing from the *area of the church*.[26] Indeed, it was the church which Barth was seeking in these years, and the more he tried he did not find it, not even later in the Confessing Church and certainly not after its second synod in Berlin-Dahlem (1934). Furthermore, Brunner's flirtation with the Oxford Movement and the Moral Rearmament signals, in Barth's view, an avoidance of the urgently decisive questions of the church struggle in which Barth feels left more and more alone. He enters into an *isolation,* which he is willing to accept for the sake of the *truth of this confession.* This explains the sharpness of his rebuttal of Brunner. Finally, it declares itself: it concerns a contradiction in "the task"; Brunner intends and wants "essentially something completely different" than he does.[27]

The importance of this nexus of the true church and theological decisions cannot be overestimated. "Is not 'love' where it concerns the church an unbelievably much *harder* affair than we all conceive? Must it not go hand in hand with an *absolute* fight for the truth?" Charlotte von Kirschbaum asks of Eduard Thurneysen, and she may be speaking here as Barth's *alter ego.*[28] For von Kirschbaum and Barth, this is a rhetorical question, but it is not that for Thurneysen. He genuinely wrestled with the struggle for the truth in the church and for the church — a struggle which Thurneysen does not want to evade under any circumstances when it thrusts itself upon him! — and how this struggle relates to theological argument. This goes far beyond stylistic questions of a theological "culture of debate," and only marginally does it perhaps have something in common with rules of etiquette and behavior. When Thurneysen speaks of the problem of polemic in the church, he then asks whether an inconsiderateness for the sake of the "task" of theology must

25. Ibid.

26. See *CD* I/1, 26.

27. Barth to Brunner, January 1, 1933 (in *Barth-Brunner: Briefwechsel,* 213-217), 214-216.

28. Von Kirschbaum to Thurneysen, December 3, 1934 (in *Barth-Thurneysen: Briefwechsel Bd III,* 772-778), 775, with reference to Calvin (775f.).

necessarily result in an inconsiderate talking with and about one another.[29] Certainly one requires clarity in theological thinking, especially in the evaluation of theological tasks and challenges! However, I would like to ask with Thurneysen: cannot such clarity combine itself with a readiness to help the interlocutor in his argument without the attitude of a know-it-all so that he might be able to recognize his own mistakes and arrive at a mutually supportable insight? Thurneysen is convinced that the insistence for theological clarity and the readiness for common insight go hand in hand; one does not attempt to arrive at clarity by the drawing of lines between people, but between views. Why cannot mistakes in reasoning be pointed out and corrected without immediately calling theological integrity into question? This does not only depend upon temperament, but can become a question of the character of theology.

Here Barth thought, and accordingly behaved, differently. His personal record repeatedly shows how he tended to subject those closest to him to harsher judgments, even rigorous condemnations, while remote dissenters were often treated more generously, or, at least, with greater complexity. It almost seems that Barth wanted to hold up before his friends, or those who held themselves as such, a mirror which distorted their views in order to expose more clearly the merest move towards dissent making it appear to be a substantial distortion. That he thereby often felt lonely was something that he accepted; there is even the impression that he appeared to seek this isolation, especially towards those who assured themselves that they were thinking along his lines without having to draw all of his conclusions.

Here, we approach the shallows of a character study or a psychogram. This Barth would have fervently refused to tolerate, and he could only react ironically to insinuations of this kind by Brunner by referring to Wilhelm Tell's statement that "the strong one is mightiest when he is alone" (Friedrich Schiller).[30] John W. Hart is surely correct with his observation that Brunner was not Barth's equal in terms of rhetoric and technical discussion.[31] Barth mercilessly played out his superiority, and he occasionally looked like a terrier shaking off an annoying little pup with a snap. Three decades later, he even regretted not testing

---

29. Thurneysen to Barth, December 1, 1934 (in *Barth-Thurneysen: Briefwechsel Bd III*, 764-772), 771.

30. Brunner, *Natur und Gnade*, 7; Barth, *Nein!*, 8; see the earlier exchange, Brunner to Barth, June 12, 1930 (in *Barth-Brunner: Briefwechsel*, 196-199), 199; Brunner to Barth, January 16, 1933 (ibid., 217-222), 221, and Barth to Thurneysen, January 30-31, 1933 (*Barth-Thurneysen: Briefwechsel Bd III*, 346-354), 352.

31. Hart, *Karl Barth vs. Emil Brunner*, 205.

his strength of arms against a better opponent.[32] That Brunner continually recruited Barth's attention and, if possible, acknowledgment, Barth either could not or did not want to admit.[33] Such things appeared to him, at best, as secondary, if not even embarrassing, not pertinent at any rate.

What is the important thing in a theological argument? Barth poses that: theology can and may not understand itself other than as a church science. And the church is only then the church — or rather, it newly becomes the church again and again — if it allows God's word to be spoken to it and listens to it alone. Only then can it address a situation of hopeless disunity and mental confusion and become the witness to the truth. In regard to this, all possible forms of considerateness are of little significance.

The exchange of letters between Barth and Thurneysen demonstrates, in reference to the example of his criticism of Brunner, that this was no easy matter for Barth. On occasion, he reveals that he suffered from the loneliness which his conduct produced and which he felt was imposed upon him. He does not arrive, however, at the thought that he might have engaged in a self-contradiction: in theological discussion, he asserts a certainty of judgment, even a self-certainty, that he in his dogmatics grants no theology on earth, no *theologia ektypos*. A church dogmatics worthy of the name can only *refer* to the truth of God which asserts itself. Dogmatics cannot substitute for this truth, and ought not want to do this. Therefore Barth calls dogma an "eschatological concept."[34] But there is virtually nothing of this to be perceived in the theolog-

---

32. In a letter, dated August 14, 1964, to Friedrich Schmid, the author of *Verkündigung und Dogmatik in der Theologie Karl Barths: Hermeneutik und Ontologie in einer Theologie des Wortes Gottes* (München: Chr. Kaiser, 1964), Barth writes that "I would have done better 30 years ago to have directed a frontal attack against Gogarten instead of against the so much weaker Brunner." Jürgen Fangmeier and Hinrich Stoevesandt, eds., *Briefe 1961-1968*, Karl Barth Gesamtausgabe (Zürich: TVZ, 1975), 264.

33. In his letter of condolence to Mrs. Margrit Brunner, dated April 16, 1966, Barth mentions that after 1934 he read all of Brunner's publications, but that he no longer had any need "to attack him, or to defend myself against him." Barth to M. Brunner (in *Briefe 1961-1968*, 328f.), 329. He had been much too busy with his own tasks to find the strength "to 'argue with him' once again. Perhaps that was what caused his suffering with regard to me?" (ibid.). To the dying Brunner, Barth conveyed yet another conciliatory word, in reminding him of God's "yes" before which every human "no" retreats. From a letter to Peter Vogelsanger, dated April 4, 1966 (in *Briefe 1961-1968*, 326f.), 326. Barth, however, never retracted his "No!"

34. *CD* I/1, 269. Barth draws this concept from his *Christliche Dogmatik*. Karl Barth, *Die christliche Dogmatik im Entwurf: 1. Band. Die Lehre von Worte Gottes, Prolegomena zur christlichen Dogmatik*, ed. Gerhard Sauter, Karl Barth Gesamtausgabe (Zürich: TVZ, [1927] 1982), 150, 62, 489, 583. See here, Gerhard Sauter, "Dogma als eschatologischer Begriff," in *Parrhesia: Karl Barth zum 80. Geburtstag*, ed. Eberhard Busch, Jürgen Fangmeier, and

Gerhard Sauter

ical argument. Barth speaks *ex cathedra*, although not with an anathema against the heretic, but with a denunciation of their views and arguments. This leads us to the second problem area: to the strategy of placing suspicion upon natural theology and to the front-lines which develop as a result.

III. Clarification over the Emerging Church Struggle

Barth was offended by the applause which Brunner received when he criticized Barth at Erlangen and Tübingen — bear in mind that it is the Tübingen and Erlangen of that period! — and regarded this as proof of Brunner's switching sides, of his conversion to the other party.[35] This reproach deeply injured Brunner, and its after-effects exerted an influence over his later approach, particularly in his theological anthropology. Was a legend of a theological stab-in-the-back being promoted here — the suspicion that false friends had secretly allied themselves with the opponent — had one's own troops attacked him and were thus responsible for such a collapse? What may appear to be an over-reaction on Barth's part can most easily be explained out of the decisive situation which not only confronted Barth every day in Germany, but which he also wanted to intensify and, if need be, force, because he saw in the confusion of German church politics — comparable to the tip of an iceberg — an actual symptom of a much deeper and far-reaching confusion.[36] He speaks of a "Babylonian confusion," by which he meant not only a linguistic disorder which renders communication impossible in the long term.[37] Rather, he has in mind an ideological endeavor to storm the heavens, a titanic rebellion which God himself must oppose — and, as it almost appears, Barth would see himself incorporated into the heavenly hosts which travel down from heaven in order radically to sweep away this collective confusion so that it finally becomes clear again who is "above" and what must remain "below."

Some years earlier Barth caricatured the theology of his teacher Wilhelm Herrmann as a pitiful enterprise to elevate itself to the height of a dogmatics:

Max Geiger (Zurich: EVZ, 1966), 173-191; later published in Gerhard Sauter, *Erwartung und Erfahrung: Predigten, Vorträge und Aufsätze* (München: Chr. Kaiser, 1972), 16-46.

35. Barth, *Nein!*, 8f. See Barth to Thurneysen, July 20, 1934 (in *Barth-Thurneysen: Briefwechsel Bd III*, 667-672), 671.

36. For example: Barth to Thurneysen, June 13, 1935 (in *Barth-Thurneysen: Briefwechsel Bd III*, 903-907), 905: "push to a decision," and "summon to a choice."

37. Barth to Thurneysen, January 30-31, 1933, ibid., 352.

"Aside from the path from above to below, there is no other way at all. Orthodox Christology is a glacier stream which flows from an elevation of 3000 m; one can do something with that. Hermann's Christology, as it stands there, is a desperate attempt to lift a stagnant lagoon to the same height by means of a hand pump. That cannot be done."[38] The pattern from above/from below becomes the Shibboleth which divides the spirits. "Natural theology" is every attempt to think theologically "from below." Whoever avoids this decision, who interposes other tasks, who seeks a "both-and" instead of an "either/or" with all its consequences, can only be a traitor to the task of theology.

Barth's front-line position is much too large a field for me to cover here. I must limit myself to a single and, in my opinion, substantial criterion. Barth defines his view of "natural theology" in an *ad hoc* manner, one which, from the outset, permits no space for Brunner's proposed distinction between a right and a wrong natural theology: "By 'natural theology' I mean every (positive *or* negative) *formulation of a system* which claims to be theological, i.e. to interpret divine revelation, whose *subject*, however, differs fundamentally from the revelation in Jesus Christ and whose *method* therefore differs equally from the exposition of Holy Scripture."[39] In this way, a ball of problems is formed by concatenating different questions with one another. There are, first of all, hermeneutical observations: the "point of contact" or the "preliminary understanding" as an inevitable initial condition of every human interpretation and every communication. Second, there are didactical tasks: "how" can theological knowledge be communicated, how can it be mediated? Third, there is a radical criticism of the tradition: not only is there a complete rejection of "neo-Protestantism," but also a principled denial of every historical-cultural-religious precondition for the knowledge of God. This Gordian knot is immediately and definitively cut through with a single blow: since theology is constituted by a *sui generis* foundation, this may not be subverted under any circumstances, not even through an alleged support that is supposed to bolster it anthropologically or by cultural history. What God by his self revelation has absolutely "established" as the given for theology, and which must be given to it again and again anew, is something which is never entrusted to a theologian, i.e., it is never at one's disposal. Rather, theological existence is first formed by virtue of theological "givens." In plain language: everything which opposes this theological *movement of thought*, as was recog-

38. Karl Barth, "Die dogmatische Prinzipienlehre bei Wilhelm Herrmann" (1925), in *Vorträge und kleinere Arbeiten 1922-1925*, 595.
39. Barth, *Nein!*, 11f.

nized as normative by Barth in his study of Anselm, is "natural theology" and susceptible to the suspicion of being a system.[40]

By this means, Brunner and indeed anyone who envisions for theology an additional complementary or merely preparatory assignment for theology in a way more or less like his, are put on the spot and pressed for a decision.[41] Theology, for Barth, does not require any protection on its flank because it exposes no open flank *if* it wants to be the theology of the word of God and nothing else, not even something next to it, before or supplementing it. Barth discursively attains clarification at this point — which he will often later reiterate — in that he seizes upon some misunderstandable terms, or if need be, only on one single opposable concept of his opponent, and, in doing this, accuses him of departing from the terrain of theology perhaps without even knowing so. In this instance, it is the "capacity for words"[42] of the human person, for Brunner a pillar of the "formal" image of God, which Barth reads as a human conquest of the address of God — and with this he ties a noose for Brunner.[43] That Brunner quickly thereafter regretted employing this admittedly unfortunate term proved of no assistance; rather, it could be assessed as a new demonstration of the linguistic confusion of which Brunner made himself culpable.

Barth's definitive rejection of natural theology, which pushes aside any analytical clarification as insignificant or even dangerous, is almost a classical example of the reduction of a problem, which is necessary and perhaps even extremely helpful in a period of crisis, but, in the long term, produces decisive

40. In *Nature and Grace*, Brunner speaks of natural theology as a "system of reason" which is sufficient in itself (32). He understands the term "system," however, differently than Barth who probably has a definition of system as employed by the philosophy of German idealism in mind. Brunner means an autonomous *structure of argumentation* that rests in itself, that is, however, limited and serves the theology of revelation as a "substructure." "System" is, as it were, one of many elements from which theology is assembled, so to speak. Barth speaks, by contrast, of one "way": of *the movement of thought* which is evoked by God's revelation and which follows after it.

41. Barth to Thurneysen, dated June 13, 1935 (in *Barth-Thurneysen: Briefwechsel Bd III*, 903-907), 905.

42. Brunner, *Natur and Gnade*, 18f., 41, and, in turn, receptivity "for the word of God" (18), "addressability" (18f.) — and fatally "capacity for revelation" (15). With Barth's criticism of this expression Brunner not only feels misunderstood, but sees himself also wrongly quoted: he did not speak of the "human capacity for revelation" which, if it were true, "would be truly gruesome," but of "the revelatory power of the works of God in the sense of Romans 1, that is to say, in the sense of the hypothetical possibility for the non-Christian, and of the positive possibility for the Christian" (Brunner to Thurneysen, cited in *Barth-Thurneysen: Briefwechsel Bd III*, 751).

43. Barth, *Nein!*, 16-20, 24-27.

reductions and leads to a confused discourse. This strategy, widely employed by Barth, proved later to be a boomerang which avenged itself on Barth: see, for instance, Dietrich Bonhoeffer's pointed accusation that Barth relies on a "revelational positivism,"[44] or, since the 1960s, the growing suspicion that Barth's appeals to the authority of the word of God that requires of humans a decision were decisionist and authoritarian and, at best, only serve to explain the autonomy of religion. It is in this sense that Barth's legacy today is dealt with by some who can only preserve his legacy by placing it in a larger theological context, possibly even moving it into the vicinity of Schleiermacher.

Considered from the perspective of "Systems Theory," operating with dualities or with "binary codes" appears as "a method of recognition" or as a "condition of self-identification," and it thus appears as a means of protecting identity — making it irrelevant for the knowledge of truth.[45] Dualities would be important only for the question of how a society, or part of one, can observe and describe itself.[46] This should give us something to think about in the argument between Barth and Brunner.

This controversy displays certain parallels to Luther's argument with Erasmus over the bondage of human will. But the question concerning how one can argue theologically about truth develops differently under today's requirements for communication, perhaps more focused than during the time of the Reformation with its relatively stable structures for discourse. An "either/or" approach, as Barth poses in relation to Brunner, risks a polarization with the political consequences of thinking of one as either a friend or an enemy, above all — as in this case — if it is coupled with a suspicion of political misconduct. But aside from that, the stratification of the battle field on which the struggle for natural theology is taking place calls for enlightenment.

IV. The Natural Theology Debate in Relation to neo-Protestantism and Thomas Aquinas

Barth wanted to bring the controversy with Brunner — representative also of his rejection of Rudolf Bultmann, Friedrich Gogarten, and other earlier

44. Dietrich Bonhoeffer, *Widerstand und Ergebung: Briefe und Aufzeichnungen aus der Haft*, ed. Eberhard Bethge, Dietrich Bonhoeffer Werke, vol. 9 (München: Chr. Kaiser, 1990), 404.

45. Niklas Luhmann, "Identität — was und wie?" in *L' argomento ontologico*, ed. Marco M. Olivetti, Archivio di Filosofia 58 (1990) 1-3 (Padova: CEDAM): 579-596, especially 591-593.

46. Ibid., 585.

theological wayfarers — to a head by asking after the impossible human possibility of the knowledge of God and orienting all other questions to this knowledge. Without God revealing himself and simultaneously veiling himself by evading all human grasping, no human can arrive at God and his truth. A point of contact which lies in human nature, however imperiled or in need of correction it might be, would be an absurdity for theology. God's grace does not impose itself upon or elevate human nature, neither does it sublimate the nature created by God so that would be perfected and at the same time preserved. From this follows Barth's deep dislike of the Thomist dictum: *"gratia non tollit naturam sed perficit."* Barth might also have been provoked by Gogarten's selection of this dictum as the motto for a collection of his essays, titled *Die religiöse Entscheidung.*[47]

In his answer to Brunner, Barth points out that Brunner has distorted Thomas Aquinas in taking him as a source of an "unbroken *theologia naturalis.*"[48] But, in the view of the relationship between grace and nature, Thomas is actually concerned with the question: can and will God not change and transform what we have incorrectly begun? Does this exclude a judgment and purification, a purification which consumes all of life's deceptions as a fire? Does not God's faithfulness to what he has created radiate over everything and on everything we do and omit to do — out of which we can claim no entitlement? All true knowledge of God can only and simply be received from God.[49] Eugene Rogers's questions move along these lines. He draws attention to the fact that Thomas is dealing more with the question of the direction of the will than he is with the question of knowledge: God's grace guides the incorrect will of humans, but does not destroy their autonomous will when he desires that the human should concur with God's saving will. To comprehend this, we must attend to God's work beginning with and going to the eschatological completion.[50]

If that is so, then it is difficult to proceed any further by only confronting "theology" and "anthropology" without also suggesting how a *theological* anthropology might be worked out. Such a position would not only have to

47. Friedrich Gogarten, *Die religiöse Entscheidung* (Jena: E. Diederichs, 1921), 2.

48. Barth, *Nein!,* 32. See Brunner, *Natur und Gnade,* 32.

49. Rogers, *Thomas Aquinas and Karl Barth,* 183. "Natural cognition of God without grace is a self-consuming artifact, *un*natural, *de*natured, a paradox." Rogers is referring here to Thomas's exposition of Romans 1:1-16 and 1:17-29 and to the *quaestio* 1 of the *Summa theologiae,* and he laments that Thomas is usually misinterpreted with reference to his acknowledgment of the natural knowledge of God in his *Summa contra gentiles.*

50. Ibid., 188.

resist making theology possible by means of an antecedent anthropology: rather, it should demonstrate how and to what extent one can speak about the human standing before God; what may be said of human being derived from God and pointing to God; how the human becomes aware of oneself here, and what light falls on the phenomena of human existence for this self-perception.

Barth, however, does not demonstrate much interest in these questions. Not during this period, at any rate, and later only in such a way that he reserves the phrase "real human"[51] for an anthropology grounded "on Christology."[52] Not a few "phenomena of the human"[53] are disregarded in the process.[54] Barth doubts that Brunner is seeking theologically defined phenomena of the true human and not just "neutral" phenomena. In his earlier controversy with Brunner, Barth does not situate theological anthropology anywhere in the debate. He perceives in Brunner, just as in Bultmann and Gogarten, an anthropology which is postulated to *ground* theology because it is *generally valid* — and this postulate is based upon a delusional doctrine of creation which gains its theological character only by devious means. Thomas, however, has nothing in common with this. He was not interested in a generally valid foundation for the knowledge of God outside of revelation. Barth's criticism could, with greater ease, be directed to the first Vatican Council,[55] and how the famous dictum *"gratia non tollit naturam sed perficit"*[56]

51. *CD* III/2 (1948), §44.3.

52. Ibid., §44.1.

53. *CD* III/2, §44.2.

54. Brunner counters, in his review of Barth's anthropology in *CD* III/2, that Barth had now caught up on that which Brunner had already aimed at in his *Natur und Gnade* and then developed in greater detail in his theological anthropology. Emil Brunner, *Der Mensch im Widerspruch: Die christliche Lehre vom wahren und vom wirklichen Menschen* (Berlin: Furche-Verlag, 1937). Emil Brunner, "Der neue Barth: Bemerkungen zu Karl Barths Lehre vom Menschen," *Zeitschrift für Theologie und Kirche* 48 (1951): 89-100.

55. Rogers, *Thomas Aquinas and Karl Barth*, 203ff.

56. Barth, who wrote at least part of his *Nein!* in Rome, refers to the *"genius loci,"* whose statement *"Gratia non tollit sed praesupponit et perficit naturam — Santa Maria sopra Minerva"* was "developed and used" by Thomas Aquinas, with his "superior systematic method and harmony" (37). The church of *Santa Maria sopra Minerva* stands on the land of the Temple of the *Minerva Calcidica*; its predecessor was built "in proximity to or even in the ruins of the old Minerva temple" (Ursula Kleefisch-Jobst, *Die römische Dominikanerkirche Santa Maria sopra Miverva: Ein Beitrag zur Architektur der Bettelorden in Mittelitalien* [Münster: Nodus, 1991], 17. See also *Santa Maria sopra Minerva*, pres. di Nilde Iotti, testi di Franco Borsi et al. (Rome: Editalia, 1990). The paraphrase, which Barth cites or which he coined, does not correspond to the language usage of Thomas, who, as far as I know, never

played out its notorious role in the Catholic apologetics of the nineteenth century.[57]

However, Brunner obviously cannot exclude the misunderstanding that he was advocating the autonomous reason of the human person. To be sure, as he emphasizes, this reason needs grace in order to be liberated from sin. Incorrect reason receives back its sense of direction which God had intended for it when he had created human beings in his image.[58] By grace persons are put in their right place and — now free from all cramp and tension — they are able to look responsibly toward God, at the world, and at themselves. This is how the Reformation doctrine of justification is distorted by neo-Protestantism. Barth sets his "No!" in opposition to *this*, and, for that reason, he wants to understand the theological doctrine of knowledge in correlation to the doctrine of justification.[59]

V. The Reception of the Natural Theology Debate

Stanley Hauerwas professes a christologically grounded "natural theology" of the variety Barth developed later in the course of his *Church Dogmatics*.[60] I can outline here only one leitmotiv of his Gifford Lectures: it is the unrestrained joy over the Christian church's appointment and calling to be *witness* of the truth, which was neither produced by, nor can be secured by, the church. Theology is therefore liberated from the burden of having to prove itself as universally acceptable, or even to implement a truth now realized. Hope for assent to the faith can be undermined by wrong arguments just as much as by apologetic strategies. At one point in this discussion Hauerwas states that "security kills the joy of faith." The witness cannot carry the full burden of proof to what he or she testifies. God himself accomplishes his

places *"praesupponere"* and *"perficere"* together. See, by contrast, ST I q.1.a.8 ad 2: *"Cum enim gratia non tollat naturam, sed perficiat, oportet quod naturalis ratio subserviat fidei; sicut et naturalis inclinatio voluntatis obsequitur caritati"*; I q. 2 a. 2 ad 1: *"[. . .] sic enim fides praesupponit cognitionem naturalem, sicut gratia naturam, et ut perfectio perfectibile."*

57. See Bernhard Stoeckle, *'Gratia supponit naturam': Geschichte und Analyse eines theologischen Axioms unter besonderer Berücksichtigung seines patristischen Ursprunges, seiner Formulierung in der Hochscholastik und seiner zentralen Position in der Theologie des 19. Jahrhunderts*, StAns 4 (Rome: Herder, 1962).

58. For example, Jae Jin Kim, "E. Brunner: Sein Denkweg und die Dialektik der autonomen Vernunft," *Korea Journal of Systematic Theology* 1 (1997): 149-166.

59. Barth, *Nein!*, 38.

60. Stanley Hauerwas, *With the Grain of the Universe*, especially 158f., 166f., 193-204.

truth. We cannot realize his truth either by arduous activity, or by the exertion of thought. This does not exclude "naturally," but demands that we speak intelligibly for those who disagree with our testifying to the truth. Because each witness, each discussion of faith, can happen alone in hope that God will let his seed, which is scattered world-wide, sprout and mature.

Fully ten years after the Barth/Brunner controversy, Hans Joachim Iwand formulated one of its unresolved issues in what I regard as a very judicious way: "The repentance demanded of theology today consists of assigning revelation to our eon and natural theology to the coming eon. The theme of the true religion is the eschatological goal of theology."[61] It is in light of this perspective that one of the ecclesially practical side-effects of this argument must be rightly assessed: if I am correctly informed, the "conference centers" of the Swiss Reformed Church, a counterpart of the German Protestant academies which developed after the Second World War, were without exception grounded and led by students of Emil Brunner. They were conceived as discussion forums for eristic theology which Brunner envisioned, as means for the fulfillment of the "other task" of theology. Theologians trained only in the Barth school, as it was reported to me, were not interested in this since they saw themselves, due to theology's one and only task, called simply and solely to the pulpit. The Swiss conference centers have, for a long time now, no longer been interested in the task Brunner held so dear. That can be counted against him as little as what can be heard from many pulpits today can be used against Barth's concise explanation of his "no" against Brunner: "No, just the *one* task all the more!"[62]

61. Hans Joachim Iwand, *Glauben und Wissen,* ed. Helmut Gollwitzer, Nachgelassene Werke, vol. 1 (München: Chr. Kaiser, 1962), 291.
62. This article formerly appeared in German as "Theologisch miteinander streiten — Karl Barths Auseinandersetzung mit Emil Brunner," in *Karl Barth in Deutschland (1921-1935): Aufbruch — Klärung — Widerstand,* ed. Michael Beintker, Christian Link, and Michael Trowitzsch (Zürich: TVZ, 2005), 267-284.

God *Is* His Decision:
The Jüngel-Gollwitzer "Debate" Revisited

Bruce L. McCormack

This is the story of a debate which never took place, a debate which remained stillborn because one of its members chose not to participate.

In December 1964, a very young Eberhard Jüngel completed work on a masterful study of Karl Barth's *Church Dogmatics* and sent it off to the publisher. The work was entitled *Gottes Sein ist im Werden: Verantwortliche Reden vom Sein Gottes bei Karl Barth: Eine Paraphrase.*[1] I call this work "masterful" because what it offered was much more than an interpretation of this or that aspect of Barth's teaching; it was nothing less than an attempt to uncover the underlying logic of the whole, the material connections of its various parts in the space of some 120 pages. It was an audacious work as well, in that it sought to show that the doctrine of the Trinity performs the same function in Barth's theology as demythologization performs in Bultmann's, viz. that of warding off false objectifications of divine being. And, finally, it was an audacious work in another sense. Jüngel's goal throughout was to use perspectives derived from Barth's dogmatics to dismantle the doctrine of God set forth by Helmut Gollwitzer in his *Die*

---

1. Eberhard Jüngel, *Gottes Sein ist im Werden: Verantwortliche Reden vom Sein Gottes bei Karl Barth. Eine Paraphrase,* 2nd ed. (Tübingen: J. C. B. Mohr (Paul Siebeck), 1967); ET idem, *God's Being Is in Becoming: The Trinitarian Being of God in the Theology of Karl Barth, A Paraphrase* (Grand Rapids: Wm. B. Eerdmans, 2001). This is, perhaps, the appropriate place to raise a mild protest against the practice of altering titles — or, in this case, sub-titles — in order to make books more marketable. "Responsible speech with regard to the being of God" is not only what the sub-title says; it is also a more apt characterization of what is ultimately at stake in this book.

Existenz Gottes im Bekenntnis des Glaubens, the third edition of which had appeared that same year.[2]

Gollwitzer was one of Barth's favorite former students, a very close friend, and he had also been the great man's choice to succeed him in Basel upon his retirement in 1961.[3] The inequality in age (Jüngel was but 30 years

---

2. Helmut Gollwitzer, *Die Existenz Gottes im Bekenntnis des Glaubens,* 2nd ed. (Munich: Chr. Kaiser Verlag, 1963); ET idem, *The Existence of God as Confessed by Faith* (Philadelphia: The Westminster Press, 1965).

3. Eberhard Busch, *Karl Barth: His Life from Letters and Autobiographical Texts* (Philadelphia: Fortress Press, 1976), 454. Barth himself laid his finger on the audacity in a letter to his good friend, Gollwitzer. "A packet just arrived from Ernst Fuchs containing the galley proofs of a book by Jüngel which — *ecce!* — takes aim at *you* and criticizes you on the basis of the *Church Dogmatics.* What next!" Karl Barth to Helmut Gollwitzer, March 1, 2, 1965, in Barth, *Briefe, 1961-1968,* ed. Jürgen Fangmeier and Hinrich Stoevesandt (Zürich: TVZ, 1975), 296. It would be a mistake to assume, however, that the bewilderment (exasperation?) registered in this comment rested on close study of Jüngel's analysis and argument. Barth had, after all, only just received the text and he need only have read the Foreword to know that Gollwitzer was being challenged. What we do know is that the book would, quite soon after this letter to Gollwitzer, become a sidebar discussion in a *Sozietät* devoted to Moltmann's *Theology of Hope.* "Every second week, a small circle meets in our dining room — around six to eight students who participate very energetically. We are, just now, discussing the book by 'Jüngel' in which the participants are generally interested. Eduard Thurneysen comes too." Unpublished letter from Charlotte von Kirschbaum to Gertrud Staewen, March 21, 1965 (KBA 9265.28). The quotation marks around the name of Jüngel is probably a reference to the fact that Jüngel himself referred to the book in his sub-title as a "paraphrase" of Barth. If so, it leaves open the question whether the statement is made in jest or in seriousness — whether, in other words, von Kirschbaum is criticizing Jüngel on the grounds that his "paraphrase" is more nearly his own theology than Barth's or so nearly identical to it that one can only speak of the work as Jüngel's in a derived sense. Be that as it may, since the book was not yet in print at the time of the discussion mentioned by von Kirschbaum, the students would have had no access to it and it seems likely that Barth would have had to provide some sort of provisional assessment of it in order for a discussion to take place. Even then, it is impossible to know with certainty how much of the manuscript Barth had read to that point in time. When, finally (some months later), Barth purchased a copy of the published work, he would then read only up through p. 72 of the German edition — which means everything prior to Part III. That would seem to suggest that the provisional assessment provided by Barth at the *Sozietät* mentioned in the von Kirschbaum letter touched only on the material which dealt directly with Gollwitzer, i.e., Part III. But since minutes were never kept of *Sozietäten,* we cannot be sure what judgment, if any, Barth registered in relation to this book. What is certain is that Barth wrote to Jüngel on April 13, 1966, to extend a special word of invitation to the celebrations of his 80th birthday which were to take place in Basel on May 9 of that year. The language is worth noting. "It would give me great joy to see you among the invited guests because I have gotten to know you as one, among the younger generation of theologians today, who has studied my work thoroughly but who is also willing and has the capacity to carry further the work that is needed today indepen-

of age while Gollwitzer was nearly 56) and attainments may, in part, help to explain why Gollwitzer chose not to respond publicly.[4] I suspect that it also may have had something to do with the fact that there could be no truly satisfactory answer to Jüngel's very persuasive analysis and argumentation![5] In

---

dently and fruitfully." Karl Barth to Eberhard Jüngel, 13 April 1966 in *Briefe, 1961-1968*, p. 328. That comment helps us to understand Eberhard Busch's claim that "Jüngel was one of the young men whose progress Barth followed hopefully, because of his attempt to re-express the doctrine of God presented in the *Church Dogmatics*, against a background of study with Rudolf Bultmann and Ernst Fuchs." See Busch, *Karl Barth*, 491. My warm thanks to Hans-Anton Drewes for pointing me to the von Kirschbaum letter and for leading me through his own understanding of what can be known of Barth's reception of Jüngel's book. One final comment: in 1978, Daniel Migliore recalled a conversation from his memorable post-doctoral year in Tübingen (summer 1965 to summer 1966). "According to a reliable report, Barth himself judged that while Gollwitzer was right *vis-à-vis* Braun, Jüngel was right *vis-à-vis* Golliwitzer." See Migliore, "Review of *The Doctrine of the Trinity: God's Being Is in Becoming*," *Theology Today* 35 (1978): 96. Unfortunately, Migliore can no longer remember who the source of the "reliable report" was. As a consequence, this story cannot possess the level of verifiability needed in historical reconstruction. But it remains suggestive, nonetheless.

4. That Jüngel had already been teaching at the *Sprachenkonvikt* in East Berlin for some three years by that point in time (and prior to the completion of his *Habilitationsschrift* in 1964) was the direct result of the building of the Berlin Wall. "When Erich Honecker, under orders from Walter Ulbricht, raised the wall, the seminary students who lived in East Berlin were cut off from their professors who lived in West Berlin. In order to ease the academic emergency, Kurt Scharf, who would later become Bishop of Berlin, appointed me to a teaching position. Just a few weeks before I had received my doctorate in theology. (A few months later police headquarters in East Berlin wanted to take the doctorate away from me.) As a consequence, I was very poorly prepared. Thus I began to burn a lot of midnight oil. Often on the evening before I still didn't know what I would lecture on the next morning (yes, academic nights are long)." Eberhard Jüngel, "Toward the Heart of the Matter," *Christian Century* 108 (1991): 230.

5. Though Gollwitzer never spoke publicly with respect to Jüngel's "Barthian" critique of his doctrine of God, his student Friedrich Wilhelm did take a swipe at Jüngel in passing, in a comment on the student revolutions of 1968. There he wrote, "Karl Marx and the epochal year 1917 are the determinants of the reality experienced today and it is precisely the young Christians, inspired by their ecumenical comrades, who are pressing for the completion of the 'turn of the times' which took place in 1917 in society itself and through society in theology and church. Bourgeois existentialism has reached its final hour. Pannenberg's 'history' offers no substitute; it is much rather a return to positions found in the pre-Marxist nineteenth century. Jüngel operates for the time being in the metaphysical controversy over being and becoming. Moltmann alone has moved ahead." See Marquardt, *Studenten im Protest* (Frankfurt, 1968), 69-70. This comment reflects a gross caricature of Jüngel's theology. As we shall see, Jüngel was seeking in his paraphrase to overcome the, in its way, highly classical metaphysical doctrine of God set forth in Gollwitzer's book by means of a *thoroughly* anti-metaphysical account of Barth's theology. To say that Jüngel operates in a metaphysical sphere in raising the question of the "becoming" or "historicality" of God's being is not only

any event, the student revolutions which occurred just three years later would bring about a "change of fronts" in Christian theology in Germany. Interest in hermeneutical discussions and the Christian existentialism which it had spawned was supplanted to a large degree by interest in "political theologies." Within the realm of Barth research, the significant problems addressed by Jüngel were set aside by many as a needless distraction. My own belief is that Barth studies has always paid a high price for not paying closer attention than it did to Jüngel.[6] In this brief essay, I would like to redress the balance to some extent.

I. The Occasion for Jüngel's Book:
Gollwitzer's Debate with Herbert Braun

The occasion for Jüngel's dramatic entry into the field of dogmatic theology was provided by a debate which *did* take place — a debate between Gollwitzer and Herbert Braun, a New Testament scholar who numbered Karl Barth among his early influences but who was to be found on Bultmann's side in the demythologization controversy of the 1950s.[7] The is-

---

unjust; it is cynical. For it asks readers to ignore the fact that it was precisely Gollwitzer's work that made necessary the challenge to metaphysics — and to do so for no better reason than that Gollwitzer had embraced the new political "reality" whereas Jüngel had not.

6. Jüngel's reaction to the nearly contemporaneous rise of "political" readings of Barth's theology is instructive — both with regard to his own intentions and also with regard to what was at stake in his own anti-metaphysical reading of Barth: "I have remained skeptical with regard to the 'political theology' which blossomed at that time and a Barth-interpretation which reached its peak in the claim that God's being is a being in the revolution. This is not because I understood theology to be irrelevant to praxis and apolitical but rather because I saw in this undertaking an exact repetition of that against which Barth had so passionately struggled, viz. that God should ever be allowed to function as a predicate of history. The point instead was to understand history as a predicate of God and, in this way, to honor the truth in faith and action. I was not prepared to replace the old compulsion to think along the lines of metaphysics with a new quasi-political compulsion to act." See Eberhard Jüngel, "Unterbrechung des Weltlebens: Eberhard Jüngel über 'Gottes Sein ist im Werden' (1965)," in *Werkbesichtigung Geisteswissenschaften: Fünfundzwanzig Bücher von ihren Autoren gelesen,* ed. Henning Ritter (Frankfurt am Main: Insel Verlag, 1990), 135.

7. The first edition of Gollwitzer's book appeared in 1963. Its strong critique of Braun's theology led to an often quite heated public debate in Mainz on February 13, 1964. The debate was recorded and subsequently published. See "Post Bultmann Locutum: Eine Diskussion zwischen Professor D. Helmut Gollwitzer (Berlin) und Professor D. Herbert Braun (Mainz)," vol. 1, ed. Horst Symanowski, *Theologische Forschung: Wissenschaftliche*

sue between them may be aptly summarized as follows. Is the word "God" simply a name we give to the event in which "faith" takes its rise in the human (Braun's view) or is the name rightly given to an objectively real Reality (Gollwitzer's position)? If the latter, can theology speak responsibly of this Reality without resorting to an outmoded form of metaphysical thinking? And if it cannot, is not the reduction of the role of theological language to description of human states of consciousness inevitable?

Read today, what is most striking about this debate is the extent of *agreement* between the two combatants. Gollwitzer is happy to concede, for example, that talk of God's "objectivity" carries with it the risk that the being of God will be confused with the objectivity of "thinglike givenness."[8] In order to prevent such an outcome, he argues that God does not "exist" in the same way that plants, animals, rocks, and human persons "exist." For these "things" owe their being to Another; God does not. Hence, when we use the word "existence" in relation to God or when we say simply "God exists," we are using the word "exists" in a "symbolic" way (Tillich); i.e., "it requires special comment, which must consist in correlative positive and negative safeguards."[9] The negative safeguard consists in the reminder that God does not belong on a list of things that "are." As the early Barth put it, "The gods exist, the one God, the Father, does not 'exist.'"[10] And Gollwitzer adds, again very much in line with the early Barth, "If he belonged in this list, then he could become an object without remaining subject."[11] The true God, in other words, remains Subject even as he makes himself the object of human knowing and experiencing.

But, second, if God does not "exist" as things "exist," if "existence"

Beiträge zur kirchlich-evangelischen Lehre 37 (Hamburg-Bergstedt: Herbert Reich Evangelischer Verlag, 1965). This publication of this volume was accompanied by a second containing further reflections by Gollwitzer and, most notably, Hans-Werner Bartsch. See "Post Bultmann Locutum: Eine Diskussion zwischen Professor D. Helmut Gollwitzer (Berlin) und Professor D. Herbert Braun (Mainz)," vol. 2, ed. Hans-Werner Bartsch, *Theologische Forschung* 38 (Hamburg-Bergstedt: Herbert Reich Evangelischer Verlag, 1965). Barth read this exchange with interest and observed privately to Gollwitzer that Braun's contributions to this debate put him in mind of a "voice from Auerbach's cellar." The reference, of course, is to the voice of Mephistopheles, who took Faust to Auerbach's cellar (a wine bar in Leipzig). See Karl Barth to Helmut Gollwitzer, March 1, 2, 1965, in Barth, *Briefe, 1961-1968*, p. 294.

8. Gollwitzer, *The Existence of God*, 202.

9. Ibid., 204.

10. Ibid. Gollwitzer is here citing Karl Barth, *Die Auferstehung der Toten* (Munich: Chr. Kaiser Verlag, 1924), 19.

11. Gollwitzer, *The Existence of God*, 204.

means something other and different when applied to him, then we must be taught how to use the word rightly. This happens in that we base all of our talk of God's existence on the basis of his "self-disclosure"[12] — and herein lies the positive safeguard. What Gollwitzer has in mind in speaking of God's "self-disclosure" is preeminently the "encounter" with God which occurs in faith.[13] What happens in that event is that God "addresses"[14] himself to a human person in such a way that she hears the word of "promise" and receives her justification. God himself is present in his address but "present" in a way that keeps him from becoming identical with any object to be found in the world of the "objectively ascertainable," the world of "things" which lay no claim on the human and which can be considered in a disinterested fashion. God is "present" in hiddenness;[15] he remains Subject even as he gives himself to be known in and through an object. And it is precisely this element of hiddenness which ensures that the relation to God *cannot* be one of disinterest. God encounters us and we are placed under judgment and made alive. To say that "God is" on the basis of this encounter is to be have one's whole situation fundamentally altered; it is to be changed.

> "God is" is not a neutral statement in the indicative which asserts in the first instance an existence as such and still leaves it an open question what that existence means for us. It immediately changes our situation and can thus only really be said in the form of confessing to that change, acquiescing in that change. The grammatical subject of this proposition is indeed from the start no empty subject but contains the whole event of revelation. Thus if a man really recognizes what this proposition says and in recognizing it accepts it, then he not only accepts an existence of God in itself, but also assents to God's being what he encounters us as in his revelation. . . . Hence we have not here to do with one of the truths which we can ascertain without any change in our own being, but with the truth which must change us in order to be able to be accepted by us, which we are not free for without more ado, which we have no desire for as we are, but for which we have been made free by itself. In the proposition "God is," the enmity between God and man is done away.[16]

12. Ibid., 205.
13. Ibid., 214.
14. Ibid., 209.
15. Ibid., 221.
16. Ibid., 214.

For Gollwitzer, "God is" is a statement which can only rightly be made — in the words of Eugen Rosenstock-Huessy — "in the vocative. Since God's favor and giving is the ground of the creation's existence, we can speak properly and strictly of that existence only as one that does not exist in itself but happens, as one that can be spoken of only in verbs and in the form of doxology."[17] Or, as Franz Rosenzweig put it in his *Star of Redemption*, "God's I remains the root word that sounds like a pedal note all through revelation; it resists all attempts to translate it into a He, it is I and must remain I. Only an I, not a He, can speak the imperative of love. That imperative must always only be: love me!"[18]

But, then, this surely ought to mean that there can be no talk of a God "in and for Himself but only of the God 'for me.'" And Gollwitzer is largely in agreement with this. But, he says,

> it is a fundamentally different matter whether this talk of God's being-in-Himself is rejected on dogmatic or on methodological grounds, i.e. whether it is rejected because of the content of what the event of revelation discloses to us concerning the confrontation of God and man, or whether it is rejected because of an anterior decision to the effect that we agree to mean by "God" not a being that has its place in the world of the objectively ascertainable, but the point of reference of our practical reason (Kant), of our moral existence, which we require and must conceive in order to give a "Whence" to our "I may" and "I must." "God" is then a concept without any objectivity, without any being of its own, used for the self-grounding of our existence as one that is morally challenged. This is conceived from the start in terms of the epistemological alternative between the objectively ascertainable and the existential, which already, before we encounter the Christian message, lays down the formal pattern for its interpretation and already determines in advance how the content of that message is to be understood. This is incorporating "the revelation of God in Jesus Christ in an already established system of the non-objectifiable" and as such, as Iwand says, is in actual fact "the victory of natural theology."[19]

I said earlier that Gollwitzer has more in common with Braun than he was, perhaps, aware of at the time. For he, too, wants to base responsible talk of

17. Ibid., 211-212.
18. Ibid., 212.
19. Ibid., 207-208.

God on the event in which faith takes its rise. He, too, resists any speculation about the being of God in and for himself and wants to limit talk of God's existence to what may be said on the basis of the *pro me* relation of God to the one addressed in revelation. The difference between Gollwitzer and Braun (which won't go away) has to do with the question of whether this limitation is really to be founded upon the event of revelation and it alone or whether it has all been decided in advance by an existentialist version of natural theology.

It should be added that Gollwitzer not only has much in common with Braun, but also with the early Barth. It is not without significance for an understanding of the differences which subsequently emerge between Jüngel and Gollwitzer that the latter first encountered Barth's theology in the early 1930s in Bonn whereas the former only met Barth in the winter semester of 1957/1958 in Basel. The significance of this difference has to do with the fact that in Bonn, Barth's theology still found its center of gravity in the event in which the Word is addressed to the individual whereas the mature Barth had his center of gravity in a highly actualistic and historicized Christology.[20] It is also understandable that Gollwitzer, as a Lutheran, should have prized the earlier theology so highly — for the early theology of Barth was more easily assimilated to the Lutheran interest in justification *by faith.*

But now, in spite of his intention to limit responsible talk of God to the God who has entered into a covenantal relation with the individual in Christ (the God *pro me*), Gollwitzer did affirm the necessity of speaking of God "in and for Himself." Or, to be more precise, he thought it necessary to affirm *that* God has a being "in and for Himself" even if he can say nothing further about it on the basis of the *pro me* relation. The "necessity" in question is one Gollwitzer thinks to arise out of the "knowledge of faith." "[W]e must not evade or shrink from saying also: *God is in-and-for-himself.* This must not be denounced in advance as a speculative proposition which forgets the *pro me* and speaks of a God who does not concern us. On the contrary, when it stands in the context of the confessing response to what God says to us, it denotes an indispensable element in the knowledge of faith."[21] Why should this be so? we might well ask. Because, Gollwitzer continues, in the event of God's address "the hearer confesses that he who stands before him has ap-

20. As Hans Urs von Balthasar rightly remarks, "As Barth continued to publish succeeding volumes of the *Church Dogmatics,* he gradually and without fanfare, but no less inexorably, replaced the central notion of 'the Word of God' with that of 'Jesus Christ, God and man.'" See von Balthasar, *The Theology of Karl Barth,* trans. Edward T. Oakes (San Francisco: Ignatius Press, 1992), 114.

21. Gollwitzer, *The Existence of God,* 217.

proached him in freedom, that in this approach, in God's being for us, he — man — received a free unmerited gift which is not grounded in anything that is necessary to God . . . but is grounded in his free, sovereign decision, in his 'groundless mercy', and for which man can therefore only be thankful."[22] It is in order to safeguard the *freedom* of God and therefore, the graciousness of the relation that it is necessary to affirm that "God is in-and-for-Himself" and not only "for us." The "necessity" of speaking of God "in and for Himself" is thus an inference drawn from the nature of the encounter itself. And it is this necessary inference which then allows (invites? tempts?) Gollwitzer to say that in this proposition "we have to do with . . . the old concept of the aseity of God as *theology* understands it."[23]

But is this even a "necessary" inference? Is it "necessary" to say "God is in and for Himself" in order to be able to say that God is free? Even more importantly: has the "freedom" of God really been defined by the being of God in the relation established in his address to the human where use is made of the "old concept" of aseity? How can the affirmation of the "old concept" of aseity *not* be a venture into the older metaphysics which Gollwitzer thinks himself to have overcome with his restriction of responsible speech about God to that which can be said on the basis of the *pro me* relation? Such questions only mount when we consider that Gollwitzer can also say "The fact that 'revelation's mode of being is definable only with reference to persons' has its ground not in the essence of God, but only in the will of God, i.e. it is not possible to argue back from it to the essence of God in the sense of how God is constituted, but only to the essence of his will, i.e. from his will as made known in history to his eternal will as the will of his free love."[24] The distinction between the divine essence and will which comes to expression in this statement is, as Jüngel would point out, "thoroughly in line with the classical concept of substance."[25] It is precisely at this point that Jüngel

22. Ibid.
23. Ibid.
24. Ibid., 186. It should be noted that I have here offered a slight — if significant — correction to the translation of James W. Leitch. Leitch has "nature" where I have "essence." But Gollwitzer's original text said (quoting from Bonhoeffer's *Akt und Sin*) "Daß 'die Seinsart der Offenbarung nur im Bezug der Personen bestimmbar' ist, hat nicht im Wesen Gottes, sondern im Willen Gottes seinen Grund. . . ." John Webster gets this passage right in his translation of Jüngel's citation of it where he has "Gollwitzer stresses that the mode of being of revelation . . . has its ground 'not in the essence of God but in his will.' " See Jüngel, *God's Being Is in Becoming*, 5.
25. Jüngel, *God's Being Is in Becoming*, 106.

would attempt a correction of Gollwitzer on the basis of his own reading of Barth's dogmatics.

II. Jüngel's Understanding of Revelation as the Basis for All Responsible Speech about God

Jüngel shifts the ground of the discussion at the very outset from the individual's encounter with God to Christology. The effect of this shift is to refine and radicalize the basic question which must arise with respect to any talk of a being of God in and for himself. Instead of asking the more general question of how the being of God in and for himself relates to his being "for us," Jüngel now asks the concrete question: how does the being of God in and for himself relate to his mode of being as the Subject of a human historical life — a Subject which experiences suffering and death? He agrees with Gollwitzer that an answer to these questions may only be sought on the basis of "revelation." But once you have defined revelation in terms of the historicized Christology of the later Barth, as Jüngel does in his "paraphrase," you may not seek to find in God anything other or more than the conditions (the power or capacity needed) to explain this Christology. If you do, you will have left the ground of this Christology and will be building on some other soil.

According to Karl Barth, "Revelation is *Dei loquentis persona* [God speaking in person]."[26] What is meant by that is made clear when Barth adds, "in God's revelation God's Word is identical with God Himself."[27] Therefore, "revelation is the self-interpretation of this God"[28] — in the sense that what God *does* as the Subject of a human life in time constitutes a perfect and complete revelation of who and what God is. This does not mean, of course, that any human recipient of this revelation enjoys an exhaustive understanding of it; none do. It means only that God the Word leaves nothing proper to him as God behind in becoming human. It means that, on the objective side of the relation established in revelation, God is fully and completely present in his very being as God. "[I]n revelation, 'the fullness of the original self-existent being of God's Word reposes and lives.'"[29] Revelation is,

---

26. Ibid., 27, here quoting Karl Barth, *Church Dogmatics* I/1, trans. G. W. Bromiley (Edinburgh: T&T Clark, 1999), 304.

27. Jüngel, *God's Being Is in Becoming*, 27.

28. Jüngel, *God's Being Is in Becoming*, here citing Barth, *CD* I/1, 311.

29. Jüngel, *God's Being Is in Becoming*, here citing Barth, *CD* I/1, 305.

thus, "not another over against God" but "the repetition of God."[30] Revelation happens in that God "reiterates" himself in the mode of being of a Subject in history.

Again following Barth, Jüngel goes on to argue that because God is himself in his act of Self-revelation, then he is both the *event* of revelation and the *revealedness* which flows from it. Therefore, in revelation, we have to do with the being of God "in a threefold way." "For God 'in unimpaired unity is the revealer, the revelation and the revealedness', or as it may also be put, 'the revealing God and the event of revelation and its effect on man'. Thus: God is subject, predicate and object of the event of revelation."[31] And so revelation is the root of the doctrine of the Trinity.

The importance of this last line of thought for Jüngel's overall argument lies in the fact that he finds in it the ontological basis in God for the revelation that occurs in time — and, more specifically, for the repetition of the being of God in history. That revelation is the repetition of God in time presupposes "a reiteration of God in eternity, 'a self-distinction of God from Himself, a being of God in a mode of being . . . in which He can also exist for us.'" In this way, the doctrine of the Trinity is made to be the ontological condition of the possibility of a revelation in time understood in Barth's sense. Jüngel goes on to describe the doctrine of the Trinity as the "hermeneutical foundation" for the whole of the *Church Dogmatics*.[32] Since hermeneutics is ontology for him — and must be, since hermeneutics has to do with the reiteration of the eternal being of God in the mode of a Subject in history — he is also saying that the triunity of God provides the ontological condition for the possibility of revelation.

Jüngel sums up the results of his investigation thus far with the claim that "the highest and final statement which can be made about the being of God is: God corresponds to himself."[33] That is to say, "God's being *ad extra corresponds* essentially to his being *ad intra* in which it has its basis and prototype. God's *self*-interpretation (revelation) is interpretation as correspondence."[34]

But things are not quite so simple as they might appear at first glance, on the basis of the account given thus far. For Jüngel also insists that "The Christology of the doctrine of reconciliation . . . points with strict necessity back to

---

30. Jüngel, *God's Being Is in Becoming*, 28, here citing Barth, *CD* I/1, 299.
31. Jüngel, *God's Being Is in Becoming*, 28.
32. Ibid., 17.
33. Ibid., 36.
34. Ibid.

the doctrine of election."³⁵ The movement of God's being in time — "The Way of the Son into the Far Country" and the "Homecoming of the Son of Man" finds its origin in an *event* which takes place in the being of God itself, an eternal event which Barth described with the language of "primal decision."³⁶ The correspondence of God with God which takes place in that God reiterates his being in time is *not* a correspondence of God's being in the mode of a Subject in history to a being of the Trinity abstracted from the eternal event of election. It is rather the correspondence of God's being in the mode of a Subject in history to a triunity of God which is itself *already* determined by the event of election. It is for this reason that Jüngel can quite reasonably ask:

> Does not this very distinction which Gollwitzer draws between the essence and the will of God (in distinguishing between the "essence of God in the sense of how God is constituted" from the "essence of his will") leave a gap in a metaphysical background to the being of God which is indifferent to God's historical acts of revelation? Clearly Gollwitzer does not *want* to say this. But can this consequence be avoided if the "essence of his will" which is understood as God's free love is not at the same time understood as the *will of his essence?* Is not God's essence *determined* precisely in his will? . . . Does not the *being* of God which becomes manifest in and as history compel us to think of God's being, in its power which makes revelation possible, as *already* historical being? . . . If we wish to think of God's being "in-and-for-itself," as postulated by Gollwitzer, in a Christian way, that is, in accordance with revelation, are we not *required* to think of this being as being which, in a certain way, is already historical being in advance, a being in which God as Father, Son and Holy Spirit is already, so to speak, "ours in advance"?³⁷

Jüngel's doctrine of "correspondence" turns out, on closer inspection, to be that of a correspondence between the being of God in revelation and the being of the triune God in the event of election. Such a view might well imply a certain *logical* priority of Trinity over election (God appears in the eternal decision of election as triune). But it does not imply an *ontological* priority of a triunity of God "in and for itself" in which God could somehow be "in-

---

35. Ibid., 14.

36. Ibid., here citing Barth, *CD* II/2, 9 and elsewhere; *CD* IV/2, 32.

37. Jüngel, *God's Being Is in Becoming*, 6, here citing (in the last sentence) Barth, *CD* I/1, 386. (It should be noted that I have lightly revised the last sentence in the Webster translation.)

Bruce L. McCormack

different to God's historical acts." There is no such ontological priority of Trinity over election in Jüngel's reading of Barth. What we need to do now is to inquire more deeply into the understanding of the relation of Trinity to election which is implied by Jüngel's reading.

III. God Is His Decision: The Relation of Trinity and Election

Jüngel does not explicitly address himself to the question of the logical relation of Trinity and election. His attention lies elsewhere — in the question of the relation of God's being "in and for Himself" to God's being in the mode of a Subject who suffers and dies. *That* is the "becoming" of which his title speaks, the "becoming" which leads to death. Still, it is possible to tease an answer to our question out of what he says about the divine election in Barth's theology.

Jüngel understands the "primal decision" in Barth's theology to be an eternal act in which God sets himself in relation "in both an inward and an outward direction at the same time."[38] "God relates to Himself in that he determines himself to be the one who elects." And "God relates Himself to humanity in that he determines humanity to be the elect."[39] But notice: "Decision does not belong to the being of God as something supplementary to this being; rather, as event, God's being *is* His own decision. 'The fact that God's being is event, the event of God's act, necessarily . . . means that it is His own conscious, willed and executed decision.'"[40] And that means further that "God's being is constituted [*konstituiert*] through historicality."[41] There is, therefore, no being of God that is somehow ontologically prior to this decision. If God "constitutes" himself as God in this decision, then there can be nothing prior to it. To be sure, God appears in this decision as triune, for Jüngel. For that reason, one might reasonably conclude that he understands Barth to have made triunity to be logically prior to election. But ontologically prior? No. "[W]e have to understand God's primal decision as an *event* in the being of God which *differentiates* the modes of God's being."[42] That is to say, it is an event which gives to each of the modes of being of the one God their particular properties.

Earlier, we saw that, in revelation, God corresponds to himself. We are

38. Jüngel, *God's Being Is in Becoming*, 83.
39. Ibid., 85.
40. Ibid., 81, here citing Barth, *CD* II/1, 271.
41. Jüngel, *God's Being Is in Becoming*, 81.
42. Ibid., 86.

now in a position to refine that statement further: "the historicality of the being of God . . . reiterates itself in the historicality of revelation."[43] The full meaning of the first half of this statement is made even more clear in the following statement: "God's primal decision is, at the same time, the 'primal relationship' between God and humanity, in which God turns to humanity and so is *already* with humanity before humanity was created. The primal decision constitutes the primal relationship of God to humanity and in this primal relationship there takes place 'primal history', in which, *before* humanity has been created, God *already* relates Himself to us. God's being takes place as *historia praeveniens* [prevenient history]."[44] Thus, the one being of God has a "double structure"[45] — a historicality of the being of God in eternity which is reiterated in time. It is this "double structure" which sets up the relation of correspondence between the being of God in election and the being of God in the mode of a Subject in time.

IV. An Unresolved Problem

I would like to say as clearly as I can that I think Jüngel has gotten Barth exactly right. At every step, it seems to me, his reading is in line with Barth's self-understanding, his own deepest lying intentions. But there is a problem with Barth's execution of his intentions which surfaces in Jüngel's account. For Jüngel expresses himself at times in ways which, if taken in isolation from the passages which have already passed before us, could be taken as implying an ontological priority of Trinity over election. I do think these sorts of statements work exceptionally. But they do need to be addressed — and explained.

To give just one prominent example, "In this determination, God's 'being-already-ours-in-advance', which is grounded in the trinitarian 'being-for-itself', directs itself, as it were, outwardly."[46] Here, the grounding in question *seems* to be ontological. And if it were, that would most certainly create the sort of "metaphysical background to the being of God which is indifferent to God's historical acts of revelation"[47] of which Jüngel rightly complains in relation to Gollwitzer. His correspondence theory and his

43. Ibid., 83.
44. Ibid., 90-91.
45. Ibid., 83, 87.
46. Ibid., 91.
47. See above, n. 37.

"double structure" only work to the extent that they are made to rest solely upon election as the ontologically "originating" event. As Jüngel himself puts it, "the decision of the election of grace not only affects elect humanity but also, at the same time, affects God in an originating way."[48] So why this apparent inconsistency?

A way forward to an answer might well begin with the reminder that this book intends to be a "paraphrase." However true it may be that it is more than that, it intends also to be that. And the truth is that Karl Barth never gave any evidence of having seen a tension between the doctrine of the Trinity set forth in *CD* I/1 and the doctrine of the Trinity made possible by the Christology of *CD* IV/1f. And so it is understandable that Jüngel should say "the doctrine of election . . . points back to the doctrine of the Trinity in the *Church Dogmatics*. . . . Thus God's moved being will certainly have to be handled — most especially in the doctrine of the Trinity — as a being moved by *God*. It is therefore not surprising that Barth's doctrine of the Trinity provides 'an answer to the question of the God who reveals Himself in revelation.'"[49] Again: Jüngel understands the doctrine of the Trinity as the "hermeneutical foundation" of the whole of the *Church Dogmatics*.[50] My point is that it is quite possible that it was convictions like these which allowed Jüngel, on occasion, to depart from his chosen path and to treat the triunity of God *as such* as the ontological ground of the correspondence between God "in and for himself" and God in the mode of a Subject in time, rather than the triunity of God that is *already* determined by the divine election. That such an outcome would undermine Jüngel's conclusions and, as we shall see in due course, his "program" in writing this book is clear. That such an outcome is possible at all is due to Jüngel's failure, at this point in time, to see that Barth's doctrine of the Trinity remains much too formal and abstract to be completely compatible with the Christology of *CD* IV/1f.

I repeat: if one starts, as Jüngel wishes to do, with Barth's later historicized and actualistic Christology as the basis for all responsible speech about God, then one can only posit in God the ontological conditions which make possible *this* Christology. In practice, that means that one cannot penetrate any further than the divine decision in which this Christology finds its ontological point of origin. Anything said about God beyond that which finds its

---

48. Jüngel, *God's Being Is in Becoming*, 84. (Webster's translation has here been lightly revised. Webster has for the phrase *in ursprünglicher Weise* "in a fundamental way.")

49. Ibid., 15, here citing Barth, *CD* I/1, 311f.

50. See above, n. 32.

root in the eternal decision would have to be said on some other basis than this Christology. Jüngel knows this — better than anyone. But he also thinks that "Barth's doctrine of the Trinity is already christologically grounded. . . ." It's not. Barth's doctrine of the Trinity was constructed step by step, from the Göttingen dogmatics, through the Münster dogmatics to *CD* I/1, in an effort to provide the ontological ground — not of his later Christology! — but of his doctrine of revelation, construed along the lines of a dialectic of veiling and unveiling. "I understand the Trinity as the problem of the indissoluble subjectivity of God in His revelation," Barth wrote in 1924.[51] And so it remained in *CD* I/1. "The task of the doctrine of the Trinity," as Jüngel rightly summarizes Barth's program in *CD* I/1, "is precisely to comprehend the subject of revelation as *the* subject who remains 'indissolubly subject in His revelation.'"[52] But that, in itself, is a reflection of the fact that Barth's center of gravity still lay, at this time, in the situation of the human recipient of revelation in the here and now of his/her existence. It did not lie in the God-human, Jesus Christ — which is why this doctrine of the Trinity is *not* Christologically grounded.

The truth is that the doctrine of the Trinity elaborated in *CD* I/1 is founded upon a highly formal analysis of the proposition "God reveals Himself as the Lord." It is this statement "or what this statement is meant to describe, and therefore revelation itself as attested by Scripture" which is "the root of the doctrine of the Trinity."[53] From it, Barth proceeds to derive analytically (as he thinks) the three moments of revelation which — if God truly reveals himself as *the Lord* (i.e., the one who indissolubly remains the Subject that he is even as he reveals himself) — must correspond to three moments in the being of the eternal God (to the immanent Trinity, in other words). But the concept of Lordship as it is employed here is indefinite and completely unspecified. It is not controlled by the thought of Self-humiliation and Self-limitation as it would be once Barth had written his doctrine of election. The power ascribed to God in this formulation is simply power in the abstract. And the notion of freedom which the formulation entails is simply that of freedom *from* external conditioning (indissolubility), not a freedom *for* the human. It is, in a word, the freedom of indifference which, as Thies Gundlach rightly says, would give a *relative* justification to those who would seek to find

51. Karl Barth to Eduard Thurneysen, May 18, 1924, in *Karl Barth — Eduard Thurneysen, Briefwechsel. Band 2, 1921-1930*, ed. Eduard Thurneysen (Zürich: TVZ, 1974), 254.

52. Jüngel, *God's Being Is in Becoming*, 34-35, here citing Barth, *CD* I/1, 382.

53. Barth, *CD* I/1, 307.

in Barth's doctrine of the Trinity the basis for an understanding of the Divine Subject in terms of "radical autonomy."[54] Gundlach is right: Barth's doctrine of election comes "too late"[55] to have an impact on the concepts of divine power and freedom resident in Barth's doctrine of the Trinity. Barth's doctrine of election in *CD* II/2 constitutes a "critical correction"[56] of the understanding of the Trinity and the being and attributes of God found in preceding volumes.

But the real test of the compatibility of Barth's early doctrine of the Trinity with his later Christology is to be found in the following critical question: could the early doctrine of the Trinity really provide the ontological ground for the later Christology? The answer to that is clearly no. The later Christology is historicized. Only a historicality of the triune being of God as founded in election could correspond to it. Or, to put a finer point on it: Jüngel's statement "God's suffering corresponds to his being-in-act"[57] can be true only *if* God's being-in-act is his being in the act of electing to suffer. But to put it that way is to suggest that it might be even better to grant election a certain logical priority over the being-in-act that is the triunity of God.

To his credit, Jüngel too would eventually come to the conclusion that Barth's doctrine of reconciliation constituted "a great recapitulation, but also a revision of the whole of Barth's theology."[58] It needs only to be added

---

54. Thies Gundlach, *Selbstbegrenzung Gottes und die Autonomie des Menschen* (Frankfurt am Main: Peter Lang, 1992), 164. For the thesis that Barth projects a modern concept of autonomy on to God, see Trutz Rendtorff, "Radikale Autonomie Gottes: Zum Verständnis der Theologie Karl Barths und ihrer Folgen," in idem, *Theorie des Christentums* (Gütersloh: Gütersloher Verlagshaus Gerd Mohn, 1972), 161-181.

55. Gundlach, *Selbstbegrenzung Gottes*, 161.

56. Ibid., 167.

57. Jüngel, *God's Being Is in Becoming*, 100. Jüngel goes on to say (very suggestively, I think), "It is...no paradox when we speak of 'God's being in the act of suffering.' This statement would be a paradox if the essence of God were a god incapable of suffering, as was sometimes maintained in the early church. . . . On the basis of Barth's inference from God's being revealed to his 'inner' being, we shall have to understand, *in* God himself, too, God's being-in-act which corresponds to the passion of the Son of God, as in a certain sense a *passive* being — passive in the sense of obedience. This passivity of obedience in God is also the highest form of activity insofar as it is *affirmed* passivity. It belongs 'to the inner *life* of God that there should take place within it obedience.'" Ibid., p. 101, here citing Barth, CD IV/1, p. 201 (the emphasis is Jüngel's).

58. Eberhard Jüngel, "Einführung in Leben und Werk Karl Barths," in idem, *Barth-Studien* (Köln/Gütersloh: Benziger Verlag and Gütersloher Verlagshaus Gerd Mohn, 1982), 53. Jüngel goes on to say, "The Christology anticipated in *CD* I/2 in nuclear form is now developed by taking up a critical stance in relation to the early church dogma and the doctrinal

that the Christology through which Barth effected this revision was itself dependent upon his doctrine of election.

In sum: it is not the doctrine of the Trinity *as such* which provides the hermeneutical foundation of the whole of the *Church Dogmatics,* but (after II/2) it is the triunity of God understood in terms of the *determination* given to it in the eternal act of election. The being-in-act of God is His being in the act of Self-determination. One cannot go behind this event, for there is nothing prior to it. And so, Christology is the epistemological ground of election and election is the ontological ground of Christology. That is the key to understanding the relation of the early volumes of the *Church Dogmatics* to the later.

That having been said, however, the magnitude of Jüngel's achievement cannot be underestimated. For the first time, the anti-metaphysical force of Barth's doctrine of election — and of a doctrine of the Trinity which has been corrected in its light — had been clearly seen.

V. Jüngel's Lasting Contribution

Jüngel's book is, perhaps, best remembered for the following claim, which constitutes the most significant result of his study. "[T]he dogma of the Trinity is the appropriate expression for the being of God. It protects the Christian doctrine of God from becoming mythological or slipping into metaphysics. . . . Paradoxical though it may sound, Barth accorded to the doctrine of the Trinity (1932) the same function which the programme of demythologizing performs in the theology of Rudolf Bultmann."[59] I think myself that Jüngel is headed in the right direction. But the claim is only true

---

formulations of, above all, Protestant orthodoxy, and made to be the foundation of the doctrines of sin, justification, sanctification, calling, the efficacy of the Holy Spirit in the congregation gathered, built up, and sent by Him, as well as the doctrine of the faith, hope and love of the individual Christian. In doing so, on the one hand, the anti-metaphysical trininitarian conception of God is intensified by the localization of the movement of humiliation and obedience unto death on the cross. On the other hand, talk of God which turns itself against an abstract 'theo-monism' is now enriched and made to be a 'theanthropology' by means of an exaltation of the man Jesus to the right hand of God, a movement which is localized in the being of the human. In both cases, the emphasis with which he had one-sidedly proclaimed the 'Godness of God' forty years earlier now experiences a *retractio* in favor of bringing to light the *particula veri* in the liberal theology he had once fought against: viz. that rightly understood, God's *Godness* includes His *humanity.* . . ."

59. Ibid., 33-34.

when the solution he advances to Gollwitzer's lapse into metaphysics has been secured by the critical correction offered in the preceding section. Only where God's triunity is never conceived of in abstraction from the eternal act of election is it the case that the dogma of the Trinity acquires the strictly anti-metaphysical force Jüngel would like to find in it. Only then is a reconciliation of aims (if not of approaches) with Bultmann possible.

But the program announced in this statement has yet to be taken up with the seriousness it deserves in the English-speaking world. Sadly, it was derailed by the politicization of theology which occurred in the late sixties. Though much has been gained through such politicization (I am thinking here specifically of the contributions of liberation theology), much has been lost too. What has been lost is a sense of the reality-referential character of talk of the *humanity* of God, of the *real* presence of the suffering God in and to human suffering, of the existence of *real* truth in the welter of conflicting opinions. Each of these dimensions of our life is finally hermeneutical in nature. And each is, for that reason, deeply ontological.

Jüngel's little manifesto is still lying on the table. It is my hope that a new generation of Barth scholars will take it up — with appreciation and real comprehension and attend to its lessons.

Conclusion

Daniel Migliore was a post-doctoral student in Tübingen from the summer of 1965 to the summer of 1966. During that time, he read with great profit both Gollwitzer's book on the existence of God and Jüngel's book on Barth. What intrigued him most about Jüngel was his attempt to narrow the distance between Barth and Bultmann. As late as 1983, when I took my comprehensive Ph.D. exam in systematic theology from him, he was still assigning Jüngel's book for the portion of that exam which dealt with theological method. To this day, I cannot think of Jüngel without also thinking with great fondness of Migliore. It was Migliore who first introduced me to Barth. In doing so, he set my course for life. And in putting Jüngel in my hands, he gave me a road-map to the *Church Dogmatics* which continues to illumine my work. Thanks, Dan! You have taught me a great deal and I will always be grateful.

The Time That Remains: Hans-Georg Geyer in the Intellectual Debate about a Central Question in the Twentieth Century

Gerrit Neven

In this essay, "The Time That Remains,"[1] I present the work of the German theologian Hans-Georg Geyer, because he is a paragon of a mode of thinking which enters the debate with one's contemporaries over central issues of the twentieth century.[2] That century was a violent one. It was a century in which the vision of modernity was obscured by two world wars and ultimately dissolved into the relativism of postmodernity. This development cuts deep into the flesh of the Christian tradition. Whereas initially Nietzsche and Marx only proclaimed the death of God, Michel Foucault and Gille Deleuze proclaim with equal force the death of man as well.[3] It is precisely under these circumstances that Hans-Georg Geyer chose the work of Karl Barth as the starting-point of his theologizing. He appreciated Barth as a theologian who does not ignore the radical denial of God and man, but enters the debate with

1. For the provenance of this title, see n. 47.

2. Hans-Georg Geyer (1929-1999) studied in Frankfurt from 1950 till 1954 with Hans-Georg Gadamer, Max Horkheimer, Theodor W. Adorno, and Wolfgang Kramer. From 1954 till 1958, he studied systematic theology in Göttingen and Berlin under the guidance of Hans Joachim Iwand, Ernst Bitzer, and Walter Kreck. From 1964 till 1967 he was Professor of Systematic Theology at the Kirchliche Hochschule in Wuppertal, from 1967 till 1971 at the University of Bonn, and from 1971 till 1982 at the University of Göttingen. From 1982 till 1988 Geyer was Professor of Systematic Theology and Philosophy of Religion at the University of Frankfurt am Main. He wrote his philosophical dissertation on Husserl (1954) and his theological dissertation on Melanchthon (1958), on whose reception of Aristotle he would habilitate in 1965.

3. See Michel Foucault, *The Order of Things: An Archeology of the Human Sciences* (New York: Vintage Books, 1994), especially the last chapter; Gilles Deleuze, *The Fold: Leibniz and the Baroque* (Minneapolis: Fortress Press, 1993).

its representatives. Unlike contemporaries like Jürgen Moltmann and Wolfhart Pannenberg, Geyer did not turn away from Barth. He did not share their criticism that Karl Barth would have locked up theology in a bastion. He did not regard Barth as a theologian who lived on the past, but rather, he valued Barth as a theologian who let the future affect his thinking.

I will not give an extensive overview of the reception of Karl Barth in Hans-Georg Geyer's thinking. It is my aim to show that Geyer is able to make fruitful use of the dialogical potential of Barth's theology. The key to this interpretation is the place of the parousia. In Barth's thinking about the various aspects of reconciliation, the parousia plays a determinative role. Following Barth, Geyer states that the Messiah's having drawn near is the precondition of a future-oriented and, therefore, dialogical mode of thinking. The parousia points to a nearness of salvation which does not, as it were, supernaturally demolish time and history, but rather breaks open time and history from within — messianically. This parousia asks for an attentive and communicative way of thinking and acting. That's why I have given this essay the biblical title, "The time that remains," from Isaiah 21:11: "An oracle concerning Dumah [silence]: Someone calls to me from Seir: 'Watchman, what is left of the night? Watchman, what is left of the night?'"

Geyer executed a transition from the closed thought-frames of metaphysics to the open and risky expectation of the Messiah, for whom each moment in time is an opening through which to enter. This expectation leads to intensive forms of discussion and debate, not just with theological colleagues, but also with thinkers like Nietzsche, Husserl, Heidegger, Horkheimer, Bloch, Sartre, and many others. The end of the twentieth century is the time which is constantly interrupted by the parousia. In the time that remains, the *novum* appears. This *novum* is not an immanent consequence of time, but it takes shape in the faith which dares to think risky thoughts. The reflection on faith thus takes on the character of an engaged theology, which is aimed at a praxis that breaks loose from the often forced patterns of thinking and acting. The focus in this reflection on faith is the humanity of Jesus Christ, whose humanity is still debated.

1. Introduction: Towards a New Mode of Thinking in the Footsteps of Karl Barth

Hans-Georg Geyer was eminently present at the center of the most important intellectual debates of the twentieth century. In these debates, he distinguished himself in that he was aware of being determined by a point that lies beyond the death of the metaphysical God. Geyer's thinking was free from the totalitarian traits of Western culture. As early as 1962, Geyer declared his agreement with Walter Benjamin's *Theological-Political Fragment.*[4] With this, Geyer distanced himself from the idea that historical convictions, scientific achievements, or political opinions had in themselves the potential to make "the jump ahead" to a time which is qualitatively new and different.[5] Our knowledge is determined by economic and political factors. The desire to know is driven by a force which excludes what cannot be calculated. Geyer is of the opinion that this force and the history of freedom contradict each other, and that the application of this force is incompatible with the freedom rights of the Enlightenment.

According to Geyer, however, the modern desire for power goes hand in hand with metaphysics of a modern sort. Metaphysics and modernity are closely related. Their relationship is one of succession. Geyer writes in a reflection on Nietzsche that both have led to a death: classical metaphysics has led to the death of God, while modern metaphysics to the death of man. The God of heaven was — according to Nietzsche — an illusion. Man has taken the place of God, but now — according to Geyer — he runs the risk of breaking down under the weight of his own drive for knowledge. Perhaps also the modern concept of man is based on an illusion. How, given these circumstances, should we move on?

At any rate, in this situation old thinking habits cannot be continued. A new mode of thinking is needed. This criticism of metaphysics (which was also part of the thinking projects of Geyer's theological contemporaries such as Moltmann and Pannenberg) was one in which the future became the paradigm of transcendence — a paradigm that informed the direction that

4. For the first time in 1962 and — insofar as I could ascertain — for the last time in 1998, in a discussion with Jürgen Seim, published under the title "Solus Christus." Cf. "Solus Christus — Das Eine Wort Gottes im Horizont der Heiligen Schrift," in *Christliche Theologie im Angesicht Israels: Festschrift zum 70. Geburtstag von Wolfgang Schrage,* ed. Klaus Wengst (Neukirchen, 1998), 3-22.

5. Cf. "Geschichte als theologisches Problem" (originally 1962), in H.-G. Geyer, *Andenken: Theologische Aufsätze* (Tübingen: Mohr/Siebeck, 2003), 52: "Faith, getting involved with and trusting upon the message concerning Christ, [is] at the same time radically renouncing the desire to discover the truth of the proclamation in past history. . . . Close to this truth is W. Benjamin's thinking, based on the best Jewish heritage: 'Only the Messiah himself will consummate all that is happening historically, in the sense that only he himself will redeem, consummate, create its relation to the Messianic.' Therefore, nothing historical can 'relate itself to something Messianic on its own account.'"

Geyer chose for his own thinking.[6] It will be shown below that in this he followed the sentence which stems from Barth's thinking, or rather from that of the early dialectical theology, according to which "our time is an implication of the *Parousia* of Jesus Christ."[7]

2. The Subjectivity of God and Man after the Twentieth Century

Geyer found himself at the heart of a discussion which had the future as its object. The idea of the death of God and the idea of the imminent death of man have not, in fact, left the theme of the future. Now, for Geyer the question was how the future can be thought of without somehow extrapolating the projects of the past. Following Karl Barth, Geyer took up a position which can also be found with great thinkers of our time. In contrast to Geyer, however, they are in the comfortable position that they can look back to the twentieth century *after* the turn of the century.

Radical Emancipation and Dehumanization

One of these great thinkers is the French philosopher Alain Badiou.[8] In his book *The Century,* Badiou establishes a conversation between several important representatives of the twentieth century. Important for my theme is the afterword of his book, "The joint disappearances of Man and God." Man and God — this is what in the end the conversation of the philosophers is all about.[9] Badiou remains in the background and lets others bring forward their ideas about the century. On the basis of these philosophical and poetic texts, many of which have become classic by now, Badiou shows what the foundational theme of the century was and what questions this period left

6. Just as with, e.g., Moltmann, Pannenberg, and Jüngel, the theologians who have dominated the discussion since Barth.

7. Cf. Geyer, "Karl Barths Umgang mit der Osterbotschaft des Neuen Testaments," *ZDTh* 13 (1997): 65-66: "To the question of the mode of this new thinking belongs the recollection of its being rooted in the remembrance (Andenken) of God's 'absolute subjectivity' in thinking-after the preceding, absolutely unpredictably concrete acting or doing in the resurrection of the Crucified One from the dead." Geyer regards Karl Barth as the teacher who tried a new mode of thinking: "He risks a new thought when he applies a new mode of thinking" (64).

8. Badiou is philosopher, mathematician, dramatic adviser, and novelist. He has become known to theologians especially through his book *Saint Paul: The Foundation of Universalism* (Stanford: Stanford University Press, 2003).

9. A. Badiou, *The Century* (Malden, MA: Polity, 2007).

behind. Badiou establishes that the death of God and the death of man form the great theme of the philosophy and the theology of the twentieth century. It goes without saying that this theme leads to the question how it should and can go on beyond this God and this man.[10]

In the twentieth century, Badiou writes, the theme of the death of man has been painted in two directions, which are related to each other disjunctively: they go together without, however, being sublated dialectically. On the one hand, there is the movement that radicalizes Kant's approaches. It leads to a construction of man in which he becomes the slave of his own emancipation. This line runs from Kant via Fichte to Sartre. On the other hand, there is the way of the radical anti-humanism of Nietzsche. Basically, its representatives argue "that the absenting of God is one of the names for the absenting of man. The joyous catastrophe affecting the divine figure (the gods, Nietzsche repeats, died of laughter), is at the same time the gay science of a human, all too human catastrophe: the dissipation or decomposition of the figure of man. The end of humanism."[11]

This either-or does not leave room for postmodern, partly religious, thinkers like Levinas or Derrida. In Levinas's appeal to God's radical otherness in order to safeguard the otherness of the human other, Badiou sees something forced.[12] In the circle round Derrida, a sort of religion of messianic delay or of *différance*, "a deferral of presence," came into existence.[13] This relation between philosophy and religion, too, is too artificial for Badiou.

Before Badiou, Geyer already distinguished these two lines. It is this attentiveness that constitutes the greatness of his thinking. Moreover, in an intensive, at times almost apocalyptic, way, he reflected on the possible consequences. The first, emancipatory line was sketched by Geyer extensively and with great care.[14] And he recognized the second, anti-humanistic line im-

10. Badiou, *The Century*, 165-178.

11. Badiou, *The Century*, 171.

12. Badiou, *Ethics* (London: Verso, 2001), 22: "The phenomenon of the other (his face) must then attest to a radical alterity. . . . This means that in order to be intelligible, ethics requires that the other be in some sense *carried by a principle of* alterity which transcends mere finite experience."

13. Cf. P. Hallward, *Badiou: A Subject to Truth* (Minneapolis: University of Minnesota Press, 2003), 157: "Nowhere is the incisive simplicity of Badiou's orientation more apparent than in his conception of time. Whereas Sartre's Philosophy is organised around the future, Bergson's around the past, and Derrida's around the deferral of presence, Badiou's subject lives in a time that is entirely saturated by the present, a time without promise, inheritance or reserve."

14. Cf., e.g., Geyer, "Norm und Freiheit," in *Andenken*, 306-332.

Gerrit Neven

plicitly in his work: in several essays he inculpates forms of knowledge which eliminate man as subject.[15] Thus, Geyer foresaw a dehumanization of the modern anthropological project. He observed that a thinking which emancipates itself from God and which at the same time is totalitarian, has driven away the concrete subject, which has a name, an identity, a thought and a dream, from large parts of science and technology. Therefore, renewed reflection can, Geyer thought, only come from beyond the end of this man. A new mode of thinking must be clearly aware of this end.

A Biblical and a Metaphysical World View

The essence of the distinction between the biblical-Christian and the metaphysical-Platonic world views is the subject of an extensive and unambiguous essay of Geyer's entitled "Atheism and Christianity."[16] According to Nietzsche — Geyer writes — the difference between the God of the Bible and the God of metaphysics would be irrelevant. According to Nietzsche, faith in God as a supersensual power in general would no longer have any real influence, since God is not ascribed any power anyway. However, it is precisely faith in such a power that would be necessary to determine the convictions and the actions of man.[17] This may be the case, Geyer answers Nietzsche, it may indeed look plausible that the distinction between "metaphysical" and "biblical" is only a subtlety. But the question is — Geyer continues — whether the ascertainment that God has lost his power over man and that the "supersensual heaven" has no meaning for the "sensual earth" must imply the death-blow to the gospel.

Geyer suggests that the answer to this question is no. For this, he reminds us that, unlike the metaphysical God, the God of the Bible *can* die. And he also makes clear that modern atheistic anthropology — whether of an existentialist or a Marxist sort — is bound to the form of metaphysical thinking. For that reason, Christian faith could impossibly be linked with this anthropology. "When the Christian faith is placed under the law of godlessness as a result of the inner destruction, then it should present itself as the religion of the identical life, that is, of the utmost which is possible and absolutely necessary in this world of contradictions that destroy each other.

15. Geyer, "Das Subjekt im Prozeß der Vergesellschaftung," in *Andenken*, 364-393.
16. Geyer, "Atheismus und Christentum" (originally 1970), in *Andenken*, 91-111.
17. Ibid., 92-93.

72

That is, as the effective and active hope that does not get tired of working out the world as a unity and a whole."[18]

Therefore, according to Geyer, Christian theology has the task, also argumentatively, to lead the Christian faith out of its dogmatic identification with a concept of religion that is still metaphysically determined. For this faith is "not a relation of man to his own being, but the perception of God's relation to the being of man as God's own act in the history of Jesus Christ which is unique in kind and in time."[19] This history teaches us that God can die, and that on the basis of this God's death, people, in faith, receive the power to be really earthly, finite, and to be able to die. According to Geyer, it is precisely this that distinguishes it from the religion of identical life, which has been informed by modernity. "Here, in the center of the Christian proclamation, in the message of the death of Jesus Christ on the cross . . . lies the orientation point of Christian thinking and speaking about God. In the Christian faith, who God is and what his essence consists of can only be thought of appropriately when we take as point of departure the view that the death of Jesus Christ on the cross is God's own act on behalf of all, which took place once and for all — as it has become clear from the beginning beyond the end, that is, from the resurrection."[20]

Thus, Geyer does not accept Nietzsche's analysis: it is inappropriate to lump together the God of metaphysics and the God of the gospel of Jesus Christ. Therefore, it is vitally important to prevent the difference, which at first glance may seem small and subtle, from disappearing from sight altogether.

3. Geyer's Project: Remembrance *(Andenken)*

Geyer's reflective project is called "Remembrance *(Andenken)*."[21] This is not the place to sketch the meaning of the word "remembrance" and its connotations in detail. The question here and now is only whether and in what way "remembrance" can lead to a new mode of thinking.

18. Ibid., 109.
19. Ibid., 111.
20. Ibid., 108-109.
21. Geyer's early works about Husserl and Heidegger cannot be discussed here. As for Heidegger, cf. especially his "Andenken," in idem, *Erläuterungen zu Hölderlins Dichtung* (Frankfurt: Klostermann, 1996).

Gerrit Neven

Remembrance as a Central Concept of Geyer's Mode of Thinking

A central part of Geyer's remembrance is the mimesis, the imitation of God in the praxis of love for one's neighbor. I think that for Geyer this mimesis takes the place which in metaphysics is taken up by ideological representation. Geyer tries to avoid ideology, because it is always an anonymous reality which shows itself veiledly in doctrines and ideologies. Thus, in his thinking Geyer does not take the way of ideological or even dogmatic representation, but — avoiding duplications — the way of mimetic presentation. Said in a Pauline way: also in thinking he is concerned with the apostolic existence, which does not *re*present, but which presents. In this context, Geyer mentions Paul's admonition in God's place: "Therefore, if anyone is in Christ, he is a new creation; the old has gone, the new has come! . . . We are therefore Christ's ambassadors, as though God were making his appeal through us. We implore you on Christ's behalf: Be reconciled to God" (2 Cor. 5:17-20).

Thus, the praxis of reconciliation mentioned here has its roots in God. In remembrance, God is a name, a *nomen proprium,* and not a concept. This name continues in the passionate plea to stop the production of fierce images and to practice the love for one's neighbor. This plea introduces in remembrance the mimesis of love (in Christ's place) in forms of a concrete praxis. So, it is not about ideological (symbolical) representations, but about presentations, it is about giving form to being as a witness to real reconciliation. Here, Geyer shows passion for the *realitas fidei:* remembrance implies for him — at least also — mimesis.

What "remembrance" entails is described by Geyer most beautifully, but also most complicatedly, in an essay on the true church.[22] The word "remembrance" cannot be found in this essay, but the immediacy of the name is exposed all the more clearly. Geyer's thesis is that the *church* presents the reconciliation that took place once and for all — called "evangelical substance" — in the active form of mimetic praxis.[23] "The specific moment of the kerygma of the Christian church, by which it distinguishes itself by its practical being from all the other mimetic functions within the whole exposition of its evangelical substance, is precisely related to the fact that the homiletic praxis of the application of the 'word of the cross' as the 'word of reconciliation' in the name of Jesus Christ, of the crucified Son, is, among all the sorts of mimesis of the gospel of Jesus Christ in and by the church, that sort [of

22. Geyer, "Wahre Kirche," in *Andenken,* 227-256.
23. Ibid., 235.

74

mimesis] in which not only the verbality, but in the verbality of the gospel its elementary nominal character shows itself with irreducible immediacy."[24]

Of course, Geyer's conception of remembrance does not entail a licence for glossolalia, but neither does conceptuality have primacy in remembrance. The mimesis is not anti-intellectual, but it wants to be a preamble to a new mode of thinking, in which there is place again for the subject — God and man. Returning to the main theme of my essay, I can say that it is by the presentation of the love of God, which in remembrance should be brought to the surface, that Geyer wants to open up our thinking to the coming of God in the parousia.

A Further Elaboration of Geyer's Mode of Thinking

How can Geyer's mode of thinking be delineated more accurately? I summarize the fruits of my readings by way of five key phrases: (1) freedom; (2) the sixties; (3) contradicting the totalitarian; (4) the epistemology of hope; and (5) the identity of Jesus Christ.

1. For Geyer, *freedom* is the hallmark of (theological) debate. He enters the thinking space of critical freedom. I restrict myself to the remark that this freedom structures the debate in which the new thinking shows itself. I could cite from the "Theses to a critical-systematic revision of the concept of church doctrine." Thesis 7.3.1 reads: "The promise that somebody gives to someone else and the trust with which the latter receives the promise, are ruled by a relationship of absolutely free reciprocity and by a reciprocal freedom which is not to be limited."[25] Here, the criticism of metaphysics is applied discourse-theoretically and betrays a deeply humanistic heritage.

2. The experiences of *the sixties* were important to Geyer. In the church they were the years of awakening ecumenism; politically, they were the years

24. Ibid., 238: "Das spezifische Moment des Kerygmas christlicher Kirche, durch das er sich innerhalb der Gesamtdarstellung ihrer evangelischen Substanz durch ihr praktisches Sein von allen anderen mimetischen Funktionen unterscheidet, hängt genau damit zusammen, daß die homiletische Praxis der Ausrichtung des 'Wortes vom Kreuz' als des 'Wortes der Versöhnung' im Namen Jesu Christi, des gekreuzigten Sohnes, unter allen Arten der Mimesis des Evangeliums Jesu Christi in und durch seine Kirche diejenige ist, in der sich nicht nur die Worthaftigkeit, sondern in der Wortsprachlichkeit des Evangeliums dessen elementare Namentlichkeit mit ireduzibler Unmittelbarkeit manifestiert." About the relationship between mimesis and name, cf. W. Benjamin, "Über das mimetische Vermögen," in: *Gesammelte Schriften*, vol. 11.1, 210-213.

25. Geyer, *Andenken*, 291.

of "democratization," of the worldwide mass protests of students and workers. Looking back, one may conclude that those years' wave of emancipation has weakened and that their goals have not been reached by a long way. The sixties, rather, inaugurated a time in which the individual I is lost in an anonymous We, a time in which — sharply said — the individuals become nothings. For Geyer, the downfall of concrete individuality falls under the category of reification.[26] The concrete subject coincides abstractly with any other subject.[27]

3. Geyer wanted *to contradict the power of what is totalitarian*. He was very sensitive to the totalitarian features of modern society. For Geyer, Horkheimer's thinking about historical developments and about processes in consciousness was exemplary. On the occasion of a re-publication of Horkheimer's works Geyer wrote an extensive essay.[28] Horkheimer had agreed to a new edition only after a long period of hesitation, because he doubted whether his theory of the thirties could be printed again at the end of the sixties without alteration. Geyer was appreciative of this doubt. Since the critical theory of Horkheimer and others is determined by a conscious connection with praxis, it "cannot abstractly remain the same what it once was, when the historical constellation in which it was once developed, has changed."[29]

After the Second World War, Horkheimer had become deeply skeptical. He speaks of the "dreary . . . knowledge" that "after the Second World War human society has taken the road to mechanical barbarism with an imperturbability that borders on deadly certainty."[30] "Doubt about the thesis which for him, too, was once a certainty, namely, that the possibility of a transfer of modern society into a humane situation would be a present possibility, has sunk in" deeply.[31] However, the will to contradict concretely has not been weakened by this. So, Horkheimer does not resign. Geyer ascertains that in Horkheimer "faith in the forces and in the reality of progress towards a better society has been lost; however, the will to [strive for] it and to know

---

26. Geyer refers, among other things, to Karl Barth's Tambach Lecture and to later writings like "Christengemeinde und Bürgergemeinde" and "Die Menschlichkeit Gottes."

27. Cf., e.g., the end of "Das Recht der Subjektivität im Prozess der Vergesellschaftung" (originally 1970), in *Andenken,* 364-393.

28. Geyer, "Elemente der kritischen Theorie Max Horkheimers" (originally 1969), in *Andenken,* 332-363.

29. Ibid., 333.

30. Ibid., 339.

31. Ibid.

and to expose without compromise all that which powerfully frustrates it, has remained."[32] This reading shows up Geyer's conviction that also in times of anxiety and disappointment because of the definitive delay of the parousia of a humane society, the will to contradict decidedly and concretely can remain.

4. About the *epistemology of hope*, Geyer debated intensively with Jürgen Moltmann and Wolfhart Pannenberg.[33] In their theology of hope, the distinction between future as an aim to strive for and future as the goal of God's exclusive act is so minute — Geyer writes — that the biblical promise can hardly be distinguished from a principle. History itself seems to enter the stage as a means of salvation. Geyer's ultimate criticism is that, in his opinion, the theological programs of Moltmann and Pannenberg are enclosed by a metaphysical correlation between God and the world. Geyer puts the critical question whether in Moltmann's theology, within the correlation of God and the world, Israel's history of promises is more than an explication of historical processes that are led by hope, which are really independent from this history of Israel. He doubts whether for Moltmann and Pannenberg the death and resurrection of Jesus Christ are really constitutive (and not just illustrative) of the exegesis of biblical texts and of the praxis of the Christian community.[34]

The common issue, with which Geyer, Moltmann, and Pannenberg knew themselves to be confronted, was the problem of the parousia, the coming or the arrival of that which is new. One may say that Moltmann and also Pannenberg have made the biblical category of the *novum* into the key concept of their epistemology of hope. Geyer greatly appreciates this, but — as has been said — he also has his objections. For Geyer, "parousia" concerns a future of which no one knows the time and the hour. Future in a biblical sense cannot be calculated.[35] Although we are vitalized by images of the fu-

---

32. Ibid., 340.

33. J. Moltmann, *Theologie der Hoffnung,* 1964; W. Pannenberg, *Heilsgeschichte und Geschichte,* 1959.

34. Cf. Geyer, "Ansichten zu Jürgen Moltmanns 'Theologie der Hoffnung,'" in *Diskussion über die Theologie der Hoffnung* (München, 1967), 64: "The moment of explication so strongly dominates the scene that the constitutive character of the history of Jesus Christ does not show up clearly enough, to say the least." Cf. also "Zur Frage der Notwendigkeit des Alten Testamentes," *Evangelische Theologie* 25 (1965): 207-238, in which Geyer discusses Israel's saga, which, as immediate word, is absolutely constitutive for Israel's language and for the promise that is written in this language.

35. Cf. Geyer, "Solus Christus," in Wengst, *Christliche Theologie im Angesicht Israels,* 19.

ture, these do not lead us into the future itself. Instead of images one could speak of hopeful revolutions. A whole repertoire of such revolutions could be introduced, all under the common denominator of liberation history. However, it is still to be shown whether this "liberation history" does really entail liberation, that is, whether it has led to freedom. Here, Geyer regards Pannenberg and Moltmann not critical enough. He critically contrasts their approach with that of Benjamin. Geyer remains faithful to the concept of a near expectation: for him, this expectation is a qualitative feature of faith, which is a prerequisite for a new, non-metaphysical mode of thinking.

5. The question of the *identity of Jesus Christ*, or of the legitimacy and the meaning of Jesus' death on the cross, has a key position in Geyer's work. This question is decisive for his turn from metaphysics to parousia.[36] Geyer states that God's new coming in the parousia is an implication of the concrete identity of Jesus Christ. How do we find this identity, this unattainable unity of God and man which is nevertheless intended in the biblical language? To answer this question, Geyer applies the Husserlian concepts of "protention" and "retention."[37]

With "protention" or "the protentional" Geyer denotes the continuity between the character of Jesus' conduct and his fate. But he does not want to interpret his death, but simply lets it stand in its facticity, that is, he depicts it as a mere fact, a breakdown, by which this life simply ends. According to Geyer, this historical fact can undergo an intensification or an "ontological deepening" "only by the event of Easter, which itself is meta-historical."[38] Only when we look back — Geyer speaks of "retention," see below — it becomes clear that the attempts to ignore this fact and to give this death a place in a higher framework can only lead to an idealization of this death, or to its degradation to an empirical fact. The declaration that in reality this death implies a "jump ahead" can — Geyer writes — only be rooted in the meta-historical domain, in remembrance, which runs backwards.

Besides the protention, or the succession of the historical occurrence and its end, there is the retention, the remembrance which runs backwards, which in and through a breakdown can see and name continuity. It is precisely the retention, which has its roots in Easter, that makes acute the question who Jesus is and what the meaning of his death is. For it does not leave

36. Geyer, "Rohgedanken über die Identität," in *Andenken*, 176-207.

37. Geyer, however, does not mention their provenance from Husserl's phenomenology. Cf. also Geyer, "Ansichten," 61.

38. Geyer, "Rohgedanken über die Identität," in *Andenken*, 204.

behind the aporia of this death. Whoever wants to hold out over against the reality of death cannot avoid the question of the truth of this death and of this cross. For doctrinal or impersonal statements are not at all possible in the face of this death. Such sentences ascertain and conceptualize. The reality of this death opposes such attempts: the anamnesis, the commemoration, of this death shows, on the contrary, that it cannot be made metaphysical or objective.

I started the delineation of Geyer's mode of thinking with the discourse-theoretical remark that it is characterized by a passion for freedom. Geyer affirms the accuracy of this remark precisely in a passage on the cross. So, with this the circle is complete. Geyer writes: "The question concerning the meaning of the cross is characterized by an infinite openness, as a result of which it keeps an undisturbed priority over against and right through all answers."[39] Openness, as opposed to the enclosure of totalitarian metaphysics! That's why knowledge concerning the identity of this Jesus can only be acquired "by participation in the process of the actuality of this meaning question in the medium of human language." The decisive category of this language is the *Verbum Dei promittens*.[40]

4. Résumé

There is a remarkable parallellism in the thinking of Geyer and Badiou about metaphysics. Badiou ends his book *The Century* with the ascertainment that in the "joint disappearances of Man and God" in the death of both these subjects lies the dissolution of a thinking which could not say goodbye to metaphysics. Badiou points to a new mode of thinking which engages with that which presents itself as true in the great revolutions of the past. In Geyer we find a surprisingly parallel passion for what is true and new. Following Barth's thought about time, Geyer advocates a thinking which attempts to produce something *risky*. Badiou, too, points to what is risky. For him — just as for Geyer — this is possible (and necessary!) precisely because he detached himself from metaphysics.[41] To be short, it is remarkable that both Geyer and the atheist Badiou, who thinks decisively

39. Ibid., 206.
40. Geyer, *Andenken*, 289-291.
41. Badiou has developed a new concept of being, in which, with mathematical rigor, room is left for what is accidental. Instead of the repetition of what is the same (law), the *Événement*, the event, is allotted a constitutive role.

anti-metaphysically, want to sharpen the thinking and open it up to a new space beyond the death of man.

As has been said, Badiou distinguishes between two anthropological lines: the anthropology of Sartre and the anti-humanistic line in the philosophy of, e.g., Foucault. These lines are close to each other. It seems that the extremely humanistic line of Sartre must dissolve into an anti-humanistic line, since for Sartre, man is condemned to freedom. According to this account, he goes from one wave of liberation to another, without ever being or being able to be really free. He is programmed as a man and he is unable to free himself from this program. This position has also been analyzed quite accurately by Geyer.[42] He says that as long as this man is programmatically bound to himself, he will never be able to be free. This is a reality of which not just Sartre was aware. The same knowledge was already uttered with great force by great Christian theologians (Luther, Paul). The man who is spoken of here is the man whose will is bound, the self-contained man who ultimately, however, is unfree: *servum arbitrium.*

Michel Foucault distanced himself from any form of anthropology: for him, the man of modern subjectivity is dead. The attempts — e.g., of French postmodernity (Levinas, Derrida) — to reintroduce the relation to transcendence he criticizes as "religion" or "theology." Badiou agrees with Foucault's criticism. He, too, is an atheist who has learnt that the God of Abraham, Isaac, and Jacob is dead.[43] At the same time, Badiou ascertains that postmodernity, which has rightly relativized and criticized every compulsion for emancipation, does not take us any further. The revolutionary urge seems to have left postmodernity; it has become boring.[44] Badiou searches for what is empty, open, which is still there, also in the time when the subject has disappeared. He searches an emptiness in which thinking finds the strength to become concrete, that is, real, not enclosed by images and representations that are continually produced outside of us and within us.[45]

We encounter this image of an emptiness as a space for thinking also in Geyer. One example among others can be found in his reflections on the

42. Geyer, *Andenken,* 310-319.

43. Cf. A. Badiou, *Briefings on Existence. A Short Treatise on Transitory Ontology* (New York, 2006), 22: "It can well be that God has been agonizing for a very long time. What is surely less doubtful is how, for centuries, we have been busy with successive ways of embalming him."

44. Cf. Frans Kellendonk, *De verhalen* (Amsterdam, 2007), and about him, Arnon Grunberg, "Het bodemloze gat achter je," *NRC Handelsblad,* 28 September 2007.

45. Cf. also Geyer, *Andenken,* 388-389.

identity of Jesus Christ. The great aporetic question for Geyer in these reflections is whether Jesus' conduct was legitimate. Was he the obedient Son or rather a Promethean rebel?[46] It has been shown that for Geyer, historical attempts are unfit to solve this problem. The question whether Jesus acted rightly or not, and whether he was condemned rightly or not, cannot be solved unambiguously.

This is a consequence of Geyer's deeper conviction that historical reconstructions cannot lead to a concrete identity. There is no other possibility than to accept this aporia, this emptiness, and to retain a prospect to a point beyond death. Geyer says that a thinking which lets itself be inspired by this *novum* should be seen within the perspective of time. Biblically spoken, this is "the time that remains,"[47] which as such is a time of intense expectation. There is no need to lose the revolutionary urge. Geyer learnt from Benjamin that the coming of the Messiah is the archetype of the "jump ahead," which is the pattern of many great revolutions.[48] The power of this parousia is effective precisely because of its humility, its freedom from every form of self-exaltation.[49]

How can we speak about this *novum?* Only in the form of an expectation without illusions. Here, one may become somewhat apologetical over against Badiou. Badiou teaches with Nietzsche that the God of Abraham, Isaac, and Jacob is dead. This God has lost his influence. He has been interiorized and will not return from this interiorization. With Geyer and following Benjamin I say: one should not start with the historical faith in the God of the Fathers. The coming of God cannot be calculated and cannot be deduced from historical assessments and processes. The judgment on the quality of our tradition and our faith is not our business, but rests with the God whom we expect.

---

46. Ibid., 197.

47. The watchword in Isaiah 21:11 reads: "An oracle concerning Dumah [silence]: . . . 'Watchman, what is left of the night? Watchman, what is left of the night?'" (NIV). Cf. from Benjamin's disciple Giorgio Agamben, *The Time That Remains: A Commentary on the Letter to the Romans* (Stanford: Stanford University Press, 2005). What remains is what separates us from the Messiah. This, more than the Messiah's being close, is the Messiah himself.

48. Geyer, "Solus Christus," in Wengst, *Christliche Theologie im Angesicht Israels*, 20.

49. Geyer, *Andenken*, 52. In Geyer and Benjamin, the time which still contains all that is possible, is sharply delineated. With Badiou, spatial categories are dominant. Moreover, Badiou knows the Messianic from Benjamin's oeuvre. He is interested in it and certainly does not see any contradiction with his own project. There is a clear affinity between biblical eschatology and a new thinking in the emptiness after the disappearance of man.

Echoes of Barth in Jon Sobrino's Critique of Natural Theology: A Dialogue in the Context of Post-Colonial Theology

Matthew D. Lundberg

From the very beginnings of Christian theology, the question of the relationship between God's revelation and the knowledge claims of human experience has been a perplexing issue. In patristic theology, it is common to point to figures such as Justin Martyr and Tertullian as examples of very different ways of engaging this question. While Justin seized upon every available feature of Greco-Roman wisdom in an attempt to make a case for the truth of Christian faith (albeit also suggesting that such wisdom was fatally flawed apart from the true philosophy of Jesus Christ),[1] Tertullian famously asserted that the traditions of Athens and Jerusalem are irreconcilably at odds with one another, and that one must therefore choose between them.[2] Lying beneath this epistemological issue of revelation and experience, and the chief reason for its thorny character, is a bundle of anthropological and christological questions: Who and what is humanity, both in itself and before God? What is implied about the being and status of humanity if one thinks that human beings have, through their experience, some kind of knowledge or sense of the divine — even if that knowledge requires correction? Or what is implied about the situation of *anthropos* if one regards human beings as utterly dependent on the revelatory initiative of God for any knowledge of the divine? And where, precisely, does Jesus Christ fit into the equation?

---

1. See especially Justin Martyr, *First Apology,* ed. and trans. Cyril C. Richardson, in *Early Christian Fathers,* Library of Christian Classics (Philadelphia: Westminster, 1953), 242-289.

2. For his famous antithetical posing of the question, see Tertullian, *The Prescription Against Heresies,* trans. Peter Holmes, in vol. 3 of *Ante-Nicene Fathers,* ed. Alexander Roberts and James Donaldson (Peabody, MA: Hendrickson, 1994), ch. 7.

These critical questions continue to resound today in what is often called "post-colonial" theology, as theologians in various parts of the world grapple with the relationship between their pre-Christian religious traditions and the crucial Christian claim to the primacy and sufficiency of Jesus Christ. Given the colonialist heritage and destructive repercussions that accompanied the arrival of Christianity to many parts of the globe, it is unsurprising that many post-colonial theologians have considered it important to stress the significance of *pre*-Christian religious experience for the authentic taking-root and continuing well-being of Christian faith. While generalizing is always accompanied by great peril, this appears to be the trend among theologians and scholars of "world Christianity" for whom Africa appears as chief paradigm.[3] For example, Lamin Sanneh claims that a key reason for the recent explosion of Christianity in Africa was the vitality of indigenous traditions, especially the strength of their pre-existing names for God, which became part of the "translation" of Christian faith to African soil.[4] Indeed, Andrew Walls points to this cultural translation — in which pre-Christian cultural realities, in being taken up by Christ, reshape Christianity itself — as the very life-blood of the Christian religion, historically speaking, although he also points to the incarnation of Jesus as the condition for all subsequent translations.[5] As a second example, Gillian Bediako and Kwame Bediako have argued that "primal" religions form the indispensable substructure of Christianity, both in Africa today but also in earlier eras.[6] Expressed in traditional dogmatic categories, the idea here appears to be that some kind of indigenous "natural theology" provides the link between the pre-Christian situation and Christian faith, a link without which the latter would flounder — although this is often interpreted, as by Sanneh, as God "preceding" the missionary.[7]

But it would be a mistake to broaden the generalization to include Latin

3. For the big picture, with Africa at its center, see Philip Jenkins, *The Next Christendom: The Coming of Global Christianity* (Oxford: Oxford University Press, 2002).

4. Lamin Sanneh, *Whose Religion Is Christianity? The Gospel Beyond the West* (Grand Rapids: Eerdmans, 2003), 18, 31-32, 42.

5. Andrews F. Walls, "The Translation Principle in Christian History," in *The Missionary Movement in Christian History: Studies in the Transmission of Faith* (Maryknoll, NY: Orbis, 1996), 29.

6. See, e.g., Gillian M. Bediako, "Primal Religion and Christian Faith: Antagonists or Soul-Mates?" *Journal of African Christian Thought* 3, no. 1 (2000): 12-16; Kwame Bediako, "The Roots of African Theology," *International Bulletin of Missionary Research* 13, no. 2 (1989): 58-65.

7. Sanneh, *Whose Religion Is Christianity?* 32.

Matthew D. Lundberg

American theology without significant qualification. Certainly some theologians, including some liberation theologians such as Leonardo Boff, have given sustained attention to the relation between pre-Christian indigenous traditions and the Christianity that accompanied European aggression, addressing the question in a way that implies some kind of natural theological bridge.[8] But in other theologians, including many of the leading first and second generation liberation theologians, one finds surprisingly little interest in bridging the gap via natural theology. One especially significant representative of such an approach is Salvadoran theologian Jon Sobrino, who in fact mounts a rigorous and hard-hitting critique of natural theology that might seem on the face of it rather startling in light of other post-colonial theological projects. One likely reason for Sobrino's approach — one that may help explain the different tendencies in Latin America than in African theology — is the comparatively longer duration of a substantial Christian presence on a larger part of the continent, as well as the tragic success of the original "Christianizers" in suppressing, destroying, or converting pre-Christian traditions. A second reason is that the main contextual concern of Sobrino, like most of liberation theology, has been less cultural and more socio-political in character — with his attention focused on responding theologically to the oppression and poverty that has been tacitly and sometimes overtly supported by the Christian church and its theology since the 15th-century conquests.

In today's climate in post-colonial theology, if the above generalizations are correct, Sobrino's position could aptly be titled a "minority report." Given this distinction, his position echoes the most famous critique of natural theology, that of Karl Barth, which was a minority report in its own right, albeit one that has decisively shaped subsequent discussions of the topic.[9] In view of the path often taken today in post-colonial theology, where some-

8. E.g., Leonardo Boff, *New Evangelization: Good News to the Poor,* trans. Robert R. Barr (Maryknoll, NY: Orbis, 1991), although he also interprets this bridge as the pre-missionary presence and act of the triune God (69-70).

9. Interpreting Sobrino's critique of natural theology as an echo of Barth must be regarded more as a theological exploration in service of a fruitful dialogue than as a search for a genetic intellectual relationship, in part because Sobrino tends to emphasize the disjunction between Latin American and European theology (see esp. Sobrino, *The True Church and the Poor,* trans. Matthew J. O'Connell [Maryknoll, NY: Orbis, 1984], 7-38). But it is worth noting that Latin American liberation theology more broadly has often confessed an admiration of Barth. As a key example, see Gustavo Gutiérrez, *The Power of the Poor in History: Selected Writings,* trans. Robert R. Barr (Maryknoll, NY: Orbis, 1983), 222-233. This should probably be attributed in large part to Barth's own impressive stance against the political tyrannies of his day.

84

thing akin to "natural theology" is given a significant role in linking the Christian claim of revelation to the claims of human experience, it is worth exploring what might be learned from the *critiques* of natural theology in Barth and Sobrino, particularly with respect to the latter's attempt to still create space for theological affirmation of the experience of the poor vis-à-vis revelation. Moreover, there is much to be gained in such an exploration with respect to that deeper question that lurks beneath all matters of theological epistemology — What does it mean to speak *theologically* and *christologically* about humanity?

In what follows, I will construct a dialogue between Barth and Sobrino by (1) examining their respective critiques of natural theology with an eye to the anthropological and christological underpinnings of each, and by (2) analyzing the insights that flow from the affinities and differences of Sobrino's approach in relation to the voice of Barth, with the aforementioned broad trends in post-colonial theology in mind.[10]

Barth's Seminal Critique of Natural Theology

Much has been written about Barth's critique of natural theology and its development,[11] including the contextual factors that contributed to the zeal of his polemic — particularly his growing distaste for German liberal theology, his disenchantment with that tradition's support of German aggression in the Great War, and his resistance to the Third Reich. While Barth's critique was a long time in the making, it made a loud splash in his dispute with Emil Brunner in the wake of the Barmen Declaration and Brunner's publication of *Nature and Grace* (1934). Barth famously spoke a loud *Nein!* to Brunner's claim that an innate capacity to receive revelation, implying a basic element of natural theology, persists in humanity even despite its sinfulness, and constitutes a necessary "point of contact" for humanity to be able to grasp God's saving revelation in Christ.[12] Barth saw his critique of Brunner to be a

---

10. Such a dialogue is fitting for the present volume due to the tremendous significance of the theology of Karl Barth and various forms of liberation theology throughout the impressive theological career of Daniel L. Migliore.

11. Among the better analyses are Thomas F. Torrance, "The Problem of Natural Theology in the Thought of Karl Barth," *Religious Studies* 6, no. 2 (1970): 121-135; and from a sympathetic but critical Catholic perspective, Henri Bouillard, "A Dialogue with Barth: The Problem of Natural Theology," *Cross Currents* 18, no. 2 (1968): 203-228.

12. Karl Barth, *Nein!*, in *Natural Theology: Comprising "Nature and Grace" by Professor*

necessary corollary to the Barmen Declaration's confession that "Jesus Christ, as he is testified to us in the Holy Scripture, is the one Word of God, whom we are to hear, whom we are to trust and obey in life and in death."[13] Barth's position had not changed substantially by the time he wrote volume II/1 of the *Church Dogmatics,* where the topic receives its fullest treatment in material that anticipates crucial themes Barth develops further in volume IV. But I shall restrict my attention to Barth's position in *CD* II/1 since my purpose here is simply to sketch in broad strokes his theological dismay with natural theology so as to be able to hear its echoes in the liberationist project of Sobrino.[14]

At the outset, it is important to be clear about how Barth defines "natural theology" so that we do not make the mistake of thinking that he rules out any connection between experience and theology — an important matter, to be sure, in comparing him to Sobrino on these questions. For Barth, natural theology is the attempt to use a non-revelatory source as the basis for making claims about God in a way that "receives the character of an independent series of statements" (II/1, 99, cf. 102). It is the purported *independence* of natural theology that is chiefly unacceptable, since it presupposes the independence of humanity from God in Christ. For Barth, the question of humanity is thus knit into the very fabric of the question regarding knowledge of God, and to address one question apart from the other is to lapse into a dubious abstraction. In his attempt to avoid theological abstractionism, Barth refuses to talk about knowledge of God that is not a function of Christ's justification of the sinner, and considers his viewpoint to represent a sharpening of the Reformation's soteriological insight in the sphere of theological epistemology (II/1, 127). Natural theology is thus a concern for Barth primarily because of what it implies anthropologically and christologically.

Since genuine knowledge of God is necessarily bound up with the reality of salvation, Barth regards it as impossible apart from *faith* (II/1, 155-59). Since God rather than humanity is the author of faith, knowledge of God in

---

Dr. Emil Brunner and the reply "No!" by Dr. Karl Barth, trans. Peter Fraenkel (London: Centenary, 1946).

13. *The Barmen Declaration,* in John H. Leith, ed., *The Creeds of the Churches: A Reader in Christian Doctrine, from the Bible to the Present,* 3rd ed. (Louisville: John Knox, 1982), art. 1 (p. 520).

14. Karl Barth, *Church Dogmatics,* ed. Geoffrey W. Bromiley and Thomas F. Torrance, trans. T. H. L. Parker et al., vol. II/1 (Edinburgh: T&T Clark, 1957), esp. §26 (subsequent references will be noted parenthetically as II/1).

faith always remains an act of "the God who gives Himself to be known in His Word" (II/1, 12). "Knowledge" in Barth's sense is never a merely cognitive matter, but is the full-orbed response of the whole person — involving also the will in loving obedience, further underscoring the inseparability of knowledge of God from salvation (II/1, 36-37). As the knowledge of faith, true knowledge of God is an act of "God's free grace," something *given* to humanity, never something that human beings can grasp via their own intellectual capacities (II/1, 22). This is for Barth a consequence of trying to think in a rigorously consistent way through the sovereignty of God over all things — including revelation and knowledge of God (II/1, 85). For God to be *God,* and the Lord of all knowledge of himself as God, means that *particular* revelation is the only way that God can be known. There is no possibility of constructing knowledge of God on the basis of analogies from human reality to the reality of God — the so-called *analogia entis* (II/1, 75-84). The only possibility of analogy in knowledge of God is "an analogy to be created by God's grace" (II/1, 85), initiated by the divine act with scripture as its touchstone, which Barth generally terms the *analogia fidei.*[15] Knowledge of God is possible only due to God's own "readiness" to make the divine self known, and never from any human readiness "that is grounded in itself" (II/1, 66).

Barth's critique of natural theology, therefore, is simply the flip side of his christocentric account of knowledge of God as a matter of faith, obedience, and grace. He acknowledges that it is certainly possible for humanity to search out a knowledge of that which transcends its own domain. But the result is not true knowledge of *God,* but a projection on the part of humanity itself — thus in actuality, an idol. Barth suggests that it is folly to think that a humanly constructed notion of the divine, which ultimately must be regarded as an idol, should be encouraged as a precursor to knowledge of the true God (II/1, 89-91).[16] He rejects the claim that a natural theological "point of contact" is necessary in a pedagogical way to facilitate the conversation between Christian faith and the unbeliever. Using natural theology in this apologetic way not only curiously requires the perspective of faith to bracket itself, but also patronizes its mortal enemy, unbelief, rather than taking it seriously as what it is — the enemy of faith (II/1, 93-96). At root here is Barth's refusal to regard humanity in "natural" or abstract terms, insisting instead

---

15. On this important notion in Barth, see Bruce L. McCormack, *Karl Barth's Critically Realistic Dialectical Theology: Its Genesis and Development 1909-1936* (Oxford: Clarendon, 1997), 16-18.

16. Cf. Barth, *Nein!,* 82.

on concrete theological terms in seeing humanity as such always as sinner, therefore one who needs to be given the *gift* of faith — saving knowledge of God (cf. II/1, 130).

In discussing the putative *biblical* evidence for natural theology (such as Ps. 19, Rom. 1–2, or Acts 17), Barth argues that if God in scripture is never regarded independently, that is, dissociated from God's revelation, it would be extraordinarily odd if *humanity* were made an "independent witness" to knowledge of God (II/1, 102, 109). What Barth calls this "improbabability" is confirmed in his mind by the fact that the "main line" of scripture never regards human beings as anything other than sinners who are in need of rescue. How, then, could humanity in itself have reliable epistemic access to God from an independent avenue (II/1, 103)? In other words, how could natural theology be affirmed as a teaching of the Bible if its very existence contradicted the core message of the Bible itself? On the contrary, argues Barth, the very point of the Bible's reference to "man in the cosmos" is to remind humanity that it is objectively changed in the saving and revelatory work of God through Jesus Christ (II/1, 111). In other words, scripture's reference to humanity as such is intended, if one is consistently seeing it from the perspective of the main message of the Bible, to remind humanity as such that it is in fact *not* humanity as such — that it is sinful and objectively redeemed by God's grace in Jesus Christ (II/1, 112, 116).

Therefore, for Barth, the only reliable way in which the "readiness of man" for knowledge of God can be successfully affirmed on Christian terms is christologically — through the one in whom human sin is finally conquered (II/1, 148-49). Thus in place of Brunner's anthropological "point of contact," Barth substitutes a christological claim: "There is for man, included in the readiness of God, a readiness of man for God and therefore for the knowledge of God" — in Jesus Christ (II/1, 161; cf. 128). Barth therefore makes knowledge of God a function of reconciliation, seen in representational and substitutionary terms. Accordingly, any independent theological epistemology (i.e., natural theology) is quite out of Christian bounds. Knowledge of God is inseparable from the question of reconciliation.

Since the two questions are inseparable, according to Barth, natural theology's claim to independent knowledge of the divine is also implicitly a claim to salvation on human terms, therefore standing as an attack on the sovereignty and sufficiency of Jesus Christ (II/1, 163-166).[17] The presupposi-

---

17. It is not accidental, therefore, that Barth's critique rings with echoes of Augustine's diatribes against Pelagius.

tion of natural theology, and one of the reasons why it has been (and will continue to be) a perennial and alluring theological temptation, is that *sinful* humanity will always attempt to ground its knowledge, of itself or God or whatever, in its own reality (II/1, 135-136). Because of the sinful impulse that energizes the project of natural theology, if it is allowed into the Christian theological arena, it will always have a cancerous character and tend to be a totalizing impulse in theology: "[I]n its exercise it at once assumes a position of monopoly" (II/1, 136).[18] It "domesticates" revelation by its underhanded way of allowing revelation a place at the theological table, thus "making revelation into non-revelation," even though it inevitably does a poor job of such superintendence because of the insuperable power of God's revelation (II/1, 139-140).

Since natural theology *affirms* "humanity as such," however, it is only powerful as an alluring illusion, in Barth's view — because "humanity as such" is mere mirage (II/1, 165). Natural theology must not be regarded as a serious possibility, because then we affirm humanity *extra Christum* as a serious possibility (II/1, 166). Rejecting natural theology matter-of-factly is to tell humanity the truth — You do *not* exist outside of Christ. If there really were a "humanity as such," then natural theology would be a legitimate project. But there is no such humanity, in Barth's view, because of Jesus Christ. It is best, then, to drop natural theology as an already repudiated possibility (II/1, 168-170).

While Barth is quite clear about the christological and anthropological reasons behind his rejection of natural theology, it is important to recognize that he does not exclude all considerations of human experience from the theological enterprise, but simply takes extraordinary care in how he relates such experience to God's unique and unsurpassable revelation through Jesus Christ. He regards the biblical statements about humanity "in the cosmos" (with which he associates the above-mentioned biblical prooftexts for natural theology) as a "side line" that only makes proper sense if we carefully consider its relation to scripture's "main line." Human experience can serve as a "secondary" and "dependent witness" to the truth of revelation (II/1, 105), but it is a witness that can only be created by the act of revelation itself. Barth speaks of the typical scriptural prooftexts as the Bible's way of articulating the "brightness" and "echo" that is produced in human experience

---

18. In his reflections on the Barmen Declaration and the German church struggle against the backdrop of the question of natural theology, Barth characterizes natural theology's totalizing impulse as a "trojan horse" (II/1, 173).

precisely by revelation in Jesus Christ — a brightness and echo that as a side line flows from and redounds upon the main line (II/1, 110). Barth argues in fact that whenever the Bible does appear at first glance to point to an independent knowledge of God apart from divine revelation, this "side line" is so thoroughly embedded in the sin and grace saga of God and humanity through Israel and Jesus Christ that it is impossible to regard it as a biblical warrant for developing a natural theology (see II/1, 107-108). That is to say, Barth regards human experience as theologically significant only if we regard it as a reality that is taken up by God through the event of revelation in order to lay bare its theological significance with respect to that revelation.[19]

What is crucial for Barth, therefore, is the *form* of the relationship between experience and revelation, and in particular that revelation itself — actualistically understood — must govern the appeal to experience. In his view, this is where natural theology falls short. Its appeal to human experience *in se* is objectionable because it (1) ignores the sovereignty of God in Christ, (2) abstracts "humanity" from its actual theological situation vis-à-vis sin and grace, and (3) facilitates both of the first two errors by its separation of the questions of knowledge of God and salvation. We shall hear echoes of these concerns in Jon Sobrino in both consonant and dissonant form.

Sobrino's Liberationist Critique of Natural Theology

The central concern that informs Sobrino's initial critique of natural theology is his concern to shore up the *revelation* of God through Jesus of Nazareth with an eye to the patterns provided for Christian discipleship by Jesus' revelatory history. Throughout his work Sobrino insists that the Jesus who lived concretely and conflictually for the kingdom of God presents in his concrete words and actions the only reliable revelation of the truth of God and the truth of humanity — that is to say, how humanity is called to live as truly human.[20] Jesus' revelatory existence includes his whole life, but as a revelation of God takes a surprising turn on the cross. Following the train of Luther and Moltmann, Sobrino develops a *theologia crucis* that he places in

19. Cf. also Barth's highly nuanced discussion of "other words," "other lights," and "parables of the kingdom" that witness to Christ the true Word, Light, and embodiment of the Kingdom. In Barth, *Church Dogmatics*, ed. Geoffrey W. Bromiley and Thomas F. Torrance, trans. Geoffrey W. Bromiley, vol. IV/3 (Edinburgh: T&T Clark, 1961), esp. §69.2.

20. For one of Sobrino's clearest statements of this matter, see his *Jesus in Latin America*, various translators (Maryknoll, NY: Orbis, 1987), 19-40.

direct opposition to the tradition of natural theology. Natural theology, which Sobrino defines as "every attempt to gain access to God on the basis of what is *positive* in history — whether we view it as nature, history, or human subjectivity," lacks the resources to fathom the negativity of the cross.[21] Natural theology's dependence upon analogy, that is, similarity between the world and God, makes it impossible to grasp the contradiction between God and the world that hangs over the cross, as well as the surprising and liberating revelation of God brought by Jesus.[22] Natural theology "[blocks] out the radical meaning of the cross for Christian existence" through its imposition of a "Greek metaphysical conception of God's being and perfection" that *a priori* rules out suffering as a possible divine experience.[23] In conceiving of God primarily via the rather abstract and unhistorical category of power, natural theology assumes that God (in order to be truly powerful) must also be attributed the category of *apatheia*.[24]

This approach, according to Sobrino, which works analogically from the wonder of creation, does not have the dialectical sharpness necessary to recognize anything of God on the cross, where power is paradoxically expressed through suffering.[25] Whereas natural theology can only grasp divine transcendence and power as God being "greater" than the world, and is easily manipulated analogically to give divine legitimation to the "greater" ones in the world, transcendence when parsed through the cross involves both a "greater" and a "lesser."[26] A dialectical conception of transcendence emerges only through the cross, and never the unaided resources of reason in natural theology, underscoring the mystery of God which natural theology feels so confident to pierce, but never can. When seen through the cross, "God becomes *more* transcendent, *more* unencompassable, *more* indescribable, *more* a mystery."[27] As Sobrino makes clearer in a discussion of the resurrection, this dialectic shows that God is not an undifferentiated "greater," but should primarily be known through the divine solidarity with sinful and suffering humanity on the cross, a solidarity which brings salvation and hope.

---

21. Jon Sobrino, *Christology at the Crossroads: A Latin American Approach*, trans. John Drury (Maryknoll, NY: Orbis, 1978), 221.

22. Jon Sobrino, *Jesus the Liberator: A Historical-Theological Reading of Jesus of Nazareth*, trans. Paul Burns and Francis McDonagh (Maryknoll, NY: Orbis, 1993), 249.

23. Sobrino, *Christology at the Crossroads*, 195.

24. Ibid., 191-193.

25. Ibid., 220-221.

26. Sobrino, *Jesus the Liberator*, 247-248.

27. Ibid., 248 (italics in original).

Through this "lesser" divine aspect, it is possible to grasp God's "love" in a very concrete way, one that energizes concrete discipleship.[28] The abstract resources of natural theology would never be able to name God as love in such a way, in their one-sided focus on the abstract "greater" that the revelation of the cross calls into question.

Formally at least, we can already see a noteworthy affinity between these beginnings in Sobrino and Barth's own critique — their shared concern to secure the primacy of revelation for all of theology, and their recognition of the conflict such primacy inevitably brings to the sinful world's expectations regarding God. Similar to Barth, Sobrino is attempting to take epistemological heed of the reality of sin. But he does so with a liberationist notion of *historical* sin in mind in connection to the *experience* of the Latin American poor whose poverty is caused by that sin — an issue to which we will return shortly. In his view, not only does the approach of natural theology founder on the revelatory event of the cross, but it also fails to resonate existentially with the poor of Latin America since in general it is incapable of dealing with any negative features of reality.[29]

In contrast to the epistemological method of natural theology, a way of knowing God that gazes first and foremost on the cross shatters all humanly constructed images of God.[30] This shattering, according to Sobrino, serves as a fulfillment of the second commandment: "[The cross] reveals nothing of what is usually presented as divine."[31] Here it is possible to glimpse the deeper rationale of Sobrino's skepticism regarding natural theology, once again with much affinity with Barth's critique — namely, the idea that human God-talk in natural theology is directed by a sinful and manipulative self-interest that grasps the positive features of created reality in an attempt to create an image of the divine that justifies and legitimizes human projects in the world. Sobrino writes: "The silence of God in connection with Jesus' cross tells us at once that we must break completely with the inertial human way of thinking about God. . . . The first thing the cross unmasks is people's selfish interest in seeking to know God."[32]

It is the sinful human tendency to manipulate the idea of God — particularly acute in the case of natural theology, without the governing

28. Sobrino, *Christ the Liberator: A View from the Victims,* trans. Paul Burns (Maryknoll, NY: Orbis, 2001), 89.

29. Sobrino, *Christology at the Crossroads,* 195-198.

30. Ibid., 219-220.

31. Sobrino, *Jesus the Liberator,* 248.

32. Sobrino, *Christology at the Crossroads,* 188, cf. 199, 221.

checks and balances of revelation — that is most determinative for Sobrino's assessment of the impotence of natural theology. Rather than falling short solely because of the lack of correspondence between the deity
revealed on the cross and the epistemic expectations of natural humanity,
it is the *sin* that is revealed on the cross that is most problematic in the
project of natural theology. Stressing that the human quest for God is un-
dergirded by the sinful attempt to avoid the truth of God, Sobrino writes
that "[n]atural theology embodies our questioning search for God. The
cross, rather than answering any such questions, prompts us to a very different sort of questioning."[33]

The doctrine of historical sin that lies behind Sobrino's critique of
natural theology is the reason, in his view, that the big problem that must
be addressed by Latin American liberation theology, in strong contrast to
much of European theology's concern with mass atheism, is idolatry.[34]
The predominantly first-world problem of atheism is largely a theoretical
and rather abstract challenge. But in the Latin American world where
death is an everyday reality, and where the social structures that produce
such a situation are generally bulwarked by certain conceptions of God
and the divine will, the problem of idolatry must be confronted in tragi-
cally concrete form. Working analogically from the idol Molech of the Old
Testament (see Lev. 20; 2 Kings 23), Sobrino suggests that idolatry — "the
creation of divinity by humans"[35] — leads to death, because it is people
with power, whose selfish interests maintain the injustice of the status quo,
who tend to create and perpetuate these idols at the expense of the underside of society which suffers and dies as a result. Since natural theology is a
rather abstract and theoretical form of thinking about God, which, furthermore, is motivated by sinful impulses that in Latin America support
unjust and oppressive systems, Sobrino's theological project of opposing
the foil of idolatry requires a much more concrete form of *revealed* theology, such as what he finds christologically in the concrete life, proclamation, and fate of Jesus of Nazareth.[36] Only when focusing on the surprising
element in revelation is it possible to take revelation seriously and thereby
guard against "turn[ing] God into a God in our own image and likeness,

---

33. Ibid., 222.

34. See Sobrino, *True Church*, 31-33.

35. Jon Sobrino, *Jesus in Latin America*, 99.

36. For Sobrino's most detailed and nuanced treatment of the issues of atheism and
idolatry in theology, see "Reflexiones sobre el Significado del Ateísmo y la Idolatría para la
Teología," *Revista Latinoamericana de Teología* 3 (1986): 45-81.

which is always easier when, as is inevitable, we concentrate on the positive elements of the revelation of God."[37]

Up to this point, we have seen certain elements of Sobrino's critique of natural theology that dovetail rather closely with Barth's critique. More so than many other European theologians, Barth, in taking up Feuerbach's critique of belief in God, hones in on the concrete problem of idolatry in addition to the largely intellectual issue of atheism. Such is unsurprising given the fact that Barth's critique of natural theology, while determined by his christocentrism, grew to maturity in the fires of the Nazi conflict. Sobrino recognizes this when he mentions Barth at certain points of his own critique of natural theology. But Sobrino appears to suggest that Barth too quickly reduces all of humanity to the same universal situation, that of sinful idolaters who have rebelled against God.[38] Given the more concrete forms of continuing idolatry — that is, those that cause untimely death for the poor — which Sobrino focuses upon as a liberation theologian, he thinks that an important distinction must be made between the world's *victims* and its oppressors, despite the fact that sin is a universal human problem that also afflicts the poor, the point that is axiomatic for Barth. It is at this juncture, especially in some of his later work, that Sobrino backs away slightly from his more universal statements about the sinful human propensity to manipulate "God" for selfish ends which informed his initial critique of natural theology. In contrast to the rest of humanity, the victims "have every right to imagine a God who is theirs, who rights their wrongs, who confers life on them."[39] While this statement appears to support a more experientially driven form of natural theology for the *poor* as victims of the world's evil, thus standing as a crucial difference from Barth's all-encompassing critique of natural theology, Sobrino clarifies that the poor have the "right" to imagine a God who liberates them "because God is like that; that is how he has been revealed."[40] It is here that the subtlety of Sobrino's view requires great care so as to avoid misunderstanding him.

That Sobrino regards the poor as in a relatively different position than the rest of humanity in relation to natural theology, despite his own skepticism regarding natural theology as a general project, makes greater sense when seen in conjunction with the epistemology of suffering that he con-

37. Sobrino, *Jesus the Liberator*, 247.
38. Ibid., 250.
39. Ibid.
40. Ibid.

nects to his theology of the cross. We have already seen his critique of the "wonder" that energizes the traditional approach to natural theology, as a wonder that tells falsehoods about the suffering reality of the world and lacks eyes for the cross. But Sobrino does admit that a certain form of "wonder," a *negative* form of wonder, is indispensable for knowing the Christian God. This form of wonder is that of sorrow.[41] Accepting epistemologically that some kind of analogy is always necessary for genuine knowledge to take place, Sobrino posits an experiential analogy in the suffering of the poor that opens their eyes to see the reality of God in the suffering Christ on the cross. It is sorrow through the suffering caused by sin that provides the "connaturality" that facilitates a recognition of God on the cross, a very different kind of connaturality than that assumed by Greek philosophy and traditional natural theology which ascends by means of a creational *analogia entis* to claims about the divine.[42]

It is in this connection that Sobrino's emphasis on the theological importance of the "crosses of history" shows itself to be an important yet extremely nuanced modification of his critique of natural theology. From very early in his career, Sobrino has stated that the historical crosses of the poor are a theological lens that facilitates knowledge of the cross of Jesus, which is the linchpin of truly Christian knowledge of God.[43] As his career progressed, however, this emphasis took more definite form in a notion, that of the "crucified people," that was often employed by Sobrino's close friend, the martyr Ignatio Ellacuría.[44] According to Sobrino, the crucified people are the body of Christ that "embody Christ in history as crucified."[45] The poor, who die as the result of historical sin before their time, are a symbol of Christ, who died before his time as the result of history's sin. By means of this notion, it appears that Sobrino regards the impoverished victims of the world's injustice and structural violence to be a window into the Christ who reveals God. There appears to be something about their experience, their suffering and its connection to sin, that is profoundly theological and therefore confers theological knowledge. Indeed, there is a sense in which they almost provide something approaching a natural theology, but through the experience of

41. Sobrino, *Christology at the Crossroads*, 199.

42. Sobrino, *Jesus the Liberator*, 249.

43. Sobrino, *Christology at the Crossroads*, 199.

44. Ignacio Ellacuría, "The Crucified People," trans. Phillip Berryman and Robert R. Barr, in *Mysterium Liberationis: Fundamental Concepts of Liberation Theology*, ed. Ignacio Ellacuría and Jon Sobrino (Maryknoll, NY: Orbis, 1993), 580-603.

45. Sobrino, *Jesus the Liberator*, 255.

suffering. In an important methodological essay, Sobrino talks about "elevating present reality to a theological concept" as a "manifestation of God."[46] It is the experience of reality's victims that alone can illuminate God, something that Sobrino regards as a "scandal" to "natural reason."[47]

Thus the question arises: Is Sobrino here setting up simply an alternative natural theology — one at odds with the tradition but still formally a natural theology? On the one hand, some sort of affirmative answer seems unavoidable. He posits, in what amounts to a historical *analogia entis* of sorts, that if reality is dependent upon God, then God will affect historical reality and be discernable, in some way, through that reality.[48] But, on the other hand, we must take great care to notice the hermeneutical nuances of Sobrino's position. It is the theological centrality of Jesus' cross, in his view, that justifies taking the reality of the world's suffering as such an important theological lens. That theological lens in turn illuminates the cross itself.[49] There is clearly, then, a hermeneutical circle at work, but one in which the theological event of the cross, as illuminated by scripture, appears to have the leading role, although Sobrino also notes that it was the experience of the *poor* in particular, not just *any* experience, that helped liberation theology to see Jesus rightly.[50] There is something staurological, we might say, about the plight of the poor that makes their experience illuminative of the cross — a sense (undoubtedly too weak from Barth's perspective) in which the cross event itself is what draws the theological significance out of that experience, an experience which in turn casts further light on the cross.

Sobrino's position is subtle because he is engaged in the complicated methodological task of differentiating between traditioned *concepts* and experienced *reality,* in order to open up the theological significance of the latter, while still giving due consideration to the former. Significantly, however, neither theological concept nor experienced reality is identical with revelation. Thus any appeal to the experienced reality of the poor as a window into knowledge of God, he says, must be "compared with" the revelation of God.[51]

---

46. Jon Sobrino, "La Teología y el 'Principio Liberación,'" *Revista Latinoamericana de Teología* 12 (1995): 124 (translation mine). He appeals in part to Vatican II's affirmation of the significance of the "signs of the times."

47. Ibid., 125 (translation mine).

48. Ibid., 123.

49. Ibid., 122-124.

50. Jon Sobrino, "La Fe en el Dios Crucificado: Reflexiones desde El Salvador," *Revista Latinoamericana de Teología* 11 (1994): 51.

51. Sobrino, "La Teología y el 'Principio Liberación,'" 123 (translation mine).

It is also not without significance that the notion that Sobrino uses to "elevate" the reality of the poor to a theological concept includes a theological touchstone — the cross event. By calling the notion the "crucified people," the cross itself seems to govern tightly the appeal to experienced reality itself. Implied in Sobrino's analogical and experiential concept is the revelatory event to which it is bound and which it is intended to illuminate. That christological event, the cross, therefore appears to control the interpretation of the sorrowful experience of the suffering poor in the world. Hermeneutically speaking, past and present, text and reality, come together in producing meaningful christological understanding, but in an ordered way.

Barth and Sobrino in Dialogue

What, then, are we to make of these convergences and divergences between Barth's seminal critique of natural theology and Sobrino's liberationist critique of the same? Both theologians have grave problems with what we might call "classic" natural theology, where unaided reason is allowed independent access to knowledge of God — access apart from God's revelation in Jesus Christ. Though their approaches to the issue involve important differences that ought not to be minimized, both insist that the question of knowledge of God cannot be separated from the question of sin. In Barth's case, the foil is "humanity as such," which he thinks claims knowledge of God in order to idolize the self; in Sobrino's case, the foil is a "humanity as such" where questions of victimhood and oppression are withheld from the theological equation. Both thus strive to avoid theological abstractionism in the sphere of theological epistemology and anthropology.

But the abstractions each opposes are worth analyzing further. Barth rejects the non-theological idea of neutral humanity — unsinful and unneedful of reconciliation — which he regards as an illusory *anthropos* in light of Christ's revelation of sin and Christ's objective salvation of humanity. While there is a sense in which Sobrino shares this opposition, he is also worried about a further abstraction that he sees also in approaches like that of Barth — a "sinful and redeemed" humanity in Christ without reference to *historical* sin.

Consideration of the latter, as we have seen, is what leads Sobrino to search out an appropriate theological way of taking up the experience of the poor. He attempts to carve out space to use the crosses and hopes of the poor as experiential analogies for Jesus' cross and resurrection, while at the same time problematizing classical natural theology in terms that strongly resemble Barth's critique. In the place of natural theology's *analogia entis*, Sobrino appeals to what might be called an *analogia historiae*. Rather than being creation-based, the analogies he uses theologically are historical in nature. As such, they more naturally have to do with sin and grace, cross and resurrection, despair and hope as seen in the world of the poor.[52] But hermeneutically, they are tightly connected to the biblical text's discussion of the same. They do not stand as an independent natural theology of history (following Barth's definition), but as a key hermeneutical piece of a broader theology of revelation: "The passion of the world is what gives realism to that of Christ; and the cross of Christ is what confers theological radicality on that of the world."[53] While Sobrino indeed argues (largely echoing Barth) that naked reason used philosophically will inevitably become a manipulative tool of sinful human self-interest, he also thinks that the poor can break down our normal self-interest and help us see past ourselves to who God really is. The poor can play this role because of the congruity between their "crosses" and the cross of Jesus through which God is decisively made known.[54] Alluding to the parable of the sheep and the goats in Matthew 25, Sobrino suggests that when the poor (rather than "nature") become the experiential mediation of knowledge of God (through Christ), the result is not natural knowledge, but a fitting kind of "con-natural" knowledge, a knowledge that comes from shared suffering, which as such illuminates the God who shares human suffering through the cross of Jesus.[55]

Despite his critique of natural theology (and its *analogia entis*), Sobrino deems it appropriate to employ these particular kinds of analogies as interpretive of the central Christian events of cross and resurrection because the interpretation itself is governed by these events themselves. In this sense, despite Sobrino's view that his approach addresses deficiencies in a more universal, Barth-like approach to humanity in sin and in Christ, it may perhaps still be appropriate to regard his approach as a liberationist approximation of Barth's *analogia fidei*. For example, in his discussion of analogical "Easter experiences," Sobrino says that "experiences throughout history clearly depend on that first one for being understood as analogous Easter experi-

---

52. Cf. the discussion of "Easter experiences" that analogically illuminate Jesus' resurrection, in Sobrino, *Christ the Liberator*, 66-73.

53. Sobrino, "Meditación ante el Pueblo Crucificado," *Sal Terrae* 74, no. 1 (1986): 96 (translation mine).

54. Sobrino, *Christology at the Crossroads*, 223.

55. Ibid.

ences."[56] Where Sobrino differs from Barth is that he is not as clear that it is a divine *act* of the Holy Spirit, rather than the inherent similarity of the analogy itself, that initializes the analogy as theologically useful. Or to put it differently, Sobrino is not quite as clear as Barth about what stands as the anchor and stimulus of the analogy. Viewed from the perspective of Barth's approach, therefore, Sobrino could be accused of being dangerously close to turning the poor subset of humanity into a "humanity as such" that has supra-revelational access to knowledge of God.

To be sure, we see at this point a crucial difference between their views, one that can only receive brief mention in this essay — namely, the extent to which and form in which Barth and Sobrino see sin as a universal and therefore leveling reality (as well as their corresponding views of "atonement" and justification). But it appears in general that Sobrino's care in presenting an ultimately christological hermeneutical connection of the poor to Jesus shows that he is not as far from Barth as one might think. Sobrino implies that the poor themselves, though they remain hermeneutically illuminative of Christ's history, also need their crosses and hopes redefined in light of Christ's history: "On the cross illegitimate interests are unmasked, and legitimate interests are reformed, but what the cross shows in any case is that our interests are broken."[57]

Moreover, there is little sense in which the experience of the poor grants free-floating or independent epistemic access to God. It is only in connection with the revealed, concrete events of Jesus' cross and resurrection that Sobrino takes the "sorrow" and "hope" of the poor up into theology — thus like Barth and more clearly than in some post-colonial theology today, revelation is still the horse pulling the cart of appeal to experience. Along with the *analogia fidei*, Barth's related categories of "dependent witness" or a derivative "brightness" are not so far from what Sobrino is attempting to argue with respect to the hermeneutical significance of the poor, even if Sobrino's statements occasionally give the impression that the relationship is rather symmetrical. But it is also important to recognize that the kinds of experiences that Sobrino is referring to — usually ones of oppression and suffering — are lamentable and reprehensible, and therefore should be seen as a form of "darkness" that is given theological weight through the revelatory darkness of the cross, rather than the creational "brightness" that Barth talks about in II/1. Thus the challenge that Sobrino's position poses to Barth's per-

---

56. Sobrino, *Christ the Liberator*, 66.
57. Sobrino, *Jesus the Liberator*, 250.

spective from his liberationist *theologia crucis* is that the experiences most likely to gain theological significance through the brightness of the Christ-event are those that evoke his cross. It is only in light of those experiences, and governed by their concrete christological realism with respect to sin and salvation, that it is appropriate to look for the positive echoes of divine glory in creation.

In any case, the methodological centrality of christology to both theologians (despite significant differences in the content and method of their respective approaches) shows the fundamentally indeterminate and unstable place that any kind of natural theology will have in any theological project that strives to see Jesus Christ as the unique and unsurpassable revelation of God. In pointing out a secondary form of abstractionism that may obtain in Barth's approach, Sobrino suggests that not all experiential windows are created equal, that there may in fact be human experiences that serve as an apt epistemic window into the divine, but only via their connection to the apex of God's revelatory activity — Jesus' cross and then resurrection. Barth's more thoroughgoing theology of sin and grace shows, on the other hand, the enduring questionability of even those human experiences, and thus further reinforces the continuing need to read all experience through the lens of the revelation of Christ. Both positions pose valuable challenges that any theological appeal to "primal" or "indigenous" or "pre-Christian" experience would do well to ponder carefully in the important task of pursuing a sensitive yet christologically appropriate way of parsing revelation and experience in a post-colonial context.

"Beautiful Playing": Moltmann, Barth, and the Work of the Christian

Cynthia L. Rigby

In 1971, three years after Karl Barth's death, Jürgen Moltmann published an essay titled "Die Ersten Freigelassenen Der Schöpfung" ("The First Liberated Men in Creation").[1] In it, Moltmann explores the theological significance of "play" in relationship to his theology of hope.[2] In 1972, the essay was published in English, along with three responses, in a volume titled *Theology of Play*.[3] At the close of the book are some comments by Moltmann, who was asked to make a final response. Disappointingly, Moltmann finds himself unable to enter into conversation with his respondents. "In my opinion, the premises from which these replies have been written are not the same as my own," he laments. "We are perhaps not even talking about the same thing. . . . I am at a loss as to what to answer. . . . The authors and I live in the same one world, and yet in completely different inner spaces."[4] Moltmann even alerts the readers that "This book . . . shows where the battle line in theology is being drawn today," going on to

---

1. Originally published by Chr. Kaiser Verlag, München.
2. Moltmann seems, in this regard, to be responding to critiques made of his otherwise well-received *Theology of Hope* (1967). Daniel L. Migliore notes, for example, that "Moltmann speaks very briefly of the joy of Christian hope . . . but he has not yet productively explored the relation between a theology of hope and theology of play" (*Theology Today* 25:3 [October 1968]: 387-389, at 389).
3. Jürgen Moltmann, *Theology of Play*, trans. Reinhard Ulrich (New York: Harper & Row, 1971). The three responses are written by Robert E. Neal ("The Crucifixion As Play"), Sam Keen ("godsong"), and David L. Miller ("Playing the Game to Lose").
4. Moltmann, *Theology of Play*, 111.

delineate the "rules of the game" he plays by, presumably in contrast to his respondents.[5]

Commentators on the book are unable to articulate what, exactly, Moltmann means by this dramatic statement.[6] What can be said with certainty, on the basis of the rules he lays out, is that he disagrees with his respondents' tendency to think about "play" both as though it has "no rules"[7] and as if it can include anything, even the cross.[8] It also seems safe to surmise that Moltmann yearns to have someone with whom to converse on this subject who shares his theological "premises."

This essay imagines how Karl Barth would have responded to Moltmann, as one who essentially played according to Moltmann's "rules of the game." Barth's provocative comments directly on the subject of "play" were few,[9] but here will be appreciated and deepened in relationship to Moltmann's insights. My operative conviction is that Moltmann would have enjoyed developing his theology of play in conversation with Barth, largely because Barth — like Moltmann — oriented all his theological excursions around the fundamental theological premise that God is sovereign. Both Moltmann and Barth believe play is possible only because, and appropriate only when, it is engaged by the creature in relationship to the sovereign Creator. It is precisely because play takes place before the sovereign God that it has certain rules, does not include everything, and accomplishes something quite specific and worthwhile. It is in playing before God, in fact, that we begin imagining what God desires — i.e., the shape of God's Kingdom. As God's desires become ours by way of imagination, our playing takes the form of creative efforts that make a genuine contribution to the Kingdom's coming.

A central concern feeding the development of this argument is the current rate of clergy burnout.[10] Many of my colleagues serving in parish ministry are therefore implicitly involved in the conversation taking place in this

5. See "Are There No Rules of the Game?" 112-113.

6. See, for example, Charles W. Kegley, "Theology: 1939-1979," *Journal of Ecumenical Studies* 16:1 (1979): 119-127, at 122-123; and William D. Dean, *Theology of Play* (book review), *Journal of the American Academy of Religion* 42 (1974): 594.

7. Keene, "godsong," *Theology of Play,* 98.

8. See Neale, "The Crucifixion As Play," *Theology of Play,* 76-86.

9. Again, Barth died just as theologies of play were beginning to emerge.

10. Pastoral burn-out is currently at crisis proportions, according to much recent literature (see, for example, Jackson Carroll, *God's Potters: Pastoral Leadership and the Shaping of Congregations* [Grand Rapids: Eerdmans, 2006]; *Clergy Burnout: Recovering from the 70-Hour Workweek . . . and Other Self-Defeating Practices* [Minneapolis: Augsburg Fortress, 2006]).

essay. It is my belief that further development of a "theology of play," as inspired by Barth and Moltmann, might contribute to supporting pastors, and all Christian ministers, in their lives and work.

Serious Play

We are playing in the world and with the world, and we are trying through free play to make ourselves fit for the totally-other.

Moltmann[11]

Outward and inward work will be done with more rather than less seriousness once a person realizes that what she desires and does and achieves thereby, when measured by the work of God which it may attest, cannot be anything but play.

Barth[12]

Recently, a presbytery[13] rejected a lecture title I gave them. I knew something was amiss when I got a phone call, rather than the usual email, from the coordinator of my visit. "Some members of the presbytery just don't think the timing is right for a lecture on 'play.' You know, with the war in Iraq, the aftermath of Katrina, the coming recession. We'd like you to do something *serious*."

I had had it in mind to lecture on Karl Barth's understanding that "our work . . . cannot be anything but play" when done with an awareness of the sovereign God.[14] My thinking, of course, had been not to ignore the suffering that was plaguing the world in 2007, but to help pastors re-envision and live into the Kingdom of God when, descriptively speaking, it is hard enough for them to imagine surviving another week in the parish. Respecting the presbytery's request, I changed the lecture title and limited the use of the word "play" in my actual remarks.

It is no wonder that the presbytery asked me to adjust my presentation, given that "play" is commonly associated with diversions and amusements, a "taking off" from the very work they are hoping more deeply to engage. And

11. Moltmann, *Theology of Play*, 16.
12. Karl Barth, *Church Dogmatics* III/4 (Edinburgh: T&T Clark, 1985), 553. Hereafter references will noted as *CD* III/4.
13. A presbytery is one of the governing bodies of the Presbyterian Church (USA).
14. Barth, *CD* III/4, 553.

surely they are right that "play" holds the promise of escape, even for the most hard-working theologians. Moltmann certainly thinks that time *away* from work is essential to our well-being as creatures created for the rhythms of labor and Sabbath rest; others warn of the importance of making a clear distinction between "work" and "play" to ensure that rest actually occurs.[15] But those who invited me did not want to be reminded, as I believe they frequently are, that they need to play if they want to be whole people who are fruitful in their work. They were eager to talk about their *work* — the content, nature, and importance of their work itself.

Is there a place for talking about "play" as *part* of our work, as Christians? Moltmann and Barth both believe there is, and that doing so is essential to faithful living. Moltmann rightly points out, in fact, that conceiving of play only as something *other* than work that is necessary for the *continuance* of work is problematic. To make his case, he reminds us of the way play has been used, historically, to anesthetize the masses against revolting against the system rather than to "protest . . . the evil plays of the oppressor and the exploiter."[16] What Moltmann advocates is not the kind of play that "recapitulates the rhythm of the working world," the way so many of our overscheduled vacations, for example, do. Rather, he proposes a theological approach to "play" that remembers "the purpose of humanity's creation" (as it says right at the front of Calvin's *Geneva Catechism*) is "to glorify God."[17] Whatever our play is about, according to Moltmann, it must honor our being, before God, as creatures created not out of necessity, but *ex nihilo* — by the playful, creative action of the Creator God. Play that is "free" in this sense does not support "a merely reproductive imagination" that simply revives us before pumping us back into the systems of the world, argues Moltmann. It fosters, rather, "an imagination productive of a more liberated world" that is more consistent with who God is and what God desires.[18]

Barth argues, similarly, that "play," understood theologically, is not about taking time off work for the purpose of returning to work, refreshed and ready to produce more efficiently. Rather, to "play" is to engage one's own activity in relationship to the activity of the sovereign God because one

---

15. See, for example, Johan Huizinga's now-classic work, first published in 1938, titled *Homo Ludens: A Study of the Play Element in Culture* (Boston: Beacon Press, 1955) and David Jensen's *Responsive Labor: A Theology of Work* (Louisville: Westminster John Knox Press, 2006), 62.

16. Moltmann, *Theology of Play*, 16.

17. Ibid., 18.

18. Ibid., 12.

exists before, and belongs to, this God. When we play for the purpose of working more we expose our ill-founded conviction that work is the most important thing of all, simultaneously building a justification for ordering our lives around ourselves and our own efforts. Work-related stress, in this scenario, can quickly become a "badge of honor" — to be tempered by spates of "play" that ensure our stress levels do not impinge on productivity. This way of living is, of course, idolatrous — a "grievous sin," according to Barth.[19] "To work tensely," Barth insists, "is to do so in self-exaltation and forgetfulness of God" despite any "faithfulness, zeal, conscientiousness and good intentions" we may bring to our work.[20] In contrast to this, when we understand that all of our work *is* play — serious play, but play nonetheless, we are consequently "released" from "the feverish state of tension" we have falsely convinced ourselves is the "only way" we can be.[21] We then work "with the relief and relaxation which spring from" the recognition of God.[22]

The release from stress that comes from knowing ourselves before God has corporate, as well as personal, benefits. For the sake of transforming the world, the pastors at that presbytery meeting may well have been willing to live stressed-out lives. But to live with such stress is actually to neglect the "fellow-humanity of right work," according to Barth, who believes God never commands us to do anything that denies humanity for the sake of something "greater."[23] Moltmann points out that history cannot be changed, in any case, by those whose goal is to "make history." This is because they will inevitably burn out. "Infinite responsibility destroys human beings because they are only human and not God," Moltmann writes.[24] History can only be changed when our work is engaged for its own sake; when it is embraced freely; when it is characterized by "a calm rejoicing in existence itself."[25] Work *is*, in such a scenario, play. Its aim is no longer to be "productive" or "ethical," but "creative" and "aesthetic."[26]

19. Barth, *CD* III/4, 552.
20. Ibid.
21. Ibid., 552-553.
22. Ibid., 552.
23. Ibid., 553.
24. Moltmann, *Theology of Play*, 23.
25. Ibid.
26. Ibid. These are the terms Moltmann uses, following Søren Kierkegaard but apparently reversing Kierkegaard's ordering of the "stages" of spiritual life. Kierkegaard describes journeying from the "aesthetic" to the "ethical," and then on to the "religious." Rather than directly contradicting Kierkegaard's ordering between the aesthetic and the ethical, here, the argument could be made that Moltmann is describing an approach to the "religious" which

But how is it, exactly, that play before God — play that is done for its own sake — can function to change history? It is one thing to expound on the therapeutic benefits of a God-centered life. It is quite another to argue that it is only by way of a "calm rejoicing in existence" that the world will be changed. What is clear in this imagined conversation between Moltmann and Barth (with those presbytery pastors and elders interjecting from the sidelines), is that an adequate "theology of play" is about far more than issues related to personal spirituality. Rather, it is about the politics of the Kingdom. It is about the "transfiguration of politics,"[27] in fact — about doing the will of God in the world as those who pray constantly the prayer that Jesus taught us, demanding that God's Kingdom come, imagining what it looks like, and participating in its reality.

Moltmann and Barth would surely agree that the play-er who understands her activity in relation to the activity of the sovereign God contributes to the changing of history not because her efforts are actually less provisional than they appear, but because the God who stands at the center of her awareness, the God in whom she "lives and moves and has her being," is the God of Abraham, Isaac, and Jacob. The God before whom we play is not just "any old God," but the triune God who is — scandalously enough — self-revealed in the person of Jesus Christ. Play in relation to this God changes history because this God has specific characteristics, opinions, and desires that will one day, we believe, be made fully manifest in the creation of a new heaven and a new earth. Play that is engaged with the awareness that God is just will become itself just play and will, in its own right, promote justice. Play that is undertaken in recognition of God's beauty will itself be beautiful. Play that recognizes God's power as the living, dynamic power of the Trinity will abhor the leveraging of sheer power and instead perpetuate "creative, sacrificial, and empowering love" that is "self-sharing, other-regarding, and community-forming."[28] In short, because true play emerges out of a centeredness in *the particular* God who is sovereign, it is not characterized by imaginative efforts to perpetuate the unimaginative. Rather, it is marked by our desire for God's desires to come to fruition, for this world to become what it really is, as loved and claimed by God.

---

incorporates the best of the aesthetic (which he believes is being neglected) as well as the ethical (which, he believes, is too readily assumed).

27. See Paul Lehmann, *The Transfiguration of Politics* (Norwich: S.C.M. Press, 1975).

28. See Daniel L. Migliore, *Faith Seeking Understanding* (Grand Rapids: Eerdmans, 1991), 63-64.

Imagining Play

Being aware of God is an art and — if the term may be permitted — a no-
ble game. . . . Karl Barth was the only theologian in the continental
Protestant tradition who has dared to call God "beautiful."

Moltmann[29]

Beautiful playing presupposes an intuitive, childlike awareness of the es-
sence or center . . . of all things. It is from this center, from this beginning
and end, that I hear Mozart create his music.

Barth[30]

We tend to associate the imagining that goes hand-in-glove with playing with
a kind of dangerous free-for-all. "Imagination knows no bounds!" the saying
goes, and our concern, related to this popular conception, is that it therefore
encompasses that which is life-denying as well as elements of the abundant
life promised by Christ.[31] Certainly, imagination has too often been utilized,
historically, to develop systems of exploitation and dehumanization. For this
reason it makes some sense that we Christians have often divorced the imaginary from the good in order (ostensibly) to protect the good.

One problem with this separation is that discussion of the good that
shuns imagination tends to present the good as though it is boring. Hans
Urs von Balthasar laments what he believes is a common malady since modernity, that "the 'good' has lost its attraction because it has been cut off
from beauty."[32] The good is not boring, according to von Balthasar, but
beautiful. God is in fact both good *and* beautiful; trying to think of either of
these attributes in isolation from the other is impossible when one is thinking of God, when one is living "from the center."[33] As John Keats famously
noted: "Beauty is truth, truth beauty — that is all ye know on earth, and all
ye need to know."[34] Apart from beauty, how can we even identify truth?
Apart from imagining God's desires in such a way that God's desires become
our own, the good might be piously spoken of, but is never truly known.

29. Moltmann, *Theology of Play*, 27, 38.
30. Karl Barth, *Wolfgang Amadeus Mozart* (Eugene, OR: Wipf and Stock, 1956), 16.
31. See John 10:10.
32. Cited in William A. Dyrness, *Visual Faith* (Grand Rapids: Baker, 2001), 90.
33. Barth, *Mozart*, 16.
34. John Keats, "Ode on a Grecian Urn," *Oxford Book of English Verse: 1250-1900*, ed.
Arther Quiller-Couch (Oxford: Oxford University Press, 1919), #625.

This last point gives way to an even more devastating problem with setting "imagination" aside in conversations about the good. That is: to do so reveals that we are still caught in the "ethical" at the expense of the "aesthetic." According to Moltmann, to be caught in the ethical is to be closed to "the images for the coming new world [which] do not come from the world of struggle and victory, of work and achievement, of law and its enforcement." It is to resist "the world of primal childhood trust."[35] Without becoming "like children," without playing, and imagining, as children before God, there is no hope that we can enter into the "totally other" Kingdom in which no infants die, no labor is in vain, and the wolf and the lamb eat together.[36] How can we, in this broken world we live in, even begin to imagine such things? It is impossible for us to do so, as hard-working, ethical adults, on the basis of our own wherewithal. "Human renewal is not intrinsic to human capacity; it comes to humanity as a gift."[37] This is why Jesus desires that we have the faith of children; that we put aside ethics in favor of aesthetics;[38] that we play in relation to the God for whom nothing is impossible.

It is actually good news for us, as finite, ethical beings, that God is not the very best thing we — even at the top of our creative game — are able to imagine. How burdensome and dangerous it would be to imagine we might imagine our way to God. Anselm taught, in direct opposition to this, that God is "that than which nothing greater can be conceived." Because God is *God*, and not whomever we might imagine God to be, we are free to be who we really are as creative creatures. Because God is beyond anything we can conceive, we are also free to distinguish our plans from God's plans, imaginatively opening ourselves to participation in the plans of a God "who by the power at work within us is able to accomplish abundantly far more than all we can ask or imagine."[39]

When we play before God, then, our fear of engaging in idolatrous imaginings is replaced by the joyous "fear and trembling" that comes with knowing God has enabled *us* "to will and to work for God's good purpose."[40] Protecting the good from the beautiful is, in this space, no longer a temptation. As play-ers before God, our imaginations are neither confined to our

---

35. Moltmann, *Theology of Play*, 35.

36. See Luke 18:17 and Isaiah 65:17-25.

37. Paul Lehmann, *Ethics in a Christian Context* (New York: Harper & Row, 1963), 322. Lehmann is here discussing the meaning of the doctrine of total depravity.

38. See note 26.

39. Ephesians 3:20, NRSV.

40. Philippians 2:12.

best efforts nor liable to lead us to sin. Instead, they are bound by the one who is unbounded, by the one who has claimed us, and fully included us, in boundless love.

At this point I can almost hear the members of that presbytery asking, "What exactly does all of this mean, when it comes to living in a real world that is really at war? What are the actual boundaries we are talking about? What *is* the content of God's desire?" Thankfully, both Barth and Moltmann insist that God's beauty and boundlessness do not imply that God's desires are ethereal and/or all-embracing. Further, they delineate very precisely the shape of the Unbounded One's desires. Barth explains, for example, that when we are "aware . . . of the essence or center of all things,"[41] we in fact know beyond question that "the command of God . . . is self-evidently and in all circumstances a call for counter-movements on behalf of humanity . . . and therefore a call for the championing of the weak against every kind of encroachment on the part of the strong."[42] To imagine dehumanizing possibilities is *never* to participate in the desire of the God who is *always* for humanization.

Moltmann similarly describes the limits to the exercise of imagination, noting that play cannot be about just anything and still be play. Simply put, play that correlates with life before God is never oppressive. Moltmann goes on to devote even more effort than does Barth to articulating what is *not* included in the realm of play. Moltmann would surely, in fact, challenge Barth's statement that "all of our work is play." Barth's general statement, at this point, might come too close to risking something Moltmann is very concerned about: namely, that "the categories of play" not be "misplaced."[43] Specifically, Moltmann holds that suffering, the passion, and especially the cross should be "left . . . out of the game."[44] "The life of Jesus in the gospels stands under the signs of the manger and cross, homelessness and murder," writes Moltmann.[45] "In the face of such suffering aesthetic categories fail rather abruptly."[46] "Play," Moltmann believes, is appropriate only to "reconciled existence."[47] In relation to the resurrection, new life, and the promised Kingdom, then, our work is play. But we are called to work also in relation

41. Barth, *Mozart*, 16.
42. Barth, *CD* III/4, 553.
43. Moltmann, *Theology of Play*, 35.
44. Ibid., 29.
45. Ibid., 28.
46. Ibid.
47. Ibid., 31.

to "unreconciled existence," to stand in "solidarity" and "pain" with those who suffer.[48]

This, of course, complicates things for us. As we have said, to let go of re-producing the world in favor of living as imaginative, creative children is al-ready challenging. Moltmann adds to this challenge that we who are players can never become children as a means of escape from the sufferings of this world. At the same time that we imagine the Kingdom, we grieve that which is not the Kingdom. As people of hope, we live with a great deal of dissatisfac-tion and despair. As people who play, we recognize that songs and laughter and games must be set aside wherever and whenever there is suffering — from the passion to the resurrection.[49] We should not become play "enthusi-asts," Moltmann warns, but should rather be "dialecticians" who recognize that "the cross remains an offense . . . until the dead rise and all begin to dance and everything has become new."[50]

And so we return, full circle, to the presbytery's reaction to my topic. Why speak of "play" in a world full of war? Or, as Moltmann puts it, "How can I play in a strange land, in an alienated and alienating society? How can we laugh and rejoice when there are still so many tears to be wiped away and when new tears are being added every day?"[51] In short, Barth's answer to this question is: we may play, because God redeemed us in Christ to be "subjects" and "righteous partners of God" in the "great event of reconciliation."[52] And Moltmann's an-swer is: we must play, if we are to change the "present system of living."[53]

Why must we play? Because our playing — our imaginative, fragile, free, and provisional actions before the sovereign God — are made by this God to be essential to the divine life and work, to the very coming of the Kingdom.

Liberating Play

> [Play is] a childlike imitation and reflection of the fatherly action of God which as such is true and proper action.
>
> Barth[54]

48. Ibid.
49. Ibid., 28-29.
50. Ibid., 112.
51. Ibid., 2.
52. Karl Barth, *Church Dogmatics* IV/2 (Edinburgh: T&T Clark, 1958), 8-10.
53. Moltmann, *Theology of Play*, 13.
54. Barth, *CD* III/4, 553.

Liberation from the bonds of the present system of living takes place by playing games.

Moltmann[55]

Recently, *The New York Times Magazine* featured an article titled "Why Do We Play?"[56] The answer given is, perhaps not surprisingly, neither Barthian nor Moltmannian. The author concludes that scientific studies on child development suggest play still "warrants a place in every child's day," though "not too overblown . . . [or] . . . sanctimonious a place."[57] The idea that adults might play, or that any of us, in our play, might somehow contribute to the coming of the Kingdom to earth as it is in heaven would, no doubt, be considered "overblown" — and certainly "sanctimonious"!

How can we conceptualize what it "looks like" to say our play before the Other, provisional as it is, somehow participates essentially in God's life and work? I would like to offer three very different sketches I hope will help illustrate the liberating power of play, as Moltmann and Barth have described it. The first ("The Egg Server") draws from my experience of watching my children play. The second ("The Piano Player") borrows a story about a homeless community from Anne Lamott. The third ("The Artist") imagines us play-ers as artists participating in the artistry of God.

Conceptualization #1: "The Egg Server"

Several months ago, in listening to my children play with their toy "kitchen," I realized what Barth meant by his assertion that our play is an "imitation and reflection of the fatherly action of God" that is, at the same time, "true and proper action."[58] Up until that point, I had understood "imitation" and "reflection" to reference practice for "real" action that will take place in the future. The *New York Times* article points out, along these lines, that one of the developmental benefits of play-acting is that it gives children the opportunity to practice the true form their acts will take, once they reach adulthood. Children's church, for example, provides opportunity for children to "mimic" regular worship so that they will be slowly formed into the future worshiping adults they will become. Following the same logic, one could

55. Moltmann, *Theology of Play*, 13.
56. Robin Marantz Henig, "Why Do We Play?" *The New York Times Magazine* (February 17, 2008).
57. Ibid., 75.
58. Barth, *CD* III/4, 553.

readily argue that worshiping adults are merely practicing to live in the fullness of the Kingdom.

I hear my four-year-old son, Alexander, pretending to fry an egg and serve it to his two-year-old sister, Jessica. He serves it from the center of what he knows to be true. He is an egg-receiver who reaches out of his participation in what is real to include his sister. His play creates a space for her. The eggs, the frying pan, and the burner are made of wood (he is a child incapable of breaking and frying real eggs in a real pan), but the play in which he engages invites her into the reality of the center in which he, the child, stands.

There is no doubt that Alexander and Jessica are, in their play, imitating and reflecting patterns of hospitality and service they have witnessed in our household. Alexander is, most clearly, imitating parental actions in pretending to make and give fried eggs to his sister. Down to the details of reminding Jessica to "be careful, it might be hot, don't forget to blow on it!," Alexander is rehearsing and absorbing who he is, how he is cared for, and how he can participate in caring for other members of his family. While his activity pales in comparison to what I — the one he is copying — can do (I can really fry real eggs), it certainly is worthwhile. I'm sure it is fair to say that Alexander is making good progress toward someday making real eggs and really serving his sister breakfast. Play is good practice for what is to come.

Except that "good practice" is not all that is going on. For in serving his sister the wooden eggs, Alexander does not simply "imitate" what his mommy and daddy have done for him, many times. He actually demonstrates hospitality. His imitation is, in the words of Barth, not only "imitation" and "reflection," but "true and right action" that itself participates in the hospitable existence that is the desire of God. In Moltmann's terms, we might even say that Alexander's simple "game playing" promotes liberation insofar as it challenges world systems in which two-year-old girls are not fed a good breakfast, or looked out for, or respected. Alexander's goal is not, of course, to challenge world systems. It is, simply, to participate in existence, and as such is transformative.

Alexander and Jessica, in their playing, create from the center. They imagine what the Kingdom looks like, and they advance it.

Conceptualization #2: "The Piano Player"

Anne Lamott tells the story of witnessing beautiful play, on her way back from getting her nails done, on a day when she is to be interviewed on a talk show with Charles Schulz. She passes, for the second time, the home of a group of homeless people who are displaying their possessions:

> I was coming up on the lean-to. I couldn't see it yet, except in my mind — the blue plastic Mary, the big bright plastic toys; the pride that was on display, each object numinous, holding something more than itself. There they were making something out of nothing; surrounded by ruins, you assemble what comforts you. . . . I thought of the lamp that was not plugged into anything; then of the boy who looked like Pig Pen, blinky and dense, then of Linus, and Schroeder, of the ferocity and poignancy of our illusions. You think a blanket will protect you? That you are really making lovely music on a toy piano? But the blanket did protect Linus; and Schroeder does play beautifully; and maybe more than anything, they keep at it. They believe.[59]

Barth held that Mozart plays the piano beautifully because he plays "from the center . . . of things."[60] But — shockingly, given that I mean no disrespect to Mozart — so does Schroeder, and so does the homeless person with his toy piano, though in very different ways. The homeless person in Lamott's story does not create the music Mozart does, both because he is not Mozart and because his piano is only a plastic toy. But he does imitate "the fatherly action of God" by displaying his splendor, along with the other members of his community. He unabashedly creates, and with what is ready at hand. He creates not, technically, *ex nihilo* ("out of nothing"), but with close enough to nothing that Lamott's intentional allusion to the character of the divine creativity is evocative. This homeless "Schroeder," this beautiful player, is participating in the Kingdom of God by pretending to play a discarded, plastic, toy piano. By celebrating his existence. By acting in freedom. By challenging oppressive systems through the celebration of his existence and the exercise of his freedom, as one who plays. This piano player is, without a doubt, making a contribution to the Kingdom by way of playing, and imagining, and recognizing the beauty that is the center of all things. Lamott's story is testimony to this. If Jessica shares in the divine hospitality by virtue of Alexander's play-acting, Lamott witnesses God's glory in the beautiful playing of this homeless person and his friends.

---

59. Anne Lamott, "The Gospel According to Pig Pen," in "Word by Word: Anne Lamott's Online Diary," *Salon,* May 1997, www.salon.com/may97/columnists/lamott.

60. Barth, *Mozart,* 16.

Conceptualization #3: "The Artist"

As those who play, who agree with Moltmann that "being aware of God is an art,"[61] we might think of ourselves as artists who are compelled to participate in the beauty that lies beyond ourselves. The Holy Spirit has come upon us; we are creatures claimed by the One who is "totally other" for productive, and not merely reproductive, purposes. In imagining the will and purpose of this Other, we begin to participate in it. This will and purpose has been made known to us concretely in Jesus Christ, who "no longer calls us servants, but calls us friends . . . because we have known the mystery of the Father's will."[62] And so we look to him, and listen again to his parables about the Kingdom, and think about the way he taught us to pray. We imagine the pearl of great price, and a woman kneading bread or searching for a lost coin, and a father rushing out to embrace his son who has come home. And in imagining, we are caught up in the reality of it all. And so we have to paint (or sing, or dance, or write, or tithe, or preach, or feed, or heal). We are driven to paint, to participate even more deeply in that which has laid claim to us. And the mystery deepens even as our participation gives way to contribution. To *contribution* — *our* contribution. Contribution that in no way compromises on the sovereignty of God, the fact that the promise and work of the Kingdom is all God's. But, as artists imagining the Kingdom of God, we know — don't we? — that the work that is all God's is, somehow, also ours.

It is appropriate, here, to say that the work of the Kingdom is *all God* and *also ours* because we are looking at it from the vantage point of the mystery itself. Imagining the Kingdom of God has led us smack dab into the middle of the mystery. And (from the vantage point of the mystery itself), the character of the God/world relationship is understood to be participatory, not transactional. In a transactional way of understanding, God does something and we do something. If God does it all, we do nothing. If we do something, God's sovereign power is compromised. In a participatory model, by contrast, God does it all *and* we are fully included in the doing of God. And not as puppets are we fully included, but as creatures created by the Creator God to be creative. It is *we* who contribute something, *we* who are artists participating in the artistry of God.

All God, and us. "Everything I have is yours," God says to us, in the words of the father to his elder son in Luke 15:31. *Everything God has is ours.*

---

61. Moltmann, *Theology of Play*, 27.
62. John 15:15.

Let us go to the party, then. Let us go, and play. Let us play, and create. Let us create, and contribute.

Conclusion

I suppose members of that presbytery would have been more amenable to my topic if they had known something of what Moltmann or Barth mean by "play." Yet it also true that there are good reasons to resist "a theology of play" even when it is properly understood. In short, playing is risky business.

To "play," as we have discussed it here, is to risk on at least two levels. First, it is to risk recognizing that our work is not all that important, understanding that it is at best provisional in the face of a sovereign God who will bring all things together in the fullness of time. And second, it is to risk recognizing that our work is of eternal significance, precisely when it is done freely and for its own sake before a sovereign God who will bring all things together in the fullness of time. It is to risk first being changed by God, and then being vehicles of change in the world.

Both of these risks are significant ones. To let go of the perception that our own work is important is, simultaneously, to let go of the guilt we experience when the quality of our output does not match up to our self-expectation. Moltmann explains that the guilt many of us walk around with keeps us from playing — it bogs us down in dissatisfaction with ourselves to the point where we "blackmail ourselves with images of what we are not."[63] People of faith, according to Moltmann, are those who risk letting go of their own self-importance to live, instead, as those who are guilt-free.

To recognize our "work of play" as essential to the divine work is also a risk. It risks recognizing how unconditionally we are loved, and how fully we are included, by the God who claims us in Jesus Christ. Grace can, when truly perceived, only overwhelm us. The risk is that we may drown in it. Becoming like children, we plunge into the water, anyway. And we begin to play. Joyously splashing around, we imagine what God desires and find ourselves participating in the promised Kingdom.

Risking life before the sovereign God offers us the blessing of existence for its own sake, the freedom to play. Free from guilt, Moltmann says, we experience faith: "a new spontaneity and a light heart."[64] People of faith "ac-

63. Moltmann, *Theology of Play,* 32.
64. Ibid.

cept themselves as they are and gain new confidence in themselves because they have been trusted more than they deserve," Moltmann explains.[65] They learn to play, and in their playing risk the ongoing transformation of themselves and the world.

I believe there is a pressing need, in the year 2009 in the United States of America, to revisit and creatively develop a theology of play. We live in a time and culture in which even people of faith believe there is "no other way" than to live lives full of stress that emphasize, above all, the importance of work. Surely, there is a better way. It is my hope that, in engaging in conversation with Moltmann and Barth on this subject, and in playfully conceptualizing what they, some decades ago, were putting forward, fresh theological approaches to understanding the relationship between our work and our play will begin to emerge.

Related to this, continued exploration of what it means to live as people of faith in a world in which the Kingdom has not yet come is sorely needed. How do we participate in this Kingdom, taking up our calling to advance its coming while at the same time remembering that we are but creatures before the sovereign God, our actions at best fragmentary and provisional in relationship to God's actions? Developing a theology of play holds promise for testifying to the great and graceful mystery of how we who can do nothing in and of ourselves can — in relationship to the God who has met us — freely participate in, and even make a contribution to, the divine work.

---

65. Ibid.

CONVERSATIONS WITH TRADITIONAL THEOLOGICAL TOPICS

"Inspired Heterodoxy"? The Freedom of Theological Inquiry and the Well-Being of the Church

Dawn DeVries

> *I am firmly convinced, however, that [my teaching about God] . . . is the kind of inspired heterodoxy that soon enough will become orthodox, even if not by virtue of my book, and even if only long after my death.*
>
> Friedrich Schleiermacher, *Über seine Glaubenslehre* (1829)

A perennial theological question is where to draw the boundaries of an ecclesial tradition, or perhaps more precisely: which voices ought we to hear and which ought we to ignore — or even silence — in our theological debates? These questions are neither new nor unique to the Reformed tradition. The Protestant Reformers inherited a long and complex tradition of heresiology, and they, in turn, although considered heretics in Rome, handed on no small volume of writing against heresies. Our Reformed confessions are peppered with deprecations hurled at deviant opinions old and new. In a single chapter of the Second Helvetic Confession, for example, Heinrich Bullinger (1504-1575) can "abhor the impious doctrine of Arius . . . and Servetus," "detest the dogma of the Nestorians," "execrate the madness of Eutyches," "by no means accept the strained, confused and obscure subtleties of Schwenkfeldt," and "condemn Jewish dreams," to name but a few of the heresies he steers around.[1]

---

1. *Confessio helvetica posterior* (1562), XI in *Die Bekenntnisschriften der reformierten Kirche: In authentischen Texten mit geschichtlicher Einleitung und Register*, ed. E. F. Karl Müller (Leipzig: A. Deichert'sche Verlagsbuchhandlung [Georg Böhme], 1903), 182-186.

While theologians today may be as contentious as they ever were, Bullinger's brand of rhetoric is mostly out of style. And yet in recent years, in the face of the growing chaos of cultural and religious pluralism, there has been a call to "reclaim the center" of our churches, to "draw a line in the sand" with reference to particular opinions deemed to be very dangerous, indeed a call for a return to orthodoxy — if perhaps a more generous orthodoxy than that of the age of religious wars, when true blue Presbyterians, as Samuel Butler (1612-1680) put it, sought to "prove their doctrine orthodox/ by apostolic blows and knocks."[2]

A call for a return to orthodoxy invites reflection on fundamental questions in the prolegomena to any dogmatics: questions about authoritative sources and norms, and about the definition of heresy and orthodoxy itself. Before getting into the substance of these matters, however, I want to draw out some other questions implicit in my title. One set of questions has to do with the meaning of the terms "orthodoxy" and "heresy." Is it best to think of these two as in simple opposition to each other? Is everything that is not orthodox of necessity heretical? Or is there something in between these two terms? Following from these is another set of questions having to do with the ecclesial response to ideas that are not orthodox. If there is, in addition to full-blown heresy, something called "heterodoxy," what are we to think of it? Are heterodoxies simply permissible differences of opinion on unimportant matters, or are they the gateway to more serious deviation, the beginning of the long slow slide into heresy? Can heterodoxy be tolerated or perhaps even encouraged in the church, or should it be restrained and silenced? These are the sorts of questions I had in mind when lifting Friedrich Schleiermacher's (1768-1834) evocative description of his own doctrine of God as an "inspired

2. Samuel Butler, *Hudibras,* with notes and literary memoir by Treadway Russell Nash (New York: D. Appleton & Company, 1868), 44. Butler was a Restoration-era man of letters who ruthlessly satirized Puritan hypocrisy in this brilliant burlesque poem. The line I allude to comes in the opening of the poem and is part of the introduction of its central character, Sir Hudibras, a Puritan knight riding out in defense of orthodox religion. The larger passage reads, "Twas Presbyterian, true blue,/For he was of that stubborn crew/Of errant saints, whom all men grant/To be the true church militant:/Such as do build their faith upon/The holy text of pike and gun;/Decide all controversy by/Infallible artillery;/And prove their doctrine orthodox/By apostolic blows, and knocks;/Call fire, and sword, and desolation,/A godly-thorough Reformation,/Which always must be carried on,/And still be doing, never done/As if Religion were intended/For nothing else but to be mended./A sect, whose chief devotion lies/In odd perverse antipathies:/In falling out with that or this,/And finding somewhat still amiss" (44-45).

heterodoxy" — a phrase I believe he means in a properly theological sense, as I shall explain later.[3]

Because I identify myself as a theologian within the Reformed tradition, I want to look at these questions in close conversation with two great Reformed theologians, John Calvin (1509-1564) and Friedrich Schleiermacher. I do not claim that their thoughts on orthodoxy and heresy are an exhaustive representation of Reformed thinking on these themes; rather, they are important benchmarks. But before mining our own tradition, I must turn to at least a cursory discussion of the concepts of orthodoxy and heresy that Calvin inherited.

I

The meaning of the terms "heresy" and "heterodoxy" was forever changed by the rise of Christianity. In Hellenistic times, among both the Greeks and the Jews, a heresy was simply a school or a sect with its own distinctive body of doctrine. To be a "heretic" was to be one who chose to join some such particular sect. "Heterodoxy," by contrast, was understood to be the holding of a different opinion than the one commonly deemed correct. In either case, there was no particular blame assigned to such alternative views.[4] But already in the

3. The epigraph to this essay is taken from F. D. E. Schleiermacher, *Über die Glaubenslehre: Zwei Sendschreiben an Lücke,* in F. D. E. Schleiermacher, *Kritische Gesamtausgabe* [hereafter abbreviated KGA], ed. Hans-Joachim Birkner, Gerhard Ebeling, Hermann Fischer, Heinz Kimmerle, Kurt-Victor Selge (Berlin: Walter de Gruyter, 1984-), Part 1, vol. 10:334. The word translated as "inspired" is *divinatorische*. Schleiermacher argued that there is a divinatory aspect in any act of interpretation by which the interpreter imaginatively projects herself into the very person of the author she is interpreting in order to understand his unique individuality. See F. D. E. Schleiermacher, *Hermeneutik: Nach den Handschriften neu herausgegeben und eingeleitet,* ed. Heinz Kimmerle (Heidelberg: Carl Winter Universitätsverlag, 1974), 105. Presumably a "divinatory" heterodoxy is one that understands the unique individuality of the Christian revelation intuitively — from the inside.

4. See the entry "Heresy" in *The Interpreter's Dictionary of the Bible: An Illustrated Encyclopedia,* ed. George Arthur Buttrick et al. (Nashville: Abingdon Press, 1962), 2:583. Cf. the entries for "Häresie" and "Heterodox" in *Wörterbuch der philosophischen Begriffe,* ed. Arnim Regenbogen and Uwe Meyer (Darmstadt: Wissenschaftliche Buchgesellschaft, 1998), 281-282, 289. Cf. the entries on "Häresie" and "Häretiker im Urchristentum," in *Die Religion in Geschichte und Gegenwart,* ed. Hans Frhr. V. Campenhausen et al. (Tübingen: J. C. B. Mohr [Paul Siebeck], 1958), vol. 3:13-21. The classic study of orthodoxy and heresy in the early church is Walter Bauer, *Rechtgläubigkeit und Ketzerei im ältesten Christentum* (Tübingen: J. C. B. Mohr [Paul Siebeck], 1934).

New Testament, the usage of the term "heresy" was changing. Paul, it is true, does use the word "heresies" to denote factions in much the same sense as earlier authors, but he clearly implies that such divisions are an evil which disturbs the unity of faith. He grants that perhaps some heresies must be tolerated for the time being, but they are never to be encouraged or relished or seen as anything other than a trial that will come to an end in the eschaton (1 Cor. 11:18-19). Paul uses two different words for factions in 1 Corinthians 11, and this led Augustine and others to draw a distinction between schisms, sects that break the fellowship of the church, and heresies, parties within the church who disagree about doctrine.[5] By the time of the writing of 2 Peter, heresies are spoken of explicitly as the destructive work of false prophets (2 Peter 2:1).

A similar transformation in the meaning of heresy occurs in the first Christian centuries. In the New Testament, heresy is pernicious doctrine, that is to say, evil or incorrect teaching that should not be received by the faithful. As the letter to Titus puts it: "avoid stupid controversies, genealogies, dissensions, and quarrels over the law, for they are unprofitable and futile. As for a man who is factious [that is, the heretic], after admonishing him once or twice, have nothing more to do with him, knowing that such a person is perverted and sinful; he is self-condemned" (Titus 3:9-11, RSV). Heresies are an evil to be avoided by the community, but this can be achieved simply by shunning the heretic whose own ideas condemn him. Gradually, however, during the first three centuries, the idea developed that heresy was really more like a disease than a mistake — and a contagious disease at that. To protect the community of the faithful, the good bishop should do whatever is necessary to root out the disease even if that means radical surgery. Jerome (c. 349–c. 420), commenting on Galatians 5:9, aptly expresses this view:

> Cut off the decayed flesh, expel the mangy sheep from the fold, lest the whole house, the whole paste, the whole body, the whole flock, burn perish, rot, die. Arius was but one spark in Alexandria, but as that spark was not at once put out, the whole earth was laid waste by its flame.[6]

By the high Middle Ages, not only theological tradition but also canon law delineated in the most careful terms both the definition of heresy and its

---

5. The words are αἵρεσις and σχίσμα. For Augustine's discussion of the distinction between heresy and schism, see his *Questionum Septemdecim in Evangelium Secundum Mattheaum*, xi.2 (*Patrologiae Cursus Completus, Series Latina*, ed. J.-P. Migne [Paris, 1844-1865], 35:1367). Hereafter cited as PL.

6. PL 27:430.

proper treatment. For Thomas Aquinas (c. 1225-1274), both heresy and apostasy are species of unbelief, but while the apostate Jew or infidel refuses to give assent to the doctrines of faith, the heretic is willing, but does so improperly by following his own opinions rather than the articles of faith as defined by the creed, duly convened church councils, or the pope. There is a possibility for differences of opinion among church theologians in "matters the holding of which in this or that way is of no consequence, so far as faith is concerned, or even in matters of faith, which were not as yet defined by the Church." But if a theologian were "obstinately to deny them after they had been defined by the authority of the universal Church, he would be deemed a heretic."[7] Thomas closes his discussion of the matter by considering whether heretics should be tolerated, or repentant heretics received, in the church. His answer, in short, is "no." The heretic has committed a sin far more grievous than any other, one deserving not only excommunication but also death. The church, it is true, desires the conversion of sinners, and so properly postpones the excommunication of the heretic until after two warnings. But a heretic who persists in his errors after these warnings ought to be delivered to the secular tribunal "to be exterminated thereby from the world by death."[8] Even a heretic who has seen the error of her ways and repented should not be permitted to return to the bosom of the church more than one time. If a relapse into heresy occurs, whether or not repentance follows, the heretic should not escape the flames.

By the middle of the thirteenth century, and continuing right through the outbreak of the Reformation in the sixteenth century, the Roman church devoted an entire institution — the Inquisition — to the extermination of heresy. Ironically, the later Middle Ages were really the golden age of heresy in the Western church. It seems that for every brush fire the Inquisition managed to stamp out, two others ignited.[9] Nonetheless, the Roman church's policy on heresy was clear: it was a dangerous threat to the *corpus Christianum* that could not be tolerated under any circumstances. As the

---

7. St. Thomas Aquinas, *Summa Theologiae* IIa-IIae, q. 11, art. 1-2, hereafter cited as *ST.* English translation, *Summa Theologicae,* trans. Fathers of the Dominican Province, 3 vols. (New York: Benzinger Brothers, 1947-48), 2:1224-1226.

8. *ST* IIa-IIae, q. 11, art. 3-4; ET, 2:1226-1228.

9. For a thorough discussion of high and late medieval heresies, see Heinrich Fichtenau, *Heretics and Scholars in the High Middle Ages, 100-1200,* trans. Denise A. Kaiser (University Park, PA: The Pennsylvania State University Press, 1998), and Gordon Leff, *Heresy in the Later Middle Ages: The Relation of Heterodoxy to Dissent c. 1250-1450,* 2 vols. (Manchester: Manchester University Press, 1967).

body of official church dogma increased in volume, however, so the range of permissible heterodoxy narrowed in scope, and heresy was taken as the simple opposite of orthodoxy — as any form of dissent to the church.[10]

On the eve of the Reformation, some Catholic voices were lifted against the extreme control the Roman church sought to maintain over religious and theological imagination. Erasmus, for example, argued that not every doctrine of the church is of equal importance, and that if an accused heretic believed the fundamental articles of the faith (in this case, as expressed in the Apostles' Creed) this should be sufficient proof of his orthodoxy.[11] But the official understanding of heresy did not change: any persistent deviation from established church doctrine was heresy punishable by excommunication and death. In 1520, Martin Luther was condemned as a heretic in the papal bull *Exsurge, Domine.*[12]

The important elements in the concept of heresy remained constant during the patristic and medieval periods, even if the actual treatment of heretics shows development. Such elements would include: the notion that orthodoxy is a fixed body of teaching embodied in the creed or established by duly convened councils or by the pope; that heresy is a refusal to submit to the church's correction and be silent when one's opinions conflict with orthodoxy; that heresy is both an ecclesiastical and a civil offense; and that heresy left unchecked will destroy the *corpus Christianum.* Further, there was an increasing tendency to see any heterodoxy as heresy. John Calvin, like most of the magisterial Reformers, shared all but one of these convictions — the one that made *him,* from Rome's point of view, a heretic.

10. See the discussion in Leff, op. cit., vol. 1, 1-47.

11. See his treatise *Inquisitio de Fide: A Colloquy by Desiderius Erasmus Roterodamus 1524,* ed. with an introduction and commentary by Craig R. Thompson (New Haven: Yale University Press, 1950; 2d ed. Hamden, CT: Archon Books, 1975), 54-73. See also the remark made in several of his letters that "not every error is a heresy," *Opus epistolarum Des, Erasmi Roterodami,* ed. P. S. and H. M. Allen and H. W. Garrod, 12 vols. (Oxford: Clarendon Press, 1906-1958), 939.81, 1033.234-43, 1202.253; English translation, *Collected Works of Erasmus,* ed. Peter G. Bietenholz et al., 86 vols. (Toronto: University of Toronto Press, 1974-93), 6:295-299; 7:108-115; 8:201-211.

12. The text of the bull is in Carl Mirbt and Kurt Aland, eds., *Quellen zur Geschichte des Papsttums und des römischen Katholizismus,* vol. 1, 6th ed. (Tübingen: J. C. B. Mohr [Paul Siebeck], 1967), 504-513.

II

Calvin's teaching on heresy is marked by an inner tension that betrays the insecurity of the evangelicals even in the second generation of the Reformation. On the one hand, he is sharply critical of the very definition of orthodoxy that fueled the Inquisition. But on the other hand, for many reasons — not least, the survival of the Reformed churches in Switzerland and France — he did not wish to present himself as anything other than a defender of the orthodox catholic faith. This ambivalence can perhaps best be illustrated by two incidents in his career, one undoubtedly more well known that the other: his conflict with Pierre Caroli over the Nicene Creed, and his complicity in the execution of the anti-trinitarian theologian Michael Servetus.

The conflict with Caroli began at a meeting before the commissioners of Bern in February 1537. Calvin attended this meeting in order to question Caroli, then an evangelical pastor in Lausanne, about his practice of advocating prayers for the dead. But in a surprise move, Caroli turned the tables and accused Calvin and his Lausanne associate Pierre Viret (1511-1571) of Arianism. When Calvin tried to counter with a passage from his Genevan Catechism, Caroli requested that all in attendance give assent to the three ancient creeds: the Nicene, the Athanasian, and the Apostles'. Calvin refused with the remark: "We swear in the faith of the one God, not of Athanasius, whose creed no true Church has ever approved."[13] Calvin did not hesitate to discuss the difficulties he had with the creed: it was too repetitious; it had the quality more of a song than of a theological confession; it perhaps was not really the work of the Nicene fathers.[14] The details of the ensuing debate between these two men need not detain us. For now it is enough to ask why Calvin reacted in this way.

Many theories have been advanced for explaining his refusal to subscribe, and undoubtedly his motives were complex.[15] Chief among them,

---

13. *"Ad haec Calvinus, nos in Dei unius fidem iurasse respondit, non Athanasii cuius symbolum nulla unquam legitima ecclesia approbasset,"* *Ioannis Calvini opera quae supersunt omnia,* ed. Wilhelm Baum, Eduard Cunitz, and Eduard Reuss, 59 vols., *Corpus Reformatorum,* vols. 29-87 (Brunswick: C. A. Schwetschke & Son [M. Bruhn], 1863-1900), 10b:83-84. Hereafter cited as *CO.*

14. *CO,* 7:315-316.

15. I am most persuaded by the account of this matter given in W. Nijenhuis, "Calvin's Attitude Toward the Symbols of the Early Church during the Conflict with Caroli," *Ecclesia Reformata: Studies on the Reformation,* Kerkhistorische Bijdragen, no. 3 (Leiden: E. J. Brill, 1972), 73-96. Cf. Jan Koopmans, *Das altkirchliche Dogma in der Reformation,* trans. from the Dutch (1938) by H. Quistorp, Beiträge zur evangelischen Theologie, no. 22 (Munich: Chr. Kaiser Verlag, 1955), 45-48; Benjamin B. Warfield, "Calvin's Doctrine of the Trinity," *Prince-*

however, if we are to take Calvin's own explanation seriously, are Caroli's grounding of the authority of the creeds not in their material agreement with Scripture, but in their having been received by the Catholic church and handed down unchanged through the centuries, and Caroli's scholastic insistence upon the actual words of the creeds as touchstones of orthodoxy.[16] As W. Nijenhuis has argued, "For Calvin and his followers . . . this authority was not automatically conferred by the antiquity of the confessions nor by their formal ecclesiastical validity but was founded upon the truth which they professed. . . . The decisive question was whether a confession was in agreement with Scripture."[17] Moreover, Calvin had no patience for those who insisted upon a literal subscription to any creed, as if human doctrines could be equal to the Word of God. But this represents only one side of Calvin's thinking, and for the other we must consider the fate of Servetus.

Michael Servetus was an educated Spanish physician and lay-theologian who wrote an infamous treatise *On the Errors of the Trinity* (1531). Taken into custody by Roman Catholic authorities, he managed to escape from prison in Vienna in 1553 just before his official condemnation as a heretic. He made the mistake, however, of stopping in Geneva on his way to Italy. Calvin, who had carried on a short correspondence with Servetus, was well acquainted with his unorthodox views, and he ordered Servetus's arrest. In a trial that lasted for months, Calvin provided the evidence against Servetus's theology, and in October of the same year Servetus was burned at the stake for heresy in Geneva. The grounds for his execution were denial of the eternity of the Son of God and rejection of catholic (i.e., infant) baptism. In this case, Calvin showed himself just as capable of being a literalist as Caroli. William Farel is said to have quipped, after hearing Servetus's dying words — "Jesus Christ, Son of the eternal God, have mercy on me" — that he could have been spared had he gotten his adjective in the right place. He should have said, "Jesus Christ, eternal Son of God, have mercy on me."[18] And Calvin's

---

ton *Theological Review* 7 (1909): 553-652; B. A. Gerrish, *The Old Protestantism and the New: Essays on the Reformation Heritage* (Chicago: University of Chicago Press, 1982), 205-206, 382 n. 56.

16. See Calvin's defense of his stand against Caroli, *Adversus Petri Caroli calumnias defensio* (1545), CO 7:289-340.

17. W. Nijenhuis, *Ecclesia Reformata: Studies on the Reformation,* 95.

18. Cited in Roland H. Bainton, *The Travail of Religious Liberty: Nine Biographical Studies* (Philadelphia: Westminster Press, 1951), 94. Bainton recounts the same incident in his *Hunted Heretic: The Life and Death of Michael Servetus, 1511-1543* (Boston: Beacon Press, 1953), 212, but here he notes that the account was from "an anonymous source hostile to Calvin."

language for describing the threat that heresy presents to the church is reminiscent of Jerome. Servetus's views are a "contagion" that must not be allowed to spread.[19]

That Calvin rejected the Roman definition of orthodoxy is beyond doubt. In his discussion of councils and their authority in the *Institutes,* Calvin asserts that the only sure principle for determining the orthodoxy of doctrine promulgated by a council is Scripture.[20] Nor does the pope rightly establish orthodox doctrine. On the contrary, the pope burdens consciences by promulgating doctrines that go beyond the express teaching of Scripture.[21] Insofar as the pronouncements of councils conform to the teaching of Scripture, they should be respected, and the burden of proof is on the theologian who wishes to take issue with them.[22] Throughout this discussion, Calvin shows himself a keen church historian. He is aware that the findings of many duly convened councils are contradictory; moreover, he knows that even at the most revered councils, decisions were sometimes made with worldly weapons rather than with the sword of the Spirit. He is realistic in assessing the likelihood that church politics is sometimes driven by Satan and not the Spirit.[23] Scripture alone, then, is the sufficient standard of orthodoxy.

Lest he be accused of evangelical subjectivism, however, Calvin turns immediately to the anticipated criticism: is not the interpretation of Scripture an equally contentious matter? How will you know which interpretation is orthodox? And in an argument that is breathtaking for its circularity, Calvin asserts that the real power of councils is to give an authoritative interpretation of Scripture:

> We indeed willingly concede, if any discussion arises over doctrine, that the best and surest remedy is for a synod of true bishops to be convened, where the doctrine at issue may be examined. Such a definition, upon which the pastors of the church in common, invoking Christ's Spirit,

19. See his remarks in *Defensio orthodoxae fidei de Sacra Trinitate, contra prodigiosos errores Michaelis Serveti Hispani* (1554), *CO* 8:453-644, esp. 471-472. See also the opening account in the register of the Company of Pastors which recounts the trial of Servetus in Geneva. He was imprisoned so that "he would not infect the world with his blasphemies and heresies" (*Actes du Procès de Michel Servet* [1553], *CO* 8:725).
20. John Calvin, *Institutio Christianae religionis* (1559), 4.9.8. Hereafter cited as *Inst.*
21. *Inst.* 4.10.
22. *Inst.* 4.9.13-14.
23. *Inst.* 4.9.8-12.

agree, will have much more weight than if each one, having conceived it separately at home, should teach it to the people, or if a few private individuals should compose it.[24]

But the last word in this paragraph returns to his earlier theme of the subordination of councils to Scripture: "I deny it to be always the case that an interpretation of Scripture adopted by vote of a council is true and certain."[25] In that denial, Calvin left the Roman conception of orthodoxy behind.

What, then, constitutes heresy for Calvin, and what does he think should be done about it? Calvin is clear that heresy is instigated by the devil, and that it is the work of reprobate sinners. It is a grave danger to the Church, and therefore ought not to be tolerated; appropriate sanctions, both civil and ecclesiastical, should be imposed against heretics.[26] While Calvin faults the Roman Catholics and some extremist Lutheran theologians for sanctioning severe punishment of heretics without a fair hearing, he is not opposed in principle either to torture or to the capital punishment of heretics.[27] Calvin perhaps comes closest to a formal definition of heresy when defending himself against the charge. He argues that the bond of unity in the church cannot be maintained without agreement in doctrine and submission to the sole headship of Christ. Thus, he and the Genevans are not schismatics, since they have cut off fellowship because of serious doctrinal differences, and they are not heretics because, throwing off the tyranny of Rome, they have pledged their obedience to Christ alone.[28] Not every doctrinal error merits extreme action: only corruption

24. *Inst.* 4.9.13.

25. Ibid.

26. *Inst.* 1.13.21-22; *Defensio orthodoxae fidei* (*CO* 8:461-479). See the discussion of Calvin's defense of capital punishment for heretics in Marian Hiller, *The Case of Michael Servetus (1511-1553): The Turning Point in the Struggle for Freedom of Conscience* (Lewiston, NY: Edwin Mellen Press, 1997), 321-326.

27. See his *Last Admonition to Joachim Westphal* (*CO* 9:150-52; English translation, *Calvin's Tracts and Treatises*, trans. Henry Beveridge, 3 vols. [Edinburgh, 1844-51; reprint, Grand Rapids: Baker Book House, 1983], 2:357-360; hereafter cited as TT). During the first five years of Calvin's oversight of the Genevan reformation, thirteen people were hanged, ten were decapitated, thirty-five were burned, and seventy-six were expelled from the city (Nathanäel Weiss, *La Chambre ardente, étude sur la liberté de conscience en France sous François Ier et Henri II (1540-1550) suivie d'environ 500 arrêts inédits rendus par la Parlement de Paris de mais 1547 à mars 1550* [Geneva: Slatkine Reprints, 1970. First published 1889]).

28. *Inst.* 4.22.5-6. Cf. his *On the Necessity of Reforming the Church* (1544), *CO* 6:521-523; TT 1:214-218.

of the most fundamental articles of Christian faith can justify withdrawal from fellowship.[29]

The problem with Calvin's understanding of orthodoxy and heresy is that it makes them matters of interpretation. If it is the clear teaching of Scripture as interpreted by the church that constitutes the standard of orthodoxy, which church possesses that teaching? And if even a majority vote of a council does not guarantee the soundness of one's interpretation of Scripture, how can one ever be certain of one's orthodoxy or heresy? It was just this epistemological weakness in Calvin's position that attracted the attention of Sebastien Castellio (1515-1564), an early advocate of religious tolerance. In the dedication to his book *Concerning Heretics: Whether they are to be Persecuted and How they are to be Treated* (1554) he remarks:

> After a careful investigation of the meaning of the term heretic, I can discover no more than this, that we regard those as heretics with whom we disagree. This is evident from the fact that today there is scarcely one of our innumerable sects which does not look upon the rest as heretics, so that if you are orthodox in one city or region, you are held for a heretic in the next. If you would live today, you must have as many faiths and religions as there are cities and sects.[30]

Even though he drew a distinction between fundamental articles of faith, other important doctrines, and things indifferent, Calvin was in no way tolerant of heterodoxy or, what is the same thing, deviation from his own theology. One could cite a variety of evidences for this, but perhaps one will suffice. In a letter of 1555, Calvin seeks to warn the evangelicals in Poitiers against the vicious rumors being spread about him and his work in Geneva. Calvin states that the man who has brought these reports to Poitiers, a certain M. de la Vau, had already shown himself a rascal in Geneva, when he had the impudence to disagree with Calvin about a doctrinal matter with the comment, "These then are your reasons; I think differently." Calvin asserts that doctrine is not a matter of one's private opinions, but of "standing by what God points out to us" and "acquiescing in the truth." To de la Vau's charge that in Geneva everyone must kiss Calvin's slipper, Calvin replies:

---

29. *Inst.* 4.1.12, 4.2.1. See also the discussion of *adiaphora* in *Inst.* 3.19.7.

30. Sebastien Castellio, *Concerning Heretics: Whether they are to be Persecuted and How they are to be Treated. A Collection of the Opinions of Learned Men Both Ancient and Modern*, trans. Roland H. Bainton, Records of Civilization: Sources and Studies, vol. 22 (New York: Columbia University Press, 1935), 129.

What he calls kissing my slipper is that people do not rise up against me and the doctrine which I teach, to grieve God in my person, and trample him so to speak under foot. Those who show themselves so hostile to peace and concord, prove that they are actuated by the spirit of Satan. He reproaches me with procuring for my books such authority, that not even the most venturesome, nor the most courageous dare to speak ill of them. To that I reply, that indeed the least we can expect is that the Seigneurs, to whom have been entrusted the sword and authority, should not permit the faith in which they are instructed to be lightly spoken of in their own city. But luckily the dogs that bark so lustily after us, are unable to bite.[31]

One cannot help but note the lack of modesty in Calvin's understanding of his own theology. He sees himself as delivering the truth from God; thus, any heterodoxy is not merely just that — another opinion — but rather a Satan-inspired plot against the church. For all his disagreement with the Roman church on the foundation of orthodoxy, Calvin actually treats dissent in a very similar way: the scope of acceptable heterodoxy is narrowed to virtually nil, and any doctrinal opinion that differs from his own is seen at best as a pernicious error, at worst as heresy.[32] Castellio's cynical observations about the mutual anathematizing of Christian sects proved prophetic: what followed the Reformation of the sixteenth century was not the recovery of the apostolic purity of the church its leaders had hoped for, but instead more than a century of bitter religious wars.

III

The two hundred years that separate Calvin and Schleiermacher, while certainly plagued by religious controversies, were also years in which significant steps were taken towards the establishment of religious liberty. John Locke (1632-1704) argues in his *Letter Concerning Toleration* (1689) that civil authority should be directed toward the temporal good and prosperity of society and that individuals (with certain exceptions) should be able to practice religion according to the dictates of conscience. The magistrate should not

31. "To the Church of Poitiers, 20 February 1555," *CO* 15:442; TT 6:145.

32. Whether or not Calvin deserves Roland Bainton's epithet "the Peak of Protestant Intolerance" (*The Travail of Religious Liberty*, 54-71), it is clear that he was a man more in tune with the spirit of late medieval Catholicism than with the new winds of Erasmian humanism on this point. Cf. Hillar, *The Case of Michael Servetus*, 285-313.

be in the business of enforcing belief, which is not, in any case, something that can be simply willed. "The business of laws," he writes, "is not to provide for the truth of opinions, but for the safety and security of the commonwealth and of every particular man's goods and person. And so it ought to be. . . . [I]f Truth makes not her way into the understanding by her own light, she will be but the weaker for any borrowed force violence can add to her."[33]

Locke concludes the *Letter* with a brief discussion of the concepts of heresy and schism. He defines heresy as "a separation made in ecclesiastical communion between men of the same religion for some opinions in no way contained in the rule itself." Thus for Protestants, who acknowledge no other rule of faith than Holy Scripture, heresy is "a separation made in their Christian communion for opinions not contained in the express words of Scripture." One can be a heretic in this sense by *forcing out* a minority who refuse to subscribe to doctrines of the majority that are not the express words of Scripture; equally, one can be a heretic by *withdrawing* from a communion because that church refuses to profess one's extra-biblical opinions. Locke is quick to add that there is a difference between the express words of Scripture and doctrines believed to be deduced from them. The latter ought never to be imposed on another,

> unless we would be content also that other doctrines should be imposed upon us in the same manner, and that we should be compelled to receive and profess all the different and contradictory opinions of the Lutherans, Calvinists, Remonstrants, Anabaptists, and other sects which the contrivers of symbols, systems, and confessions are accustomed to deliver to their followers as genuine and necessary deductions from the Holy Scripture. I cannot but wonder at the extravagant arrogance of those men who think that they themselves can explain things necessary to salvation more clearly than the Holy Ghost, the eternal and infinite wisdom of God.[34]

Locke's was certainly not the only voice lifted against dogmatic Christianity. The Latitudinarians and Deists in England and the Pietists in Germany, each for their own particular reasons, argued against the hegemony of Protestant orthodoxy. By the time Schleiermacher published his *On Religion:*

33. John Locke, *A Letter Concerning Toleration* (Latin edition: Gouda, 1689), in *Great Books of the Western World*, ed. Mortimer J. Adler, vol. 33 (Chicago: Encyclopedia Britannica, 1952), 15.
34. Ibid., 22.

Speeches to Its Cultured Despisers in 1799, pleas for tolerance and a religion of reason had given way to the supercilious dismissal of religion as the domain of uneducated bigots. Clearly, Schleiermacher developed his thoughts about heresy in a different context than Calvin's. Yet even in Schleiermacher's Prussia, accusations of heresy carried civil consequences: such charges could land one's books on the censor's list, or prevent one's appointment to a teaching post in a university theological faculty.

Schleiermacher's conception of orthodoxy and heresy cannot be grasped apart from his understanding of religion in general. In the *Speeches,* he argues that religion is not a particular body of knowledge, nor a specific variety of action, but rather a form of consciousness — specifically the feeling and intuition of the infinite. To be religious is not to believe certain doctrines or to act in particular ways but to sense the underlying unity in the multiplicity of finite things. Unlike the Protestant scholastics and the Deists alike, Schleiermacher refuses to reduce religious faith either to fundamental articles of belief or to morality. Doctrines, creeds, and other statements of belief are, for him, second-order reflection on the immediate experience of faith. Mere subscription to articles of belief, then, could provide no sure measure of a person's faith. And a person's inability fully to articulate his doctrinal beliefs could not provide sufficient evidence for doubting his piety.[35]

If doctrines do not function to establish or define faith, what is their purpose? Schleiermacher argues that systematic theology serves the church by providing critical norms for its proclamation, both in word and in deeds. The language of worship and proclamation is intended to edify and persuade; it is poetic or rhetorical language that can lead to misconceptions without the limits set by critical theological reflection. The theologian strives to give an account of the Christian way of believing in the most precise terms possible in order to provide norms for regulating the imprecise language of preaching, worship, and devotion. The question then arises: What norms, if any, limit the theologian's description of the Christian way of believing? It is in the context of answering this question that Schleiermacher discusses the concepts of orthodoxy, heresy, and heterodoxy, but he gives each of the concepts definitions and evaluations quite different from those of Thomas or Calvin.

Doctrines are thoroughly historical products for Schleiermacher, and

35. F. D. E. Schleiermacher, *Die Religion: Reden an die Gebildeten unter ihren Verächtern* (1799; 4th ed., 1831) in KGA I/12:41-149. English translation, *On Religion: Speeches to Its Cultured Despisers*, trans. John Oman (New York: Harper & Row, 1958), 26-118.

therefore no doctrinal statement is a perfect, once-for-all symbolization of Christian faith. The dogmatic theologian seeks to give an account of the Christian faith commonly held in a given church at a particular time. What is orthodox, then, is simply the prevailing doctrinal consensus in that church, while heterodoxy is any view that departs from this consensus.[36] Schleiermacher was aware that for some this would seem an insufficient definition since it is not related to a fixed norm of orthodoxy. But he notes that the distinction between "orthodoxy" and "heterodoxy" in his sense of the terms can be observed even where there is no fixed doctrinal norm, and thus the definition of the terms cannot depend upon such a norm.[37]

The orthodox and heterodox impulses are equally important for theology. Without the orthodox impulse, one could discover no true unity of Christian faith; but without the heterodox impulse, there would be no development of doctrine. Theologians who tend one-sidedly to one impulse or the other do damage to the church: the one-sidedly orthodox theologian by retaining dogmas that are antiquated relics unable to be understood in connection with other parts of the faith, the one-sidedly heterodox theologian by rejecting well-grounded pronouncements of the church that can and must be understood in relation to other aspects of belief. Thus, Schleiermacher says, "every dogmatic theologian who either innovates or exalts what is old, in a one-sided manner, is only a very imperfect organ of the church. From a falsely heterodox standpoint, he will declare even the most appropriate orthodoxy to be false; and from a falsely orthodox standpoint, he will combat even the most mild and unavoidable heterodoxy as a destructive innovation."[38]

Thus far it sounds as if there is no absolute standard against which a theologian's account of Christian faith must be measured. But we must now introduce the concept of heresy, for it is heresy that provides an absolute boundary: the church theologian is obligated to exclude any truly heretical elements from his system. Given Schleiermacher's understanding of orthodoxy, heresy clearly cannot be understood as deviation from the orthodox norm. For one thing, the orthodox norm is not fixed and unchangeable. Moreover, some deviation, as in the case of heterodoxy, can be a good and healthy thing for the development of doctrine. So what is heresy? For

36. F. D. E. Schleiermacher, *Kurze Darstellung des Theologische Studiums zum Behuf einleitender Vorlesungen* (1811; 2d ed. 1831), KGA I/6:398; English translation, *Brief Outline on the Study of Theology*, trans. Terrence N. Tice (Richmond, VA: John Knox Press, 1966), 74.

37. Ibid.

38. KGA I/6:399-400; ET, 74-75.

Schleiermacher, heresy is any doctrine that cannot be explained from the distinctive essence of Christianity and cannot be conceived as compatible with it, even though it claims to be Christian and wants to be regarded as such by others. Heresy is anything that contradicts the essence of Christianity, even while the appearance of Christianity remains.[39]

Once again, Schleiermacher was well aware that this is a formal definition of heresy, and one that is likely to vary depending upon how the essence of Christianity is construed. This problem, he states, cannot be avoided. However, once the theologian has determined what for her constitutes the essence of Christianity, any idea that would destroy it cannot be contained in the system of doctrine. In Schleiermacher's own definition of the essence of Christianity everything is connected with the redemption accomplished by Jesus of Nazareth.[40] Consequently, he discerned four "natural types" of heresy that could interfere with the essence so defined. On the one hand, one could deny that humanity needs redemption (Pelagianism) or that humanity can be redeemed (Manicheanism), while on the other hand one could understand the Redeemer as so different from us that he cannot truly bring us redemption (Docetism), or so like us that he himself stands in need of redemption (Ebionitism).[41] At every point in the development of the system of theology, these four types of heresy must be eliminated.

Schleiermacher deals at length with the question of the ecclesial response to heresy in his *Practical Theology* in a section on the influence of church government on the establishment of doctrine. The governing bodies of evangelical churches, he argues, have two main responsibilities: the first is to exercise the binding authority that maintains the church's continuity with its originating ideals; the second is to remain open to the free spiritual influence that individual members can exercise on the whole body. In fact, the evangelical churches were born from Luther's exercise of just this kind of individual free spiritual influence; therefore, Protestants ought to be especially careful to preserve the possibility of free expression.[42]

---

39. KGA I/6:348-349; ET, 37-38.

40. F. D. E. Schleiermacher, *Der christliche Glaube nach den Grundsätzen der evangelischen Kirche im Zusammenhangen dargestellt*, in KGA I/13.1:93-102. Cited hereafter as Gl. by paragraph and subsection. English translation, *The Christian Faith*, ed. H. R. Mackintosh and J. S. Stewart (Edinburgh: T&T Clark, 1928; reprint, 1999), 52-60.

41. Gl. §22; ET, 97-101.

42. KGA I/6:436-437; ET, 106-107. Cf. F. D. E. Schleiermacher, *Die praktische Theologie nach den Grundsätzen der evangelischen Kirche im Zusammenhangen dargestellt*, in *Friedrich Schleiermachers sämmtliche Werke*, 31 vols. (Berlin: Georg Reimer, 1834-1864), I/13, where the

Schleiermacher points out that from the beginning, evangelicals were opposed to the Roman Catholic way of thinking about doctrine. For the evangelicals it was a fundamental principle that the Word of God alone could establish doctrine, and that no human being had the right to lay down or enforce articles of belief that went beyond Scripture.[43] Therefore, from the age of the Reformation, Protestants have put enormous importance on biblical scholarship, and on the theology that grows out of it. But biblical interpretation, too, is a developing thing, and so it is not in the evangelical spirit to adopt a fixed authoritative interpretation of Scripture. It is always possible that, under the guidance of the Spirit, the church's biblical scholars and theologians will come to new insights.[44]

During the years that Schleiermacher labored as a professor and pastor in Berlin, the Lutheran and Reformed churches in Prussia united. Although this was an occasion of great celebration, for many it was also a cause for suspicion and mistrust, and not surprisingly, there was soon a strong movement calling for confessional subscription as a means for preserving the purity of the church. From the beginning, Schleiermacher was a strong opponent of this view. He regarded the demand for literal subscription as slavish and mechanical — thoroughly opposed to the original spirit of the Reformation.[45] The confessions, or "symbolic books" as he called them, do have an important role to play in the church, but it is not the role of establishing "reine Lehre." In their origin they were directed outward, not inward: they intended to show how the evangelical congregations distinguished themselves from Roman Catholics and from revolutionary groups. They were never intended to regulate the faith of those inside their own churches: in fact, their tendency was precisely in the opposite direction. Schleier-

---

two divisions of the section dealing with church government are entitled "The organized activity of church government" (534-703) and "The free element of church government, or the free spiritual power that individuals exercise over the whole" (704-725). Hereafter cited as PT. Cf. "Warnung vor Selbstverschuldeter Knechschaft," *Predigten in Bezug auf die Feier der Übergabe der Augsburgischen Confession* (Berlin: Reimer, 1831), in *Friedrich Schleiermacher: Kleine Schriften und Predigten*, ed. Hayo Gerdes and Emanuel Hirsch, 3 vols. (Berlin: Walter de Gruyter, 1969), 3:13-24. Hereafter cited as *Kleine Schriften*. English translation, *Reformed But Ever Reforming: Sermons in Relation to the Celebration of the Handing Over of the Augsburg Confession (1830)*, trans. with intro. and notes by Iain G. Nicol, Schleiermacher Studies and Translations, vol. 8 (Lewiston, NY: The Edwin Mellen Press, 1997), 21-33.

43. PT, 625.

44. PT, 625-626, 641ff.

45. PT, 637, 646. See also his essay, "Über die eigentümliche Wert und das bindende Ansehen symbolischer Bücher," KGA I/10:117-144.

macher concludes that "the evangelical church remains evangelical only when it accepts the mobility of dogma through biblical interpretation. . . . If one adopts a static literalism, then it is no longer a living presentation of the faith [*Vorstellung*], but simply repeated words."[46]

What, then, is the role of churchly authority in regulating doctrine? Schleiermacher does not mince words: the only task of churchly authority in this regard is to ensure academic freedom and the free exchange of theological research.[47] It is true that if one permits such freedom, it is impossible to prevent all corrupt teaching in advance. But the health of the church will be preserved if congregations are connected in a larger fellowship, so that the corrupting influences of the individual are outweighed by the common spirit of the community.[48] Schleiermacher also argues that well-executed pastoral care can forefend the evil effects of corrupt teaching. People are less liable to be misled by heresy if they have been well formed in Christian faith. The risk of corrupt teaching has to be taken for the sake of the development of doctrine, the heart of evangelical identity.[49]

Those who contribute the most to the process of doctrinal development, according to Schleiermacher, are academic theologians and theological authors. He does not use the term "academic theologians" in the sense in which it is commonly used now, for a group distinct from "church theologians." He simply means theologians who work in an educational institution, while theological authors are those who write on contested questions in the church.[50] In order best to serve the church through their free spiritual influence, theologians must strive to be "princes of the church": i.e., people who combine religious interest and a scientific spirit with the ability to balance both theoretical and practical activity.[51] The academic theologian must strive in teaching to draw ministry students into critical engagement with Scripture and tradition without thereby destroying their faith.[52] The theological author must avoid publishing his work in media that would reach beyond its intended audience, but rather should present his ideas to those who can make correct use of them. Moreover, theological writing ought not to be purely polemical, but should seek to discover the good that is contained even in the

46. PT, 641.
47. PT, 656-658.
48. PT, 658-659.
49. PT, 659-662.
50. PT, 709-724.
51. KGA I/6:329-330, 443; ET, 21, 112.
52. PT, 709-719, esp. 711-12. Cf. KGA I/6:443; ET, 112.

ideas it seeks to refute.[53] All of these warnings to theologians give evidence of Schleiermacher's keen awareness of the possible dangers of free theological inquiry. It can be disturbing to immature Christians; it can produce scandalous public controversies. For the most part he leaves the containment of possible dangers entailed by free theological inquiry to the discretion of the theologian herself. However, he does note that church authorities exercise control over ecclesiastical appointments, and thus can prevent those whom they deem truly dangerous from occupying the pulpit.[54]

The balance between binding authority and free-theological inquiry, like the balance between heterodoxy and orthodoxy in an individual theologian's work, is intended to ensure the continuity of the evangelical tradition through change. The theologian must strive to demonstrate the connection between the old and the new.[55] Sometimes truly insightful theological work will lead the theologian to hold an opinion contrary to the majority in his church, a heterodox opinion. But since majority votes are never a guarantee of the correctness of doctrine, it is altogether possible that what is heterodox will one day become orthodox.[56] Schleiermacher warns that the church should not quench the Spirit in its drive to define dogma in a permanent way.[57] The Spirit, who is bringing about the consummation of the church, always has something new to communicate through the engagement with Scripture. The evangelical church and its theologians, therefore, ought to stand ready to receive these new insights.

What, then, can be done about heresy? Schleiermacher argued that charges of heresy ought to be infrequently urged. It is not easy, in the midst of the fray, to be altogether clear about where one's own theological viewpoint is located in the spectrum, and one always judges another in relation to one's own position. The theologian certainly has an obligation to seek to exclude heresy from his own work, but for the most part a judgment of charity should prevail towards others. The truth shines in its own light, and false or "diseased" views of Christian faith will simply die on their own when contrasted with the power of the truth.[58]

53. PT, 720-724; cf. KGA I/6:444; ET, 113.
54. PT, 657.
55. PT, 712-713.
56. PT, 649.
57. PT, 644-645. For Schleiermacher's understanding of the Holy Spirit, see Gl. §§121-125; ET, 560-81.
58. PT, 655-659. In this section, Schleiermacher discusses the power of a connectional system of church government, such as the Presbyterian system, to restrain the errors of indi-

Schleiermacher's vision of the theological task takes its beginning point in the formal principle of the Reformation, *sola scriptura*. But while Calvin came to a sense of certainty about the scriptural account of many doctrines, Schleiermacher maintained that even the best theological statements remain provisional, subject to correction in light of fresh readings of Holy Scripture.[59] "The reformation goes on," he argued, and so the church itself must be ready to be reformed again and again according to the Word of God.[60] Openness to genuinely new insights requires an ability to tolerate or even to encourage a measure of heterodoxy. And lest churchly authority censor even the useful heterodoxy that leads to doctrinal development, it should not be too eager to condemn and exclude those whom it perhaps wrongly brands as heretics. The Spirit guides the church forward and can be trusted to preserve it in spite of human error.

IV

If I may return now to the questions with which I began, there are several observations that can be made in light of our consideration of Calvin and Schleiermacher on orthodoxy and heresy. Let me begin with the definition of orthodoxy. It is clear that both Calvin and Schleiermacher affirm the principle that the Word of God alone, as attested in Scripture and preaching, is the foundation of true orthodoxy. Neither the witness of the "ancient and undivided church," nor the antiquity of particular doctrinal formulas suffice to establish them as essential and unchangeable norms for Reformed theologians. I can find no support in Calvin or Schleiermacher — nor in the Reformed confessions, for that matter — for the argument, put forward by some, that the decisions of the first four ecumenical councils ought not to be revisited or rethought. To place any human word, even the word of a revered council, on a par with the Word of God is not in keeping with the Reformed

---

vidual pastors or congregations. The Spirit at work in the larger community leads toward truth. Cf. Gl. §§153-155; ET, 687-692. On this point, Schleiermacher echoes Calvin's views (*Inst.* 4.8.12).

59. PT, 651-655. "Es sind in der evangelischen Kirche Veränderungen des Lehrbegriffs nur zulässig, sofern Veränderungen im Schriftverständniss sind; das Anknüpfen an die Schrift ist das Princip" (PT, 654).

60. *Gespräch zweier selbstüberlegender evangelischer Christen über die Schrift LUTHER IN BEZUG AUF DIE NEUE PREUSSISCHE AGENDE: Ein letztes Wort oder ein erstes* (1827), SW 1/5:625.

habit of mind. Both Calvin and Schleiermacher recognized, as good church historians, that history is written by the winners, and that the winners in church history constitute the "orthodox" majority. Nonetheless, they both also affirmed that majority vote alone is no guarantee that one has the pure Word of God.[61]

Next we come to the question of heresy. It is clear that neither Calvin nor Schleiermacher recommended heresy as a useful body of thought to the church. Each one in his own way viewed heresy as destructive and dangerous. But the problem of rightly identifying real heretics was handled differently. Calvin, more in keeping with the spirit of the late Middle Ages, believed that tests of orthodoxy, based on doctrinal formulas approved by him, were adequate evidence to try and convict heretics; further, he insisted that if heretical opinions were not completely silenced, the church would be ineluctably drawn to them and so destroyed. For Schleiermacher, there was a difference between doctrine and faith, so that doctrinal formulas would never be sufficient tools for condemning another man's piety. Moreover, he was skeptical about human ability to pronounce another's doctrine heretical. Since our judgment is relative to our own theological perspective, it is never entirely possible to assess another's doctrinal opinions objectively. The category of heresy, therefore, is most useful as an internal norm applied by the dogmatic theologian to her own work, where it provides an absolute boundary for the way in which she speaks about Christian faith. Schleiermacher spoke of heresy as a "diseased condition" of Christianity, but he did not share Calvin's fear that its seductive power is irresistible. On the contrary, he was confident that as the church moves ahead toward its divinely appointed consummation, heresies will condemn themselves and diminish in power, while the truth will shine forth ever more brightly.

For Calvin, as for many theologians in the late-medieval church, heterodoxy tended to collapse into heresy. Dissent from official dogma was frowned upon in Geneva no less than in Rome. Although Calvin certainly respected several fellow Reformers with whom he disagreed, he nevertheless believed that those within his own jurisdiction ought either to agree with him or to be silent. Castellio was driven from the Genevan Academy for his heterodox interpretation of the Song of Solomon; Jerome Bolsec (d. 1584) was banished for objecting to Calvin's doctrine of predestination; countless

---

61. See Schleiermacher's sermon "Von dem Verdammen Andersgläubiger in unserm Bekenntniss," in *Kleine Schriften*, 108-122, esp. 112-113; *Reformed But Ever Reforming*, 127-140, esp. 130-131.

citizens of Geneva were called before the Consistory to justify themselves when objecting to one or another of Calvin's views.[62] In fact, after the banishment of Bolsec, the Little Council passed an ordinance forbidding anyone to speak against Calvin or his *Institutes*.[63] Schleiermacher sees heterodoxy as something fundamentally different than heresy and not as the first step into it. To be heterodox is to have a different opinion than the majority in the church, while to be heretical is to believe things contradictory to the heart of Christian faith.

The Reformers themselves were not *orthodox* but *heterodox* theologians! Calvin's view of what constitutes orthodoxy disagrees not only with the majority vote of his contemporaries in the Christian church, but also with the overwhelming majority throughout the ages. This is not, however, the skeleton in the closet of the Reformed churches, but their distinctive gift: the gift of openness to being reformed according to the Word of God. Heterodoxy, then, is not only an unavoidable fact but also a necessary ingredient in any truly Reformed theological discussion, for it is the heterodox impulse that remains open to new hearings of God's Word. For this reason, so far from banishing those who disagree, the church ought to cultivate their vigorous and thorough theological debate, and protect the right of individuals to dissent even from the confessions of the church.

Of course, Schleiermacher's views on heterodoxy will not be popular with those who today are urging confessional subscription as the antidote to pluralism. To take their side for the moment, one has to admit that the right of every individual to think for herself has been taken to extremes that even Schleiermacher the Romantic could not have imagined. Many churchgoers, without so much as a course in the history of Christian thought, feel competent to demur at the theological views of Augustine, Calvin, and many other heroes in the Reformed pantheon, and to create for themselves personal confessions of faith. But in this context, I am not so much concerned with issues of catechesis or Christian formation as with the vocation of the church's theologians. Should we henceforth demand, for the sake of preserving our historic Reformed identity, that our theologians subscribe to the Reformed

62. For a discussion of Castellio's quarrel with Calvin, see Bainton, *The Travail of Religious Liberty*, 124. The best study of Calvin's controversy with Bolsec is Philip C. Holtrop, *The Bolsec Controversy on Predestination from 1551 to 1555: The Statements of Jerome Bolsec, and the Responses of John Calvin, Theodore Beza, and Other Reformed Theologians*, vol. 1 in two books (Lewiston, NY: The Edwin Mellen Press, 1993).

63. CO 21:525. See the discussion in Williston Walker, *John Calvin: The Organizer of Reformed Protestantism (1509-1564)* (New York: Schocken Books, 1969), 320-321.

confessions (or perhaps only to one of them) and cease and desist thinking anew about matters the confessions have defined? Or should our churches' governing bodies define once and for all the "essential tenets" of Reformed faith and censure any theologian who speaks against them? It seems that to move in this direction would be contrary to the spirit of Calvin and Schleiermacher and to the witness of the Reformed confessions themselves. Our historic commitment to be reformed according to the Word of God demands our openness to the possibility — no, more, the probability — that even our best confessions got some things wrong. The Reformation goes on.

If theology is to be something more than a mindless repetition of formulas from the past, heterodoxy is inevitable. The potential risks involved in really creative theological reflection need to be squarely admitted. It is possible that such theology will be more disturbing than reassuring to some congregations. It is possible that theologians will make mistakes that will in fact corrupt the faith. It is also possible that a theologian, loosed from servile compliance to "orthodox norms," will give a brilliant account of the faith of the church that speaks to a new generation with power and persuasion. Schleiermacher was right to speak of the values that should form the church theologian: religious interest or *faith,* scientific spirit or *reason,* and the ability to balance theoretical and practical considerations, which is *wisdom.* Theologians steeped in these values, however heterodox their views on the current shibboleths of orthodoxy, need not be feared for their corrupting influence. And theologians who do not have these values are unlikely to make any mark on the community of faith.

Can heterodoxy actually be "inspired"? We may not be prepared to argue that Schleiermacher's doctrine of God constitutes an inspired heterodoxy destined to become orthodox. But surely we can think of other theological opinions for which people were disciplined or punished in the past that have now become seemingly self-evident orthodoxy. Were these heterodox theologians actually instruments of the Holy Spirit? Can we say for sure that they were not?

What Is the Meaning of Revelation?
H. Richard Niebuhr, Modernism,
and Nicene Christianity

George Hunsinger

The meaning of revelation as set forth by H. Richard Niebuhr continues to have remarkable appeal. His book *The Meaning of Revelation,* which first appeared in 1941, has enjoyed a steady readership for more than six decades, being newly reprinted in 2006, an impressive run by any reckoning.[1] Because the book is at once accessible yet also elusive by turns, a critical examination may not be amiss. Its central theological contents will here be assessed from the standpoint of Nicene Christianity.

The two Niebuhr brothers — Reinhold and H. Richard — might be regarded as religious thinkers who worked largely within the genre of wisdom literature. Each in his own way had much wisdom to offer that was undoubtedly compatible with Nicene Christianity. On the other hand, neither of them would seem entirely satisfactory from a Nicene standpoint. It should not be forgotten, in this respect, that neither of the Niebuhrs wished to be regarded as a theologian, each preferring instead to be thought of as a social ethicist. While that would not be problematic as far as it went, it did not prevent either of them from taking a stand on vital doctrinal issues.

Perhaps the best critical assessment of Reinhold Niebuhr's theology per se is the neglected work by Shirley C. Guthrie, *The Theological Character of Reinhold Niebuhr's Social Ethic.*[2] Guthrie did a fine job of explaining the

---

1. H. Richard Niebuhr, *The Meaning of Revelation* (New York: The Macmillan Company, 1941); with a new Introduction by Douglas F. Ottati (Louisville: Westminster/John Knox Press, 2006).

2. Shirley C. Guthrie, *The Theological Character of Reinhold Niebuhr's Social Ethic* (Winterhur: Verlag P. G. Keller, 1959).

theological concerns that would arise from a Nicene standpoint. Nothing quite comparable seems to exist for H. Richard Niebuhr, though a survey of his specifically theological contribution can be found in Libertus A. Hoedemaker, *The Theology of H. Richard Niebuhr.*[3]

Also by way of introduction, it can be said that H. Richard Niebuhr qualified, broadly, as an academic liberal theologian, even though he had many interesting criticisms to make of liberal theology. He once targeted theological liberalism, for example, when he famously wrote: "A God without wrath brought men without sin into a kingdom without judgment through the ministrations of a Christ without a cross."[4] Clearly, Niebuhr's brand of liberalism was going to be one without superficiality, sentimentality, or cant.

As a final introductory comment, it should be noted that Niebuhr is not easy to interpret, because it seems that he may have been theologically ambivalent at crucial points. He not only said different things in different places, but also had a penchant for couching his ideas in subtle and inconclusive rhetoric. The syntax could be complex, almost to the point of obscurity or studied indeterminacy. Niebuhr was often suggestive and allusive rather than straightforward and direct, typically telling the reader what he rejected without being quite clear about what he intended to affirm.

Reticence — or not wishing to assert more than one feels one can really take responsibility for — was a hallmark of the academic liberal mind. Though more nearly revisionist than rejectionist, Niebuhr seemed to approach traditional or Nicene Christianity in a way that combined personal loyalty with a troubled sensibility. He seemed skeptical toward Christian belief in its particulars while affirming its more general implications.

It is noteworthy that Niebuhr's best students tended to resolve his ambivalences either to the left or to the right, with James Gustafson and Gordon Kaufmann falling into a much more open skepticism than Niebuhr evidenced, while in turn Hans Frei and Paul Ramsey operated more clearly than their esteemed teacher within the bounds of traditional Christianity. One often feels that in his measured tones Niebuhr might be presupposing more than he was prepared to state. One of his distinguished colleagues, also a former student, once remarked to me that "Niebuhr was more orthodox in spirit than in doctrine."

3. Libertus A. Hoedemaker, *The Theology of H. Richard Niebuhr* (New York: Pilgrim Press, 1970).

4. H. Richard Niebuhr, *The Kingdom of God in America* (New York: Harper & Row, 1937), 193.

George Hunsinger

I. The Meaning of Revelation in Niebuhr and Nicene Christianity: A Study in Contrasts

With these considerations in mind, let us turn to the question of how the argument in *The Meaning of Revelation* shapes up against the received standards of Nicene orthodoxy. The observations offered here are confined almost entirely to that work alone. No attempt is being made to comment on Niebuhr's output as a whole. As already suggested, there are complex cross-currents running through the body of his work. Some of them may be more in convergence, others more in divergence, with Nicene Christianity than appeared in his revelation book. Furthermore, no attempt will be made to cover the book's entire argument. Attention will be paid primarily to how the ideas of "revelation" and "God" are defined and interrelated, particularly with respect to Jesus Christ.

As a point of reference, we may take this statement from Karl Barth:

> The doctrine of the Trinity is what basically distinguishes the Christian doctrine of God as Christian, and therefore, what already distinguishes the Christian concept of revelation as Christian, in contrast to all other possible doctrines of God or concepts of revelation.[5]

According to this view, any proposal about "the meaning of revelation" must be measured against the Nicene doctrine of the Trinity. That doctrine effectively supplies the standard of theological adequacy or inadequacy. Insofar as the Holy Trinity is set forth as revelation's content, its meaning will, from the standpoint of Nicene Christianity, be theologically adequate. Insofar as its content may be non-trinitarian, however, or perhaps even anti-trinitarian, the standard of theological adequacy will not be met.

It goes without saying that if a position should turn out to be theologically inadequate, that does not mean it contains nothing worthwhile. It can obviously contain valid insights and fruitful modes of thought without ceasing to be inadequate as a proposal about revelation when everything is taken into account.

As it happened, *The Meaning of Revelation* contained only one explicit statement about the doctrine of the Trinity. It came near the very end of the book. Here it is in full.

---

5. Karl Barth, *Church Dogmatics*, I/1, 2nd ed. (Edinburgh: T&T Clark, 1975), 301.

The doctrine of the Trinity is no satisfactory or final formulation of this understanding [our effort to understand (God's) nature], but is more satisfactory than all the ancient and the modern pantheons wherein we ascend beyond the many gods or values to someone who is limited by them. The unity of the God who appears as Father, Son and Holy Spirit is not the unity which we conceived as the common source and spirit of beauty, truth and goodness, especially not as we conceive truth, beauty and goodness in our own image. And so the oneness which the God of Jesus Christ demands in us is not the integration of our purposes and values but our integrity, singleness of mind and purity of heart.[6]

This passage is not easy to make out for some of the reasons already suggested. It consists very largely of statements about what is not the case. We are left pretty much on our own to puzzle out what the author thinks may actually be the case. Furthermore, the syntax is challenging, even as the rhetoric is ambiguous, with the tone being oracular, leaving a general impression of profundity. What can be teased out of this passage? At least this much:

First, the doctrine of the Trinity does not seem to be denied but in some sense to be affirmed. Nevertheless, it may be asked, in what sense? The only explicit formulation might be felt to carry modalistic overtones: "the *unity* of the God who *appears* as Father, Son and Holy Spirit." Modalism may be defined as the view that God is essentially one in eternity, while only *appearing* as Father, Son, and Holy Spirit in history. Modalism is above all concerned to uphold the idea of God's essential unity. If Niebuhr wished to avoid leaving the impression of possible modalism, he did little to counteract it in this statement, which seems concerned primarily with God's oneness — an observation that would be irrelevant were it not corroborated elsewhere.

With respect to the doctrine of the Trinity as a "formulation," it is said to be neither satisfactory nor final (though it is tantalizingly regarded as preferable to other unspecified views). Nicene Christianity would agree that, in some sense, no particular theological formulation is ever "satisfactory," nor is any ever "final." But it would also say, with Philip Schaff, that "This fundamental and comprehensive dogma secured the unity and the full life of the Christian conception of God; and in this respect it represents, as no other dogma does, the whole of Christianity."[7] Niebuhr's revelation book

6. H. Richard Niebuhr, *The Meaning of Revelation* (New York: Macmillan, 1941), 184-185.

7. Philip Schaff, *The History of the Christian Church*, vol. 3 (Grand Rapids: Wm. B. Eerdmans, 1988), 670.

contains no such statement, nor as far as I am aware is any to be found elsewhere in his writings.

The passage cited seems to suggest that God's unity is finally inconceivable, and especially that it is not the kind of unity we might be inclined to devise when we did so "in our own image." However, it is not clear what to make of this remark, since neither Arianism nor modalism would deny that God's unity is inconceivable, nor that it would be a mistake to conceive of the divine unity idolatrously "in our own image." What the idolatrous mistake might be remains elusive.

Finally, the passage ends rather oddly by changing the subject. It shifts from the unity of God to "the oneness which the God of Jesus Christ demands in us." This turn is indeed puzzling. What happened to the doctrine of the Trinity? It has vanished as abruptly as it emerged. "The God of Jesus Christ," however, is a telling phrase to which we will return.

We may infer that Niebuhr is more interested, throughout the book, in dispositional and anthropological matters like "our integrity, singleness of mind and purity of heart" (all worthy themes, to be sure) than he is in setting forth the doctrine of the Trinity as the content of a distinctively Christian understanding of revelation.

What about Jesus Christ in this book? Is there any passage where his deity as the second "person" of the Trinity or as the eternal Son is set forth and openly affirmed? As it happens there is none. Instead there are a few ambiguous comments whose drift, insofar as it can be worked out, tends toward denying Christ's incarnation and his resurrection, while Christ's atoning sacrifice or reconciling work on the cross receives no real mention at all.

Before quoting some passages from the book, a summary statement will be attempted based on a wider reading of Niebuhr's writings: For Niebuhr, it seems that Jesus was the center of loyalty but not the object of faith. He was the revelation of God but not the person of God in self-revelation. He was the church's companion, prototype, and source but not the incarnate Savior who died for our sins and was raised again bodily from the dead.[8] He was fully human, perhaps divinely human, but in the end, it would seem, also merely human.[9]

8. James Gustafson's reminiscence is telling: "I recall Niebuhr saying to me on his return from the Evanston Assembly of the World Council of Churches, with real passion, 'Christ, Christ, Christ! Church, church, church! Nobody speaks about God anymore! When I was young it was religion, religion, religion!'" See Gustafson's foreword to a new edition of *Radical Monotheism* (Louisville: Westminster/John Knox, 1993), 5.

9. For a sympathetic account of this uncertainty, see Hans W. Frei, "The Theology of

In the revelation book, as elsewhere, Niebuhr often spoke about "the God of Jesus Christ,"[10] but never about Jesus Christ as God. For him, Jesus was the instrument, though not the content, of divine "self-revelation."[11] Jesus was never presented as the object of worship or as the central reality of revelation (as opposed to being its vehicle). The content of revelation was finally something other than Christ himself.

While, if pushed, there is perhaps a semi-Arian trace in Niebuhr's view of Christ's person, there are passages (not prominent in the revelation book) where Niebuhr wrote about Jesus as the "Son" in a way that might suggest something more nearly like a Nestorian tendency. (As used here, "semi-Arian" would mean that Jesus was somehow of "like essence" with, though subordinate to, the Father, while "Nestorian" would mean that Jesus and the Son were two different "persons" or acting subjects, united only by a coincidence of wills.)

A modalistic tendency in the doctrine of the Trinity would perhaps be more in line with the Nestorian than the semi-Arian tendency in Niebuhr's statements about Christ's person. In any case, the language is almost always vague and elusive, so that it seems best to reserve final judgment. One can indicate no more than "tendencies" while leaving the question unresolved.

From the standpoint of traditional Nicene Christianity, however, it must be wondered why such important matters should be allowed to languish in uncertainty. Consider the following remarks. "But despite its pragmatic values a definition of revelation in terms of the person of Jesus is manifestly inadequate."[12] Or again: "the definition of revelation as the self-disclosure of Jesus is rationally and morally inadequate."[13] Here Niebuhr came very close to denying core convictions of Nicene Christianity.

He wanted "revelation" to be defined in non-propositional terms: "Revelation of the person of God through Jesus Christ does not include commu-

---

H. Richard Niebuhr," in *Faith and Ethics*, ed. Paul Ramsey (New York: Harper & Row, 1965), 115-116. Frei points to a place in *Christ and Culture* (New York: Harper Brothers, 1951) where Niebuhr allows that his essentially "moral analysis" of Christ's character would not necessarily be incompatible with a "metaphysical" analysis of Christ's person. On this slender basis Frei asserts that Niebuhr's christology would "meet the test" of conforming to Chalcedon (115). Frei is on more solid ground when he suggests that Niebuhr leaves us with an essentially "economic Trinitarianism," a polite way of saying "modalism" (98).

10. E.g., *The Meaning of Revelation*, 85.

11. Cf. ibid., 152.

12. Ibid., 148.

13. Ibid., 149.

nication of the propositions that Jesus was born of a Virgin, that the Scriptures are inerrant, and that history is catastrophic."[14] Maybe not. But just what do these negations rule out, and what in turn do they actually rule in?

Denying the "Virgin Birth" has typically gone hand in hand with denying the Incarnation. Rejecting a fundamentalist view of inerrancy, moreover, would tell us nothing about what a proper idea of Scripture as God's Word would look like. (Niebuhr's view of revelation in this book is notable for its curious silence about how Holy Scripture might be seen, if at all, as God's Word.) Furthermore, the relevance of Niebuhr's point about "history" is not clear. Niebuhr would apparently prefer to see history as tragic rather than catastrophic. Little hangs on this. More importantly, however, one notes an apparently instrumentalist use of the preposition "through," whereby "God" is said to be revealed "through" Jesus Christ, no more, no less.

Similar questions arise about the relationship envisioned between the meaning of revelation and the cross of Christ. In the book Niebuhr stated that "God's son" was "slain by our iniquities," but nowhere do we find it stated that he was slain "for our iniquities."[15] It is said that God's beloved son was not allowed to "exempt himself from the suffering necessary" for the work of completing and redeeming creation.[16] Yet what that "necessity" for Christ's suffering might have been is nowhere explained. These sketchy remarks are about as close as the book comes to discussing the saving significance of Christ's death. By contrast, for Nicene Christianity, reconciliation as accomplished on the cross is at the very heart of what revelation must be about. "Sacrifice" and "propitiation" are listed as among the outmoded ideas of a "primitive past."[17] From a broadly Nicene standpoint, however, neither Passover nor the eucharist, to say nothing of the cross, can properly be understood without them.

The theme of Christ's resurrection was another matter that would seem more essential to Nicene Christianity than to Niebuhr: "We see the power of God over the strong of the earth made evident," he wrote, "not in the fact that he slays them, but in his making the spirit of the slain Jesus unconquerable."[18] This remark was about as close as Niebuhr would come in the book to affirming anything like Christ's resurrection, i.e., that the "spirit" of the slain Jesus was "unconquerable."

14. Ibid., 174.
15. Ibid., 166.
16. Ibid. Are there echoes in this statement of Schleiermacher?
17. Ibid., 178.
18. Ibid., 187.

In short, whether it was a matter of the incarnation, the atonement, or the resurrection, the meaning of revelation, for Niebuhr, did not seem to include anything like the full deity of Jesus Christ, his atoning sacrifice, or his transfigured bodily identity in and through his resurrection. On these grounds a Nicene doctrine of the Trinity would hardly be possible. The meaning of revelation, for Niebuhr, had little to do with God's triune identity.

One last point: Note that Niebuhr's concept of revelation heavily privileged the present tense. Consider the following remark:

> The God who reveals himself in Jesus Christ is now trusted and known as the contemporary God, revealing himself in every event; but we do not understand how we could trace his working in these happenings if he did not make himself known to us through the memory of Jesus Christ; nor do we know how we should be able to interpret all the words we read as words of God save by the aid of this Rosetta stone.[19]

Elsewhere revelation is described as being essentially "a contemporary event."[20] The implication seems to be what while God is our contemporary, Jesus is present only by way of "memory." By contrast, for Nicene Christianity, revelation has essentially three tenses, with the life-history of Jesus Christ there and then occupying the controlling center. By virtue of his resurrection and ascension, moreover, the living Christ also determines the present and the future.

By so heavily privileging the present tense, Niebuhr effectively threw the covenant with Israel (on which no weight is placed in the book) into the same kind of oblivion, with respect to revelation, as is undergone by the Trinity and the authority of scripture. Note that in the passage cited, the "Rosetta stone" (Christ as the clue to scripture) is accorded importance mainly because it allows us to gain a glimpse of how God may be "revealing himself in every event." Any scandal of particularity is dissolved, it would seem, in standard modernist fashion, by reinterpreting the particulars of biblical revelation in terms of some larger conceptual scheme (as opposed to the other way around). Moreover, how seriously is Niebuhr to be taken when he states that God is being revealed "in every event"? Are there not some events so evil that they do not reveal God? (In other writings, especially *The Responsible Self*, Niebuhr's God approaches being identical with Fate.)[21] Finally, Niebuhr's

19. Ibid., 154.
20. Ibid., 41.
21. Niebuhr, *The Responsible Self* (New York: Harper & Row, 1963).

"presentizing" of the meaning of revelation would seem also to be a way of essentially "existentializing" it. From the standpoint of Nicene Christianity, the dispositional, chastened, and restrained aspects of Niebuhr's theological anthropology are in fact arguably the book's strength, but would hardly be adequate to define the meaning of revelation.

At this point, the following observation may be ventured. Suppose someone said some things that were valid though not sufficient, and yet asserted them as if they were sufficient. A complex situation would be created. Insofar as the valid elements were valid they would remain valid. But insofar as sufficiency were claimed for them, the assertion would be false. Because Niebuhr's theological anthropology is arguably one thing while the meaning of revelation is (from a Nicene standpoint) quite another, it might be best finally to receive the book as wisdom literature rather than as adequate for doctrinal theology. Indeed, from a Nicene standpoint, the concepts of God and revelation in the book are, as has been suggested, either non-trinitarian, or sub-trinitarian, or finally perhaps even anti-trinitarian, though in any case underdeveloped. Nevertheless, there would be no reason, in principle, not to learn from Niebuhr's theological anthropology, as long as the meaning of revelation, as confessed by the Nicene faith, were properly set forth and affirmed.

II. The Rise of Historicism and the Retreat to Inwardness: On the Distinction Between Internal and External History

The preface to H. Richard Niebuhr's *The Meaning of Revelation* contains the following remark:

> Students of theology will recognize that Ernst Troeltsch and Karl Barth . . . have been my teachers. . . . These leaders in twentieth century religious thought are frequently set in diametrical opposition to each other; I have tried to combine their main interests, for it appears to me that the critical thought of the former and the constructive work of the latter belong together.[22]

Niebuhr does not explain how he thinks he might be reconciling Troeltsch and Barth in the book. He leaves it up to his readers to work this out. The question might be phrased like this: In what ways does Niebuhr converge with these two thinkers, in what ways does he diverge from them, and in

22. Niebuhr, *The Meaning of Revelation*, p. x.

what ways might he be seen as combining their main interests? Although Niebuhr's response to Troeltsch will be examined, some suggestions about how Niebuhr might be related to Barth will set the stage.

Niebuhr's Convergence with Barth

In the first part of this essay it was suggested that theologically the connection was not always great. Niebuhr did not share Barth's robust commitment to Nicene Christianity. One searches in vain, whether in this book or in any of his writings, for an unambiguous affirmation of the full deity of Christ (the touchstone of the trinitarian faith). For Niebuhr (as noted), while Jesus was the object of loyalty and devotion, he was not the incarnate Son. He was the source but not the content of revelation. Accordingly, from a Nicene point of view, what we find is a relatively weak view of the incarnation, of the atonement, and of Christ's bodily resurrection. All this is rather far from Barth.

For Nicene Christianity, it might be said that Jesus is logically indispensable. He was a unique person who accomplished our salvation in a way that only he was equipped to do. We find this affirmation represented in the 1998 PCUSA Study Catechism.

Q 29. What do you believe when you confess your faith in Jesus Christ as "God's only Son"?

A. That Jesus Christ is a unique person who was sent to do a unique work.

Q 30. How do you understand the uniqueness of Jesus Christ?

A. No one else will ever be God incarnate. No one else will ever die for the sins of the world. Only Jesus Christ is such a person, only he could do such a work, and he in fact has done it.[23]

---

23. Compare these affirmations with a similar section in the Heidelberg Catechism (1563):

Q 15. What kind of mediator and redeemer should we look for then?

A. One who is truly human and perfectly righteous, yet more powerful than all creatures, that is, one who is also truly God.

Q 16. Why must the mediator be truly human and perfectly righteous?

A. God's justice demands that a human being must pay for human sin; but a sinful human could never pay for others.

Q 17. Why must the mediator also be truly God?

A. So that the mediator, by the power of divinity, might bear the weight of God's wrath as a human being, and earn for us and restore to us righteousness and life.

As here set forth, Jesus is logically indispensable, because only a divine-human person could have accomplished his unique saving work. Deny his uniqueness as the incarnate Son and by the same token one has denied the unsubstitutable uniqueness of his saving work in bearing the world's sin and bearing it away.[24]

Nevertheless, even if Jesus were not logically indispensable, he could still be materially decisive. While for Barth he was both, for Niebuhr he was at least the latter. Although it was not inconceivable that some other person might have played, or might yet play, a similar spiritual role, as a matter of contingent fact only Jesus, for Niebuhr, was the one who revealed that ultimate reality was finally benevolent toward us, despite all strong appearances to the contrary.

That was Niebuhr's basic quandary. How can we believe in the benevolence of God? How can we believe in it when our earthly life is beset by so much tragedy, misery, loss, destruction, and death? Without ever quite explaining how, Niebuhr found in Jesus the decisive clue. By the powerful example of his unswerving faith in God, despite his being rejected, abandoned, and betrayed, and finally condemned to death on a cross, Jesus revealed that God was to be trusted no matter what, and he inspired in us the same faith as was in him. He thus became the object of our loyalty and devotion. In that sense (though only in that sense), Jesus was materially decisive. Although he was much more than that for Nicene Christianity (and so for Barth), at this point we have a moment of convergence.

Another point of limited convergence concerned the nature and function of religious language. Like Barth, Niebuhr held, in the end, that religious language was informative, that it made truth claims, that it had propositional content. He seemed to reject what has been called the "expressivist" view. In contrast to someone like Tillich, he did not think we needed to correlate non-informative religious symbols with informative concepts, or expressions of inner experience ("metaphors") with formulations of cognitive content (concepts).[25] Although Niebuhr's stance with regard to proposi-

24. Note that the word "unique" is ambiguous. It can be used in either a relative or an absolute sense. When used relatively, it points to a special occurrence within a larger class, as when each person's thumbprint is unique, yet still within the larger class of thumbprints. When used absolutely, as when Nicene Christianity speaks about the uniqueness of the incarnate Son as a divine-human person, it means "exclusively unique" or *sui generis*, for it is talking about something that by definition is one of a kind. Niebuhr can use the term "unique," but seems to mean it only in the more relative sense of "materially decisive." See for example *The Meaning of Revelation*, 126.

25. For the expressivist, concepts without metaphors were empty, whereas metaphors

tional content was not simple, and although he did not explicitly use the idea of analogy, in the end he seemed closer to "realism" than to either "literalism" or "expressivism."[26]

The clearest apparent rejection of the logic of expressivism in *The Meaning of Revelation* came when Niebuhr affirmed his own view over against "social mysticism":

> It cannot be enough to say that in revelation we meet the divine self, for if this meeting is pure immediacy which does not provide us with truths about God it would remain incommunicable and unable to provide the reasoning heart with principles of understanding.[27]

Whatever else this statement might mean, it seemed to affirm that "truths about God" were not absent from the meaning of revelation. This interpretation of Niebuhr was supported by his favorable quoting of Herrmann, where we read that revelation was "*not* the stimulation of numinous feelings" though it was "necessarily accompanied by religious feelings."[28] Recall that expressivism needed independent interpretive concepts precisely because it effectively defined "revelation" in terms of numinous or religious feelings, which were expressed in (and evoked by) non-informative religious symbols. So again, Niebuhr seemed to be distancing himself from expressivism. Finally, whatever else we might think about the eloquently stated convictions at the book's conclusion, they certainly assumed that revelation had cognitive content in and of itself, content which should continually prompt us "to rethink all ideas about deity."[29]

It would seem that although revelation's content (in effect, for Niebuhr, what it affirmed about God, freedom, and immortality) was in line with theological liberalism, Niebuhr's view of revelation (contrary to many lib-

---

without concepts were blind. It came down to a matter of the head without the heart (concepts) and the heart without the head (metaphors), so that the two had to be brought into mutual correlation. In Tillich, for example, "God" as someone who spoke and acted was a non-informative symbol, whereas "the Ground of Being" was the informative concept needed to interpret it. God did not really speak and act (that would be "absurd literalism"), but since we are persons, it was *as if* God did so in our religious "experience." The phrase "as if" would give us the syntax of equivocation in the expressivist viewpoint.

26. For these distinctions, see George Hunsinger, "Beyond Literalism and Expressivism," in *Disruptive Grace* (Grand Rapids: Wm. B. Eerdmans, 2000), 210-225.

27. Niebuhr, *The Meaning of Revelation*, 175-176.

28. Ibid., 152.

29. Ibid., 187.

eral views) was not essentially non-cognitive. Accordingly, his view of religious language was in some sense "realist." Religious language for him had propositional content, even if that content was a matter of perpetual discernment and refinement by the reasoning heart.

Niebuhr therefore converged with Barth insofar as they both affirmed three things:

(a) that Jesus was materially decisive for revelation,
(b) that revelation involved truths about God, and
(c) that religious language was not merely expressive but informative.[30]

There were also divergences, however, insofar as Barth went on to affirm:

(a) that Jesus was not only materially decisive for revelation but also logically indispensable,
(b) that truths about God could not be restricted by the deliverances of historicism, and
(c) that revelation informed us about a God who was trinitarian in and of himself to all eternity, not simply in relation to us (and our "experiences").

The latter point was examined previously in part one.[31] The point about historicism, to which we now turn, involved Niebuhr's critical appropriation of Troeltsch.

30. Niebuhr and Barth would also agree that revelation encountered us as whole persons. It was no more a matter of the heart without the head (expressivism) than of the head without the heart (some versions of literalism). For both theologians revelation was always a matter of the cognitive, the affective, and the practical: in effect, the head, the heart, and the hand. For various reasons, Barth downplayed the affective dimension more than did Niebuhr, while Niebuhr perhaps in the end privileged the practical dimension more than Barth would. These were differences, however, within what was essentially a shared holistic stance regarding the meaning of revelation in its mode of address.

31. As previously noted, Hans Frei suggests that Niebuhr's theology tended toward "economic trinitarianism." See Frei, "The Theology of H. Richard Niebuhr," 98. Frei's essay is still perhaps the best analysis of Niebuhr's theology to have been written.

By way of digression it might be added that in recent theology another type of "economic trinitarianism" has emerged. It is not modalistic in tendency, but instead has tritheistic and sometimes subordinationist implications. It is not modalistic, because modalism presupposes a strong conception of the "ontological divide" between God and the world. The newer economic trinitarianism, by contrast, systematically blurs or relativizes this dif-

Niebuhr's Convergence with Troeltsch

Despite the cognitive aspects in Niebuhr's conceptions of revelation and religious language, a certain anti-propositionalist strain appeared in his argument at the same time. Although revelation was not merely the stimulation of numinous feelings, neither was it "the communication of supernatural knowledge."[32] What revelation meant "cannot be expressed in the impersonal ways of creeds or other propositions but *only* in responsive acts of personal character."[33] Along the same lines we read that "revelation is not the communication of new truths and the supplanting of our natural religion by a supernatural one."[34] Niebuhr's evident aversion to the "supernatural" converged with the historicism that we find in Troeltsch. Niebuhr disavowed any propositionalism that would affirm "supernatural" interventions in the realm of "external" history.

Historicism, as vigorously set forth by Troeltsch, involved three main components: analogy, probability, and correlation. A long, if somewhat difficult, passage from Troeltsch may be quoted, which sets these components forth.

> For the means by which criticism becomes possible at all is the application of analogy. The analogy of that which happens before our eyes . . . is the key to criticism. The illusions, . . . the formation of myths, the deceptions, the party spirit, which we see before our eyes are the means of recognizing such things also in the tradition. Agreement with the normal, usual, or at least variously attested, happenings . . . as we know them, is the mark of probability for happenings which the critic can recognize as

---

ference. It involves what might be called the "historicization of eternity," because it seems to take eternity as no more than a transcendent dimension that runs along in tandem with history (on which it is in some sense dependent). Eternity and time, God and the world, appear to be two interrelated dimensions of one and the same reality. Though not co-equal the difference between time and eternity becomes merely relative, arriving finally at a point of dialectical identity. At the same time the divine unity is made to rest entirely on *perichoresis*, since the ideas of divine simplicity and aseity (and therefore God's radical otherness) are discarded. Economic trinitarianism of this second, "panentheistic" type can be seen (in various ways) in the early Pannenberg, the later Moltmann, Jenson, and LaCugna. For a trenchant critique of panentheism, see Barth, II/1, 312.

32. Niebuhr, *The Meaning of Revelation*, 152.

33. Ibid., 153, italics added. Barth would not say "only" here. For him it would be "both/and." He would say: "not merely in creeds but also in responsive personal actions."

34. Ibid., 182.

really having happened or can leave aside. The observation of analogies between past events of the same kind makes it possible to ascribe probability to them and to interpret the unknown aspects of the other. The omnipotence thus attaching to analogy implies, however, the basic similarity of all historical events, which is not, of course, identity . . . but presupposes that there is always a common core of similarity, on the basis of which differences can be sensed and perceived.[35]

From this passage the three components of historicism can be lifted out:

- Analogy. The idea of analogy as here conceived was essentially something metaphysical. It posited that all events in history were "of the same kind." They were all fundamentally similar. They exhibited "a common core of similarity."
- Probability. This basic similarity between events present and past was a necessary condition for making probability judgments. All judgments about historical events were merely probable, and events could be judged as probable only if they agreed with "normal, usual, or at least variously attested happenings as we know them."
- Correlation. Historical criticism had therefore to reject as "mythical" any claims that supernatural events had occurred. Events of that kind could not be correlated with present events as we know them. Historicism had therefore to reject all faith in miracles, as well as any claim that God was directly revealed in one series of events over against all others.

Hans Frei has suggested that Troeltsch's analysis of historical method may lie behind Niebuhr's distinction between internal and external history. He wrote:

Troeltsch saw in scientific-historical method a grave threat not merely to miracle-trusting faith or a stringent orthodoxy, but to the claims for the historical uniqueness of Jesus Christ by the later nineteenth-century tradition. Undoubtedly Niebuhr felt that the historical method of Christian faith could not challenge this point of view, (which Troeltsch shared with so many others in modernity) in regard to the objects of historical knowl-

---

35. Ernst Troeltsch, "Über historische und dogmatische Methode" (1898), *Gesammelte Schriften,* vol. 2 (Tübingen: J. C. B. Mohr, 1912), 729-731. Quoted by Jürgen Moltmann, *Theology of Hope* (New York: Harper & Row, 1967), 175-176.

edge. It is unwarranted dogmatism to except the event "Jesus Christ" from
the laws of analogy, interrelation and probability that govern our knowledge of historical events. Instead of disputing the correctness of this understanding of the object, Niebuhr suggested that side by side with the
"external," scientific method there is an existential, participative "internal" understanding of history.[36]

Frei went on to note that shifting revelation from external to internal history
would not have satisfied Troeltsch.

> The claim for a special apprehension in history and internal participation,
> Troeltsch contended, is no better founded than the orthodox argument
> for cosmic miracle. He thought that the simple transfer [of miracle] from
> nature to spirit was the common core of the nineteenth-century Christian
> historical tradition. Niebuhr's Christology and doctrine of grace in *The
> Meaning of Revelation,* and other writings of that period, indicate how
> close he is to the position Troeltsch rejected.[37]

For the nineteenth-century tradition of academic liberal theology, whose
most distinguished representative was Schleiermacher, the rise of historicism
had meant a retreat to inwardness. As Frei suggested, Niebuhr aligned himself
with this tradition. In doing so he diverged greatly from Barth without, it
would seem, finding a position that would have satisfied Troeltsch. At this
neuralgic point he combined the main interests of neither thinker.

The alternative to the inward turn, Frei suggested, would have been to
dispute the correctness of this understanding of the object, in other words,
to challenge the underlying assumptions of historicism. Barth of course did
exactly that at great length, but for a brief, incisive, and accessible rebuttal of
historicism, it would be hard to surpass Jürgen Moltmann.[38]

Conclusion: The Humility of Relativism as a Point of Convergence

Historicism, for Troeltsch, led inexorably to cultural and historical relativism
in theology. Although Niebuhr was undoubtedly influenced by Troeltsch at

36. Frei, "Theology of H. Richard Niebuhr," 89-90.
37. Ibid., 93. According to Frei, Niebuhr interprets revelation as a kind of internal miracle. While Barth would not disagree, he sees revelation primarily as an "objective miracle," so
to speak, because it is identical with the advent of Jesus Christ.
38. Moltmann, *Theology of Hope,* 172-182.

this point, he did not adopt Troeltsch's relativism uncritically. Instead he deepened it by transposing it onto a more directly theological basis. This point was well explained by Frei:

> In worship, ethics, and theology we must remember that it is the one sovereign and gracious Lord who confronts us in all things. Theocentric or religious relativism is inescapable not because there is no absolute, but because there is one exalted being who *is* absolute, who defeats and converts our natural polytheism and forces us to acknowledge that all values and beings, even our thoughts and confessions about him, are relative.[39]

While at this point, Niebuhr converged with and went beyond Troeltsch, he also stood, as it turns out, in significant convergence with Barth. For much the same reasons as Niebuhr gave, Barth agreed that all our thoughts and confessions about God were merely relative so that they needed to be questioned and reconsidered again and again. "The truth itself," wrote Barth, "demands complete openness."[40]

> We do not secretly ask: How can I progress further on the right path which I am, of course, already treading? It necessarily means that even in relation to our best works and the most sacred of our hypotheses and convictions we confess that we are sincerely sorry and repent, not of the grace of God which has hitherto sustained and controlled us, but of the way in which we have treated the grace of God even in our best works and the construction of our most sacred hypotheses and convictions.[41]

Theocentric relativism led Niebuhr to rely on grace alone as the only factor that could convince us about the truth of the gospel. Frei attributed this aspect to the influence of Troeltsch. "Niebuhr's confessional, nonapologetic theology, his completely nondefensive understanding of culture has undoubtedly been deeply influenced by Troeltsch."[42] Perhaps so. At the same time, however, the very same aspect — confessional, nonapologetic, nondefensive — was very much a hallmark of Barth's theology. Perhaps at this point, at least, Niebuhr had indeed found a way to combine the main interests of the two thinkers from which he wished to take his bearings.

---

39. Ibid., 87.

40. *CD* II/2, 648.

41. *CD* II/2, 646. Barth, of course, keeps theological certainty and self-critical humility, orthodox conviction and healthy relativism, in dialectical tension.

42. Ibid., 89.

Interpretatio in bonem partem:
Jürgen Moltmann on the Immanent Trinity

Thomas R. Thompson

When I reflect upon the theological career of Daniel Migliore, among the many merits of his scholarship, teaching, and interaction with students, one virtue comes quickly to mind: his fairness. Migliore always impressed me as a fair hermeneut, as a charitable reader of texts, whether that text were a personal face or a dense thicket of morphemes. He reinforced for his students the maxim of reading a text first in its best possible light before affixing one's critical gaze, which is to say that he engaged in a hermeneutics of hospitality before he turned to a hermeneutics of suspicion. One never got the impression that he peremptorily applied a litmus test to another's theology — though he was, in the final analysis, concerned with fidelity to the Christian ecumenical and Reformed tradition.

In this essay I would like to offer what I think is a fairer read of a provocative theologian on a critical issue. Ever since the publication of his influential *Theology of Hope* (1964)[1] and *The Crucified God* (1972),[2] Jürgen Moltmann has been sorely criticized for either lacking or having an inadequate doctrine of the immanent Trinity, thereby compromising God's freedom vis-à-vis the world. Karl Barth famously noted this lacuna in response to *Theology of Hope:* "Would it not be wise to accept the doctrine of the immanent trinity of God?"

1. Jürgen Moltmann, *Theology of Hope,* trans. James W. Leitch, Preface to new paperback edition trans. Margaret Kohl (New York: HarperCollins, 1991); hereafter cited within the text as *TH.*

2. Jürgen Moltmann, *The Crucified God,* trans. R. A. Wilson and John Bowden, Preface to new paperback edition trans. Margaret Kohl (New York: HarperCollins, 1991); hereafter cited within the text as *CG.*

— expressing his disappointment that Moltmann was apparently not the anticipated "child of peace and promise."[3] And Hermannus Miskotte was quick to sound this similar note in response to *The Crucified God,* wherein the Trinity seemed to originate only in the course of redemptive history: "But God appears in the end to have become the prisoner of this history."[4]

Such criticisms became standard fare in assessing Moltmann's theology, and they continue to be voiced today even after his theology has largely run its course. This can be seen, for example, in three more recent works. In a republished essay, Paul Molnar continues to maintain that Moltmann lacks an orthodox doctrine of the immanent Trinity:

> Moltmann honestly believes that the historical event of the cross and the heart of the triune God can be understood together in a single perspective. If they can, then there is no distinction between the immanent and economic Trinity. And there is no God independent of the world.[5]

Similarly Robert Letham, for whom such a criticism has become so dazzlingly axiomatic that he even attributes it to Moltmann's sympathetic interpreter Richard Bauckham in egregious misquotation: "According to Bauckham, Moltmann makes the same mistake as Hegel — that of making world history the process by which God realizes himself."[6] And in a more nuanced treatment, John Cooper also concludes that Moltmann's theology "entails that God requires a world, that he actualizes his implicitly triune nature in world history"[7] — thus blurring the distinction between immanent and economic Trinity. Such examples could be multiplied.

3. Barth's letter to Moltmann of 17 November 1964, Karl Barth, *Letters 1961-1968,* ed. J. Fangmeier and H. Stoevesandt, ed. and trans. G. W. Bromiley (Grand Rapids: Eerdmans, 1981), 175-176.

4. Hermannus Heiko Miskotte, "Das Leiden ist in Gott. Über Jürgen Moltmanns trinitarische Kreuzestheologie," in *Diskussion über Jürgen Moltmanns Buch "Der gekreuzigte Gott,"* ed. Michael Welker (Munich: Chr. Kaiser, 1979), 85.

5. Paul D. Molnar, "The Function of the Trinity in Jürgen Moltmann's Ecological Doctrine of Creation," ch. 7 of *Divine Freedom and the Doctrine of the Immanent Trinity: In Dialogue with Karl Barth and Contemporary Theology* (Edinburgh: T&T Clark, 2002), 221.

6. Robert Letham, *The Holy Trinity: In Scripture, History, Theology, and Worship* (Phillipsburg, NJ: P&R Publishing, 2004), 305. In *The Theology of Jürgen Moltmann* (Edinburgh: T&T Clark, 1995), 24-25, Bauckham is merely citing this common criticism of Moltmann, but immediately goes on to state his own opinion: "He does not dissolve God into world history, but he does intend a real interaction between God and the world" (25).

7. John W. Cooper, *Panentheism: The Other God of the Philosophers* (Grand Rapids: Baker Academic, 2006), 258.

While Barth's and Miskotte's criticisms are fair ones, based as they are on Moltmann's early theology, these last three I regard as less than fair, given the breadth of Moltmann's theology. By way of contrast, I will argue that a discernible shift in Moltmann's trinitarianism takes place *post Crucified God,* one in which he develops not only an appropriate doctrine of the immanent Trinity — capturing its essential orthodox truth — but one which arguably improves upon the foibles of the traditional interpretation. Only by reading Moltmann in light of these further developments does one accord him a fair interpretation of his trinitarianism and his understanding of the immanent Trinity. In sketching out the main lines of my argument, I will also identify a few collateral issues that critics cite as further evidence of Moltmann's compromise of the Creator/creature distinction.[8]

The Development of Moltmann's Trinitarianism

There is in Moltmann's *theologia viatorum,* as he is fond to describe his own theological endeavors, a discernible genesis and evolution of his trinitarianism. These can be traced in three phases and typified as the *emergence, broadening,* and *clarification* of Moltmann's trinitarianism. Key interpretive issues hang on a recognition of this development in Moltmann's thought.

Moltmann's ascent to theological notoriety came swiftly upon the publication of his *Theology of Hope,* the first of his well-known trilogy of works that tackles "the whole of theology in one focal point."[9] Taken alone, however, one looks in vain in *Theology of Hope* for any explicit affirmation or theology of the Trinity. In fact, Moltmann's comments and strain of thought in this foundational work even appear deprecatory of this doctrine as traditionally attired. This is evident in the first place in Moltmann's quibble with Barth over the immanent Trinity, which distinction Moltmann contended "is always in danger of obscuring the historical and eschatological character of the Holy Spirit, who is the Spirit of the resurrection of the dead" (*TH* 57) — a comment reflective of his central concerns in *Theology of Hope.* Barth's firm rejoinder, "Would it not be wise to accept the doctrine of the immanent

---

8. The following is drawn largely from Thomas R. Thompson, *Imitatio Trinitatis: The Trinity as Social Model in the Theologies of Jürgen Moltmann and Leonardo Boff* (Ph.D. diss., Princeton Theological Seminary, 1996) — a dissertation directed by Daniel L. Migliore.

9. Moltmann describes this as the prevailing method of the first phase of his theological career, crediting Bauckham for the insight. See *History and the Triune God: Contributions to Trinitarian Theology,* trans. John Bowden (New York: Crossroad, 1992), 168-176.

trinity of God?" admittedly haunted Moltmann: "I suspect you are right but I cannot as yet or so quickly enter into this right."[10] The question whether Moltmann has developed an acceptable doctrine of the immanent Trinity has haunted his trinitarianism since.

But beyond this direct and isolated comment, it is questionable whether the ontological direction of Moltmann's thought in *Theology of Hope*, taken by itself, even allows of any near trinitarian confession. Given the radically historical and eschatological orientation of his program of rethinking God and revelation through the category of promise, Moltmann tends to depreciate any personalist approach to the doctrine of God as entailing an unacceptable model of revelation — that affording but an ahistoric self-disclosure of a static eternal being. Instead, the future and historical faithfulness or "selfsame-ness" of God *(Selbigkeit)* overwhelms any transcendental selfhood *(Ichhiet)* (cf. *TH* 116), resulting almost exclusively in dynamistic descriptions of deity as "the power of the future," and the like, in the ontological fashion of Ernst Bloch (cf. *TH* 16). Although Moltmann admits to an *Einseitigkeit* in *Theology of Hope*, which becomes more understandable in light of its primary foils — namely, any doctrine of God that resembles Parmenides'; or notion of revelation that smacks of religious epiphany — the lack of any personalist account of God, of which the Trinity is the eminent expression, hounds Moltmann's early theology, even ironically through *The Crucified God*.

To be sure, Moltmann does recognize the need to think through the form the Trinity would take given his eschatological program, as is clear in his reply to Barth, as well as in formal discussion over the *Theology of Hope*.[11] But the *emergence* of Moltmann's trinitarianism would not come from any immediate or conscious attempt to work out the kinks of this explicitly non-trinitarian baseline; rather, it would enter in more serendipitous

10. Moltmann's letter to Barth of 4 April 1965 (Barth, *Letters,* 348), worth quoting at greater length:

> The nub of your criticism caused me the most cogitation, namely, that in place of eschatology — to escape its dominating one-sidedness — the doctrine of the immanent Trinity should function as an expository canon for the proclamation of the lordship of Jesus Christ. I must admit that in studying C.D. at these points I always lost my breath. I suspect you are right but I cannot as yet or so quickly enter into this right.

11. *Diskussion über die Theologie der Hoffnung,* ed. Wolf-Dieter Marsch (Munich: Chr. Kaiser Verlag, 1967), 215-222.

fashion from a different, albeit complementary angle: a theology of the cross. It is when Moltmann turns his attention to a *theologia crucis* in apposition to the resurrection motif of *Theology of Hope* that his thought becomes explicitly trinitarian, as he himself acknowledges:

> For me, the work on this theology of the cross meant a surprising turning-point. Having asked in many different ways what the cross of Christ means for the church, for theology, for discipleship, for culture and society, I now found myself faced with the reverse question: what does Christ's cross really mean for God himself? . . . And from the cross of Christ I also found access to the trinitarian life of God.[12]

It is his theologically *in-tensive* account of the cross which first demands of Moltmann a more differentiated concept of God, a development which finds its first fullest and most poignant expression in *The Crucified God*. In its title chapter, Moltmann takes up this striking locution of Luther, but considers that the *theo*logy consistently entailed by the cross necessitates a more explicit trinitarianism than the tradition has accorded:

> When one considers the significance of the death of Jesus for God himself, one must enter into the inner-trinitarian tensions and relationships of God and speak of the Father, the Son and the Spirit. . . . The more one understands the whole event of the cross as an event of God, the more any simple concept of God falls apart. (*CG* 204)

Initially, therefore, it is the cross for Moltmann which "stands at the heart of the trinitarian being of God" and which "divides and conjoins the persons in their relationships to each other and portrays them in a specific way" (*CG* 207). Or, in Moltmann's favorite formula of this period: "The material principle of the doctrine of the Trinity is the cross of Christ. The formal principle of knowledge of the cross is the doctrine of the Trinity" (*CG* 241).

Around this trinitarian "revolution in the concept of God" (*CG* 152) required by the cross converge a number of Moltmann's signature themes: the passion of Christ reveals the God of pathos, whose suffering capacity to identify with a godforsaken world alone broaches the theodicy question posed by an Auschwitz, thereby enabling us to transcend the modern impasse of theism and atheism — all rich themes on which Moltmann himself

---

12. Jürgen Moltmann, *Experiences of God,* trans. Margaret Kohl (Philadelphia: Fortress, 1980), 15-16.

waxes passionate. It is here also that he first laments with Rahner the practical irrelevance of the Trinity in Christian consciousness (*CG* 236), and endorses Rahner's famous axiom as a corrective measure (*CG* 240).

But for all the profundity of *The Crucified God,* a number of questions remain about the trinitarianism it delineates. For one, Moltmann still appears loath to describe God, even here as Trinity, in any strong personalistic way:

> In that case, what sense does it make to talk of "God"? I think that the unity of the dialectical history of Father and Son and Spirit in the cross on Golgotha, full of tension as it is, can be described so to speak retrospectively as "God." . . . In that case, "God" is not another nature or a heavenly person or a moral authority, but in fact an "event." (*CG* 247)

Though Moltmann qualifies this impersonal language somewhat, any qualification is only weakly personalistic. In *The Crucified God* the Trinity is largely described in dialectical terms as an "eschatological process" (e.g., *CG* 249).

This leads to a second problem area in this second influential work: its loud Hegelian overtones, as reflected, for example, in the following:

> If one describes the life of God within the Trinity as the "history of God" (Hegel), this history of God contains within itself the whole abyss of godforsakenness, absolute death and the non-God. *"Nemo contra Deum nisi Deus ipse."* Because this death took place in the history between Father and Son on the cross on Golgotha, there proceeds from it the spirit of life, love and election to salvation. (*CG* 246; cf. also 252-256)

Moltmann's extended application of dialectical identity (cf. *CG* 25-28), his process and panentheistic language for God (e.g., *CG* 77), in addition to his frequent and express use of Hegel, all lend to his trinitarianism a formal similarity to that of the latter, for whom the Trinity served a more symbolic function in interpretation of the world process, a "principled" use not unlike the following: "Understood in trinitarian terms, God both transcends the world and is immanent in history. . . . He is, if one is prepared to put it in inadequate imagery, transcendent as Father, immanent as Son and opens up the future of history as the Spirit" (*CG* 256). But the most serious and consistent criticism of Moltmann's resemblance to Hegel in *The Crucified God* is a perceived collapsing of the Trinity into world history, where, in the terminology of Rahner's axiom, the economic Trinity is *strictly identical with* the immanent Trinity, with no seeming transcendence of the latter over the former.

Finally, it is the third movement of this dialectical Trinity that occasions a third basic objection to Moltmann's formulation: for all *but* practical purposes it appears binitarian. Next to the interaction between Father and Son, the Spirit appears in attenuated fashion, as mere effect of the life and love proceeding from the Christ event (cf. *CG* 244-246; 254-256). Moltmann even gives the impression that the Spirit's provenance is the cross, which reinforced the greater suspicion of some that the Trinity at large finds its actual origin in this dialectical event.

In sum, Moltmann's early *dialectical Trinity* is burdened by a Hegelian stigma, and by classical standards appears quite unorthodox. Hence the valid critiques of Barth and Miskotte. But this is not Moltmann's last word on the Trinity.

A second phase witnesses a *broadening* or expansion of Moltmann's appropriation of the Trinity, which is quite distinguishable from its debut. Beginning already in *The Church in the Power of the Spirit* (1975),[13] but finding its fullest articulation in *The Trinity and the Kingdom* (1980),[14] Moltmann's early dialectical Trinity, which was largely confined to the events of cross and resurrection, and which fell prone to many of the same criticisms of Hegel's Trinity, is broadened into what may be called a *narratological Trinity* — Moltmann's trinitarian accounting of the biblical witness to the larger historical-redemptive relationships of Father, Son, and Spirit. In my reading, any problematic Hegelian stigma is erased here in a more expansive and fully personalist portrayal of the Trinity. It is here that Moltmann definitively unveils his social trinitarianism. This could almost be considered a *Kehre* in Moltmann's trinitarian thought, except that he continues to underscore the earlier dialectical themes of cross and resurrection, albeit in a fuller-bodied trinitarian context. It might be better to say that certain Hegelian insights are taken up by Moltmann (dare one say *aufgehoben?*) into a larger trinitarian framework that bears a much more evident kinship with the confessional tradition. We will return to these two works in demonstrating the development of Moltmann's immanent Trinity.

13. Jürgen Moltmann, *The Church in the Power of the Spirit,* trans. Margaret Kohl (New York: HarperCollins, 1991), 50-65; hereafter cited within the text as *CPS.* In the 1990 Preface to this work Moltmann indicates that this is really where his efforts began on the Trinity which led to the formulations of *The Trinity and the Kingdom* (*CPS* xv).

14. Jürgen Moltmann, *The Trinity and the Kingdom,* trans. Margaret Kohl (San Francisco: Harper & Row, 1981); hereafter cited within the text as *TK.*

A third phase in Moltmann's thinking encompasses all reflections on the Trinity subsequent to *The Trinity and the Kingdom* which refine and offer *clarification* of the doctrine laid out in that definitive work, and which think through its consequences for other theological loci. It is significant that *The Trinity and the Kingdom* is the first work in Moltmann's "series of systematic contributions to theology," which represents for him a new genre of theological expression. In this more traditional and systematic approach to theology, *The Trinity and the Kingdom* plays a foundational and integrative role for Moltmann's continuing reflections on a variety of other doctrines, which in turn clarify and give nuance to his basic trinitarian statement. Though there is no significant migration from the doctrine laid out in *The Trinity and the Kingdom,* it is necessary to read that mature position in the light of subsequent applications, as opposed to that of the emergent or exclusively dialectical phase, where one might retain the suspicion that Moltmann was waxing more poetically (*à la* Hegel) than doctrinally on the Trinity, as many continue to read him. A recognition of these developments in Moltmann's trinitarian thought coupled with a hermeneutical "reading back" to *The Trinity and the Kingdom* are necessary for a proper interpretation of his mature proposal, and especially for his endorsement of an immanent Trinity. Since the development of Moltmann's immanent Trinity takes place in dialogue with Rahner's well-known axiom, some discussion of its validity is necessary. This is especially the case because some render Moltmann guilty (of economic trinitarianism) by sheer association with this axiom, given the peculiar penchant of many of those who embrace it.

The Validity of Rahner's Rule: The Economic Trinity Is the Immanent Trinity and Vice Versa

Karl Rahner's lament that, for all practical purposes, contemporary Christians were "mere monotheists" became something of a rallying cry for the present trinitarian renaissance. It also occasioned his ameliorative axiom concerning the congruity of the economic and immanent Trinity. Rahner's immediate concern was to overcome the scholastic dichotomy in the doctrine of God between the treatises *De Deo uno* and *De Deo trino* in which the former, coming first in the guise of a natural theology, preempted the importance of the latter. The result of this *modus procendi* was to promote a "mere" or non-trinitarian monotheism, since what takes *theo*logical precedence is the unicity of the divine nature and its particular character. States Rahner:

But then one really writes, or could merely write, a treatise *"De divinitate una,"* since the unicity of the divine being justifies this procedure, and make it very philosophical and abstract in development — which is of course what happens — with very little concrete reference to the history of salvation. It deals with the necessary metaphysical attributes of God, and not very explicitly with the experiences of the history of salvation which have come from God's freely adopted relations to creation. . . . But then the theology of the Trinity cannot but give the impression of being able to make merely formal [i.e., non-ontological] assertions about the divine persons. . . . And even these assertions seem to deal with a reality entirely centred on itself, a Trinity which is not opened to anything outside, and of which we, the outsiders, only know something through a strange paradox.[15]

This scholastic approach leaves in question whether God *for us* — revealed as Trinity — is truly representative of God *in se.* The primary objective of Rahner's axiom is to dispel this doubt: the economic Trinity *is* the immanent Trinity; what we see in salvation history is God as God genuinely is, which is to say, the Trinity is a real mediation of God's salvific life.[16]

To illustrate the validity of Rahner's axiom, we can isolate particular moments of trinitarian extrication (economically) from the more philosophical construal of deity that assumed preeminent (and "immanent") status in Western theology. It has been the imposing and impersonal conception of God as metaphysically *One,* described principally as indivisible, immutable, and eternal, as drawn from the Greek philosophical tradition of contrast with the transient and perishable world of the *Many (via negativa),* that has created the most havoc for the trinitarian confession. The reconsideration of these attributes, each of which definitionally implies the others, offers a helpful perspective on the legitimacy of Rahner's axiom.

Rahner's own employment of his axiom in his constructive statement of the Trinity is most simply, though less admittedly, an assault on the traditional doctrine of divine indivisibility.[17] If the economic Trinity is a true revelation of God's being, divine unity must be more differentiated — "three-personal" — than that of the indivisibility of the divine nature. Rahner's "proof" of his axiom in this respect is the Incarnation, a "mission" or "send-

---

15. Karl Rahner, "Remarks on the Dogmatic Treatise 'De Trinitate,'" in *Theological Investigations,* vol. 4, trans. Kevin Smyth (New York: Crossroad, 1982), 84.

16. Idem., *The Trinity,* trans. Joseph Donceel (New York: Herder, 1970), 38.

17. See ibid., 45-46.

ing" *proper* to the Son (as Logos), not merely appropriated to him, and "not simply the result of the efficient causality of the triune God working as one nature in the world,"[18] as would be the case within the framework of the Augustinian doctrine of the *indivisa* of divine works *ad extra*. But how ironic that the linchpin of Trinity doctrine — the Incarnation — that which first gave rise epistemologically to the trinitarian confession *(ordo cognoscendi)* must now be defended ontologically *(ordo essendi)* due to a conception of divinity that impugns its fundamental integrity. At its most basic level Rahner's axiom merely affirms that the economic *Trinity* is the immanent *Trinity,* that God's threefoldness towards us is indicative of an integral and *real* threefoldness in God's own being, as opposed to an implacable oneness (unicity).

A similar case occurs with immutability, which is the theological context in which Moltmann, elaborating a *theologia crucis,* first embraced Rahner's rule. As but one participant in the theopaschite "revolution in the concept of God" (*CG* 204), Moltmann finds this classical theistic axiom catastrophic for the basic claims of Christian faith. Not only must it render the Incarnation disingenuous or docetic, but it trivializes the *crux* of the Christian gospel — the passion and resurrection of Christ. God's ability to change, to genuinely enter history and experience its vicissitudes ought not to be neutralized or denigrated by a superseding notion of supreme being. In view of the economy of redemption, the Trinity cannot concomitantly be understood as a "closed circle" in heaven, since God is no *Deus incurvatus in se,* but a tri-personal history opened to us (*CG* 255). What we observe in the narrative history of Scripture is a faithful witness to who and what God is. In this sense, the economic Trinity is the immanent Trinity.

Divine eternality conceived of classically as "timelessness" is the third major attribute of the One to which the logic of Rahner's axiom is a helpful corrective. The simple conception of eternity as timelessness in which all temporal things are to God *simul totem* appears disingenuous to the interactive progress of redemptive history and puts in question God's real, meaningful relation with creation. But there is no reason to suppose that the trinitarian drama of creation and redemption — an ostensibly poignant give-and-take between God and creature — is at the same time *(simul totem)* transcended by a divine experience that is unaffected or unmoved by the former; to hold thusly makes of salvation history something of a side show. However construed, divine eternality cannot be defined in opposition to

---

18. Idem, "Remarks," 87-88.

creaturely temporality. In respect to God's historical, temporal experience, the economic Trinity is simultaneously the immanent Trinity.

The legitimacy of Rahner's *Grundaxiom* is summed up well by Catherine Mowry LaCugna. Trinitarian theology, she argues strenuously, disavows the coexistence of "two levels" of the Trinity separated by an "unbreachable ontological difference," as though there were "an intradivine sphere, unrelated to the creature."[19] To the degree that Rahner's basic concern is in view — namely, that the Trinity be liberated from a philosophically incongruent doctrine of God so as to become redolent for the entire range of Christian belief — his axiom is viable: God *pro nobis* is consistent and commensurate with God *in se*. But is the economic Trinity *fully* coextensive with the immanent Trinity? Is Rahner's "vice versa" also as viable — that the immanent Trinity *is* the economic Trinity? Here we begin to bump up against the limitations of Rahner's axiom, limitations which Rahner himself, it has frequently been pointed out, violates.

Taken by itself, it is difficult to discern how strict of an identity Rahner's formula proposes between the immanent and economic Trinity. If the "vice versa" is merely tautological, then a good-faced interpretation is possible, since this would merely confirm the legitimacy of his rule from the point of view of the economy of redemption *(ratio cognoscendi)*. But if Rahner's vice versa makes an additional identity claim — namely, from the point of view of the immanent Trinity *(ratio essendi)* — then this would proffer a strict identity between the two, compromising the freedom of God in creation and redemption, and resulting in a mere economic trinitarianism — the very condition that necessitated this distinction in the first place. In this most basic respect the economic Trinity *is not* the immanent Trinity: the former does not fully — that is, ontologically — exhaust the latter, since the latter antedates the former in the order of being. This is to say that the Trinity eternally and infinitely transcends a finite, temporal creation.[20]

19. Catherine Mowry LaCugna, *God for Us: The Trinity and Christian Life* (San Francisco: Harper, 1991), 210.

20. There are two central doctrines which particularly depend upon and reinforce this trinitarian distinction and whose denial — either flat out or *de facto* by means of a subtle or radical reinterpretation — signals an economic reductionism. The first is the doctrine of *creatio ex nihilo*, which guarantees that creation is not necessary to God's essential being (as Trinity). The second is the eternal (pre)existence of Christ, including the idea that the person-forming principle of Jesus of Nazareth is enhypostatic in the *eternal* Son of God and anhypostatic of human nature, ruling out any christological adoptionism of ontological dimensions.

What follows from this epistemologically is that we should not suppose that our knowledge of the economic Trinity is *identically exhaustive* of the immanent. Though we may rightly assume that the divine economy is a true revelation of God's essential being as Trinity, it is presumptuous to contend that to the degree we comprehend that economy we comprehend God per se. The latter, however, tends to be a weakness of economic trinitarians, who, leaning toward an adoptionist christology as well as the notion of God's self-constitution in history, epistemologically "capture" the infinite in the finite since the ultimate essence of God — as Trinity — is an amalgam of God, humanity, and history, which is to say, of Creator and creature. The economic Trinity *is not* the immanent Trinity in that the former cannot fully mediate the mystery of the latter, though it does so truly and faithfully.[21] We must acknowledge on God's part a moment of accommodation, and on our part a moment of epistemic silence (doxology).

To summarize: I consider that a balanced perspective on the relationship between the immanent and economic Trinity maintains a *correspondence* between the two while rejecting their *strict identity*. There is a congruity, agreement, harmony between the trinitarian economy (God *pro nobis*) and God's eternal trinitarian being (God *in se*), but the ontological transcendence of the latter — antedating as it does a *creatio ex nihilo*, and especially signaled by the eternal preexistence of the Son of God — also guarantees its epistemological transcendence. While the Trinity we know in the economy corresponds to who God really is, this true and reliable knowledge does not exhaust the trinitarian mystery. The question that now remains is whether Moltmann achieves this balance in distinguishing the immanent and economic Trinity.

Moltmann on the Immanent/Economic Distinction

We noted earlier that prior to the emergence of his trinitarianism, Moltmann's project of rethinking God, world, and revelation in pervasively historical and eschatological categories led him to question the relevance of the classically-conceived immanent Trinity, since its ever-looming transcendence appeared to mitigate the historico-eschatological character of re-

---

21. A simple example of this principle would be as follows: We cannot assume that the relationship between the Father and the *incarnate* Son as witnessed in Scripture — and most intimately in John's Gospel — exhausts the incomprehensible glory of their relationship pre- and post-Incarnation (cf. John 17:5), though it faithfully attests to the fundamental nature and quality of that relationship in the mode of the Son's humanity.

demption (*TH* 55-58). This was the point on which Barth personally challenged Moltmann, and to which Moltmann confessed stupefaction as to how an immanent Trinity would fit into his basic theological program. In that same correspondence, however, Moltmann indicates the direction of an answer. Without weakening the thoroughly eschatological nature of redemption, his attempt would be to "so expound the economic Trinity that in the foreground, and then again in the background, it would be open to an immanent Trinity."[22] Yet Moltmann did not immediately follow up his own suggestion. Even in the emergence of his trinitarianism via the *theologia crucis* the question of the transcendent status of the Trinity dogged his theology, and Moltmann's formal endorsement of Rahner's axiom in *The Crucified God* only heightened the suspicion of many that any ontological Trinity was strictly identical with its economy, that for Moltmann the Trinity's provenance, like unto Hegel, was history itself (*CG* 240; cf. *TK* 160).

Moltmann only begins to address the issue of the immanent Trinity positively in the third work of his original trilogy, *The Church in the Power of the Spirit*. There, in modified terminology, he affirms the fundamental tenet guaranteed by this distinction:

> As God appears in history as the sending Father and the sent Son, so he must earlier have been in himself. The relation of the one who sends to the one sent as it appears in the history of Jesus thus includes in itself an order of origin within the Trinity, and must be understood as that order's historical correspondence. Otherwise there would be no certainty that in the messianic mission of Jesus we have to do with God himself. . . . The *missio ad extra* reveals the *missio ad intra*. The *missio ad intra* is the foundation for the *missio ad extra*. . . . From the Trinity of the sending of Jesus we can reason back to the Trinity in the origin, in God himself, so that — conversely — we may understand the history of Jesus as the revelation of the living nature of God (*CPS* 54).

The "Trinity in the origin" as condition of its sending is Moltmann's preferred term for the "immanent Trinity," since the latter had in *theo*logical conception become severed from the economy of redemption. Moltmann polemicizes here the classically-conceived immanent Trinity as a "closed circle" — perfect, self-satisfied, and shut up in heaven. It is this circle that he wants to ensure is open to the trinitarian economy, both *a quo* and *ad quem* (*CPS* 53-56). In an essay written the same year he concurs that the basic in-

---

22. Moltmann's letter to Barth of 4 April 1965 (Barth, *Letters,* 348).

tent of the economic/immanent distinction "developed with theological cogency"; he simply wants to rethink its logic further in light of the history of Christ.[23] But any doubt of Moltmann's basic orthodoxy on this trinitarian score ought from here on be allayed: the Trinity "in the sending" presupposes and corresponds to the Trinity "in the origin" — that is, to "the preexistent relationships in God himself."[24]

Moltmann's disparaging comments about the "immanent Trinity" in his mature trinitarian statement, therefore, including his attempt to reconceive and rename this reality, are clearly in reaction to the immanent Trinity as it has been metaphysically overlaid. But the theological method that posits Parmenides' One, states Moltmann, which is really a natural philosophy based on human experience of the world, is illegitimate in application to the Trinity:

> It imposes limitations on the triune God which are laid down, not by him, but by human experience of the world. This results in insoluble problems such as whether the impassible Son of the eternal Father can have suffered on the cross, whether the immutable Father can love his creation, and whether the eternal Spirit can liberate a world that is essentially dependent. The general metaphysical distinctions between God and the world become false if they are applied to the history of the Son. (*TK* 159)

It is principally a problem of attributes, Moltmann agrees, that confounds the relationship between the economic and immanent Trinity.

Thus Moltmann's embrace of Rahner's axiom, at least in its safest assertion (*TK* 160). God's nature can be read off the economy of redemption as a true revelation of deity. Such a theologic is implied in Moltmann's everpersistent question: What does this (the suffering of Christ, the history of the world, and so forth) mean for God? By this question Moltmann attempts to break the Augustinian impasse between divine works *ad intra,* which though differentiated are strictly inner-trinitarian, and works *ad extra,* which are executed indivisibly by the one divinity. He argues instead for the correspondence (*TK* 25), interchangeability (*TK* 95-99), and reciprocity of the two (*TK* 127), as, for example, regarding Christ's passion. Indeed, the works of the Trinity *ad extra* "correspond to the *passiones trinitatis ad intra*" (*TK* 160); God's actions in the world reveal true determinations and affections in God's

---

23. "The Trinitarian History of God" (1975), in *The Future of Creation,* trans. Margaret Kohl (Philadelphia: Fortress, 1979), 87-88.

24. Ibid., 84.

own being. It is in this sense that Moltmann talks — at times in an octave too high — about the cross reaching "right into the heart of the immanent Trinity" (*TK* 159); Christ's passion cannot be excluded from God's essential life and being, as though this were another "inner, self-sufficing life" (*TK* 108).[25]

Accordingly, Moltmann offers his own version of Rahner's axiom: "Statements about the immanent Trinity must not contradict statements about the economic Trinity. Statements about the economic Trinity must correspond to doxological statements about the immanent Trinity" (*TK* 154), to which he offers this clarifying commentary:

> we may not assume anything as existing in God himself which contradicts the history of salvation; and, conversely, may not assume anything in the experience of salvation which does not have its foundation in God. The principle that the doctrine of salvation and doxology do not contradict one another is founded on the fact that there are not two different Trinities. There is only one, single, divine Trinity and one, single divine history of salvation. The triune God can only appear in history as he is in himself, and in no other way. He is in himself as he appears in salvation history, for it is he himself who is manifested, and he is just what he is manifested as being. . . . Consequently we cannot find any trinitarian relationships in salvation history which do not have their foundation in the nature of the triune God, corresponding to him himself. . . . The true God is the God of truth, whose nature is eternal faithfulness and reliability. (*TK* 153-154)

Yet, unlike Rahner, Moltmann secures *trinitarian* transcendence. This he assured us of earlier in *The Church in the Power of the Spirit*, and is quite evident in his own criticism of Rahner's constriction of immanent and economic Trinity.[26] It is also confirmed by other key doctrinal indicators. For example, though he may advocate panentheistic perspectives on creation so as to tie divine agency more immanently therein, Moltmann nonetheless af-

---

25. For an example of a statement an octave too high, consider the following: "Before the world was, the sacrifice was already in God. No Trinity is conceivable without the Lamb, without the sacrifice of love, without the crucified Son. For he is the slaughtered Lamb glorified in eternity" (*TK* 83). Taken alone, this appears a careless assertion.

26. Concerning Rahner's constructive statement, Moltmann observes: "If the self-communication of the Father is the one and only direction of the Trinity, then a particular light is thrown on Rahner's thesis that 'The "economic" Trinity is the "immanent" Trinity and vice versa.' The process of self-communication is the very essence of God, and the divine essence consists of the trinitarian process of self-communication . . . [so that] the distinction between God and the world is in danger of being lost too" (*TK* 147-148).

Thomas R. Thompson

firms the essential tenet of *creatio ex nihilo* and thereby ensures the appropriate immanent/economic distinction.[27] And concerning the preexistence of the Son in his eternal Sonship, Moltmann is unequivocal. His repudiation of Arianism as a trinitarian heresy is enough to affirm this doctrine (*TK* 132ff.). For Moltmann there never was a time in which the Trinity was not; the perichoresis of Father, Son, and Spirit "exists in itself even without us."[28] Their eternal fellowship is the transcendent condition for the Trinity's manifestation in creation: "God loves the world with the very same love which he himself is in eternity" (*TK* 57).[29]

27. For his affirmation of *ex nihilo,* see, e.g., *God in Creation,* trans. Margaret Kohl (San Francisco: Harper & Row, 1985), 14, 74. Note also *TK* 107: "In order to understand the history of mankind as a history in God, the distinction between the world process and the inner-trinitarian process must be maintained and emphasized." Moltmann's panentheism is not of the same class as process theology. God does not create, long for "his Other," or suffer creation out of a deficiency of being (*TK* 23, 45).

28. *The Spirit of Life: A Universal Affirmation,* trans. Margaret Kohl (Minneapolis: Fortress, 1992), 290; hereafter cited within the text as *SL.*

29. As Moltmann notes, the Arian alternative is fraught with difficulties both soteriologically and practically: "A christology of this kind cannot provide any foundation for the redemption that makes full fellowship with God possible; it can only offer the basis for a new morality, for which Jesus' life provides the pattern and standard" (*TK* 133-134). Likewise the flip-heresy of Sabellianism: "Who or what the One God himself is cannot be perceived, because it cannot be communicated. Consequently the recognition of the manifestations of God *as . . .* cannot communicate any fellowship with God *himself* either" (*TK* 136). Trinitarian perichoresis as *fullness of fellowship* is precluded in both Arianism and Modalism because in their cases the economic Trinity is not the immanent Trinity; in each the former is relativized by an overweening monotheism, leading either to a depreciatory diffusion of Christ (Sabellianism) or to an idolatrous deification of creation via Christ (Arianism). Only the eternal perichoresis of Father, Son, and Spirit (i.e., the immanent Trinity), Moltmann contends, guarantees the glory of salvation:

> We have understood the unity of the divine trinitarian history as the open, unifying at-oneness of the three divine Persons in their relationships to one another. If this uniting at-oneness of the triune God is the quintessence of salvation, then its "transcendent primal ground" cannot be seen to lie in the one, single, homogeneous divine essence *(substantia),* or in the one identical, absolute subject. It then lies in the eternal perichoresis of the Father, the Son and the Spirit. The history of God's trinitarian relationships of fellowship corresponds to the eternal perichoresis of the Trinity. For this trinitarian history is nothing other than the eternal perichoresis of Father, Son and Holy Spirit in their dispensation of salvation, which is to say in their opening of themselves for the reception and unification of the whole creation (*TK* 157).

Moltmann clearly distinguishes inner-trinitarian love of "like for like" and extra-trinitarian love of "the Other" (*TK* 58-59, 106). Those who deny the eternal character of the former ne-

Where Moltmann challenges us in his understanding of the "immanent Trinity" is in his conceptual recasting of it in terms of doxology. Given what he considers its tainted metaphysical accretions, Moltmann prefers to speak of the immanent Trinity in terms of the patristic category of *theologia*. "Real theology [theologia]," he states, "which means the knowledge of God, finds expression in thanks, praise and adoration" (*TK* 152). Whereas the economic Trinity is the focus of kerygmatic and practical theology, doxological theology is the counterpart of the immanent Trinity — responsive and participatory praise not merely for God's good gifts, but for God's goodness *in se* as revealed by the *oeconomia Dei* (*TK* 152-153). This association of the immanent Trinity with doxology is given by Moltmann, not uncharacteristically, an eschatological twist:

> If it is the quintessence of doxology, then the doctrine of the immanent Trinity is part of eschatology as well. The economic Trinity completes and perfects itself to immanent Trinity when the history and experience of salvation are completed and perfected. When everything is "in God" and "God is all in all," then the economic Trinity is raised into and transcended in the immanent Trinity. What remains is the eternal praise of the triune God in his glory. (*TK* 161)

This statement, taken out of context, could easily be read in a reductionistic way, as though Moltmann were of that ilk who posits trinitarian self-constitution in history. But such an interpretation is clearly counter-manded by other Moltmann statements, including the following: "If the immanent Trinity is the counterpart of praise, then knowledge of the economic Trinity . . . precedes knowledge of the immanent Trinity. In the order of being it succeeds it" (*TK* 152-153). What one needs to recall in this connection is that apocalyptic dynamic of Moltmann's trinitarianism: the historical question of God is not that of God's existence *per se* (or *in se*), but of God's *monarchia* — divine rule or reign (economy) — which has been put at risk until the Son hands over the kingdom to the Father that God may be all in all (1 Cor. 15:28). *In this sense,* God's lordship has (voluntarily) become bound up with creation's salvation and will not be fully manifested, confirmed, or reconfirmed until the eschaton. Hence Moltmann's concern that the immanent Trinity be "open" — personally — not only for its sending,

---

cessitate creation as the object of divine love. Moltmann decries the deification of the world and humanity that this implies (*TK* 107). An eternal Trinity is the necessary transcendent condition of the salvific and exemplary love of God.

but also for its eschatological reunion or glorification inclusive of creation. The eternal immanent Trinity is not only manifested in the economic Trinity as a true revelation of God's nature (Love), but the economic Trinity, now embracing God's "Other," has real — consequential or subsequential — effects on God's personal (not essential) being. It is in this sense that Moltmann's hyperbolic statements about the cross being resident in the immanent Trinity are to be taken: "What happens on Golgotha reaches into the innermost depths of the Godhead, putting its impress on the trinitarian life in eternity" (*TK* 81; cf. 160-161).

Moltmann's final preference therefore is for a more flexible and nuanced trinitarian framework than what he considers afforded by the more traditional immanent/economic distinction. He proposes that we think in terms of the "monarchical," "historical," and "eucharistic" concepts of the Trinity, all of which presuppose a "primordial Trinity," and which are fulfilled in "trinitarian doxology" (*SL* 289-306).[30] Of these latter two, the primordial Trinity (formerly, the "Trinity in the origin") guarantees the ontological transcendence of the Trinity, whereas the doxological Trinity accentuates its epistemological transcendence. A brief word about the latter. Though the ontological transcendence of the Trinity is enough to preserve its mystery, the epistemological transcendence that Moltmann envisions as affirmed in doxology is also eschatologically oriented:

> This makes it clear to us that our human and historical concepts can never grasp or apprehend God himself, and it therefore leads us to fathomless wonder over God, in apophatic silence and in eschatological hope for the beatific vision. . . . It can be the theology of *faith* but not yet the theology of *sight*. It is *theologia crucis* but not yet *theologia gloriae*. It can be *theologia viatorum*, but is not yet *theologia patriae*, it is *theologia ektypa* not *archetypa*, for the glory of God has not yet appeared, and not yet is "the whole earth full of his glory" (Isa. 6.3) (*SL* 300).

---

30. States Moltmann, "We shall abandon the conceptual framework used hitherto — the pattern of essence and revelation, being and act, immanent and economic Trinity — because these dualities prove to be too wide-meshed a grid" (*SL* 290). Moreover, he considers that these distinctions derive from a general metaphysic rather than a specifically Christian theology (*SL* 343, n. 38). For Moltmann the "monarchical Trinity" is the Trinity in the sending, whose economic movement is from the Father, through the Son, in the Spirit (*SL* 290-295). The "historical Trinity" equates to his Joachimesque doctrine of the kingdoms (*SL* 295-298). And the "eucharistic Trinity" is the economic response or thankful return of creation in the Spirit, through the Son, to the Father (*SL* 298-301).

Trinitarian doxology is a spontaneous implicate of the eucharistic Trinity: thanksgiving erupts into worship and praise of God "for his own sake" as "our gaze passes beyond salvation history to the eternal essence of God himself" (*SL* 301-302). Trinitarian doxology, states Moltmann, "is the *Sitz im Leben* for the *concept of the immanent Trinity*" (*SL* 302). In this doxology we perceive the "eternal moment," an ecstatic awareness of who God is oblivious to time's ebb and flow. But such a vision does not entail an absolute absence of movement on God's part: "In trinitarian doxology the linear movements end, and the circular movements begin" (*SL* 303). And what are these circular movements? They are nothing other than "the self-circling and self-reposing movement of [trinitarian] *perichoresis*" (*SL* 304). Perichoresis is the last and glorious word for Moltmann on the immanent Trinity: "It is through the trinitarian doxology that we first perceive the immanent Trinity as it rests and revolves in itself, and whose unity lies in the eternal *community* of the divine Persons. The essential nature of the triune God *is* this community" (*SL* 309). And with this Moltmann has come full circle in his desire to understand the immanent Trinity as open to the economic, both *a quo* and *ad quem*.

Conclusion

Though it takes some sorting out, due mainly to his terminological and conceptual variation, Moltmann's understanding of the relationship between the economic and immanent Trinity achieves that appropriate balance we proposed in analysis of Rahner's axiom. These then are the main lines of Moltmann's understanding of the immanent Trinity in the context of his mature trinitarianism that must be acknowledged in any fair assessment of his theology.

There are, of course, other, collateral issues that critics routinely cite as evidence to support their suspicion that Moltmann is but a sheer economic trinitarian. For example, they will flag his self-styled panentheism as evidence of his heterodoxy, especially given his polemic against "monotheism."[31] Or they will highlight Moltmann's use of the kabbalistic notion of *Zimsum* as corroboration that he blurs the Creator/creature distinction.[32]

31. See, e.g., Molnar, *Divine Freedom*, 198, 209; Cooper, *Panentheism*, 237-258; Letham, *Trinity*, 301-304.
32. See, e.g., Molnar, *Divine Freedom*, 205; Cooper, *Panentheism*, 246-247, 52-54; cf. also Letham, *Trinity*, 300-301.

And they almost always identify his discussion of divine freedom, love, and the creative act (principally in *TK* 52-56) as a problematic model of the God-world relation.[33] While I think that each of these areas can be adjudicated in Moltmann's favor so as not to invalidate my analysis here, such an endeavor, to be fair, would require a whole other paper.

Many will, nonetheless, consider these lines of argument as too charitable a read of Moltmann. But I regard them as an interpretation that must enter into any fair consideration of Moltmann's trinitarian theology. This is the sort of theological dialogue that Daniel Migliore encouraged in his students, a hermeneutics of hospitality in pursuit of the triune God who has offered us the divine hospitality.

33. E.g., Molnar, *Divine Freedom*, 210-216; Cooper, *Panentheism*, 245-246; Letham, *Trinity*, 301-302.

God's Body or Beloved Other?
Sallie McFague and Jürgen Moltmann on God and Creation

David J. Bryant

Theological concern about the state of nature is a recent development in the history of Christian thought. One important stimulus for its emergence is an influential essay published in *Science* by Lynn White Jr. in 1967.[1] White argued that "Christianity bears a huge burden of guilt" because it helped to create attitudes that enabled human abuse of nature. The gist of his argument is that Christianity devalued nature by dissociating it from gods and spirits and separated humans from nature by identifying them as the image of a transcendent God. Theological responses to White's charge have often accepted his critique of the dualism in traditional Christianity and set about either eliminating or fundamentally revising concepts of divine transcendence. An emphasis on divine immanence has, of course, been the corollary to such moves. These theological constructions have often argued that their revisions are necessary to develop an adequate view of human responsibility for nature's well-being. In spite of such arguments, some Christian theologians have sought to develop a concern for creation while drawing heavily on traditional understandings of divine transcendence. Jürgen Moltmann is a case in point. Sallie McFague, on the other hand, has developed a far-reaching reconceptualization of transcendence, insisting that this move is necessary if Christianity is to face up to its ecological responsibility. Clearly not persuaded by such arguments, Moltmann has maintained that the traditional conception of God's otherness is a necessary ground for hope. At the

---

1. Lynn White, Jr., "The Historical Roots of Our Ecologic Crisis," *Science* 155 (1967): 1203-1207.

same time, he proposes some significant revisions of the doctrine of God in other respects, especially in relation to God's immanence.

We will be better positioned to assess such claims about what sort of concept of God is needed to provide a foundation for caring for creation after taking a closer look at how these theologians understand God's relation to the world. This paper, then, will examine how Moltmann and McFague conceive God's transcendence and immanence and the implications of their doctrines of God for human ecological responsibility.

Divine Transcendence

Eschatology provides the horizon for Moltmann's early development of the concept of God's transcendence. His theology of hope looked to a future not grounded in the realities of the present state of the world, a future opened by God's action in Jesus Christ and hence defined as the future of Jesus. God is a reality ahead of us, coming to us out of a future that breaks into the present, bringing what is genuinely new. In this framework, Moltmann conceives God's transcendence as divine futurity, which is not confined to the possibilities inherent in nature or history.[2]

Conceiving God in these terms has implications for other dimensions of transcendence as well. The God who stands ahead of us, beyond the limits of the world as presently experienced, must also be "behind" and "above" us. In other words, God must be a free Creator whose creative activity continues throughout the history of the universe if God is to be the source of a radically new creation. Thus, Moltmann unabashedly affirms the doctrine of *creatio ex nihilo* and also emphasizes the importance of continuous creation, wherein God is active in the geological and biological history of the earth as well as the history of humankind.[3]

God creates freely. Yet this does not mean that God creates arbitrarily. On the contrary, God's trinitarian existence is a life of love that cannot rest content to share love only among the persons of the Trinity. God's love seeks a genuine other, a reality that is not God, in order to express itself fully. The

2. Jürgen Moltmann, *Theology of Hope: On the Ground and the Implications of a Christian Eschatology,* trans. James W. Leitch (New York: Harper and Row, 1967), especially 216-224.

3. Jürgen Moltmann, *God in Creation: A New Theology of Creation and the Spirit of God,* trans. Margaret Kohl (San Francisco: Harper and Row, 1985), especially 72-79, 86-95, and 206-214.

work of creation, therefore, is free in the sense that it is the unhindered self-expression of the triune God who is love.[4] The otherness of creation does not entail full separation from God, however, for creation is connected to movement within God and the world's history unfolds through the reciprocal relations of Father, Son, and Spirit. The initial movement arises from the need for creation to have space and time to exist.[5] Thus, God limits Godself through self-contraction, which Moltmann develops along the lines of the Cabbalistic doctrine of *zimzum,* describing it as a sacrificial act on God's part.[6] Unlike Cabbalism, on the other hand, he develops this notion in a Trinitarian way: the Father creates; the Spirit is the sustaining energy and source of ongoing creativity; and the Son redeems and brings all to consummation through the activity of the Spirit. These concepts also lead us to the way Moltmann conceives God's immanence, to which we will return below.

Moltmann dares to provide detailed descriptions of the future of creation in its eschatological redemption, a boldness born of faith that the future is disclosed in the risen Christ. As he presents it (at length in *The Coming of God*), the ultimate goal of creation radically transcends anything we might discern in the present state of our world — specifically, a resurrection in which all creation shares. The work of the Spirit, acting as the Spirit of the crucified and risen Christ, will culminate in the Son's act of delivering a redeemed creation to God in the final realization of the divine purposes. The good news in Moltmann's vision is the redemption of everything in an eternal state of union with God. Furthermore, God redeems each being in its concrete, historical particularity. That is, all things retain their unique identity as constituted by their historical existence after they are transformed into a new, eternal being. Thus, historical existence is affirmed rather than eradicated by eternity.[7] The unqualified and universal sweep of Moltmann's affirmation regarding redemption is both breathtaking and puzzling, considering the range of beings within creation. Does he mean to include all the many viruses and other pathogens in the redemption of "all things"? If not, how and where would he draw the line? If so, how do they retain their historical identity when redeemed in a new order that does not include their es-

4. Jürgen Moltmann, *The Trinity and the Kingdom: The Doctrine of God,* trans. Margaret Kohl (San Francisco: Harper and Row, 1981), 52-60 and 105-108.

5. This concept appears throughout Moltmann's works, but see especially *The Trinity and the Kingdom,* 97-128.

6. *The Trinity and the Kingdom,* 108-111; and *God in Creation,* 86-93.

7. Jürgen Moltmann, *The Coming of God: Christian Eschatology,* trans. Margaret Kohl (Minneapolis: Fortress Press, 1996), 263-267 and 334-339.

sential operations? And does he mean to include each individual pathogen that has existed and will exist? God and the world will, at any rate, finally exist in such an intimate state of eternal togetherness in this hopeful scenario that, according to Moltmann, they will share in a perichoretic union, each indwelling the other. All things will be in God and God will be in all things.[8] Such an eschatological vision clearly requires a strong affirmation of transcendence. It is possible only if God is a genuine Other to creation, One who brings into being what was not, empowers and guides creation in its unfolding history, and ultimately transforms it in a consummation exceeding what creation could ever be on its own terms.

Sallie McFague develops a significantly different eschatological vision rooted in a different conception of God's transcendence. It is a bit misleading, in fact, to begin a discussion of McFague's view of God by looking first at the issue of transcendence, for she places primary emphasis on immanence. Furthermore, she devotes more attention to criticizing the dualism of traditional conceptions of divine transcendence than to developing her own understanding of transcendence. She argues that the traditional dualism of God and the world (expressed, for example, in the doctrine of *creatio ex nihilo*) supports pernicious dualisms of spirit and matter, humans and nature, and some humans over others. The result is a hierarchical vision of existence that legitimates domination and a devaluation of material existence.[9] The traditional Christian understanding of God's transcendence, along with its attendant dualisms, is thus part of what contemporary Christians must reformulate in a fundamental way if we are to find resources for genuine liberation within Christian faith. Part of the needed reformulation involves highlighting divine immanence as the central insight about God for our time. There are, nevertheless, at least three ways in which she delineates a place for God's transcendence.

One approach derives from her use of metaphors, which she frequently reminds her readers are combinations of dissimilars that, at least when truly alive with the shock of new insight, resist any attempt to define their meaning with precision. They are invitations to look at things in a certain way rather than concepts with clear boundaries. One of her favorite expressions for underscoring this point is that a metaphor both is and is not true; and

8. Jürgen Moltmann, "The World in God or God in the World? Response to Richard Bauckham," in *God Will Be All in All: The Eschatology of Jürgen Moltmann*, ed. Richard Bauckham (Edinburgh: T&T Clark, 2005), 41; and *Coming of God*, 335.

9. Sallie McFague, *Models of God: Theology for an Ecological, Nuclear Age* (Philadelphia: Fortress Press, 1987), 109-112.

one cannot draw a clear line between the is and is not. Anything we may say about God, then, can at best throw light on limited dimensions of the God-world relationship. Moreover, God is not an existent within the world of existents, so that our language, which derives from and is most at home dealing with the realm of finite realities, cannot adequately speak of God.[10] On the contrary, we must take metaphors from the world of experience and apply them to what is beyond all experiences of finite existents when we attempt to speak about God. To avoid the idolatry of confusing our conceptions with divine reality, we must remember that God always is more than whatever we may think or say. Thus, even if we use a marvelously apt metaphor which provides true insight into God's way with the world, it is also not true.[11] This caveat forms a strong foundation for avoiding the mistake of confusing human conceptions with God, and it clearly points to a sense in which God is transcendent, but it also leaves one a bit uncertain about what McFague really is (and is not) affirming about God when she develops her metaphorical doctrine of God. A realization that she is talking about how God relates to the world, rather than God in Godself, may alleviate the uncertainty somewhat; but some ambiguity still remains.[12]

Another form of divine transcendence to which McFague appeals is spatio-temporal in nature: that is, we cannot limit God to the present or to our corner of the universe, for the divine life encompasses all times and all places.[13] Moreover, the future is open, and the Christian paradigm gives Christians a vision that can motivate action for a better future, a new creation effected by our actions.[14] This is similar to Moltmann's conviction that eschatological hope can motivate action for a better present. Whereas Moltmann defines the future as the future of Jesus, however, McFague does not perceive it as oriented toward an ultimate fulfillment. McFague's criti-

10. See especially Sallie McFague, *Life Abundant: Rethinking Theology and Economy for a Planet in Peril* (Minneapolis: Fortress Press, 2001), 3-24.

11. Sallie McFague, *The Body of God: An Ecological Theology* (Minneapolis: Fortress Press, 1993), 131-136; and *Models of God*, 33-39 and 60-61.

12. She says at one point that "we do not know" whether "the world is God's body or . . . God is present to us in the world." On the other hand, the metaphor of the world as God's body may fit with an understanding of the Christian faith for our time and may prove "illuminating and fruitful when lived in for a while." *Models of God*, 60. To claim a metaphor is true, then, seems to amount to saying it is useful (which includes being consistent with the best knowledge of the day). To say it is Christian requires making a case for its conformity with what one takes to be the meaning of Christian faith for our time.

13. McFague, *Body of God*, 133.

14. McFague, *Body of God*, 198-202.

David J. Bryant

cism of traditional theology suggests that she would regard Moltmann's vision as anthropocentric and incompatible with an affirmation of the importance of historical existence.[15] She appears to hold a position similar to Catherine Keller's, who argues that transforming all individual beings into an eternal existence, thereby recreating them into something other than they were as historical beings, ultimately renders inconsequential what they were.[16] Moltmann tries to address this issue by insisting that the fulfillment of all things comes at the end of a history between God and the world, wherein both become what they are even in eternity. Keller's critique, however, has merit; for Moltmann needs to clarify and provide support for his eschatology by engaging in a more careful exploration of how temporally finite beings might become eternal without losing their identities.[17] In any case, for McFague, divine transcendence in relation to the future has to do with the temporal future of a finite universe, and hope is focused on the whole rather than individuals. The future is open, and we may hope for better tomorrows, transient realizations of God's will for creation, but there are no guarantees or ultimate consummations.

McFague also alludes to a third dimension of divine transcendence when examining the difference between the operations of nature and ethical norms for human life. In this context, she introduces Jesus as a parable of God and a model for Christian life, especially in his association with the poor and marginalized. The weak and vulnerable, for whom nature shows no regard, are for Christians where one especially discerns the presence of God. A disclosure coming from beyond what we can discover in nature is the source of this discernment — one that points to a transcendent source for this ethical demand.[18]

15. McFague, *Life Abundant*, 158-159.

16. Catherine Keller, "The Last Laugh: A Counter-Apocalyptic Meditation on Moltmann's *Coming of God*," *Theology Today* 59 (1997): 385-386.

17. We should acknowledge that those who deny a transcendent fulfillment of creation also wrestle with a similar problem. Since the earth will one day be destroyed by the death of the sun, and the universe will die out in a big freeze or a big crunch, one whose expectations are confined to the possibilities within the universe may finally wonder about the ultimate meaning of existence. The earth and the rest of the universe have billions of years ahead of them, of course, and one may enjoy life as a gift even with the awareness of nature's final fate. Still, nature is temporally finite and is not likely to bear up well under the weight of ultimate concern. For both positions, what we do now matters for present and future generations; and both face challenges when articulating meaningful connections between what we are now and the ultimate fate of the universe.

18. McFague, *Body of God*, 160-161 and 171-174.

These theologians represent two distinctively different approaches to Christian tradition. Moltmann makes extensive use of traditional understandings of transcendence, though he reformulates them by integrating them into a vision of creation existing in its time and space within a Creator who has made room for it — a panentheistic framework of sorts. McFague, on the other hand, wishes to offer a more fundamental transformation of the tradition. She proposes a form of panentheism in which God's otherness is defined by the insistence that God, understood as "reality and the source of reality,"[19] is beyond all concepts, and calls humans to practice an inclusive love not evident in the rest of nature. Transcendence largely serves to denote the inability of humans to capture God for their own ends, the open horizon of the future, and the unique responsibilities humans have among earth creatures. Moltmann articulates a definite hope for the ultimate fate of creation, which McFague cannot do. Speaking about the future of earth's environment, she notes at the end of one major work, *The Body of God*, that there is a very good chance that human societies will not act sufficiently to prevent the "decay of our planet."[20] Whether the long-term condition of nature is better or worse than this sad scenario depends on humans; and there is no consummation that will redeem creation (or humans). Although Moltmann's view of transcendence leads to a quite different conclusion, it does not preclude the possibility that humans will, in fact, destroy the earth.[21] Beyond any such catastrophic consequences, however, lies a redemption brought about by God, the One who can ultimately overcome the worst that humans can do. Indeed, the One who has the power to bring about the world *ex nihilo* also has the power to recreate it in a way that preserves what has been while overcoming the evil that has been interwoven with it. Moltmann's descriptions of the final triumph of God's purposes appear to exceed what any mortal should claim to know. On the other hand, the hope for a consummation of all things coming from beyond nature and history is not necessarily tied to the specific details of Moltmann's eschatological vision.

What about the practical consequences of these views of transcendence and hope? Is one or the other better for grounding action on behalf of a suffering natural world? McFague's view does underscore the importance of how we treat nature, for our decisions will lead to consequences from which

19. McFague, *Life Abundant*, 18.
20. McFague, *Body of God*, 207.
21. McFague, *Coming of God*, 234.

there can be no escape, either now or in an ultimate consummation of God's will for creation. Moltmann's theology, on the other hand, may be vulnerable to the charge that it weakens motivation for addressing our environmental crisis because it ultimately looks for a deliverance that does not depend on us. Furthermore, his position threatens to dissolve the importance of history since time is overcome in eternity. First appearances can be deceiving, however, and that may be so in these theologies. Alongside the importance of human action that we see in McFague's approach, we must place the possible enervation of motivation arising from a potential pessimism about the future. One may be tempted to give up in a state of despair in view of human societies' apparent inability to comprehend fully or respond adequately to the fate we are currently shaping. What can an individual, or even groups, hope to accomplish in the face of the intransigence of large political and economic collectives? Moltmann's vision of hope provides a sense that all is not lost. This may prove important for motivation if we can also make sense of his insistence that what we do now is conserved in eternity.

In part, what is at issue is whether everything we do must be regarded as of ultimate importance in order for us to be motivated to make fundamental changes in the way we deal with creation. The argument that hope for eternity undermines efforts to address environmental concerns draws its force from the assumption that to act we need to assume that only our deeds can make a difference. There does not appear to be any good reason to regard this assumption as well founded, however, especially in light of the fact that many people who have hope for a genuinely transcendent future are active in addressing environmental issues. Moreover, Moltmann himself emphasizes that caring for creation is a fundamental concern for Christians in our time. He leaves no doubt that addressing environmental problems is a critical aspect of being faithful, whatever one may hope will be the ultimate destiny of creation. He grounds this, in part, on his conception of God's immanence.

Divine Immanence

Moltmann and McFague both argue that God's presence in creation provides a critical foundation for our sense of responsibility toward nature. Thus, they are alike in their emphasis on the importance of God's immanence. They differ, however, in the way they conceive and develop their conceptions of God's presence in creation. Whereas Moltmann develops a Trinitarian approach to divine immanence, drawing much from Christian tradition, McFague depends more on a metaphorical approach that proposes new images for a Christian understanding of the God-world relation that is adequate for our contemporary situation.

McFague grounds her conception of God's immanence on a central metaphor: the world is God's body. The universe is God's embodied existence, which we can envision in terms of our own experience of embodied being. On the other hand, God's body is unlike any bodies we know since it includes all that exists.[22] Moreover, this is a metaphorical rather than a conceptual claim, so we must not press the point too far. It is difficult to know when we have done so, and hence difficult to know exactly how to appraise this image of God and the world. McFague does not mean that the world is literally God's body, so she does not wish to defend all implications one might draw from this affirmation when understood as a concept. Nevertheless, she is proposing the metaphor as a way we should truly regard the world in its relation to God, and as a real guide to action. Even if it remains rather vague at the conceptual level, then, it is still possible to judge it in terms of its ability to connect people with the world in a coherent, comprehensive, and fruitful way, that is, in terms of pragmatic criteria.[23]

Among the several images that emerge naturally from this root metaphor are the pictures of God as the spirit of the world and of the world as the material form of God's being.[24] We must continue to remind ourselves that these are metaphors, for as concepts they encourage a pantheistic understanding of God (which McFague eschews). Thus, McFague affirms that God has a material form of existence; yet she also denies that we should directly, unambiguously identify God and the world. She proposes that we conceive of God as the animating spirit within the world but denies that we should think of God as confined within the world. Rather, we should approach these metaphors as limited ways of imaging God's intimate presence within creation, with the result that we experience nature as sacred, possessing intrinsic value, and worthy of our love and protection. Indeed, at one point she identifies having faith in God with regarding the world as possessing intrinsic goodness.[25]

The sacred quality of material creation receives further support through

22. McFague, *Models of God*, 69-78; and *Body of God*, 16-22, 131-141, and *passim*.
23. McFague, *Models of God*, 26-27.
24. McFague, *Body of God*, 141-150.
25. McFague, *Life Abundant*, 133.

McFague's rejection of traditional conceptions of God's creative activity that, she argues, lead to a dualistic conception of matter and spirit. Thus, she rejects the doctrine that God created the world out of nothing.[26] Her alternative is to conceive of God as giving birth to creation, for the universe, "expressive of God's very being," comes from God as from a "womb." This presents a somewhat odd picture of God giving birth to Her own body, but McFague appeals once more to the metaphorical nature of her argument, insisting that what she is proposing "is that the birth metaphor is both closer to Christian faith and better for our world than the alternative picture."[27]

McFague also proposes a number of other metaphors that emphasize God's intimate presence in and to the world. Three are especially important for her: God as mother, lover, and friend.[28] These images are in one sense not new at all. It is possible to find examples of each metaphor in the Christian tradition, particularly in the tradition's mystical representatives. Further, a well-known hymn among Protestant evangelicals intones, "What a friend we have in Jesus," thereby illustrating the ease with which one might understand McFague's metaphors in an individualistic manner. Such a construal would represent a serious misunderstanding of McFague's position, however, as she makes abundantly clear. Acknowledging that God as lover can be understood in individualistic terms, for example, she emphasizes that God loves the world rather than simply individuals, and we in turn love God by loving creation as a whole.[29]

Moltmann grounds his development of God's immanence on the cross and resurrection of Jesus. In *The Theology of Hope,* the resurrection tends to predominate since the logic of promise and fulfillment, manifest in the history of Israel but revealed especially in the resurrection of Jesus, is at the heart of that work. Moltmann's later works, however, show more concern to avoid the impression that hope expresses an easy optimism that inadequately faces the world's suffering. Thus, *The Crucified God,* his next major work, argued that the one who was raised was the crucified Son of God. In the cross, God became one with the Godforsaken, experiencing abandonment and death, and the resurrection reveals that this is the necessary way to the future of hope. Thus, resurrection is connected with the way of the cross and reveals the necessary path of active hope until the final eschatological

---

26. McFague, *Models of God,* 109-110.
27. McFague, *Models of God,* 110.
28. McFague, *Models of God,* 91-180.
29. McFague, *Models of God,* 128-129.

fulfillment of history, when all provisional fulfillments are taken up into a completion transcending what history can effect. The critical point here is that history's denouement depends on God's presence to creation in the life and death of Jesus.[30]

The significance of God's presence in Jesus is dependent on God's relationship to the world as its Creator. Moltmann conceives of God as a transcendent Creator, as noted above, but there are also intimate connections between God and creation. In the first place, God makes space and time for creation by an act of self-limitation in which God suffers the withdrawal of God's being in order to allow the existence of an independent other. Thus, creation exists within God, but in its own space and time. The motivation for creation, God's desire for a genuine other to love, becomes the dynamic behind God's history with the world. The act of creation, then, is open to deeper realizations of God's love in history, especially the life and death of Jesus, which point, in turn, to the ultimate fulfillment of creation in the Eschaton.[31]

God's presence as Creator also takes the form of continuous creation, an ongoing activity of God in nature through the Spirit. Moltmann ties the Spirit's continuing creative action to the evolutionary development of life. The dynamics of evolution show that the universe is an open system in which we see increasing levels of communication.[32] The Spirit is at the heart of this process, not through "supernatural" activity but through "a silent and a secret" suffering action that communicates new possibilities to the world.[33] Moltmann asserts, "Through the energies of his Spirit, [God] is present in the world and immanent in each individual system." At the same time, this is possible because the universe is open to a transcendent God, so that we cannot conceive God's immanence without also including divine transcendence. In Moltmann's words, "[I]t is . . . impossible to conceive of God's evolutive immanence in the world without his world-transcendence."[34]

God's action in the world is Trinitarian in nature and anticipates a more profound presence in Jesus, who, along with Israel's prophetic expectations, grounds hope for an even greater presence of God at the end of history. It is

---

30. Jürgen Moltmann, *The Crucified God: The Cross of Christ as the Foundation and Criticism of Christian Theology*, trans. R. A. Wilson and John Bowden (New York: Harper and Row, 1974), 53-75 and *passim*.

31. Moltmann, *The Trinity and the Kingdom*, 108-128; and *God in Creation*, 86-93.

32. Moltmann, *God in Creation*, 205.

33. Moltmann, *God in Creation*, 211.

34. Moltmann, *God in Creation*, 206.

God's existence as Father, Son, and Spirit that enables the transcendent Creator to be also the immanent Son of God and Spirit. Their relationships have a dynamic character tied to creation's history, so that God also experiences glory in the final consummation. Moltmann has a fondness for describing the eschatological fulfillment of God's purposes as a time when God will be "all in all," for that phrase envisions a full interpenetration of God and the world.[35]

Caring for Creation

Human connections with the environment exercise a significant (but not exclusive) influence on both theologians and come to the surface frequently in the development of their conceptions of God. Both express a central concern to present a conception of God — and humans as the image of God — that will provide groundwork for a strong environmental ethic; and both are convinced that aspects of the Christian tradition have hindered, if not blocked, the development of such an ethic. They do not always agree about which aspects have been problematic, however. Indeed, Moltmann incorporates elements of the tradition that McFague rejects as an obstacle to genuine concern for the natural world. More specifically, Moltmann maintains a form of dualism in his understanding of God's transcendence and of the ultimate destiny of creation, whereas McFague argues that such dualisms undermine our sense of responsibility for creation. Moltmann, on the other hand, argues that faith in God's power as the transcendent Creator and Redeemer, who will ultimately bring about the consummation of creation whatever our failures, is important for hope that will motivate action even in the face of discouraging realities. Each position makes some important points, but neither is fully convincing since connections between action and overarching worldviews are more complex than these arguments seem to allow. This complexity is apparent in many cases where people with different fundamental convictions join forces to address social issues, such as action on behalf of civil rights or international peace.

McFague is surely right that there are forms of dualism that undermine concern for the state of the earth. For example, the form of dualism present in the apocalypticism of the *Left Behind* series of novels has apparently encouraged some evangelicals to oppose the growing environmental move-

35. Moltmann, *Coming of God*, 334-336.

ment within the evangelical wing of Christianity. On the other hand, the increasing concern for the environment in evangelical circles is a sign that some conservative Christians, who remain strongly dualistic in their understanding of God and the world, have found resources within their faith to ground a sense of responsibility for the state of creation. The existence and apparent vitality of such groups make problematic blanket assertions that all dualisms are antithetical to environmental action.

Moltmann makes a good point about the importance of hope as a ground for action. The conviction that God is ultimately in control of creation and will redeem it, whatever our failures, would certainly be a ground for hope. But would such hope work against a sense of responsibility for the state of the world? If by sense of responsibility one means a belief that earth's ultimate fate rests on human shoulders, without expectation of redemption from beyond and in spite of us, then we must say yes. Also, anyone who thinks that belief in a transcendent redemption of creation would dissolve the integrity and importance of finite beings and temporal events would be inclined to answer in the affirmative. It is unclear, however, why we need to take human actions and temporal events as ultimately determinative to have a sense that we are responsible for our world here and now. Even those who do not believe that earth's destiny finally rests on human shoulders may nevertheless have a strong sense that we are responsible for what we do to creation. They develop and locate their sense of responsibility in a way that differs from McFague, as we see in Moltmann's theology, but they can possess a sense of responsibility nonetheless.

To be sure, those who believe that God wants the earth to careen toward disaster, setting the context for an ultimate, apocalyptic divine intervention, would not be likely to share this sense of responsibility. Their perspective arises from combining a belief in God's otherness with a particular vision of history, not simply from belief in God's otherness. The issue turns, then, not on what one thinks about the nature of God, as an isolated article of faith, but on the larger context within which believers place their conception of God and the particular ways in which they make connections between their theology and their situation in the world. Moltmann makes connections, through his conception of God's immanence and his affirmation that what happens in history is conserved as well as transformed in redemption, which can ground an active concern for creation. He also provides a clear basis for hope; but does this mean that McFague's position does not?

It is apparent that there is room for despair in the worldview that McFague develops, for she seems, at times, to be on the verge of it. On the other hand, the existence of active environmentalists who share her outlook would seem unlikely if despair were its necessary result. She does, after all, hold to the conviction that the future is open, that we can make a difference, that we must make a difference if we want a livable world. It should not be a surprise, then, that many environmentalists do not have hope for the ultimate redemption envisioned by Moltmann, yet remain active and hopeful in their efforts to build a better future. Again, we need to acknowledge that it is too simple to draw a straight line from a worldview, in this case one lacking hope for a transcendent redemption, to consequences for action. The larger framework within which this article of faith exists is determinative.

Conclusion

McFague and Moltmann share a desire to be responsible to the tradition and the best insights of our time. At the same time, they each approach tradition and the current situation in fundamentally different ways. Moltmann grounds his theology primarily in the witness of the tradition to Jesus as the Christ, along with Israel's experience of God's promise, and uses the history of theology and contemporary perspectives as important ingredients in his Trinitarian theological construction. McFague wishes to begin with contemporary experiences of God's love and allow the tradition, especially as recorded in the Bible but also including the history of theology, to serve as examples of how one can express, in terms appropriate to today, our own experience of God. As a result, contemporary understandings of humans and the world (as expressed in the natural sciences and certain political philosophies, for example) exercise a far more determinative influence in her theology. Still, she does insist on the importance of continuity with the tradition. For example, she maintains that Christians must look to Jesus as a parable of God and a normative guide for human life.

These theologies face some important questions, only a few of which I can list here: Does McFague draw even more from the tradition than she acknowledges when she stresses the need for solidarity with the poor and when she describes the spiritual experience that each generation seeks to express in their own terms as the love of God? Does she manage to avoid some of the dangers of pantheism which she expressly wishes to avoid? Does she trim Christian hope to the point that we are in danger of feeling trapped in our present horizons? Does her desire to emphasize human responsibility lead her to overestimate human power and control? Does Moltmann adequately come to terms with the scientific understanding of evolution in his understanding of God's continuing creation? Does his conceptualization of the ultimate triumph of God's purposes presume to know more than finite mortals can? Has he boldly rushed in where the best representatives of Christian faith have wisely feared to go? Does his conception of the redemption of history truly anticipate its redemption rather than its elimination?

As Christians discuss and debate these and other important questions, many will also be grappling with how to assess the pragmatic significance of theological options. Moltmann and McFague are concerned about the consequences of theological claims, and both are concerned about the state of nature. This examination of these two theologians has provided evidence that pragmatic criteria alone will not serve as a helpful way of discriminating between these (and undoubtedly other) theologies, at least when we are considering what will motivate and shape caring for creation. The gain in realizing this fact is that people with different theological positions can recognize that they should avoid claiming to possess the one kind of theology that is necessary for addressing our ecological crisis and, when working to improve our relationship to the natural environment, can focus instead on building coalitions with those who share their concerns. From an environmentalist perspective, it is encouraging that people who are drawn to such different worldviews can still share in this common cause. This fact does not make theological differences unimportant, for they possess other dimensions than their environmental implications, but it does mean that people with diverse theologies can work together as they continue to engage in conversation about their fundamental convictions regarding God, the world, and human life. In their theological give and take, they would be well served to realize that quite different theologies can have positive environmental impacts and to look, in such cases, for other ways to assess theological claims.

In Search of a Non-Violent Atonement Theory: Are Abelard and Girard a Help, or a Problem?

Gregory Anderson Love

Killing, and Being Killed, as Salvific

The Frankish king Charlemagne chafed with imperial ambitions for the Saxon territories to his north. For thirty-three years he waged a campaign of terror to subdue the Saxons and force them, at point of death, to be baptized into his Latin form of Christianity.[1] In 782 CE, Charlemagne took forty-five hundred Saxons as prisoners and had them beheaded in a single day. In 804 CE, he deported ten thousand Saxons into Frankish territories.

The Carolingian theologians shifted the meaning of the Eucharist from a celebration of the sanctifying powers found in Jesus' incarnate and resurrected life to a focus on his tortured death. This crucified Christ was useful for subduing the Saxons, for he was presented as both victim and judge of the Saxons' rebellious violence against the Franks. If the Saxons remained unrepentant for their roles in Christ's death and against the Franks, they were killers of Christ and their military violation was sanctified.[2]

Three centuries later in 1095, Pope Urban II transmuted warrior bloodletting from unequivocal sin to devotional act. In calling warriors to carry out the First Crusade, he made killing enemies of Christ and of the Church a

---

1. 772-805 CE. In 800 CE, Charlemagne (742-814 CE) was crowned head of the new Holy Roman Empire.

2. For the Franks' change in the theological meaning of the Eucharist and the colonizing use of Christianity, see chapter 9, "The Expulsion of Paradise," in Rita Nakashima Brock and Rebecca Parker, *Saving Paradise: How Christianity Traded Love of This World for Crucifixion and Empire* (Boston: Beacon Press, 2008).

holy act which can free a sinner from all penance for sin. Within this context of knightly violence and shifting Eucharistic interpretation, *the giving of death became the means by which a person enters into life.* If a crusader kills, he wreaks vengeance for Christ's murder on God's behalf and imitates the terror of Christ's judgment upon those souls unrepentant for their role in his execution. If a crusader dies in battle, he shows a commitment up to death for God's honor, displaying love and devotion to Jesus for his gift of death.[3]

St. Anselm provided a new theological model of the salvation story which could incorporate such changes in ritual meaning and ethics. Anselm knew of the Paschasian debate over the Eucharist as the "real presence" of the crucified body.[4] He also lived in a cultural context in which serfs owed obedient loyalty and honor to feudal lords; an emerging monetary system began to burden the same peasants with overwhelming debt; and church officials were becoming at ease with a warrior aristocracy.[5]

In *Cur Deus Homo* (1098 CE), Anselm interpreted human sin as destroying God's beautiful creation and, through the insolence of such vandalism, as a failure to appropriately honor God. Our sins — both as personal act and original nature — are too grave for self-punishment to be sufficiently compensatory. As an act of mercy on behalf of his kin, however, Jesus offered to God the gift of his death, a self-offering on the cross which pleased God and earned a reward sufficient to pay all of humanity's debt. Through this gift of death, humanity was restored to fellowship with God and granted new life.

3. On Pope Urban II and his call for the First Crusade, see ibid., chapter 10, "Peace by the Blood of the Cross," esp. 262-265. Bernard, asked by the Pope to preach widely in support of the Second Crusade in 1146, coined the phrase *malecide* (killing an evildoer) to replace *homicide* (killing a human being) to reflect the new interpretation of crusading violence as a sign of love and devotion to God rather than a spurning of God's law. See ibid., 285.

4. In the 830s, Carolingian theologian Paschasius Radbertus wrote a tract on the Lord's blood and flesh, arguing that the same flesh that suffered on the cross is "the body given for many," the "blood shed." In the Eucharist, "the lamb is sacrificed daily on the altar by the priest in memory of the sacred passion" (quoted in ibid., 235). Echoing Isaiah 53, the Roman rite spoke of Christ as "a pure victim, a holy victim, an unspotted victim" (ibid., 234).

5. On the latter, for example, while Anselm took refuge with the Pope from English threats, he and Urban once camped out together to watch Roger of Apulia lay siege to Capua. The Archbishop of Canterbury could enjoy war as great entertainment. See Anthony Bartlett, *Cross Purposes: The Violent Grammar of the Christian Atonement* (Harrisburg, PA: Trinity Press, 2001), 95; and Brock and Parker, *Saving Paradise*, 266. On Anselm's atonement theology linked to the Crusades, see James Carroll, *Constantine's Sword: The Church and the Jews* (Boston: Houghton Mifflin Press, 2001), 284-289. In my forthcoming book on atonement, I reconfigure Anselm's theory toward a nonviolent model, but this exceeds our topic here.

When the warriors of the First Crusade reached Constantinople, Anna Comnena, daughter of Emperor Alexius I, described this fusion of imperial violence, self-sacrificing devotion, and atonement theology seen in the priests who accompanied the knights:

> [A] Latin Barbarian will at the same time handle sacred objects, fasten a shield to his left arm and grasp a spear in his right. He will communicate the Body and Blood of the Divinity and meanwhile gaze on bloodshed and become himself a "man of blood."[6]

But the Eastern Christians, like the Saxons three centuries before, were not the only ones to resist these reinterpretations of killing, Eucharist, and Christ's death.

Abelard's Suffering Christ and the God of Love

Peter Abelard rejected crusading and Anselm's atonement theology as unethical and unreasonable. Abelard had different understandings of God's character and of the source of divine-human estrangement. Abelard perceived the divine as a God of love and clemency, a merciful father rather than a stern lord of judgment and punishment. Further, God's love is eternally boundless, even for sinful humanity. Such perfect love is not diminished by sinful acts, nor in need of payment to restore its honor; it is everlastingly complete and generous. The problem is not sin's accumulated debt, but its hardening effect upon the human heart.

God saves by moving the human heart from fear to love, and the death of Jesus makes this change of heart possible. While God displays God's compassion for humanity through Jesus' words and actions, the death of Jesus creates a deeper love for God than would have been possible without it. Jesus proves the extent of his, and of God's, love for humanity *by his willingness to endure anything on humanity's behalf,* including his suffering and death. Seeing Jesus as a victim undergoing unjust suffering, sinful witnesses may feel compassionate *pity* for Jesus as tortured victim, mixed with a sense of *guilt* for their role in his death, plus a desire to seek forgiveness, and make amends and act differently. Salvation thus occurs when compassion and contrition before the flogged Christ move the sinner from self-love to a pure,

---

6. Quoted in Brock and Parker, *Saving Paradise*, 272.

selfless love. Love is therefore defined as a willingness to suffer unto death for the sake of the "other," as Christ did. God illumines the true nature of this love and enkindles hearts for love by sending the Son not only to live compassionately, but above all to die holding such a virtuous, selfless love.[7]

Since J. Denny Weaver's *The Nonviolent Atonement,*[8] numerous recent theological works across the spectrum have searched for a nonviolent model of the means by which God reconciles humanity to Godself and to the created order. They have sought to repudiate the marriage of imperial violence, devotional self-sacrifice, and the salvific meaning of the cross which developed in Christian history between Charles Martel and Anselm, and continues up to this day. Could Abelard, who rejected crusading and the compensatory understanding of Christ's death, guide us today to such a nonviolent theory of atonement? In his 2001 book *Cross Purposes: The Violent Grammar of Christian Atonement,* Anthony Bartlett argues for a nonviolent, neo-Abelardian model rooted in Rene Girard's theories of sacrifice and mimetic violence. In sharp contrast, in their 2008 work *Saving Paradise: How Christianity Traded Love of This World for Crucifixion and Empire,* Rita Nakashima Brock and Rebecca Parker identify Abelard as even more problematic than Anselm in wedding notions of salvation with violence. I find both sets of arguments to be flawed. While Brock and Parker are right that Abelard and Bartlett are more dangerous than even Anselm, the Abelardian model contains truths effective in guiding us today to a nonviolent theory of atonement. Bartlett's theory unwittingly and ironically fuses salvation with violence, precisely because his theory depends upon a male view of sin and salvation. His book exhibits no cognizance of feminist theory or theology. However, his theory also has insights, gained from Abelard, needed for an atonement theory which severs the fused relation of violence and redemption introduced in medieval Europe and continued to the present.

Abyssal Compassion and the Death of Christ

Bartlett uses the theories of the early Freud and anthropologist Rene Girard to argue that at the heart of cultural origins lies collective violence. Behind and beneath cultures is "a panhistorical conspiracy simultaneously to com-

---

7. For Brock and Parker's discussion of Abelard's alternative atonement model, see *Saving Paradise,* chapter 11, "Dying for Love," esp. 291-298.

8. J. Denny Weaver, *The Nonviolent Atonement* (Grand Rapids: Eerdmans, 2001).

mit murder, regret it, and make use of it."[9] Freud and Girard identify rivalry as the root of violence. Humans imitate not only other people's behaviors, but also their desires: We notice and find enticing what others find attractive. However, multiple persons or groups all attempting to possess the same desirable objects — certain foods, particular mates, fruitful territories — leads to continuous cycles of conflict fueled by envy and impotent hatred.[10]

As persons or groups imitate a respected role model in seeking a prized object, and fight over that object, a new imitative behavior emerges which astonishes all involved by quelling the all-out warfare. Someone attacks a victim who is singled out by an arbitrary aspect of difference or weakness, and the others imitatively join in the bloodshed. While previously, tribes were focused on obtaining a desired good, and they perceived multiple enemies, the turn to violence against the marked person or minority group deflects attention from the original object and the base traits it brought out. "He," or "She," or "They" are the source of our violence! The peace which follows the collective killing, so unexpected, is deemed sacred, and is the first cultural moment.

The ritual of sacrifice — whether of animals or humans — repeats the original crisis of violence and its resolution. Victims are chosen who are similar to yet distant from the majority in the group. Religion — the sacred, the gods of mythology — helps the culture to remember the founding crisis, its violence, and the following group rules about violence, while forgetting the fact that the violence upon the victim is unjustified murder.[11]

The story of the exchange of a violent death upon a surrogate for the

9. Bartlett, *Cross Purposes*, 7. Freud proposes an original act of murder, determined simply by rivalry, which then draws a genuine corporate complicity in bloodletting. See Freud, *Totem and Taboo: Resemblances between the Psychic Lives of Savages and Neurotics*, trans. A. A. Brill (New York: Vintage Books, 1946), and *Moses and Monotheism*, trans. Katherine Jones (New York: Vintage Books, 1967).

10. Mimetic desire is found not only in humans but across the biological spectrum. For its documentation with guppies, see Lee Alan Dugatkin, *The Imitation Factor: Evolution Beyond the Gene* (New York: The Free Press, 2000).

11. For Bartlett's discussion of Girard's theory of mimetic desire, violence, scapegoating, and religion, see *Cross Purposes*, 6-11, 27-37. Girard's anthropological theory of the social function of religion to clarify taboos and maintain social cohesion through identification of group boundaries — "us" versus "them" — shares similarities to Durkheim's. See Emile Durkheim, *The Elementary Forms of the Religious Life*, trans. Joseph Swan (New York: Macmillan Co., 1912). Bartlett, like Girard, believes that the "human abyss" of uncontrolled violence, barely kept in check by lies and the killing of the innocent, is a learned rather than instinctual social trait.

reconciliation of alienated factions is repeated not only in religious rituals and symbols — such as the mass and cross — but in theological explanations. Bartlett sees such an exchange meaning of Christ's death in Anselm's atonement theory, in which redemption is gained through violence. According to Bartlett, violence is always on the edges of life as God is continuously angry at humans for their disloyalty, until the surrogate is killed, pleasing God. God is compensated on behalf of human sinners for what God has lost, and thus does not need to return violence for violence.[12] Further, what was an arbitrary and contingent act becomes lifted up into a divine necessity: The surrogate had to die, and it was planned before the ages as the mechanism to bring peace.

For his neo-Abelardian model, Bartlett flips this Anselmian theory on its head; for Jesus effects not the solidification of the principle of mimetic exchange, but rather its forfeiture.[13] The key moment at which the entrenched patterns of mimetic violence are overturned is that of Jesus' suffering and death, a moment in which two contingent events of compassion occur.

The first contingent act of compassion comes from Jesus. In Christ, God reverses the patterns by which humans abandon and violate other humans. Jesus does this by *an act of unreserved hospitality,* a primary and unconditional opening to the "other."[14] Even at the point of his death, he refuses to violate others, to turn a fellow human subject into an object. This fundamental act of hospitality Bartlett also identifies as love, *agape,* and the giving of oneself freely and fully to another.[15]

12. On Bartlett's identification of mimetic exchange as the crucial vehicle of thought and the theological grounding for Christian praxis of violence, see *Cross Purposes,* 62-63; for its use throughout early and medieval church history in chapter 2, "Imitatio Diaboli." For his discussion of Anselm's incorporation of mimetic exchange and resulting metaphysical establishment of divine violence in his concept of "satisfaction," see 76-86.

13. In contrast to Anselm's atonement theory, Bartlett approvingly asserts that Abelard turned the framework of conflictual mimesis for understanding the salvific meaning of the cross "upside down" (*Cross Purposes,* 88). And as he says later about his model, the "moral influence" theory comes forward (223). On Jesus' act as a forfeiture of all exchange mechanisms, see 87.

14. On the core trait of Jesus' compassionate act as hospitality to the other, see (e.g.) ibid., 38, 234.

15. The contingent act of compassion as an act of love is mentioned frequently. On the act as *agape,* see ibid., 158, where Bartlett calls the act "a liberation of the self from self," which is "the content of a nonviolent account of atonement." On the act as a giving of the self unconditionally to the other, Bartlett writes that when Jesus encounters another, "he yields himself" to the other "without reserve" (153). For the act of compassion as simulta-

Jesus acts with compassion toward the innocent victims of the violent scapegoating mechanism — and toward all the abject, condemned and violated — by handing himself over to the killers as a victim like them. Through his *identification with them* and opposition to the killers, Jesus reasserts the victims' full human worth.[16]

However, simultaneously, Jesus refuses to reduce the violent perpetrators to the status of less-than-human. As in the moment of his arrest when he tells Peter to put down his sword, then kneels to repair the severed ear of the soldier holding a blade toward him, Jesus has compassion even for those who display only the will-to-power. His compassion here takes the form of *a forfeiture of violence*. For Jesus, violence itself is an outrage.[17] Further, at the spiritual and relational level, Jesus does not seek revenge; indeed, he exhibits care, the opposite of revenge. Despite feeling abandoned by God and experiencing the world's indifference, when Jesus breathes his last breath without asking God to avenge him — "Father, forgive them, they know not what they do" — he loves his enemies and refuses to participate in all patterns of violent exchange.[18]

In this forgiveness without measure, this refusal to call vengeance upon his tormentors or demonize them, Jesus dreams of the enemy as friend, "an impossible identification with an as yet nonexistent 'weakness' of the enemy whereby a true identification that is not rivalry or scapegoating might become possible."[19] By employing this imagination, Jesus refuses to collude with the powers of violence.[20] While this compassionate act judges the per-

---

neously an abyssal gift of self, an unconditional gift of love, and a surrender of the self without remainder, see 39. The contingent, non-metaphysical, socio-historically situated aspects of Christ's compassion at death make Bartlett's reconfiguration of Abelard acceptable to J. Denny Weaver.

16. On the cross as an act of compassionate identification and suffering with victims, see for example ibid., 39, 142, 151-153, 156, 158, and 221.

17. On his compassion entailing a forfeiture of violence, see for example ibid., 4, 159, 183. For Jesus repairing the Temple soldier's ear, see Luke 21:47-54.

18. Luke 23:34. On Jesus refusing to ask God to avenge his murder, see Bartlett, *Cross Purposes*, 260. On Jesus' renunciation of vengeance and instead offering forgiveness without measure to perpetrators, see 39, 131, 153-154, 159, 169, 219. On Jesus renouncing revenge despite his feelings of divine abandonment and experiences of human abandonment, see 166. Jesus not only asks God not to take vengeance as he dies; when he returns alive after the resurrection, he does not seek revenge on his murderers. See 153-155.

19. Ibid., 157. In his imagination, Jesus returns to the time prior to violent mimesis and leaps forward to the not-yet-existent future when such cold objectifications of the "other" have ceased.

20. Bartlett references Girard on Jesus' refusal to collude with the principalities and powers, Ibid., 40.

petrator through its illuminatory power, it is not the judgment of condemnation.[21] And while the act changes all of history, it is not part of an overarching divine plan, for if Jesus' response of bottomless love were demanded or necessary, it would lose its character as compassion. Instead, in his moment of human abandonment and death, Jesus contingently gives of himself in a free forgiveness that defies the system of violent exchange.[22]

To a significant yet limited extent, Jesus' act of abyssal compassion has creative effect. Jesus' act of infinite nonviolence receives the violence without calling for retaliation, thus dissipating it.[23] In this act as he dies, Bartlett finds "the fulcrum of the universe" and "an anarchic new starting point" for the human race, for Jesus breaks the bonds of violent mimesis and allows a different direction to emerge in human history.[24]

Yet the abyss of love must outlast the abyss of violence if it is to become conclusive.[25] The saving effect of Jesus' abyssal compassion thus depends upon the second contingent act of compassion, which comes from the humans who see Jesus.

Jesus' act of abyssal compassion on the cross awakens within the human hearts of those who see this act the possibility of a corresponding compassion. The transformation of the witnesses' hearts is both cognitive and volitional, for Jesus' act of love has both illuminative and invitational power.[26]

21. See ibid., 138.

22. Bartlett insists that Jesus' act of compassion is not a metaphysical event, or part of an eternal ideal. It is a particular, contingent, human act which emerges in the moment. See ibid., 24, 149, and 251.

23. In the limitlessness of nonretaliation, violence fails to win (ibid., 169). "The infinite subjective forgiveness by the victim" resolves the "others' violence in the victim" (251).

24. See ibid., 41, 138, and 240 respectively. The Crucified interrupts chronological time and initiates "the an-archical future" (240). In the cross, "the categorically new emerges" (41), "an immense novelty" (25): redemptive compassion and forgiveness in human affairs. Jesus effects "an absolute novelty of human selfhood" (18), thus changing the abyss of human abandonment and violence from within such an event, and causing redemption to arise in that moment. His death is thus "the real crossroads in human life" (152), where the new choice emerges to repeat his abyssal compassion.

25. See ibid., 168.

26. On the saving transformation of human existence entailing not merely Christ's act of compassion — his death on the cross — but also the opening of the human mind, heart, and will in compassion to the man Jesus in his full subjectivity, see ibid., 25, 86-88, and 158-159. On the cross evoking love and hope in fellow victims of violence through Jesus' solidarity with them, see 221. On the perpetrator's experience of unconditional love, infinite nonviolence, nonretaliation, and forgiveness opening the possibility for a corresponding response of love, see 39, 221. It is not merely the forgiveness, love, nonviolence, and

The suffering of Christ strips the sacred veneer off the scapegoating rituals and discloses the truth about the violent origins of human culture. Through his bottomless response of nonviolence and love, Jesus reveals his lack of guilt for the group's violence. The victim is innocent. Therefore, Christ's sufferings cannot fit the logic of a divine plan of collective redemption — a divinely planned sacrifice of the guilty which defers divine violence for sin. With the loss of this logic, the possibility of a salvific experience opens. When the victim's death is not viewed as the way to collective redemption, but as murder, it becomes clear that all human culture is based in violence, and that violence must be given up.[27]

Through his limitless love on the cross, Jesus not only strips the religious veneer off the killing of innocents; he beckons toward an alternative way to live rooted in an endless compassion for all rather than in mimetic violence. When the witnesses at Golgotha perceive Jesus' suffering love, they notice not only society's patterns of vengeance and brutal exchange, but that

---

nonretaliation which evoke compassion, but these things *as Jesus suffers* that evoke it. See Bartlett's discussion of the "aesthetic of Christ the man of Sorrows" for Christ's dimension of beauty as sorrow, and its captivating power (176-178). Bartlett quotes Oscar Wilde: "He does not really teach one anything, but by being brought into his presence one becomes something" (176-177). Describing an encounter with the abyssal love of Christ, who "took the entire world of the inarticulate, the voiceless world of pain, as his kingdom," Bartlett writes: "The Man of Sorrows can transfigure pain into beauty, and in such a way that promises a pathway beyond pain into liberation" (177). "An aesthetic of Christ, on the contrary, is led to the point where everything is lost, and it is on this basis that reality may be transformed, that something new may occur" (182). "[I]t is the very suffering of the victim, engineered by the sacred but responded to with infinite nonviolence (without sin), that is the nuclear point at which the cosmos finds re-creation" (203).

27. The vindication of the scapegoat, who is the object of collective violence, opens a possible "salvific moment" in which the sacred order built upon violence may be deconstructed for the witnesses. See ibid., 37-41, 86-88, and 134-138. The progression of biblical narratives moves toward the precise disclosure of the innocence of the victim, and the social violence, greed, and vengeance funding human culture, through the witness of the prophets and the uplifting of the innocence of Abel, Joseph, Job, Isaiah's Suffering Servant, and Jesus. From this collection of biblical narratives comes the Western history of concern for the victims of civilization's onslaught, rather than the "super-men" who have always been cultures' heroes. On Girard and Bartlett's interpretation of the biblical narrative giving a unique identification with the innocent victim, and its attending "apocalyptic vision" of cultural violence — disguised as sacred — leading toward universal death, see ibid., 28, 38-41, and 134-138. Bartlett quotes Bonhoeffer on the transformative power of the cross: "There remains an experience of incomparable value, that we have learned to see the great events of world history for once from below, from the perspective of those who are excluded, suspected, maltreated, powerless, oppressed, and scorned, in short the sufferers" (261).

Jesus acts differently. The possibility is then opened that they may respond with an act of volition: to take their place in solidarity with the non-retaliatory victim, and repeat his response to violence.

While Jesus' death seems like a defeat of non-violent love in face of brutal imperial will-to-power, and while the cross does not bring an ontological change, it does bring a new anthropological starting point into history, and this is its power. The love of Jesus brings clear eyes to his witnesses and the possibility of an *imitatio Christi*. Unlike with Anselm's theory, the contingent act of love by Christ in his last moments holds no guarantees or metaphysical assurances. Christ's example may leave the sinner unmoved. The human response of compassion is itself contingent, and cannot be forced. Further, Christ's bold act is ineffectual without that human response. Yet historically, Jesus' act opened up a new form of community devoted to Christ and determined to counter an endless pattern of hostile desire with a chain of forgiving love, and that chain's very different social world.[28]

Embracing Paradise: The Powers of Life within a Community of Ethical Grace

While Anthony Bartlett's neo-Abelardian use of Girard attempts to separate love and violence, it has the opposite effect. This criticism explains why Brock and Parker move in such a different direction to create a nonviolent theory of salvation.

In *Saving Paradise*, Brock and Parker agree with Bartlett on certain key issues. They agree that salvation is not about being spared from the punishing fury of a judgmental God, but about God effecting the flourishing of life in this world. Salvation thus involves the transformation of human personal and social practices here on earth. They agree that salvation ushers in a new

---

28. On the contingent human act of compassion in face of the cross constituting an entirely new way of human community, see ibid., 141-142, 153-159, 165-166, 221, and 254-255. On the effectiveness of Jesus' saving act dependent upon the response of the human witnesses and their creation of a new form of community rooted in abyssal compassion, see 88, 170-171, and 219-222. Bartlett says that the new Christian community of nonretaliatory response lasted for over three centuries and became a minority tradition throughout the continuing church history (220). For a Girardian model similar to Bartlett's, see S. Mark Heim, *Saved from Sacrifice* (Grand Rapids: Eerdmans, 2006); and chapter 14 in *Cross Examinations: Readings on the Meaning of the Cross Today*, ed. Marit Trelstad (Minneapolis: Fortress, 2006).

form of community grounded upon social practices which have shed scapegoating and mimetic violence. They agree that truth, beauty, and love are the forms of power which kindle that new communal ethos, and that such forms of power are by nature noncoercive.[29]

Brock and Parker criticize only one element of Bartlett's (and Abelard's and Girard's) theory of atonement, but it devastates the theory by attacking its core concept. Brock and Parker disagree with Bartlett concerning *the nature of the love* which powerfully saves humanity. Like Bartlett, Brock and Parker agree that violence only begets fear, annihilation, stalemate, dominance, and more violence. The love which opposes the powers of empire is nonviolent and nonretaliatory, for it refuses to reduce any human being — victim or perpetrator — to an object.[30] Apart from these shared elements, Brock and Parker repudiate Bartlett's definition of love.

Bartlett, like Abelard before him, defines sin and love according to typically male perspectives. Sin is self-centeredness. With this view of sin as the framework, love acquires its virtue in the refusal to think of the self and limitless persistence in thinking only of the "other(s)." True love dies. It is the selfless *agape* in which one's efforts for others continually betray a background of self-sacrifice.[31]

Abelard and Bartlett define love as an internalized condition of the heart of an isolated lover or hero, apart from the give-and-take found in webs of relationships. For them, a loving heart's ability to effect change is found in its disclosive and absorbing powers. True *agape* only gives, without needing anything from the beloved. Thus, *one proves one's love for another by one's willingness to endure anything for the other's sake.* Further, employing Girard's theory, Bartlett argues that self-sacrificing, suffering love has power to change the pattern of mimetic exchange *by absorbing the violence of the perpetrator.* The isolated lover or hero does not stand in bitter defiance to such unjust violation of the self, but rather in "fathomless yielding."

---

29. On truth as a form of power, see Brock and Parker, *Saving Paradise,* 49, 406-407. On beauty as a form of power, see xix, xxii, 49, 98, 105; ch. 6; and 207, 393, and 419. On love as power, see 49, 98, 391.

30. On violence begetting only more violence, see ibid., 13, 74, 393; see also Brock in Trelstad, *Cross Examinations,* 242. On powerful love as nonviolent, see Brock and Parker, *Saving Paradise,* xix, 47, 77, 121, 169-170, 184.

31. On sin as self-centeredness, see Brock and Parker, *Proverbs of Ashes: Violence, Redemptive Suffering, and the Search for What Saves Us* (Boston: Beacon, 2001), 32-34; and Brock in Trelstad, *Cross Examinations,* 248. On love as selflessness, self-sacrifice, and agape, see Brock and Parker, *Saving Paradise,* 52, 279, 302.

The violation goes no further, stopping in the dead body of the non-retaliatory victim.[32]

Through its ability to disclose love to others and end the cycle of violence for them, it is thus *the suffering of the victim* — the abnegation of power to resist violation — that has saving effect. Because this model erroneously identifies power exclusively with coercive power, and thus love and power as opposites, redemptive love meets the abusive use of power with a refusal to use power.[33] With such a definition of saving love, Bartlett, following Abelard and Girard, has dropped the Carolingians' killing for God as an act of devotion, but kept the self-abasement. A lover sets aside his or her relational and social needs and rights. He or she passively surrenders all power to resist violence. Such a definition of virtuous love contravenes assumptions of power by the oppressed. It erroneously suggests that life — of the victims or the perpetrators of violence — can be saved by passivity. And, by portraying suffering as holy, with the power to save, it sanctifies relations of victimization. Far from separating the Carolingians' marriage of love and violence, it deepens it, for "If self-annihilation, whether willed or coerced, is love, then it is identical with violence."[34]

32. On a person proving her or his love through a willingness to endure pain or death, see Brock and Parker, *Saving Paradise*, 284, 293-295. On love absorbing violence, thus ending a furtherance of the cycle of violence, see 296-297. Brock and Parker quote Bartlett on this (492n.51), and also Miroslav Volf (437n.40), who writes: "By suffering violence as an innocent victim, [Jesus] took upon himself the aggression of the persecutors. He broke the vicious cycle of violence by absorbing it . . . the sacralizing of him as victim subverts violence" (quoted from Volf, *Exclusion and Embrace: A Theological Exploration of Identity, Otherness, and Reconciliation* [Nashville: Abingdon, 1996], 291-292).

33. To become Christ-like is to give up all power through surrender, obedience, and humility. Love wins through its goodness, but a goodness defined as lacking in wisdom and power, for Abelard erroneously identifies knowledge with manipulative knowledge, and power exclusively with coercive power. "[T]o be good is not to be wise or powerful," writes Abelard (quoted in Brock and Parker, *Saving Paradise*, 296). Brock and Parker also quote Douglas John Hall (in Trelstad, *Cross Examinations*, 257]: "The theology of the cross is a theology of love, not power. . . . Love . . . to achieve its aim must become weak" (437n.40). On love's saving attribute identified with the utter helplessness and resourcelessness of the suffering victim, see also Brock and Parker, *Saving Paradise*, 52, 176-177, 279, 284, 296, and 304.

34. Brock in Trelstad, *Cross Examinations*, 248. On Abelard dropping the killing but keeping the self-abasement, see Brock and Parker, *Saving Paradise*, 305-306. On love's abnegation of power entailing an abnegation of the self's needs and rights, see ibid., 293; on the selfless acquiescence to violation, see ibid., 52, 404, and Brock in Trelstad, *Cross Examinations*, 248; on the contravening of oppressed people's empowerment and the suggestion that life can be saved by passivity, see Brock and Parker, *Saving Paradise*, 437n.40, 52, 80.

The union of love and violence is only compounded in the second contingent act of compassion in Bartlett's neo-Abelardian theory, that of the human witnesses for the suffering Christ. In witnessing the abyssal compassion exhibited by Christ who suffers innocently, people may be moved by an interior sense of pity combined with remorse. They may then move their hearts from self-centeredness to selfless love, and be open to demonstrating that love by a willingness to die.

However, once again love is misconstrued as *the fusion of selves* which occurs between perpetrators and victims, a perverse bonding which leaves all participants stuck in heart-breaking patterns while hierarchical and abusive power structures remain intact. Victims are discouraged from rising up in non-violent but determined resistance to their own violation. Instead, they are encouraged to acquiesce to violence in passive, forgiving love because such suffering love is virtuous (like Christ's), and has power to change and redeem the hearts of their torturers. Since compassion is erroneously defined as the full, empathetic identification of the self with the suffering of others, in Bartlett's model perpetrators bond emotionally with their victims, finding a perverse "wholeness" by connecting with the ones they mar. Their response may take the form of benevolent paternalism, or reflect a narcissistic swing from a sense of self as victim to a "need to be more selfless." But because the compassion is predicated on a relation with an inherent imbalance of power — violator to victim — neither the perpetrator nor victim acts with true love — the kind that uses power rightly to resist sin, repair harm, deconstruct relations of dominance and submission and replace them with those of mutuality and equality.[35]

Despite their attempt to gain a nonviolent atonement theory, the Christ who is embraced by Abelard, Girard, and Bartlett is still the holy victim of human sin, as was true of the Carolingian theologians with the revised

---

35. On Christ's compassionate suffering opening the possibility of a corresponding sentiment of pity mixed with guilty responsibility in sinners, and a move toward selfless love, see ibid., 281-288, 294-295. On such a response once again reflecting the fusion of selves which occurs between abusers and victims, see ibid., 296-297, 304, 397; Brock and Parker, *Proverbs of Ashes,* 155-156; and Brock in Trelstad, *Cross Examinations,* 248-249. On such fused relations functioning to encourage victims to "bear suffering for the sake of love" by associating virtue with passive, forgiving love and seeing innocent suffering as salvific, see Brock and Parker, *Saving Paradise,* 52, 201, 280, 305; *Proverbs of Ashes,* 15-42; and Brock in Trelstad, *Cross Examinations,* 248. On fused relations functioning to encourage benevolent paternalism (a compassion for and giving to victims while retaining hierarchies of superiority) or narcissistic self-absorption, but not love, see *Saving Paradise,* 201-202, 295-296, 303, 397-398.

Eucharistic theology for the Saxons, and of Anselm's theory. When salvation is located in moments of suffering and violation, an atonement theory which abets human violence is inevitable.

Instead of locating saving power in a moment of torturous death, Brock and Parker locate it in experiences of new energies for living. A victim's suffering and fathomless yielding do not save. Rather, actions save, the exercise of human powers and responsibility rooted in wise discernment of what supports the great cycles of life that sustain human existence, and what destroys them. This powerful agency which opposes scapegoating and mimetic violence is directed by an alternate ethic of life which goes beyond a mere love which does not retaliate. The love which saves is the love which embraces this world passionately — the life of the self, of others, and of the earth. Salvation occurs when humans rise up and claim the reinstatement of the image of God effected in Christ, claiming freedom in whole-bodied, passionate life, and self-possessed power. In other words, salvation happens when humans respond to the demonic use of force with a fullness of the self, not with the self's negation.[36]

One learns to embrace life and act to protect it through encounters with the Spirit of life. Manifest in Jesus and given by him to the disciples, the power of the Spirit is a form of power that is generative of new energies for living in all that share it. Those who experience the beauty and vivifying power of the Spirit "breathe . . . the healing air of paradise." Rather than an abnegation of power, *life in the Spirit of generative power* shows the limits of the principalities and powers, *precisely by affirming the freedom and dignity of human beings.*[37]

---

36. Brock and Parker term the alternate ethic of life "ethical grace." We are called to sustain life on earth ("ethical"), a call grounded in our experiences of the core goodness of life on earth (the world's web of life-giving relations which are "gracious"). On humans acting according to ethical grace as restoring paradise, see *Saving Paradise*, xviii, xxii, 25, 28-31, 66, 106-107, 158, 175-176, 250. Salvation occurs when humans rise up to claim participation in the powers of life and divinization of humanity reestablished by Christ; see xix, 14-15, 89, 106-107, 146, 191-202, 395-396. Such loving moral agency demands not only wisdom and power, but also the virtues of self-control, physical stamina, emotional maturity, and mental focus (124-125).

37. Quote from ibid., 82. Empire is not opposed one wit by the sufferings of the innocent, but it is countered by the flowering of communities rooted in the Spirit. On experiences of the beauty and life-giving, generative power of the Spirit — the gift of Christ — as restoring moral agents, see 37-38, 49, 89, 169-170, 191-202, 249-252. On coercive power finding its opposition in generative power rather than the abnegation of power, see 22, 169-170.

The Spirit of life is encountered in the beauty of the divine rhythms of the world, and in the ordinariness of life: music, fragrance, food, visages which delight the eye, offers of love by others and moments of mutual assistance.[38] Even more so, the Spirit with her generative powers is experienced in new forms of community rooted in equality, shared power, generosity, and mutual care. Public utilities are shared, and male dominance ends. The loving action which counters transpersonal violence is defined socially as *the sharing of vulnerability and the using of one's power to help others within the community.*[39] Rooted in the integrity of the self and its connections to others, love acts in empathy and with sufficient self-possession to nurture all life and alleviate pain. Such an agential, rather than merely interior, definition of love entails wisdom and power by necessity, as well as a community of friends through which such love, wisdom, and power are generated.[40]

To rise up and claim the divinizing powers of the Spirit and the healed *imago Dei* within themselves, the members of the new communities must be ready to resist forces that want to keep certain persons and groups disempowered. The new communities of life are never helped by abyssal self-sacrifice or romanticizing victims. Rather, they are helped by nonviolent *resistance* to the coercive forces of empire (not a bare nonviolent response). Loving persons act to get victims out of violating relationships, to heal victims, and to change the structures of imbalanced power which cause harm to victims.[41] Because of one's love for all life, one chooses to live in the paradise renewed by Christ (the reign of God), rather than according to the rules of the stratified Roman economic-political "household." The lover refuses to surrender her or

38. See ibid., 98, and esp. chapter 6.

39. Such a definition stands in contrast to Abelard's, Girard's, and Bartlett's definition of love as forgoing the rights of the self in limitless yielding to, and forgiveness of, acts of violation by the "other."

40. On the new communities of shared, generative power as the locus of saving experiences of paradise and the Spirit and the basis for ethical action on behalf of all life (rather than the individual acts of isolated heroes), see Brock and Parker, *Saving Paradise,* xvii, xix, 44-49, 83, 128, 130, 178, 186, 201, 238, 298, 303, 386, 410, 418; and Brock in Trelstad, *Cross Examinations,* 242. The bonds are those of mutual friendship rather than domination and submission, and the resources for sustaining life are shared by all (see Brock and Parker, *Saving Paradise,* 8, 17, 44-49). These communities which help life flourish in the face of imperial power, violence, and death are birthed by the Spirit. Jesus founds such a community, but his is not exclusive. For communal and agential — as opposed to Abelard's, Girard's, and Bartlett's individual and interior — definitions of love, see ibid., 99, 130, 290, 297, 302-304, 392-393.

41. On compassion entailing not fathomless yielding and limitless forgiveness, but nonviolent resistance to forces which violate, see ibid., 26, 47, 158, 193, 191-202, 241, 299.

his freedom, to sever connection with the Spirit and to abandon the new community of paradise on earth. She or he says "No" to violence against the self or others in the community, or the negating of one's rights to life. She or he demands justice — not punitive, but rather restitutionary.[42] Such a portrait of love could not get farther from Bartlett's abyssal compassion.

Brock and Parker see in Jesus a human being who uses generative power and wisdom to restore human life to paradise. In sharpest contrast to Abelard, Girard, and Bartlett, Brock and Parker find Jesus exercising such saving compassion everywhere except the cross. Jesus restores the image of God in human flesh, then shares that renewed capacity with others through his gift of the Spirit. For this act, the doctrines of the incarnation, Jesus' life and ministry, the resurrection, and Pentecost are central. Jesus' love evokes wholeness during his acts of physical healing and raising of the dead, his teaching and shepherding, his appreciation of beauty and his non-violent resistance to the coercive powers. He acts to create a new community rooted in ethical grace, breathes the gift of the Spirit upon the members, and offers the sacraments of baptism and Eucharist as portals into the paradisal powers he unleashes. If for Abelard, Girard, and Bartlett, abyssal compassion makes its contingent, epoch-shattering appearance in Jesus' words, "Father, forgive them, they know not what they do," for Brock and Parker, the saving power of divine compassion is seen paradigmatically in Jesus' Temple encounter with the money-changers, his miracle of the loaves and fishes, and the life-affirming acts of the women at the cross who refused to let the Roman Empire erase Jesus' identity.[43]

42. On the choice to live within the new community which is part of the renewed paradise which straddles the worlds of the living and the dead entailing a rejection of violence against the self in face of coercive powers and principalities, see ibid., 66, 80, 404-410; and Brock and Parker, *Proverbs of Ashes,* 39-42. The affirmation of life also entails the demand for restorative (or restitutionary) justice when perpetrators violate victims. The community holds the perpetrator accountable by demanding restitution, though in a nonviolent manner. The community also prays for that person. See Brock and Parker, *Saving Paradise,* 102, 181-186; and Brock in Trelstad, *Cross Examinations,* 250.

43. On the location of saving powers of paradise in Jesus' incarnation, see Brock and Parker, *Saving Paradise,* 131-135 and 143; chapter 7; and 247-248 and 259; in Jesus' resurrection, 53-54, 61, and 253; in the Pentecostal gift of the Spirit, 177. On their location in Jesus' healings, miracles, raising of the dead, teachings, and feeding the five thousand, see 60-62, 169-170, 175-179, 249-252. On their location in baptism, see 41, chapter 5, and 175; and in the Eucharist, see chapters 6-7, and pp. 236-238. On these are paradigmatic texts for the power of divine love: Jesus and the money-changers (44-49); miracles of the loaves and fishes (30-31); and the women at the cross (52-55).

Divine Hospitality and the Cross of Christ

Both sets of arguments are flawed, yet each also contains key insights which fund a reconstruction of Abelard's theory. Bartlett is right in two major ways, yet so are Brock and Parker. My reconstruction of Abelard's model contains four moves which draw upon these insights, while avoiding their fatal flaws. It concludes with a fifth move which goes beyond Bartlett, Brock and Parker.

Bartlett is correct that *the basic structure of Abelard's theory points toward one possible nonviolent model of atonement.* Abelard rightly perceives that love and grace are not mere sentiments, but forms of power which can redeem humans stuck in sin by evoking within sinners a transformation of the heart. The basic structure of Abelard's argument is this: Divine grace redeems by disclosing a human world of "ungrace" built upon violence and complicity with violence, and by simultaneously offering an alternative way to live not based upon violence. The gracious act shatters human self-deceptions and enkindles the will to switch to a life based upon grace.

This basic structure captures many elements supportive of a nonviolent conception of salvation. Salvation is not about divine punishment of sinners, but the transformation of the ungracious human order. Salvation ushers in a new form of community, one of grace which leaves behind scapegoating and mimetic violence. The structure rightly captures the nature of love as entailing risk, even when the one who loves is God, for love is a form of transformative power which depends upon the joining response of the one loved.

However, while Abelard, Girard, and Bartlett identify a basic structure helpful for a nonviolent atonement theory, they fail at describing the nature of the love which redeems — a flaw so basic it devastates their arguments, as Brock and Parker rightly argue. While love is nonviolent and non-retaliatory, love is not identified with the bare refusal to participate in mimetic violence, for such an identification defines love as the abnegation of power. Further, the human problem goes deeper than the isolated heart turned-inward. Avarice and envy are problems, but as Girard points out, they also manifest themselves in structured relations of super- and subordination. The love which counters coercive power is likewise inherently collective, found in communities in which life is embraced and fellow subjects share power equally and give aid reciprocally. *Love entails this refusal to break the subject-to-subject structure of relationships,* the structure of distinction-in-unity, which forms the true power of community and of beauty itself.

True love, grounded in experiences of beauty and life-giving relations, rises up to claim one's right to participate in the flow of life-giving power within community, and to nonviolently resist those who use coercive force to prevent such participation.

Jesus' last hours of suffering and death are insufficient to encompass the powerful love by which he refuses to break the subject-to-subject structure of relations. In sharp contrast to Abelard, Girard, and Bartlett, Brock and Parker rightly perceive the action by which Jesus saves humanity from sin as entailing the entire sweep of Jesus' story, and the attending doctrines. His actions save, not his suffering or victimization. It is during his life and after his resurrection that Jesus enacts his striking love of life which discloses a world of "ungrace" and evokes a healing and corresponding love in those he encounters. Jesus' love doesn't die, it *acts:* It brings wholeness through his physical healings and raising of the dead, his appreciation of beauty and his nonviolent challenge to coercive structures — such as when he chases the money-changers from the Temple. His love acts to create a new community rooted in ethical grace, to breathe the power of the Holy Spirit upon this community, and to empower it further with gifts of baptism and Eucharist. The miracle of the loaves and fishes accurately portrays the nature of the divine love which saves nonviolently, for it shows Jesus confronting empire not with an opposing coercion, nor with an abnegation of power. Jesus confronts the Roman structures of domination and submission by increasing a community built upon a different source of power, that of the Spirit of Life, and a different ethic, one that is hospitable and gracious.

While Brock and Parker correctly locate Jesus' love which acts to passionately embrace life, to create communities in which all members share equally in the resources needed for life, and to resist nonviolently forces which oppose such communities, *Jesus' last hours of suffering and death are essential for comprehending that life-act of life-embracing love.* As a form of power which depends upon the response of the recipient, compassion entails the risk of failure. However, in a world built upon scapegoating, codes of retaliation against the "other," and structures of dominance and subordination, those who act compassionately also risk their life. Jesus lives with integrity in this love of all life. Because of this integrity, he refuses to cut himself off from God who is the source of life, from his neighbors who live within the web of life, or from the new community based upon ethical grace (which forms the foretaste of the reign of God). As a passionate love of all life, this love entails the protection of one's own life as well as that of others.

But sometimes the act of supporting another's life, or refusing to yield one's embrace of the new communal ethos of life, puts a person in the path of those who find such love subversive of the hierarchical power structures from which they benefit. To step aside when threatened is to abandon the neighbor to the onslaught of coercive forces, or to abandon one's integrity and the new community. To put it differently, sometimes there are no good choices in the fight to preserve life (as the struggles of Dietrich Bonhoeffer, Martin Luther King Jr., and Oscar Romero display).

Jesus loved life and repudiated the pattern of mimetic violence, and in this choice of response to empire, he improvised. When threatened, he protected himself when he could, such as when he "disappeared from the crowd" when locals wanted his head, or when he slipped beyond Herod's jurisdiction to Caesarea Philippi after Herod executed Jesus' cousin John. However, Jesus also took risks of his life when he felt that protecting his own life would endanger the lives of others, his integrity, or his connection to his new community. Such is the case when, shortly after his brief stay in Caesarea Philippi, he heads towards Jerusalem, even as he perceives that such a journey risks his life.[44] As Bonhoeffer discovered in the months in New York before he returned to Nazi Germany just before the war, and King discovered at his late-night kitchen table after a death threat, and Romero discovered as right-wing guards offered to let him go as he continued to hear the sounds of his brothers being tortured, sometimes a choice to protect one's own life comes at the self-defeating cost of severing connections to one's integrity, one's neighbors, the new community of love, and the God who calls us toward each of these.

As was true of each of these men's sufferings and deaths, so Jesus' torture and death are not salvific. But Jesus' refusal to abandon the weak to the forces of empire, or curse his torturers, is salvific. This refusal is a constituent part of his life-act of compassion. If Jesus had attempted to avoid the cross at all cost, within such a contentious class of communities based upon different forms of power, then the character of his life would have been changed. *His willingness to risk his life because of his love of others, his love of his own life's integrity, his love of the God of life and of the new community of hospitality, is essential to the nature of love.* When the witnesses perceive in Jesus a love which seeks the

---

44. On Herod's execution of John the Baptist, see Mark 6:14-29 and Matthew 14:1-12. On Jesus moving with only his disciples soon after to Caesarea Philippi, see Mark 8:27-33 and Matthew 16:13-23. Instead of staying in Caesarea Philippi indefinitely, he turned his face to Jerusalem: "From that time on, Jesus began to show his disciples that he must go to Jerusalem and undergo great suffering at the hands of the elders and chief priests and scribes, and be killed, and on the third day be raised" (Matt. 16:21).

freedom of all — victims and perpetrators of violence — and a person who refuses to betray anyone, including himself and his own integrity, they perceive their own willingness to betray, and the bankruptcy of a communal life built upon such an ethos. This is why Abelard, Girard, and Bartlett are correct in perceiving the moment of the cross as saving. Jesus' suffering is not loving or salvific; but his willingness to risk suffering for the sake of his commitments is constituent to his life-act of love, a love that is redemptive. Surprisingly, in their arguments that martyrs like Perpetua hold to faithfulness to the new paradisal community against temptations to apostasy while under trial, Brock and Parker make the same point.[45]

Finally, if the revelation of truth which transforms the hearts of those who encounter Jesus is the revelation of general and universally accessible truth, then neither the cross, nor even the life of Jesus, are necessary for such a disclosure. In emphasizing that Jesus is just one avenue through which the Spirit of life works to create new communities of ethical grace, Brock and Parker signal just such a non-essentiality. However, *if what is revealed in Jesus' life-act is not only the general character of God as compassionate, but also a new act by God in Jesus to effect an ontological change in the human situation and the God-world relation, then Jesus' life-act — including his death — has a different disclosive character and power.* Abelard was ambiguous on this, which is why subsequent critics wondered if his atonement theory was merely "subjective." The love disclosed in Jesus' suffering is God's constant love for the world, but perhaps there is something new in God undergoing suffering for love's sake? If suffering and even death are brought into the inner-life of God through Jesus' life, death, and days in a tomb, or if the cross becomes an act not only of homicide but of deicide, then the cross itself contains some kind of ontological change which is particular to that historical moment, and which has disclosive and world-altering force.[46] Girard and

45. See Brock and Parker, *Saving Paradise,* 65-71, 78, 80, 97, 120-121, and esp. 165-167, 179, 200-202.

46. From Luther to today, "theologians of the cross" describe an ontological change occurring at the cross at progressively significant levels. As a result of God's kenotic movement, God takes into God's own life and history finitude and suffering (Barth, Hall), relational rupture and loss (Moltmann), the annihilating power of nothingness and death (Jüngel). For a discussion of this progressive movement, see Alan E. Lewis, *Between Cross and Resurrection: A Theology of Holy Saturday* (Grand Rapids: Eerdmans, 2001). Barth sees the death of Jesus as an act of universal human suicide, fratricide, and deicide. See for example *Church Dogmatics* IV/1 (Edinburgh: T&T Clark, 1956), 397-99. Combining neo-Abelardian models with reconfigured models of *Christus Victor,* sacrifice, and satisfaction also integrates into the former the necessary element of "ontological change."

Bartlett hint at this by describing Jesus' abyssal compassion at his death as bringing a contingent, yet epoch-changing, introduction of a unique and novel way of being human, one which can then be imitated in the new community. Under the conditions of finitude and flesh, God in Jesus introduces into creaturely history a form of human love which seeks the empowerment of all living things and which will not falter into betrayal. When this element of ontological change is brought inside the Abelardian structure of love as a power, the Abelardian theory conveys a nonviolent atonement, and separates the Carolingians' marriage of imperial violence, self-sacrificing devotion, and divine salvation.

The People of God in Christian Theology

Katherine Sonderegger

When the holy city of Jerusalem descends from the new heaven, the prophet John writes, it will be surrounded by a great high wall, and on the gates to that wall will be inscribed the names of the twelve tribes of Israel, and on its foundation stones, the names of the twelve apostles of the Lamb. When Christian theologians consider the *locus,* the "people of God," this eschatological and prophetic text of Revelation should form its very core. To be sure, other scriptural warrants come readily to mind: 1 Peter 2, with its redolent echoes of Exodus and Hosea; Romans 9–11, a near *locus classicus* for Christian reflections on Judaism; the pentecostal outpouring of the Spirit on Israel in Acts 2; and the great hymn to unity in Christ's body in Ephesians 2. Indeed we may consider Revelation 21, our core text, to be a meditation upon Ephesians 2:19-20: "Thus you are no longer aliens in a foreign land, but fellow-citizens with God's people, members of God's household. You are built upon the foundation laid by the apostles and prophets, and Christ Jesus himself is the foundation-stone" (NEB). Yet these texts do not provide for us Christians the apocalyptic force and eschatological *telos* that Revelation 21 does; and it is these notes — the marks of apocalypse and eschaton

---

I am honored to be included in a collection dedicated to Daniel Migliore, an exemplary theologian, colleague, and teacher. In his exploration of scriptural laments and the practice of Liberation Theology, Dan gives eloquent voice to the "people of God." Many thanks, too, to the Society for Systematic Theology for its invitation to read the original version of this paper at its annual meeting, and for the many comments that improved and strengthened this revision.

— that properly order and animate the doctrine of the people of God. Within this structure the other scriptural passages find their proper balance and place. The "people of God" is an eschatological category above all else, and it is from this Omega point that Christians should begin our work.

I. The Relation of People of God and Church

To recognize the *locus,* people of God, as a reality of the end times is to acknowledge indirectly the novelty of this category for Christian systematic theology. Christians have long recognized the "people of God" as a title for ancient Israel; we have used the phrase to capture the nation-forming power of the covenant between God and Israel; patristic authors have styled the pilgrim life as a wandering "people of God."[1] But Christian systematic theology, particularly in the modern period, has turned to the doctrine of "the Church" rather than "the people of God" when the corporate life of Christians before God is examined. There is a long history to ecclesiology — we will explore some of that in a moment — but primary for us here is the recognition that when Christians develop systematic reflection on the world, its nations, and destiny, it moves nearly effortlessly into an analysis of the place of the Church in the world, the world in the Church. Friedrich Schleiermacher, here as elsewhere, expressed the modern temper when he interpreted the final consummation of the age as a comprehensive ecclesiology: the earthly dialectic of Church and world will end; the world will become the Church.[2] The "people of God," so much as it survives the advent of the doctrine of "the Church," lives on as a description of the laity — the *laos* — who do not enter the ordained ranks of the hierarchy. The peoples or nations of the earth live on, in modern systematics, as "the world," the subject of God's providential rule.

Two exceptions break this rule: Augustine's *City of God* and the Second Vatican Council's Dogmatic Constitution of the Church, *Lumen Gentium.*[3] No surprise that these exceptions frame the reflection of the Church catholic at the beginning and end of Latin Christendom; no surprise that these two

---

1. Thanks to David Burrell for pointing me to this tradition.

2. F. D. E. Schleiermacher *The Christian Faith,* trans. H. R. Mackintosh and J. S. Stewart (Edinburgh: T&T Clark, 1928); *Der christliche Glaube,* ed. R. Schaefer (Berlin: de Gruyter, 2003), Part II, §§164-169.

3. *The Documents of Vatican II,* ed. A. Flannery (Grand Rapids: Eerdmans, 1975), 350-426.

belong in the same class, as the Vatican draws explicitly on Augustine's magisterial work. We will examine both, and borrow deeply from Augustine's eschatological hunger, as for him, the city of God lives among us as a wayfarer, a pilgrim whose eyes long for another country.

But we would not give the doctrine of the people of God a full airing if we did not acknowledge here, before any examination of Revelation or later theology, that the intersection of people of God, Church, and nations is a complex and troubled one.

We may begin our analysis with a near axiom of the higher critical school: that Jesus of Nazareth did not intend to "found a Church." Now, I could never pretend to reproduce here the tangle of historical, theological, and exegetical arguments that lie behind this axiom. But central for our cause is the conviction — widely held among Christian scholars of the New Testament — that Jesus must be understood within the world of Second Temple Judaism, and more, be understood as a faithful, observant Jew. His preaching, healing, and exorcisms, and prophetic acts of feeding, Temple cleansing, and Supper fellowship, all point to the core of his ministry: the kingdom of God. The kingdom, with its anointed ruler, the messiah, is the people of God, under the Lord God, its eternal King. It will take no long study to see that for systematic theology the assimilation of this kingdom to the doctrine of the Church will not be an easy road. Alfred Loisy is remembered for his maxim, "Jesus announced the kingdom; and it was the Church that came"[4] — but for him this is not the ironic quip it is often thought to be. Nor can it be for us. If the Church is to be the main expression of Christian corporate life before God, and if Christians are to be faithful disciples of this one Jew as Lord of Church and world, then we must ask how the people of God, ruled by God as Righteous King, stands in relation to ecclesiology, its creeds, rites, and orders.

One relation of Church to people of God has been given the name — "supersessionism" in our day — and though a well-worked field in contemporary systematic reflection on Judaism, it cannot be considered completed or over-worked whenever Christians consider the people of God. Turning to the Pastoral Epistles and to the teaching of the early Church we can see the foreshadowing of the crisis that supersessionism posed to Jews and Judaism in Christian lands. I want here to distinguish supersessionism from another kindred notion, the "righteous" or "faithful remnant," a phrase more Pauline

---

4. "Jésus annoncait le royaume; and c'est l'Eglise qui est venue." Alfred Loisy, *L'Evangile et L'Eglise,* 5th ed. (Paris: Emile Nourry, 1929), 153.

and prophetic than supersessionism, a term heavily conceptual and doctrinal. Nor do I wish to suggest that supersessionism is a uniform concept, referring univocally to a single Christian doctrine and practice, nor do I mean to use it as a "shame-word," by which any teaching could be silenced without hearing or defense.[5] Indeed, I believe that properly the Christian doctrine of the people of God will comprise a certain form of supersessionism, and that the book of Revelation sets out just how this reign of the Lord and the Lamb will replace and succeed both Temple and Church.

But the Christian doctrine of supersessionism that remains improper for systematics, I argue, is one that solves the dilemma of the kingdom and the Church by proclaiming the Christian Church as the *replacement* of Jews and Judaism as the beloved covenant people of God. More dangerous still is the Christian proclamation that Jews are the "people who become the no-people" — a reversal of New Testament usage — and live as those "accursed" and exiled by God. Such teaching is the stuff of medieval iconography, cathedral statuary, and Luther's late polemic; it is bed-fellow with the "teachings of contempt" circulated early and late by Christian haters of Jews and Judaism; it is the beginning of Christian repentance to repudiate this teaching of curse and contempt and exile completely.

But when this is said we have not begun to answer the riddle of proper Christian teaching about the Church and the people of God, nor their relation to the finality and "absoluteness" — to borrow an earlier generation's phrase — of Jesus Christ to the nations, all nations, tongues, and peoples of the world. We cannot answer that riddle completely here; perhaps not completely in this age. But we can begin by prying apart the doctrine of Church and doctrine of Christian people of God; and through that distinction, set the people of Israel and the people of Christ in movement toward the heavenly Jerusalem. We will seek to join together Christology and the peoples of God in an eschatological vision, grounded by Revelation and guided by Augustine. In the end, we shall say that the doctrine, people of God, only lies in completeness ahead of us. It is the *telos* of the Church, the healing of the nations, and the fulfillment of the covenant. In the end, it simply is the doctrine of Jesus Christ, his Person with his people, built upon the 12 tribes of Israel and the 12 apostles. It is an eschatological, apocalyptic teaching.

---

5. To see some of the many shades of the term, consult Kendall Soulen, *The God of Israel and Christian Theology* (Minneapolis: Fortress Press, 1996).

II. The People of God in Augustine and Vatican II

To start with the apocalytic is to break rank with the mass of modern academic theologies of Church and kingdom. For the book of Revelation is rather an unwanted guest in much modern theology. If Paul scholars suffer from "Galatian embarrassment" — if they do — modern academic theologians suffer Revelation forgetfulness. There are, certainly, recent exegetic works on the book: Elisabeth Schüssler Fiorenza, Richard Bauckham, and Stephen Cook have all published extended works on Revelation and apocalyptic literature.[6] But systematic theologians in the modern era have turned their attention, on the whole, to the Apostle Paul and the kingdom sayings of Jesus to anchor their dawning awareness of the eschatological. Nor is such "Revelation ignorance" new: the Apocalypse of John worried the magisterial Reformers. In our day, the older voices in the Christian tradition may speak more clearly and persuasively than the modern about this work.

Augustine shows us another route into the Apocalypse. After a lengthy and testing ecclesial life, Augustine undertook a complex literary and historical work — "the longest single work to survive from Greco-Roman antiquity," James J. O'Donnell tells us[7] — the twenty-two books of *City of God*.[8] Here we find the concept, people of God, taking center stage: all human beings live as citizens within a city whose aim and destiny is either the self or God alone. Certainly, the *City of God* should not be reduced to the schematic of the earthly and heavenly city, as though this oscillation were the book's only theme. Indeed, Augustine waits until the second part of the work to introduce fully the two cities. This massive work in fact covers a wider swath of the territory that occupied Augustine's restless imagination than this duality alone. Nor is it merely, or primarily, a defense of the faith in light of the "fall of Rome"; Augustine's exegetical and historical interests ranged much further than this. Yet, the *City of God* does provide the Christian conception of

6. Elisabeth Schüssler Fiorenza, *The Book of Revelation: Justice and Judgment* (Philadelphia: Fortress Press, 1985); Richard Bauckham, *The Theology of the Book of Revelation* (Cambridge: Cambridge University Press, 1993); Stephen Cook, *The Apocalyptic Literature* (Nashville: Abingdon Press, 2003).

7. O'Donnell qualifies that phrase: he refers to a work "presenting a sustained argument unified around a coherent single theme." James J. O'Donnell, "Augustine, City of God," published on the "Augustine, City of God, A New Commentary" website: http://ccat.sas.upenn.edu/jod/augustine/civ.html.

8. I have used the Dods translation: Augustine, *The City of God* (New York: Modern Library, 1950).

history — the "overarching narrative" — so prominent in much post-liberal Protestant theology in the United States. The *civitas* is born in the eternal heavenly realms, and as a heavenly city, travels with and within the earthly community until its final burnishing and revelation at the end of days.

In recounting the rich intertwining of the cities, Augustine shows his delicate touch in allegorical and typological exegesis, his wide-ranging curiosity about ancient empire and kingdom, and his enduring and ambivalent love of the Roman classics. Spanning all these, and holding them together, is Augustine's eschatological vision. All human history, worldly and biblical, is driven forward by its future consummation in the *amor Dei*, where the love of self is taken up into the love of neighbor, the *polis* of ambition and power into the *oikonomia* of self-sacrifice and humility. Augustine breathes another air in this work than in his *Confessions* or early soliloquies: his genius for inwardness turns outward to the corporate and visible. In the *City of God*, Augustine examines the history of Israel in light of the history of Assyria and Rome, their leaders, aims, conquests and defeats: his *civitas* is the people, ordered by institution and tradition, whether of humanity or of God. The welter of inner drives and conflicts is harnessed for a larger pilgrimage, the movement of whole peoples to hope and long for heavenly places. Like the *Confessions,* the *City of God* encloses its subject matter in the Psalms. The songs of sighing, of desire and yearning, animate the cities in their movement across time, and bind them to joys that pass not away, the *communitas* of eternal Zion.

Augustine does not imagine that these pilgrim cities can be easily or neatly distinguished. Just as the mystery of the divided self resides within a single human life, so the cities indwell the unitary peoples of the earth. The envy and murderous rage of Cain live within Israel, so that Cain and Abel mark the incursion of the fall of the angels in creaturely time.[9] The Church, sown in wheat and tare, cannot be cleanly pried out of its place within Babylon or Rome: it too knows the disorder of the love of glory and the praise of others, the chief sin Augustine named as his own in the *Confessions*. The two cities indwell each other, too, in their longing for permanence and rest. Augustine did not mistake the pagan philosophical culture — the earthly city — for a crude worldliness. He knew full well that the platonism of his young adulthood awakened in him the yearning for another country; even as a rhetor, Augustine was a resident alien, seeking that other city. Augustine's mature work shows his sober recognition of the ambiguity of human his-

9. For these themes, see Books XI, XV-XVIII.

tory, the inner and outer joys and sorrows of its peoples, and its unity in longing for deliverance. There are two, Augustine wrote — he never ceded the dualism in creaturely existence — yet these two are unified in our earthly pilgrimage. It is the work of the eschatological Judge to set wheat apart from tare, and at the end of days to gather the aliens into a Holy City, the heavenly Jerusalem.

Thus, Augustine shows us the way into the eschatological category of the people of God: there are two realities, with eschatological roots; they remain two, yet they are also one; they indwell one another in inescapably historical existence; and their existence is both provisional and eternal, moving through time to a permanent *telos* in the heavenly people of God. The *typos* is unmistakably corporate. Though human drives and hopes are neither reduced nor explained away, the individual and her inwardness is not the gauge of measure. Rather, in Aristotelian fashion, humanity is set already within the body politic and it is in this communal whole that peoples are forged and redeemed. These are the eschatological themes of the book of Revelation — Augustine's work is unthinkable without it — and we will follow Augustine's lead in the theological exposition of the *locus,* "people of God."

But we cannot explore the Augustinian account of the people of God, or Augustine's own reading of the book of Revelation, without examining the modern treatment of the "people of God," the encyclicals of Vatican II. We have said that Augustine's *City of God* formed only one of the exceptions to Christian silence about the *locus,* people of God; the other was *Lumen Gentium,* the modern Augustinian doctrine of the Church. Here the people of God is firmly assimilated to the Church, a joining at once innovative and costly.

The title itself — *A Light to the Nations* — takes Isaiah's promise to Israel, and to its servant, and applies it effortlessly to the Church. Relying perhaps on the universal reach of Israel's light (I will give you as a light to the nations that my salvation may reach to the end of the earth) and its explicit application to the infant Christ in the Nunc Dimittis, *Lumen Gentium* begins its exploration of the Church with the confident confession that "Christ is the light of humanity" and prays that the Vatican Council may take its part in the great work of "bringing to all men that light of Christ which shines out visibly from the Church."[10] Chapter I of the document closes its remarkable catena of scriptural allusions to the Church with this invocation of Au-

10. *Lumen Gentium* 1, p. 350.

gustine: "The Church, 'like a stranger in a foreign land, presses forward amid the persecutions of the world and the consolations of God' announcing the cross and death of the Lord until he comes."[11] This citation from the *City of God* serves as introduction to the first material chapter of the Encyclical, Chapter II, "The People of God." Section 9 is worth quoting at some length:

> God has willed to make men holy and save them, not as individuals without any bond or link between them, but rather to make them into a people who might acknowledge him and serve him in holiness. He therefore chose the Israelite race [*plebem*] to be his own people and established a covenant with it. He gradually instructed this people — in its history manifesting both himself and the decree of his will — and made it holy unto himself. All these things, however, happened as a preparation and figure of that new and perfect covenant which was to be ratified in Christ, and of the fuller revelation which was to be given through the Word of God made flesh. . . . Christ instituted this new covenant, namely the new covenant in his blood; he called a race [*gentibus plebem*] made up of Jews and Gentiles which would be one, not according to the flesh, but in Spirit, and this race would be the new People of God.[12]

As Calvin saw in the "assembly of Israel" the Church, so *Lumen Gentium* saw in the covenant Israel the Church: "As Israel according to the flesh which wandered in the desert was already called the Church of God, so too, the new Israel, which advances in this present era in search of a future and permanent city, is called also the Church of Christ."[13] In this language we have clearly entered the neighborhood of supersessionism, but we must also say that we have not seen that claim fully established here.

Lumen Gentium as a whole echoes the fuller treatment of Christian teaching toward non-Christian traditions, the path-breaking *Nostra Aetate*,[14] in its appeal to those outside the Church who yet remain tied mystically to it: "There is first that people to which the covenants and promises were made, and from which Christ was born according to the flesh: in view of the divine choice, they are a people most dear for the sake of the fathers, for the gifts of God are without repentance."[15] Never clarified within this document is the

---

11. *City of God*, 18.51.2.
12. *Lumen Gentium* 9, pp. 358, 359.
13. *Lumen Gentium* 9, p. 360.
14. *Nostra Aetate*, in *Documents of Vatican II*, 738-742.
15. *Lumen Gentium* 16, p. 367.

proper balance of new people or new Israel to "Israel according to the flesh," nor can we specify here precisely how the Church as the people of a "new and perfect covenant" is to regard the teaching and practice of the people brought up out of the house of bondage into the land of promise. These doctrines — the finality of Christ and the finality of God's gifts — must be made explicit in any full, Christian doctrine of the people of God, and we will take them up at their proper place. But here, we must pause to examine the force and cost of the Vatican's teaching that properly and finally the new people of God is the Christian Church.

So firmly anchored in our minds is the link between people and Church that we scarcely hear how remarkable this claim is. We Christians speak of the members of the Church as "the laity" — the *laos* or people — and we often refer to the whole Church as "clergy and people," or in more Petrine language, as "a holy nation" or "God's own possession," or "people." We assume, that is, that the varying nouns used in the New Testament for groups of persons — *gens, ethnoi, laos, ochlos* — refer in the post-biblical era to the *ekklesia,* the assembly of Christ usually translated as "Church." To make this link, and to firmly assimilate the biblical collectives to the Church, is to point to creed, proclamation, and sacrament, clerical orders and members, rites and traditions, effective calling and confession as the identity and substance of the people of God. Just this association is spelled out in the remainder of *Lumen Gentium:* the document's chapters treat the hierarchy, the religious orders, the priest and laity, with their dignities and duties, and finally Mary as the sign and comfort of the pilgrim people of God. There is, then, no membership in the people without entrance into the Church by baptism; no pilgrimage toward the heavenly city apart from the trials and triumphs of the Church; no earthly city that is also and in its own place the *communitas* of God. The place of Israel and, more acutely, of post-biblical Judaism within the people of God, so construed, is severely straitened in such a doctrine; supersessionism drawn closer. So too the eschatological vision of the people of God is narrowly Church centered. The final reign of Christ is a sacerdotal rule over the Church. Such eschatology lays its emphasis upon the Holy Jerusalem as the true and purified Church, the Pauline "bride of Christ," the mystery of Christ and his Church. In all this, we see the marker of a modern, Latin ecclesiology.

It is a maxim of Church history that a full doctrine of ecclesiology had to wait on the Reformation when the very notion of the Church's unity could be both threatened and affirmed. To be sure, the late antique doctrine of the Church anticipates this modern development — we have seen its flowering in Augustine's *City of God* — but the Reformation era made explicit the doctrine that the One Church could be visibly divided amidst Christendom. The search for authenticity and unity harkened back, of course, to the ancient Church — the "undivided Church" as it is called in a rather romantic note — and the four-fold sign of the true Church recited in the Nicene Creed was tied to the Vincentian universality, antiquity, and ubiquity of Christian teaching.

Significant for our topic is the conviction, particularly among the Puritan dissenters, that the Church properly and transcendently referred to the body of the elect, the saints of God, who alone constituted the true people of God, the city set on a hill. Central to this doctrine was the Augustinian theme of wheat and tare sown together: the visible Church was vital to Reformers on all sides, but it could never replace in Puritan eyes the assembly of the holy ones, known, called, and sanctified by God alone. Here we see the out-working of a divided, and often disestablished, Church which draws to itself the symbol, idiom, and scriptural ideal of the covenant people of God. Indeed it may well be the effect of modern disestablishment on Roman Catholic ecclesiology that brings *Lumen Gentium* so close to Reformed teaching about the holy people of God. The rise of the modern secular state parallels the rise of the modern Church: as the nation-state has moved outside religious profession, so the Church has claimed for itself the religious realm, and those who belong to it are the people who follow, confess, and worship God in Christ. It has not always been divided so.

III. The People of God in Medieval Christendom

At times early and late in Christian history there have been signs of the biblical distinction between people and Church, kingdom of God and creed. One can be detected in the European Middle Ages. Now, there is much mischief in romantic longings for all things medieval, but here I believe Christians could benefit from a backward glance. Medieval Christendom was distinctive, historians tells us, in its "dual monarchy": society was governed by both crown and mitre, each taking its part in Christian *auctoritas*. Princes of the realm were Christian leaders, certainly; even more, they were anointed bearers and instruments of God's providential ordering of society. From these twin powers flowed the struggle known to generations of school children as the "lay investiture controversy," a struggle that paid quiet tribute not simply to the worldly power of bishops but to the sacerdotal authority of kings. A society governed in this fashion ushers in new elements to its ecclesiology.

The Christian people spill out beyond the borders of the Church. They are the subjects of a realm, led by a Christian governor, and in their birth as in their worldly institutions — guilds and courts and carnivals — they are already within the godly. The Christian Church serves this people; it is not identical to it. The clergy guard and offer the cultus, make intercession for rulers and the ruled, and the religious orders tend the sick and the wayfarer. Now I do not mean to suggest that Christendom was in fact an idyll of just this kind! Of course it was the frail and complex and fallen society we know to expect from our own day. But in its material structure, medieval Europe recognized the people of God as a human society in which Church and Realm *subsisted*. We have here a pattern, drawn within Christian history, of a people of God distinct from yet not separated from the Church, the body of Christ. As we shall see, this pattern does not belong to the Middle Ages exclusively. Yet in the European high medieval era, the people of God is most clearly and properly set out as distinctly worldly in the older meaning of secular: the earthly age under the reign of Christ.

Such distinction without separation should strike chords of remembrance for Christians: it is the biblical portrait of the covenant people Israel. From the call of Abraham forward, Scripture portrays a nation or people — the use is roughly synonymous in Hebrew texts — that has been called out, fashioned, and preserved as God's very own, his possession of all the peoples of the earth. Israel is not its Temple only or its Tabernacle; the sacrifices offered by its priests are not Israel *in nuce*. Rather these priests and prophets serve and lead the nation. In Scripture, we are told of a people once numerous in Egypt, enslaved by the king who knew not Joseph, borne out on eagles' wings. That whole people, of all sorts and conditions, stand before Sinai to receive the Torah; that whole nation is enumerated in tribes and houses and fighting legions as they enter Canaan. We are told of the judges who ruled this people, sitting in the gate judging right; of kings who were at once the godly will of and the rebellion of the people against its God; of the commandments, statutes, and ordinances that govern this people; of the exiles, homecomings, and triumphs of this nation; the days of empire and slavery; of Temple, priest, and Levite; of prophets and seers: all these are elements within the history of a whole people and nation, and just this is the covenant of God with Israel.

It is sometimes said — think of Leo Baeck or Martin Buber or, in more somber tones, of Adolf von Harnack[16] — that Judaism differs from Chris-

---

16. Leo Baeck, "Romantic Religion," in *Judaism and Christianity,* trans. Walter Kaufmann

tianity in just this way: that Judaism is a people, Christianity an institution; Judaism a constitution, Christianity a belief; Judaism a practice and way of life, Christianity a confession and system of doctrine; or more pejoratively — sometimes to Christians, sometimes to Jews — Judaism is worldly, Christianity transcendent and other-worldly. There is truth in this contrast — to study Talmud and to learn the catechism is to enter into that contrast — but it can be overdrawn.

Scripture and theological tradition have remembered another way. To read the author of Hebrews ring the changes on this great narrative of Israel is to see how Christians first saw themselves too as people, tribe, and nation of God, the God of Israel. The medieval west in its Christian establishment preserved conceptual room for a people of God alive beyond the borders of the Church. And even in the era of the "modern nation-state," the resonance of a Christian people, moving across generations towards its heavenly end, ruled and fed by magistrate and pastor, has never fallen entirely silent in Christian speech. Consider, among the English people, the appeal to the people of God in John Keble's National Apostasy sermon: this is 1 Samuel as a Christian text for a religious people.[17] *Mutatis mutandis* Abraham Lincoln's great Second Inaugural Address sounds the note of an entire people borne up and chastened by God's providential rule. What the medieval era preserved within Christendom, and the modern nation-state honored at times of crisis, the book of Revelation expresses in full voice. The people of God as a foundational theme in Christian dogmatics finds its richest source in St. John's Revelation.

IV. The People of God in the Book of Revelation

The book begins — surprisingly for our purposes — with an extended reflection on the Church. It opens with the prophet receiving messages for the seven churches of Asia Minor from the One like the Son of Man, the First and Last. These messages are entirely historical and concrete: they address ecclesial assemblies (perhaps under the Roman rule of Domitian) who fare at times well, at times poorly, in their discipleship as members of a fledgling

(Philadelphia: Jewish Publication Society, 1958); Martin Buber, *Two Types of Faith,* trans. N. Goldhawk (London: Routledge & Paul, 1951); Adolf von Harnack, *What Is Christianity?* trans. T. B. Saunders (New York: G. P. Putnam's Sons, 1912).

17. John Keble, *National Apostasy Considered: In a Sermon Preached in St Mary's Oxford, 1833* (London: Mowbray, 1931).

church. I would hazard that anyone who has spent time within a local parish recognizes these assemblies. The members are sometimes bold and courageous; at times lukewarm and tame; they follow odd but alluring ideas; strong personalities stir up conflict; and in them all, their works come under judgment, and they rarely are flattered by the searching light of Christ. These churches, though clearly assemblies of the cities of the eastern Roman empire, find their identity and idiom in the history and conflict of Israel. Indeed the opening invocation of Jesus Christ rings the changes on the covenant language of Israel, already echoed in 1 Peter: "he made us to be a kingdom, priests serving his God and Father." The Church is conceived in near exclusive terms as Israel-shaped.

Striking in this way is the evocation of ancient Israel in the figural use of Jezebel — a foreshadowing of Babylon the Great — and of contemporary Israel in the diagnosis and fear of "Jews who are no Jews." To the Church in Thyatira the prophet is to write in the name of the Son of God, "I have this against you: you tolerate that woman Jezebel, who calls herself a prophet and is teaching and beguiling my servants to practice fornication and to eat food sacrificed to idols." To the Church in Philadelphia: "I will make those of the synagogue of Satan who say that they are Jews and are not, but are lying — I will make them come and bow down before your feet and they will learn that I have loved you." To this Christian world, already bathed in the idiom of covenant Israel, is suddenly brought the world and language of the "faithful remnant," those who have not "bowed the knee to Baal," to borrow the telling phrase from 1 Kings, and to Jews who are not Jews, but, in that fateful phrase, members of the "synagogue of Satan." No reader of the New Testament can hear such language without detecting echoes of Romans and 1 Peter where the image and force of a "righteous remnant" is set in a different key. These echoes are vital to any full Christian doctrine of Jews and Judaism; but here we can focus more closely on the distinctive use of the remnant in Revelation.

The prophet is told that the earthly, historical Church — the refuge of the faithful remnant — faces temptation on two sides: the empire and the unbeliever. While some Christians may have faced persecution or martyrdom — the worthy, perhaps, who walk in robes of white — the Laodiceans appear all too comfortable with an age of empire and global trade: "For you say, I am rich, I have prospered, and I need nothing." The Christian Church is not to make easy friends with the world; rather its identity is to be hewn out by ancient Israel's prophets and their icy rebuke of the callous rich. Even the unbeliever and the "false teachers" of that mysterious "Nicolaitanism" are clothed in the language of Israel: "You have some there," Christ tells the angel of the Church in Pergamum, "who hold to the teaching of Balaam, who taught Balak to put a stumbling block before the people of Israel, so that they would eat food sacrificed to idols and practice fornication."

The Israel-shaped identity of the Church reaches its sharpest point in the repudiation of "false Jews," those who claim membership in the house of Israel yet belong to the house of lies. This fearsome language, certainly, carries another charge when it is spoken between the "fraternal enemies"[18] of a modern church and synagogue. But here we may well wonder whether the prophet John does not see his contemporary Church at its most "Israelmorphic" in its act of discerning the true from false teacher, the true disciple from the false. It may be, as some historians say, that the "synagogue of Satan" in Revelation 3:9 shows evidence of the conflict and final rupture between Church and Synagogue. But, more dogmatically, we may see evidence, rather, of the early Church affirming its membership in the whole people Israel just in this, that they assume the place of the remnant which testifies to the fidelity of Israel's Lord.

The claim by Christians to be a "faithful remnant" may not in itself, then, be supersessionist. Indeed, if the Pauline interpretation is correct — and I believe dogmatically and morally it is so — the remnant exists in order to sustain and purify the whole. As Elijah carried in himself the Lord's promise to make of Abraham and Sarah's descendents a mighty nation, so the believers in Christ, and perhaps in Paul himself, the promise to the whole people Israel is borne and preserved. In an explicit echo of God's chastening love of Israel, Jesus Christ testifies to the Laodiceans that he "reproves and disciplines those he loves." As the whole lump is sanctified through the first fruits, Paul writes in Romans, so the remnant of Israel, lodged within the Church, may belong, even as adversary, to the whole house of Israel. The Church as remnant echoes its Lord in participating in this mysterious relationship of representation — to act for and for the sake of — that Christians recite in the creedal affirmation of the Incarnation and Passion. This Church, then, sown in wheat and tare, may still recognize itself as part of the covenant people Israel, such that the tares — even those "learned in the deep things of Satan" — may remain Israelites, however unworthy, and those proud Christians, however "wretched, pitiable, poor, blind and naked," may remain among those disciplined in love. Like Augus-

---

18. The phrase is Franz Rosenzweig's. See *The Star of Redemption* (Notre Dame: Notre Dame Press, 1971), 415.

tine's pilgrim Church, commingled from heavenly and earthly cities, the seven churches of Revelation commingle the true and false believers within its walls but also beyond, in the whole covenant people Israel. The duality remains, Augustine teaches; yet in the mystery of this pilgrimage toward God, the two indwell one another as one.

All this talk of Church and Synagogue, of remnant and whole, dramatically falls away when a door opens in the heavens and, in the Spirit, John is given sight of the heavenly court. Here all talk of the earthly assembly fades away. The heavenly realm John is shown contains the full furnishings of apocalyptic disturbance: red dragons and living beasts; great storms of voices like thunder; terrible creatures with wings and hair and teeth; nightmarish plagues and symbols; and mighty cities roaring and burning with the smoke that goes up forever. Such visions, hypnotic as they are, do not wholly absorb the seer into heavenly things and places: these visions are, in Stephen Cook's fine phrase, the Divine "climactic intervention into the world."[19] Think of the four horsemen, riding out to do their terrible work at the opening of the seven seals. As if to sum up the suffering of the world: "I looked, and behold, a pale horse: and his name that sat on him was Death, and Hell followed with him. And power was given unto them over the fourth part of the earth, to kill with the sword, and with hunger and with death and with the beasts of the earth" (Rev. 6:8). The entire Apocalypse interweaves the heavenly and earthly — the awesome destruction of Babylon is at once transcendent and historical; the Temple earthly and heavenly — such that we see, in this distorted and luminous imagery, how God's sovereignty is exercised in the crisis of the earth. It is perhaps unnecessary to add that all this is expressed in the vivid language of Israel, especially of Daniel and his visions of the end-time. The convulsions of the earth are inscribed with the pattern of Israel's suffering: the people's exile and wandering, persecution and famine, disobedience and luxury, and final vindication and rest. The earthly city, even at its most ungodly, is depicted through the imagery of Israel and its enemies: on earth, the two cities are one.

But we here are granted a glimpse of the heavenly city, the people of the new heaven and new earth, and it is this eschatological vision that is most central for our task. Chapter 21, already cited at the beginning of this essay, crystallizes the vision of the heavenly people of God but this vision is scattered in fragments throughout the book. Remember that John is drawn into the heavenly vision on the Lord's Day: the revelation is itself a liturgical act

19. Cook, *Apocalyptic Literature*, 22.

of the people. The Divine throne room is suffused with worship. Day and night the elders and the living creatures fall down in worship, raising as their hymn the prayer of Isaiah in the Temple. Indeed we might say that the whole courtroom of the eternal places is a liturgical hymn: the vision of the throne room is structured by the four great hymns of the courtiers, and the prayers of the millions and millions, in heaven and on the earth and under the earth and in the sea, the worship that goes on forever and ever. Yet there is nothing of what a modern age will call the "institutional Church": there are no worship leaders here or priests to carry out sacrifice; no Church buildings or officers. The Church does not appear in the opening of the seals and the great battle of the armies of the dragon and of Christ. Significantly, the Temple and Tabernacle of heaven *do* appear as an *inclusio* around the great battle of heaven and earth, opened in judgment and proclamation. Yet these sightings of the Temple during the great ordeal serve to heighten the contrast at the end time. Then, neither Temple nor Church appear in the pure heavenly city that descends from the renovated cosmos: for God is its light and the Lamb its lamp. All this is worth a second look.

The first thing that strikes the Christian reader in these chapters is the distinctive pluralism of the heavenly throne room. Accustomed to thinking in broad, general categories — clergy and laity; head and members — Christians often think of *sameness* when they turn to the heavenly places. All are angels; or more carefully, like angels. But Revelation shows us not homogeneity or even serried ranks, favored by the medievals in their eschatological doctrine. Rather we have an *aliquot,* a happy jumble of kinds and groups around the Divine throne. There are angels, there are four and twenty elders, four beasts with eyes, each with different apocalyptic form, and seven spirits that are sent forth into the world. Then come horsemen, and the 144,000 sealed servants of the tribes of Israel, and the multitude beyond number, clothed in white, a woman clothed with the sun, the great King Faithful and True with his army, and then at the last the judges on their thrones who did not worship the beast, and the nations and kings, written in the Book of Life.

Here we are given an image of the people of God, a multitude of many groups and kinds, each with their calling and task, never sublated into the other or harmonized or ranked into a single orderly procession. This people is drawn from the tribes of Israel and the nations of the earth, from "every family, language, people, and nation." Such is the assembly that gathers around Christ the Lamb. As in his earthly ministry, so in his heavenly rule, Christ gathers to him the many — the lost and dispossessed, yes, but also the centurion and Pharisee, the Ethiopian courtier, the wealthy dyer of purple

— and these remain his while remaining this distinct lot. While "nothing unclean" enters there, we may well imagine that in this great army and assembly of the last days, there enter all sorts and conditions: the high and low, the timid and bold, the wounded, lame and whole, the skeptic and credulous, the elder and younger brother, the 11th hour worker and forerunner, the Jew and gentile; all in many mansions and sheepfolds. We can of course reduce this observation to a banality: the people of God is diverse; and diversity is good. But Scripture invites us deeper.

Christ, the First and Last, draws to himself, from that earthly time, a whole that is irreducibly complex and multiple. Just as the whole city, the *polis,* Mark tells us, crowded into Simon Peter's doorway to meet the One who taught with authority, so the eschatological city is a crowd of peoples, saints unified in their Object but not in their subjectivity. So too the Gospels, though harmonized by the Reformers in their commentaries and Tatian in his synoptic narrative, remain multiple and complex. No more is ancient Israel's narrative an unvarnished whole, but rather an unfolding from First to Last with multiple versions and layers and attestations, each resonant to the other but not finally reducible to it. More pronounced still is the narrative enfolding of one part in each in Revelation, so that time itself in the heavenly city is discordant, overlapping, and complex. In Daniel, in Ezekiel, in Revelation, time shimmers with an odd light — who has not stumbled at the "time, two times, and a time and a half"? — and that oddness seems to point to visionary literature and its transcendence. But we can say more.

The multiplicity of the earthly and heavenly court of God, and the scriptural witness itself, parallels at greater depth what Kant called the schematism of the categories: the noumenal and ideal categories of reason must be put into relation — *schema* in Greek — with the temporal and spatial; they must become historical, temporal, and sequential.[20] The parallel must be treated with a light touch, of course! But we might say in this Kantian vein that the worldly and creaturely realm that comes by the Spirit into the presence of the Lord and the Lamb must be "schematized": broken into temporal sequence, spread out under the conditions of historical humanity, into families and nations and tongues, into Church and Synagogue, into states and principalities, and remain on earth not utterly one but spatial, wide-ranging, and complex. Just this multiplicity *is* the relation of creature to Creator, the many to the One, the witnesses to the Truth, the earthly

---

20. Immanuel Kant, *The Critique of Pure Reason* (New York: St. Martin's Press, 1956), Book II, Chapter 1.

city commingled with the heavenly, the people to the Lord God of Israel. *A fortiori* this complexity dominates earthly life. But even in the heavenly realm, where Death and mourning and first things are passed away, a certain creaturely distinctiveness remains amidst the luminous unity.

We might see a shadow of this theme in an important variant in the final vision of Revelation. The book concludes with the great hymn of the heavenly city, the new Jerusalem descending like a bride: "See, the Tabernacle of God is among mortals, he will tabernacle with them; they will be his *peoples,* and God himself will be with them." In the final consummation of the covenant, whend is Gohimself the Tabernacle and Temple, the happy throng invited to the Supper of the Lamb remains plural, a multitude of peoples brought to God. To place all this in a more scriptural idiom, we might say that in Christ Jesus there is neither slave nor free, male nor female, Jew nor Greek; but all are one in him. This eschatological unity takes place in the Spirit and in Christ — the world is shattered and made a new whole in this glancing light of the age to come — yet the world remains in our age and culture divided, complex, multiple.

And we may think too of the older use of "schema" when we consider the Lord and Lamb on the throne in the heavenly places. Following the Protestant attraction to the humanist logician Petrus Ramus, older dogmaticians such as Polanus and Ames and Turretini said that when God is in relation — *schema* — with creatures, what is one in God must be said as two.[21] Here we have a multiplicity that is not irreducible *in se* but remains so *pro nobis.* The Divine perfections, the acts of election, the works of creation and redemption: these metaphysical elements are utterly and uniquely one in God but epistemologically multiple and dialectical for us. When the prophet John looks on the Divine throne-room, he expresses his vision with near technical, scholastic precision: always the throne has seated upon it the Lord God and the Lamb, and the perfections given the Ancient of Days are mirrored in the Lamb, the Lord's light, and the Lamb's lamp. Just so, Jesus is depicted at once as Lamb and Righteous King and Child, at once one and many. The vision granted John does not elevate him above the conditions of the creature; still he must see the surpassing one as the two, God and the Lamb.

---

21. See, for example, François Turretini, *Institutes of Elenctic Theology* (Phillipsburg: P&R Publishers, 1992-1997); and William Ames, *Marrow of Theology,* ed. J. Eusden (Boston: Pilgrim Press, 1968).

V. Conclusion

In the end, when we consider the people of God in eschatological light, we must ask about this heavenly city which is at once two and one. Recall that the gates to the city are inscribed with the names of the twelve tribes of Israel, three to a side. And this wall has twelve *foundations;* these bear the names of the twelve apostles. Within this wall is the city the prophet again measures, this time with a rod of gold. Rather than the Temple of the earth, measured at the out-break of the great war, John now measures the heavenly city, the gates, and the walls. A perfect cube of translucent gold, the city measures 12,000 stadia on every side. Dazzling with gems and pearls and luminous gold, the city sees no night nor change of day: it is lit from within by the Unity-in-distinction of the Light-Lamp of God. This is the city that has no Church and no Temple. God himself dwells with the peoples; he *is* the divine tabernacle. No reader of the New Testament can miss the Johannine echo here: the Word became flesh and tabernacled among us — the Greek is the same — and it is this Incarnate Word who declares himself the Temple, destroyed and risen again on the third day.

In the final chapter of Revelation we see with crystalline clarity and rigor the exegetical foundation of Augustine's own theology of the people of God. Here, drawn together in dazzling display are the themes that undergird Augustine's two cities. Recall that Augustine held that history is composed of two realities with eschatological destinies; they remain two, yet they are also one; they indwell one another in inescapably historical existence; and their existence is both provisional and eternal, moving through time to a permanent *telos* in the heavenly people of God. The *typos* is unmistakably corporate. Humanity is set already within the body politic and it is in this communal whole that peoples are forged and redeemed. The book of Revelation expresses these eschatological themes in its own vivid, apocalyptic idiom.

On the opening of the seventh seal, the blast of the seventh trumpet, the prophet John is shown the final vision of the covenant, the final, eschatological image of the people of God. Flesh and blood are to dwell with God and see him face to face. "I shall be your God and you shall be my people," the sum of the covenant, is realized in this Holy Jerusalem. It is secular in the old sense: the *polis* of the peoples. It is God-saturated: not mediated but direct vision of God is its perfect worship. It is Israel, the twelve tribes as entrance and crown. It is the apostolate, the twelve disciples as basis and ground. It is the tree of life, the hidden gift of Eden; it is the redemption of life East of Eden, the "leaves are for the healing of the nations." It is First and Last, even as its Lord is Alpha and Omega. It is Jew and gentile; but these as caught up in the Unity-in-distinction of the Divine Life itself. Beyond knowledge and experience, they are one even as the Son and Father are one; yet they are distinct, preserved and hallowed in their own place in the Holy City. The finality of Christ is the finality of Israel: when God will be all in all, when Church and Synagogue drop away, the Faithful and True Witness will be just this, God dwelling with his own, the many yet one people of God.

Will All Be Saved, or Only a Few?
A Dialogue between Faith and Grace

Jürgen Moltmann

Translated by Margaret Kohl

Faith says: "The one who believes and is baptized will be saved; but the one who does not believe will be condemned" (Mark 16:16). So: "Enter by the narrow gate; for the gate is wide and the way is easy that leads to destruction, and those who enter by it are many. But the gate is narrow and the way is hard that leads to life, and those who find it are few" (Matt. 7:13f.).

Grace replies: But we also read: "God desires all men to be saved and to come to knowledge of the truth. For there is one God and one mediator between God and men, the man Jesus Christ, who gave himself as a ransom for all, the testimony to which was borne at the proper time" (1 Tim. 2:4-6).

Faith: God can only help those who let themselves be helped. Grace is an offer from God in the final hour. The person who rejects the offer is lost. The person who seizes it will be saved. Faith is the presupposition for salvation; unbelief leads straight to hell.

Grace: My dear Faith, do you think that God's will is so feeble that even though he wants to help all human beings, he is unable to do so without their cooperation? Do you think that human beings are so strong that they can do what they like with God's gracious will? Who are you, human Faith, that you can set yourself up like this above God's will, and make God your servant? What God wills, he will also do, for God is God. Surely you believe that too?

Faith: I believe that "a man is just by faith apart from the works of the law," as Paul writes in Romans 3:28 — "by faith alone," as Luther translates it. "He who through faith is righteous will live" (Rom. 1:17). That is to say, God justifies only those who believe. Unbelievers remain subject to the wrath of

God. I am just because I believe. I am certain only of my own faith, and take it seriously.

Grace: Thank you for bringing up the question of faith, Faith. For what does faith believe? According to the apostle Paul whom you quote, faith believes that "God justifies the ungodly" (Rom. 4:5). And according to the same Paul, faith believes that "the righteousness of one man — that is, Jesus Christ — leads to acquittal and life for all" (Rom. 5:18). Human beings do not experience grace because they believe but in order that they may believe. It is only when they experience grace that they are able to believe. They cannot do so on their own initiative. If they could, my grace would be quite superfluous.

Faith: But it is I, Faith, who make the difference between salvation and damnation. Doesn't your grace come by way of the word of the gospel, which calls people to faith but does not coerce them? It is through conviction that people arrive at faith, not through force. It is no merit to a person if he believes, but it is still his own fault if he doesn't believe and is doomed. So the grace that is proclaimed is still focused on the free will of a human being who can or cannot believe.

Grace: My dear Faith, didn't the same Martin Luther you are appealing to write a famous book in 1525 against Erasmus called *On the Bondage of the Will*? Of course a person has free will in dealing with things, and also in the human atmosphere of trust, but God is God, and neither an object nor another person. Before God, men and women realize their true condition: the sin that cuts them off from God, and which they are unable to overcome. So God must liberate the will which sin has enslaved. The forgiveness of sins and the healing of the sick is the beginning of faith. It is all grace — grace that calls you, and grace that empowers you to believe.

Faith: "No one is predestined by God to go to hell. It is only a voluntary turning away from God, a deadly sin, persisted in to the end, which leads to damnation," says the Catholic catechism of 1992. And the 1995 declaration of the Anglican Doctrine Commission, "The Mystery of Faith," even maintains: "Nevertheless it is our conviction that the reality of hell (and indeed heaven) is the ultimate affirmation of the reality of human freedom." What do you have to say to that?

Grace: I am astonished. Earlier, the unfathomable resolve of God was at the center of ideas about judgment. It is God who elects and condemns, who saves and judges, and human beings bowed to his resolve in reverence before him. Today, it is the responsible human being who is at the center. Free, sovereign human beings are the architects of their own happiness or the diggers of their own graves. If they want to go to heaven, they believe and lead a good life. If they want to go to hell, they persist in some deadly sin. God is turned into the other-worldly executor of this sovereign human being's will. Heaven and hell become images reflecting the freedom of the human will over against God. Is this supposed to be an anthropological turning point? Then God becomes superfluous and my grace is dispensable. I cannot find anything Christian in these ideas. They would seem to derive from the Egyptian Book of the Dead rather than from the Bible.

Faith: If my faith is my own decision, then this decision is also bound up with a division: on the one side faith and on the other side unbelief. Haven't these decisions and divisions any significance for eternity? Doesn't God judge according to the decision of faith, and in his judgment divide the sheep from the goats?

Grace: I am God's grace: my eyes are not fixed on the good deeds of human beings or their decision whether to believe or not. I am God's mercy on all miserable and lost men and women. And because of that I am universal: "God has consigned all men to disobedience, that he may have mercy upon all," says my witness Paul, in Romans 11:32.

Faith: But that can't be! Wasn't your somber companion always at your side — the wrath of God, the dark side of God, God's hidden face, *hester panim?* After all, everything is not just sweetness and light. Sinners still feel that they are in the hands of a wrathful God. Where there is light there must be shadow as well. Where there is good there is also evil. Where heaven beckons, hell must threaten too. If there is no eternal torment, then there is no eternal bliss either.

Grace: Do you say that out of insight into grace or for the sake of the symmetry, as Augustine once did? God's wrath and his grace do not have the same weight. "His anger is but for a moment, and his favor is for a lifetime" (Ps. 30:5). My wrath is not hate; it is nothing other than my wounded love. So my anger does not stand side by side with me as an equal partner; it stands behind me, because it has been overcome. I have overcome in myself my pain over the sins of my children, and run to meet them full of compassion. That is the very point of the raising of the Christ crucified for sinners. So in the world too, good and evil can never have equal weight. Evil is the negation of good. There is an old English word (out of use now) which talks about evil as "ungood." But there was never a word "unevil" for good. Just because good is eternal, evil cannot possibly be eternal. Because God's salvation is eternal, hell cannot be equally eternal, for then its misery would have a share in God's eternity. Because salvation is eternal, disaster has an end. Death, misery, and hell have an end because grace is eternal.

Faith: Well, in my theological tradition, the Last Judgment is still a judgment of the divine wrath, *a judgment according to the works* of human beings. *"Dies irae, dies illa, solvet seclum in favilla"* — a day of wrath, on that day the world will dissolve into ashes — so people sang in the Middle Ages. God calls human beings to account for everything they have done and have not done. He punishes and rewards according to his final retributive justice: good with good, evil with evil. Then the good people will enter into the kingdom of glory. The godless will be cast out into the realm of eternal darkness. The Last Judgment will bring with it the end of this world. Except for angels and human beings, everything belonging to this world will be burnt up by fire and will dissolve into nothingness. The structure of the world will no longer be required once the blessed in heaven look upon God directly, face to face. So the decision of faith has eternal significance, and so has the decision not to believe. Everything which men and women do is of ultimate importance. All will have to account for themselves before God at the final judgment.

Grace: From my perspective, it is not primarily a matter of the doers of good or evil works; it is a matter of the victims of evil and violence. So I would begin with the judgment that follows suffering. For the victims of sin must receive justice. Justice must be done to those who have suffered violence. They must be raised up, and given their rights, healed and brought back to life. The perpetrators will not ultimately triumph over their victims. The one who will triumph is Christ, who is on the side of the victims. For the victims of sin, his justice is not a retributive justice, but a justice that creates justice and heals wounds, wipes away tears and creates new life for the murdered. Why? Because at the Last Judgment the Judge is Christ, the crucified Son of man, and with him appear "the least of his brothers and sisters," the poor, the sick, and the prisoners (Matt. 25). The perpetrators will be judged in the presence of their victims. They will be led out of their injustice and put right. "If any man's work is burnt up, he will suffer loss but he himself will be saved' (1 Cor. 3:15). I, Grace, free the victims of sin and the slaves of sin from the power of the sin which enthralls them. The Last Judgment has to do with the godless powers of sin and death. And from all godless powers the earth must be purified. The Last Judgment is not the end of the world; it is the beginning of the new creation of all things. After the judgment that creates justice and puts the unjust right, the divine promise will be fulfilled: "Behold, I make all things new" (Rev. 21:5). The verdicts at the Last Judgment do not have to do with the past, and not merely with human beings; they are also related to this future and to the whole globe (Ps. 96:10-13), so that a new earth on which righteousness dwells may come into being.

Faith: Then isn't there a hell anymore? What happens to unbelievers? I admit that the ideas and images of hell which we find in churches and theologies resemble a religious torture chamber from which not even death can liberate people. The Byzantine Church Father Chrysostom said that hell was "the land of eternal death in which there is no life, the place of darkness in which there is no light, an abyss out of which the sighs of the damned rise up, without their finding anyone to hear them. There all the senses are tormented, sight through eternal darkness, hearing through weeping and the gnashing of teeth, smell through the stink of sulfur, taste through the bitterness of eternal death, feeling through eternal torment." The Lutheran Augsburg Confession of 1530, Article 17, puts it more briefly: "But ungodly men and the Devil will be condemned to hell and to eternal punishment." In 1995, the Doctrine Commission of the Church of England finally did away with hell, replacing it by "total non-being." However we imagine hell, even if we abstract all its horrible fascination and all its sadism, what remains is still an inescapable remoteness from God, and a God-forsakenness that knows no way out; it is this that threatens the godless and unbelievers after death. Talk about hell is indispensable if we are to make the seriousness of the human situation before God plain.

Grace: My dear Faith, when you think about hell, why do you think about the unbelievers and worry about their fate? Look at Jesus Christ, who died for you and for unbelievers, and descended into hell, and who in his resurrection opened for you all the future of life. "Look upon the wounds of Christ — there for thee has thy hell been overcome," wrote Luther in 1519. Why did Christ descend into hell? Because he holds in his hands "the keys of death and of hell" (Rev. 1:18). What does he do with these "keys"? He throws open the portals of death in order to waken the dead, and opens the gates of hell in order to liberate the godless from their remoteness from God. Through his descent into hell Christ himself becomes the hope of the despairing. No one has to "abandon hope" — the words Dante set above the entrance to hell. All can join in the Easter jubilation: "Hell, where is thy victory?" (1 Cor. 15:55). Christ comes to seek that which was lost. It would be a tragedy for him if any were lost beyond his finding. By raising Christ from the dead, God has in this one person overcome death itself, and in him, God has begun his new creation, in which death will be no more. By raising him from hell, God has through this one person destroyed hell and begun the new world in which God "will be all in all" (1 Cor. 15:28). In this divine omnipresence there can be no regions that are far from God. The annihilation of death and the destruction of hell are part of Christ's cosmic rule. That rule does not just have to do with the fate of human beings; its essence is the surmounting and annihilation of all the powers that are hostile to God and godless, so that God's true and enduring creation may be just and indestructible. God's new world is heaven on earth, and in that world there is no longer any underworld of death and hell.

So, finally, Grace says to Faith: You are my dearest child. In all human beings I call to you, wait for you and hope to see you. You are my echo, my resonance, my longed-for response. It is for your sake that I come. In the bright day I go round with the lantern of the gospel and seek you in the hearts and minds of all human beings, great and small, women and men, Jews and Gentiles, the learned and the unlearned. When I have found you I have found my joy, and we celebrate the festival of eternal life.

And then Faith says to Grace: I owe everything to you, my redeemer, my liberator, my mother. I am nothing. You are everything. You are there not only for me. You are universal and without conditions, and run ahead to meet all and everyone. If I can be saved through your mercy, who, then, cannot be saved? Whom do you not then embrace?

So universal Grace and particular Faith join their voices and say: We praise and extol the just and merciful God, Father, Son, and Holy Spirit. Everything in heaven and on earth and under the earth will be thrown open, for you glorify yourself in them all. In your glorification lies the salvation of all men and women and the beauty of all things. They reflect your perfection and to you they raise their songs of praise.

Wholly Called, Holy Callings: Questioning the Secular/Sacred Distinctions in Vocation

Stephen L. Stell

"Does God really care what job I get? I mean, as long as I'm 'good with God' and treating other people right . . . and as long as my job doesn't make me do something immoral . . . does it really matter to God what I end up doing work-wise?"

That was the first question raised as I queried my upper-level class, "Finding the Good Life," on their vocational interests and concerns. As the conversation progressed, a number of related issues emerged. Does "vocation" mean that God has a *specific* profession in mind for my life? Moreover, if God is calling me to a particular career, does that mean I am also called to a particular job or worksite? Does a person have multiple vocations at once — career, spouse, community and church callings — and, if so, how do these various callings interact and affect one another? Can you lose or miss out on a vocation to which God is calling you? Is losing a *sense* of calling the same thing as losing the vocation itself? Can you actually have a vocation even if you don't *feel* called to anything? Can a vocation change and, if so, what causes that to happen?

More practical questions soon arose. What is the connection between God's calling on the major decisions in one's life (college, career, spouse) and the multitude of daily choices that you must make — small decisions which end up shaping your course in life in unknown ways? (So, for example, the college you choose or even the classes or extra-curricular activities selected may play a role in finding your spouse.) In such interpersonal matters, does the notion of divine calling suggest that God has one particular spouse in mind for you? Or are there perhaps several (several hundred? several thousand?) that would be equally suitable out of the six billion people on the planet? Does God guide you toward a particular person or only towards the qualities and characteristics of people that would be suitable, leaving the actual choice up to you?

After this flood of questions, someone felt the need to define our terms and clarify their uses. Is calling a one-way communication — God speaks and you hear — or is God's calling a form of dialogue that draws upon an ongoing relationship with God? In the course of making everyday choices, is there a difference between God's "calling" and God's "guidance" or "direction" or "will" concerning particular decisions? How do you deal *theologically* with the fact that your choice of college may end up affecting your choice of a spouse? Does that mean that you have a divine calling not only toward a particular person, but also toward a particular college and that together with your career choices these are mysteriously linked in some kind of divinely orchestrated causal nexus? Such complex sequences of personal choices makes God's calling dependent on a host of unpredictable circumstances and a baffling array of psychological, sociological, and situational influences and responses. How can one make sense of God's call within this expanding universe of interrelated choices, causes, effects, and random events?

Exploring Available Options

The process of thinking through such questions is more complicated today than in previous eras. Indeed many of our current theoretical and practical dilemmas concerning vocation simply did not exist within former conceptions of the world — a world which was simpler and in many ways more neatly organized. The neo-Platonic universe of early Christianity provided an ordered framework that helped to define the meaning of one's life by one's position within this order. When one dwells within a fixed, well-planned world ordained by God, the divine call can be readily determined from the providential circumstances of one's life; God's calling coincides with one's placement in this sacramental universe. The God who created this ordered reality also providentially sustains it through divinely appointed offices or stations that people uphold as they perform their respective roles. One's clear calling from God is thus structured by the constancy and ordered consistency of this divinely appointed world.

In the not-too-distant past, then, people often entered professions by apprenticing with available family relations. One's gender, socio-economic status, education, training, birth position, etc. — each interrelated with the others — became determinative for pursuing one's livelihood. Job possibilities and goals were thus envisioned from the perspective of one's place in this providentially structured universe. In this situation, there was a "natural" move from one's position in the world to one's profession — a move that was readily experienced as divine calling. Living within this well-ordered existence, it was reasonable to discern one's calling in life from the "givens" of one's circumstances. Conversely, as people gained their identities from these "givens," their lives reinforced the ordered realities constituting a divine call.

Such circumstances in life also functioned to reinforce a notion of calling within marriage and interpersonal relations. In arranged marriages, "calling" was determined by the divinely ordained authorities who prescribed one's mate. Yet even apart from arranged marriages, the "right" spouse was defined by a number of limiting prescriptions such as age, religion, race, socio-economic status, educational level, national and political associations, etc. which served to focus the call. Moreover, given the small towns, rural environments, and lack of mobility during much of Christian history, there were further limitations on the number and variety of spousal options. In these circumstances, to discern the "one right person" — like the "one right job" — was much easier and more intelligible than in the current universe of constantly expanding and complexly interrelated options.

This perception of being *called to* the concrete circumstances in one's life as well as receiving a *call from* these concrete circumstances was given a boost by the theology of Martin Luther. In many ways, Luther maintains the medieval divinely ordered universe while extending God's calling to even more people. Luther's rejection of a hierarchical distinction between clergy and lay people — the priesthood of all believers — inevitably broadens vocation beyond religious callings. Or more accurately, Luther expands the notions of *religious* calling to include *all* Christians and not just those of religious orders. Discerned from the perspective of faith, the farmer has a vocation to be part of God's providential care by feeding God's children; the tailor helps God to clothe them; husbands and wives, sons and daughters, politicians and priests, have their respective callings which fulfill God's good intentions in this providential order.

In challenging the unique status of ecclesiastical callings Luther's reformation expanded the ways in which *all* people are now *called to* a specific station in responsibility before God. Yet at the same time, this focus on specific stations restricted and reified people's "place" *in* the world, thereby solidifying the ways in which divine calling could be extrapolated *from* the world and one's concrete circumstances therein. Thus a view of providence which expanded vocation also restricted it by reinforcing one's "station" in the world (Luther's *Stand*), thereby limiting the scope and flexibility of God's call and reinforcing the status quo.

Luther's application of vocation to the common worker thus had little to do with modern ideals of equality, social mobility, or freedom of choice in the work-world. Instead Luther's expanded formulation of vocation emerges from a re-conception of God's relationship to the world (e.g., the priesthood of all believers and God's grace operating therein) which nevertheless continues to assume the basic framework of a largely static, providentially ordered world. Luther's new theological insights concerning this divinely ordered universe, though significant, were small compared to the far-reaching changes that were shortly to emerge and transform future conversations concerning vocation.

As modernity develops and other relations between God and the world take hold, more fundamental changes break in and alter the worldly structures in which vocation is envisioned. A world of ongoing evolution, for example, dissolves any notion of calling determined by one's place in a static universe. The ascendancy of evolution in scientific and historical thought also provides a context fostering greater human responsibility for the future. Similarly deism in religion re-conceives God's relationship to the world, leaving humanity more free and God's purposes less predictable and less prescriptive concerning the concrete details of existence.

A world increasingly envisioned as open, changing, and changeable provides a new interpretive framework for conversations on vocation. Successful revolutions on the political front, the rise of the middle class, increased social mobility and societal flexibility, new contact and cross-pollination among diverse cultures, alternative ways of conceiving the world scientifically, culturally, and religiously, all form interpretive contexts in which one's "place" is not so clearly defined. Moreover, these changing contexts provide a new rational framework for one's interpretations of vocation, making previous arguments less credible and convincing. Accordingly changing conceptions of the world automatically alter conceptions of divine calling. With the shift from the medieval to the modern world, or from modernity to postmodernity, former positions on vocation are deemed to be implausible and/ or irrelevant.

Today as never before one's place in the world is not so much "given" or "discerned" as it is *forged* by individual choices and actions. As previous notions of vocation become unhinged within a dynamic expanding universe of responsible actions and unpredictable cultural evolution, vocational discernment and explanation become considerably more complex. Current post-modern interpretive frameworks make the assessment of a "natural" sense of calling — whether in personal relations (such as marriage) or in work — virtually incoherent.

These conceptual tensions are matched by the practical pressures of changing economic realities. In today's world, people change careers — not simply jobs, but professions — four or five times over the course of their lives. And they do so through newspaper ads, online job postings, established business contacts, personal connections, and serendipitous circumstances. A similar set of dynamic factors influence the course of our relationships (spouses, partners, friends, colleagues, etc.). Indeed the unmanageable flux of complicated factors shaping one's opportunities in life makes vocational discernment like reading tea leaves, and comparably mystifying as to God's place in this whole process or our place in God's processes, however those divine processes may be conceived these days.

How, then, are we to understand the fluidity of these theoretical and practical situations in terms of *theological* callings? Is God somehow divinely orchestrating this multiplicity of factors that influence one's job opportunities and "callings"? At best, doesn't "calling" in this context become a dynamic series of echoes bouncing off ever-changing possibilities and evolving situations? If so, is it rationally compelling to refer to such interacting resonances as "a calling"? Or, on the other hand, does theology need to proceed on the bases of what is most accessible to our understanding? If one has conceptual difficulties *making sense of* a position within our current intellectual worlds, is that an adequate reason for rejecting it? If so, the exponential increase in our available choices and the increasing complexity of factors defining our choices (psychological, sociological, genetic, circumstantial, cultural, personal/familial, etc.) makes any specific notion of God's calling extremely difficult to delineate and defend.

Narrowing the Field

Given these vocational complexities, many would argue that it makes sense to understand divine calling in narrower terms: as directing one's life toward God, and not trying to unravel the broad, convoluted intricacies that define our personal relations and workplace roles. In our present context defined by an exponential increase in both available choices and the contributing factors shaping those choices (psychological, sociological, cultural, familial, circumstantial, etc.), it becomes all the more attractive to eliminate a notion of divine calling that tries to encompass the detailed particulars of one's life. Instead we can develop a "minimalist" or "essentialist" view of divine calling which focuses on being "good with God" (as voiced by the first question in my upper-level seminar). Such a perspective is given more careful and sustained development in Gary Badcock's *The Way of Life*.[1]

According to Badcock, "at best one's work can be understood as vocation only in a secondary and derivative sense."[2] In the primary sense of vocation, "Christian calling refers to the reorientation of human life to God through repentance, faith, and obedience; to participation in God's saving purpose in history; and to the heavenly goal. . . ."[3] This heavenly call, then, "is nothing less than to love God and one's neighbor, as Jesus teaches — or alternatively, to respond to the Word of grace with faith and obedience . . . in other words, to live the Christian life."[4]

In Badcock's argument, God need not care whether you become a mechanic or a postal worker. Professions are only significant as they influence your relationship with God. Whatever divine prescriptions may exist for the course of your life, they will not be concerned with mundane details. "Modern society has long since abandoned such ideas of providence, and Christian theology has generally followed suit."[5] Although beginning a dialogue with Luther, Badcock quickly shuts the conversation down. "His whole conception of vocation as a religious duty is totally foreign to modern culture."[6] For Badcock, "a great gulf yawns between Luther's conception and the values of the contemporary world."[7] This chasm makes meaningful dialogue impossible and calls for a theological re-formulation of vocation adequate to our current context.

In contrast to God's exhaustive specification of vocational choices,

1. Gary Badcock, *The Way of Life: A Theology of Christian Vocation* (Eugene, OR: Wipf and Stock, 2002; previously published by William B. Eerdmans, 1998).
2. Ibid., 9.
3. Ibid., 9-10.
4. Ibid., 10.
5. Ibid., 40.
6. Ibid., 44.
7. Ibid.

Badcock's faith-centered understanding of vocation is much more accessible both in theory and in practice. On the practical side, Badcock relieves the pressure to find the "one right job," thereby avoiding the plaguing complexities of definitive discernment. We may seek vocational testing to tell us what jobs will be most enjoyable, most fulfilling, or most coincident with our "signature strengths,"[8] and we are free to act upon such findings. But these psychological insights do not tell us what God wants or intends for our lives. They are rather practical bits of information that we can integrate with many other variables to facilitate *our* decision-making process.

On the theoretical side, Badcock's narrower religious perspective on vocation is more comprehensible than any complicated interpretive framework which can make sense of the impenetrable mysteries of detailed divine callings. A framework which is more comprehensible can also be more relevant, more applicable, and more persuasive, offering numerous practical and theoretical grounds for affirming Badcock's theology of vocation.

The strengths of Badcock's position are thus clear and credible, and many find it wholly persuasive. Paradoxically, however, many of my theology students initially affirmed Badcock's perspective for its practical benefits and theoretical accessibility, but when it came to formulating their own plans for the future they felt the need to go beyond him. One student, contemplating teaching within the challenging contexts of an inner city school, wrote the following:

> No one wants to teach in a school like that, myself included. However, the more I think about it the more I am certain that this is what I am supposed to be doing. Not because I necessarily think that God is directly calling me to be a teacher in a poor school. I agree with Badcock that God probably doesn't care too much. But more because if the purpose of me going into education is to make a real difference for students, and those schools have a real need for help, I cannot justify using my gifts elsewhere.

From Badcock's perspective, one can be a Christian and have a strong relationship with God regardless of where one teaches, or even *if* one teaches. Yet notice the ironic situation that arises here. My student cares deeply about those in need but imagines a God whose caring is not as resolute or demanding as her own. Moreover, contrary to Badcock's separation of the secular and the sacred, her specific expressions of care are not separa-

8. Cf. Martin Seligman's *Authentic Happiness* (New York: Free Press, 2002), especially 134-161.

ble from her faith in God. Based on her background, it becomes clear that both her value system and her "heart" are shaped by the works of God's Spirit in her, including the formative role of religion in her life. Her conviction of where she needs to work comes from God whether we give it the name of "calling" or not.

The end product of God's direction, then, seems something like this: even within a framework that supposes God's lack of specific direction concerning individual job choices, particular decisions nevertheless seem to be the result of God's (indirect) direction. Could it be, then, that there exists a more subtle, less naïve conception of divine calling to specific careers that is more faithful and intelligible than the ones rejected by Badcock?

Widening the Conversation

Badcock certainly does not dispense with God's guidance in our lives. For Badcock, the values of the kingdom of God must "inform and even determine the shape of Christian vocation."[9] Calling, then, is determined by God's commands, and "both the universals and our own ruling principle have their source and their root in God."[10] While this makes vocation *God's* calling, it also gives humanity a firm responsibility. This human role addresses a lack that Badcock perceives in Karl Barth's theology; Barth's development of vocation "fails to give human beings as God's creatures and as objects of divine love their due: in effect they are denied any real status in themselves in the Barthian system of thought."[11]

By equating divine calling with God's moral demands, Badcock emphasizes human roles and responsibilities, but at a significant cost. If Barth lessens human responsibility,[12] Badcock clearly diminishes the divine voice. In

---

9. Badcock, *The Way of Life*, 52.

10. Ibid., 72. Badcock continues this equation of divine command and call. "Properly speaking, of course, it is only when the task laid upon a person is taken to be something commanded by God that the question of a *calling* strictly arises. It is God, God alone who calls, for only God has the right to demand the unconditional obedience and sacrifice that make up the life lived in faithfulness to a calling."

11. Ibid., 54.

12. While criticizing Barth's refusal "to treat humanity in itself as a subject of interest" (ibid., 57), Badcock overlooks the fact that Barth intentionally rejects the very notion of "humanity in itself." Humanity is created to be the covenant partner of God and the divine-human relationship is constitutive for the very nature of humanity. To treat "humanity in it-

Badcock's system, vocational discernment becomes a form of moral calculus rather than the active direction of God, and a theology of vocations becomes a subset of moral theology. God's call is for love "to be expressed where it matters most."[13] But discerning where and how it "matters most" becomes the heart of vocational discernment for which Badcock's perspective offers little aid. "How one moves from the universal principle to the particular situation or context, of course, is always the problem in moral theology, and here too the same problem arises. So perhaps the problem is one that, like the poor, will always be with us."[14]

Here God seems plagued by laryngitis. The divine call is not so much comprised as it is compromised by worldly human elements. By focusing on the religious aspects of calling, and by making a strong distinction between secular and sacred, Badcock all but banishes the calling to particular professions. Rejecting a friend's sense of calling as a fireman, for example, Badcock insists that vocation "is the call to do something that can be directly characterized as religious in quality — for example, some action to which the Word of God directs us."[15]

However, what counts as "religious in quality" depends on one's view of the relationship between God and the world, sacred and secular, heavenly and worldly. Badcock's dialogue with Luther broke down over this issue — Luther's view of divine providence in our world was no longer intelligible. So, too, the conversation with Barth was truncated by a perception that God's voice drowned out humanity's. What does Badcock say about the relationship of sacred and secular? Are there intelligible alternatives that might legitimately re-shape divine calling?

Contrasted with Badcock's concept of vocation as "fundamentally about the call to faith and eternal life and then derivatively about the call to the service of the gospel,"[16] Lee Hardy insists that the call to service is at the heart of Christian faith. While agreeing that God calls to faith, "we are also as Christians commanded, and therefore called, to love and serve our neigh-

---

self" is thus, from Barth's perspective, to distort humanity rather than giving humanity its due. The conversation that develops herein includes a Barthian emphasis that truly sees God working in and through humanity.

13. Ibid., 120.

14. Ibid., 69-70.

15. Ibid., 106. He continues: "It would be more accurate, therefore, to speak of the calling that his work as a fireman allowed him to fulfill: to show love, to do good, to train for ministry, and to work in Christian service in the church and in the workplace."

16. Ibid., 39.

Stephen L. Stell

bors with the gifts that God has given us."[17] "We are called, then, not only to be certain kinds of persons, but also to do certain kinds of things."[18]

If each Christian is gifted with particular talents, abilities, interests, and concerns as well as a distinctive worldly situation in which to employ these, God's specific callings in this world become a more intelligible option. Hardy draws upon the Puritans' distinction of "general" and "particular" callings[19] in order to elucidate God's direction for our everyday life. "With the distinction between the general and the particular calling in mind, talk about 'vocational choice' — in the sense of choosing a particular occupation in which we will exercise our gifts — is both biblically appropriate and religiously important."[20]

At this point in the conversation between Badcock and Hardy, one is tempted to assemble the arguments and biblical interpretations used in support of worldly callings from God and juxtapose them with the positions that reject such worldly callings. Yet simply reporting positions and counter-positions rarely moves a conversation forward. Rather it is often more helpful to analyze the underlying frameworks that shape their respective arguments and interpretations. What are the assumptions concerning God's relationship to the world which undergird and direct the course of these conversations?

As one sees from Hardy's exposition,[21] work gains its meanings from the conceptual and theological worlds in which it exists. Applying this to Badcock, one sees that his view of work is likewise shaped by the nature of the sacred/secular relations that he assumes. According to Badcock, God's call in the Bible "is generally to a sacred rather than a secular role, a role that is discontinuous with the ordinary social sphere, and even with natural human existence as such." Thus, to seek the things above "means *not* to seek the

---

17. Lee Hardy, *The Fabric of This World* (Grand Rapids: Wm. B. Eerdmans, 1990), 80.
18. Ibid.
19. Ibid., 80ff. "The general calling is the call to be a Christian, that is, to take on the virtues appropriate to followers of Christ, whatever one's station in life. . . . The particular calling, on the other hand, is the call to a specific occupation — an occupation to which not all Christians are called" (80-81). Cf. Douglas Schuurman's chapter on "The Bible on Vocation" in *Vocation: Discerning Our Callings in Life* (Grand Rapids: Eerdmans, 2004), 17-47.
20. Ibid., 81. He continues: "At certain junctures in our lives we are confronted with the need to identify our gifts and choose an occupation; and an occupation can provide us with the concrete opportunity to employ our gifts in the service of our neighbor, as God commanded us to do. This holds not only for the occupations within the church, but in society as well."
21. Ibid., 3-76.

things that are on earth."[22] The New Testament preoccupation with heaven "ultimately renders the finitude of the world ultimately undesirable, or at best provisional."[23] Human constructs and this-worldly truths are thus "relative, contextual, and linguistic" and do not constitute the "soil in which to grow the hope of heaven."[24] With this kind of interpretive framework, it is not surprising when Badcock concludes that "the Christian calling in the Bible is very much a religious rather than a secular concept, with a heavenly rather than a this-worldly frame of reference."[25]

Yet Badcock's justification for his position contains the seeds of an alternative approach. "We are, after all, concerned with *God* here, and not with the world — though to be concerned with God is also necessarily to be concerned with the world that God created and redeemed."[26] On the one hand, Badcock consistently juxtaposes the divine and the human. We are concerned with God "and *not with* the world," with a religious "*rather than* a secular concept," with a heavenly "*rather than* a this-worldly frame of reference." Yet when he claims that "to be concerned with God is also necessarily to be concerned with the world that God created and redeemed," he undermines his own assumptions. If creation and redemption are not extrinsic relations for God — as if we could talk about God's inner Self apart from these activities — but if God *is* Creator and God *is* Redeemer, then God's very Self is bound up with the world. One would therefore say, "We are, after all, concerned with *God* here, and *therefore* with the world."

This conjunction of God and the world shapes a distinctive theological framework. While Badcock seeks a theology of vocation that relies "less on historical reconstruction and sociological analysis and more on the structures of Christian theology itself,"[27] others dispute that "theology itself" excludes such worldly input. Indeed reflection upon the Creator of our world and the redeeming God of history may actually demand that the insights of historical and social-scientific analyses inform our understandings of God's callings in this world.

Insisting that our historical-cultural conceptions of God always shape our views of work and vocation, Hardy highlights how Renaissance portrayals of God as the all-powerful creator correspondingly altered the view of

22. Badcock, *The Way of Life*, 83 (emphasis his).
23. Ibid., 87.
24. Ibid.
25. Ibid., 88.
26. Ibid., 88-89.
27. Ibid., 29.

work,[28] shaping new Reformation voices. In God's providence, grace-filled human lives are lived to God's glory as they carry out God's creative activity through human work. "Through work we respond to God's mandate to humanity to continue the work of creation by subduing the earth; through work we realize ourselves as image-bearers of God; through work we participate in God's ongoing creative activity; through work we follow Christ in his example of redemptive suffering for the sake of others; through work we serve God himself as we serve those with whom he identifies."[29] Here earthly work is not contrasted with the divine but is constituted by its relations with God.

As intended by God's providence, humanity is not self-sufficient but is created with needs and limitations that draw us together into a life of mutual service. As we enter into this interdependent life — both within the body of Christ and within society — our talents and gifts serve others and theirs serve us. Operating harmoniously, we together carry out God's work in this world and thus give glory to God in and through our worldly labors. Here the interactions of human and divine provide a framework in which God calls us to specific worldly tasks.[30]

Not every dimension of this divine calling and its providential framework is crystal clear. "Our vocation is complex, not simple. It may have a focus, but it will also have many facets."[31] Social-scientific analyses of interests and abilities may shed light on the mystery of one's vocation, but vocation will never be a solved problem — not only because the world is constantly changing,[32] but because the intelligibility of vocation requires concepts like divine providence which will never be fully understood. Hardy's question, raised in a different context, is equally insightful here. "Might the life of prayer and meditation not only be a way of fulfilling one's general calling, but one's particular calling as well?"[33] Though Hardy has in mind the option

---

28. Hardy, *The Fabric of This World*, 27. "No longer the passive and distant pure mind, God was conceived of as a cosmic craftsman, who, in an impressive display of wisdom and power, brought the entire universe into existence. . . . According to these Renaissance thinkers, human beings were not to become like God through mere thinking, but through productive activity."

29. Ibid., 76.

30. Cf. ibid., 60, 84-85.

31. Ibid., 119.

32. Cf. ibid., 118. "Life is dynamic. It changes over time. The various facets of a person's vocation will interact with each other in different ways as that person enters into new relations with other persons and as those persons change. The old answers to the question of work will not always be adequate to new situations."

33. Ibid., 119.

of a monastic life today, his question can be appropriated to highlight the irreducible element of a divine voice in any vital and realistic-to-experience definition of vocation.

Exposing the Silent Partner in This Conversation

There is a third voice that needs to be recognized in this conversation — and here I must restrain myself from bringing in a multitude of fine authors who have written on this subject. In Dan Migliore's dialogues in *Faith Seeking Understanding*, there is a hidden voice behind that of the participants he brings into conversation — and that is, of course, his own. Dan's insight, creativity, and wit are present throughout those dialogues and *his* voice is what makes *their* voices come alive and speak so powerfully.

Though I can make no claims to Dan's creativity, in many ways the chosen dialogue between Badcock and Hardy becomes a forum for my own voice.[34] Like Dan I have tried to be faithful to the dialogue partners themselves, but I have constructed the conversation according to my own concerns and commitments. And now I want to expose "that man behind the curtain" — who you were not supposed to notice or pay any attention to previously — as the one who has actually been pulling the levers and manipulating the voices. This is not only to make the conversation above more transparent, but also to carry the conversation forward, acknowledging that Badcock and Hardy are also *my* dialogue partners.

In various ways, Badcock and Hardy represent tensions in today's theological scene, tensions which unavoidably surface in current reflections on vocation. Badcock is committed to theology that is accountable to the experiences of our contemporary world and intelligible in their light. He rejects Luther because his static providential world is no longer viable today. He rejects Barth because the divine voice seems to overpower humanity in ways that are no longer culturally/theologically acceptable. Yet in the process, Badcock's quest for intelligibility ends up silencing the divine voice in terms

---

34. This notion of "my own" voice demands more investigation than I can give it here. I am a product of social-political-economic forces; I am a product of a multitude of cultural-historical assumptions (some visible and some invisible); I am a product of numerous particular traditions to which I am committed and by which I am shaped; my voice is in many ways a product of the hundred-million-dollar-plus investment in the vocations market made by the Lilly Endowment's Programs for the Theological Exploration of Vocation; to name but a few.

of callings to worldly professions. God calls us to be Christians, pure and simple. While there may be tensions with specific theological traditions, who can argue that this is not the most comprehensible approach to Christian vocations?

Well, I can . . . because I am one of those, like Badcock's fireman friend, who has experienced a very specific call to my worldly profession. Of course, I would not normally use the phrase "worldly profession" because I do not agree with the heavenly/worldly distinctions that Badcock assumes and imposes. My experience — very real, very explicit, and very powerful to me — is, of course, a product of the traditions in which I stand (including specific traditions of divine calling). It is an *interpreted* experience, a *traditioned* experience, as all experiences are. So when Badcock is challenging my experience of being called by God to my teaching profession, he is not calling me a liar or a fool. He is rather deconstructing my experience by challenging certain traditions upon which that experience is based.[35]

Primary among the theological traditions which constitute my experiences and undergird my conceptions of calling is the doctrine of the Trinity. Trinitarian emphases on the importance of the created world and the integral interrelationships of God's works in creation, redemption, and sanctification make Badcock's separation of God and the world difficult to maintain. The incarnation of God in Jesus Christ, the Christian's union with God through Jesus Christ, Jesus' presence in the Body of Christ, and the encounter with Jesus in the "least of these" (Matthew 25:31-46) mean that Badcock's insistence on the separation of sacred and secular, of God and the world, is finally not intelligible, at least within *this particular* framework.[36]

Coincident with these Trinitarian emphases, I would argue both theoretically and experientially that knowledge of God and knowledge of self are interrelated, as Calvin suggests. A Reformed theological perspective "takes captive" the wisdom of the world so that there is nothing that we learn from the sciences or social sciences that is not to be brought into relation with God as the Creator, Redeemer, and Sustainer of this world. In such a framework the human and divine, God and world, are inextricably bound together in both theory and in practice.

My biblically shaped world also includes an affirmation, if not an expla-

35. Note that this language and interpretation are my own; they are not explicitly present in Badcock's exposition.

36. Badcock may be accurate when he perceives this co-inherence of God and humanity in Jesus Christ to be unintelligible within the modern world, though the postmodern world offers greater openness.

nation, of God's providential role in and through our world. And here, of course, one reaches the margins of intelligibility. Yet one must ask if such rational limits represent a deficit for theology which must always be eliminated. When is it proper to erupt in words of praise — "O the depth of the riches and wisdom and knowledge of God! How unsearchable are his judgments and how inscrutable his ways!" (Romans 11:33) — and when is this a cop-out? If God by definition is beyond our comprehension, then delineating the limits of our understanding is as much a part of the constructive theological task as affirming, explaining, and defending our positions. Yet such intrinsic limitations are not readily accepted by an Enlightenment-shaped modern world.

While I accept Badcock's criterion of intelligibility, then, I insist that what *is* intelligible varies with one's interpretive framework. Badcock's framework separating sacred and secular "solves" many problems facing vocation today. But it is an intelligibility catered to the modern secular world — as defined by Badcock's polarity of secular and sacred — that is not equally intelligible for those dwelling within certain Christian traditions.

I would therefore like to close with an additional perspective on this discussion — a perspective which has actually been shaping the conversation throughout. In light of the dialogue up to this point, I want to suggest a framework of intelligibility which presents alternatives to some of Badcock's positions and expands upon certain of Hardy's affirmations, as we together seek theological insights which are intelligible, faithful, and inclusive.

The Universality of Christianity *and* the Particularity of Its Expressions

By subsuming vocational choices within moral theology, Badcock affirms the centrality of universal principles in guiding our particular decisions. "It is not so much the particular 'way' that matters, but the universal principle of love at stake in it all. . . ."[37] Thus God gives general commands for humanity as a whole to follow, leaving us the flexibility to follow those commands in our particular situations. Badcock simply presents it as a "fact" that "the will of God as the Bible presents it is mainly general rather than specific; for on the whole, it relates to humanity in general rather than to particular individuals."[38]

37. Badcock, *The Way of Life*, 116.
38. Ibid., 82.

However, if Badcock were to allow a little historical analysis to creep into his theology, the "facts" would look very different. While he is correct that very little in the Bible is addressed to particular individuals, virtually nothing is addressed to humanity in general. Instead, biblical commands are usually directed toward particular historical-cultural-linguistic communities: the people of Israel; the body of Christ: particular communities or specific churches; or occasionally individuals or groups therein. Yet there appears to be a purpose, even a necessity for Badcock to imagine that the divine commands address humanity in general. For if "humanity" is the recipient of these commands, then the commands are untouched by the specifics of individual cultures. The universal can be portrayed as free-floating in a cultural-historical vacuum which then legitimates its application anywhere and everywhere, with no *particular* application being of any special importance. And consequently our callings can remain "religious" (according to his definition), untouched by any contamination by concrete worldly realities which are, after all, only the setting for one's religious obedience or observance.

But in point of fact the so-called "universal" commands of God are expressed in very particular cultural forms to specific historical communities in a language which assumes their cultural specificity and anticipates an equally specific response. So the universal is both known and expressed in and through the particular. Indeed one might claim for both the Jewish and the Christian faith that God has made the particular to become the universal; and accordingly when a particular cultural expression or demand is declared to be universal, it does not thereby lose its particularity or the scandal associated with it. Likewise my response in being called to Christ evokes a specificity which does not compromise the universal, but concretely constitutes its specific meaning for my life in the particularities of the present.

From this perspective, it is misleading to describe Christianity in terms of universal principles. It did not arise in that way, nor do we appropriate it as such. People enter into the Christian faith as they encounter particular aspects of a Christian cultural-linguistic community; it is these very particular experiences which constitute Christianity as they know it. The Christianity which they come to know is not first a universal, but the coming together of many particular experiences into a coherent whole. Likewise their Christian response of obedience is not a response to some universal but is a direct response to the specific aspects of Christianity as these intersect with particular aspects of their life. It is not too far of a stretch, then, to suggest that the response that God demands is a very specific response.

Douglas Schuurman illuminates this interaction of faith and explicit obedience by referring to Bonhoeffer. "Bonhoeffer affirms two propositions: 'only he who believes is obedient; only he who is obedient believes.' Obedience is not the chronological consequence of belief. Rather, faith is the condition of obedience, and obedience is the condition of faith. In fact obedience is not only the consequence of faith; it is the presupposition of faith."[39] If this is the case, then encounter with Christian faith comes in and through the specifics of an obedient life lived in the here and now. This corresponds with the insights of liberation theology which affirm that one does not first know the theoretical truths or universal principles of Christianity and then deduce how one should act. Rather it is in faithfully following Christ in the specifics of one's historical-cultural setting that one begins to encounter and affirm universal principles. Jesus did not call his disciples by laying out the theoretical truths that were to guide their steps in all particular situations. Rather he said "Follow me" in these particular paths that we will trod together . . . and they thereby slowly began to catch a glimpse of Jesus' universal significance.

From this perspective it is misleading to speak of moving from the universality of Christianity to its particulars because Christianity itself is constituted by particulars. As George Lindbeck and others have noted, we enter into a religious community through the particularities of its culture and language and traditions. Hearing God's voice in the particulars of one's life is therefore expected because that is precisely how one came to encounter God. One does not first understand the universal that "God is love" and then subsequently apply it to the particulars of life. Rather it is the experience of certain particulars of love — expressed in the life of Christ, in the Christian community, and in our own lives — which lead us to affirm and define the universal of love according to these particularities and then continue to express that love in specifically apt ways within our world. Because we both start with particulars and end with particulars, the particularity of God's call in our world seems readily intelligible in this framework.

As the particulars of our world lead to faith, the polarity of sacred/secular collapses and the door is opened to historical/social-scientific contributions to our discernment of divine calling. As a matter of descriptive fact, God's calling to repentance and faithfulness often comes through a long process of smaller calls — many of which would not be immediately recog-

---

39. Douglas J. Schuurman, *Vocation: Discerning Our Callings in Life* (Grand Rapids: Wm. B. Eerdmans, 2004), 24.

nized as "religious" (e.g., a certain dissatisfaction with life, a sense of discomfort or lack of fulfillment, small changes in one's perspective or orientation, etc.). What if God's claim on our lives emerges from a series of calls that are not all overtly religious but are nevertheless part of God's callings, even when not recognized as such? The work of the Holy Spirit (the "sacred") in encountering us outside of Christ's framework (the "secular") and bringing us to Christ (the conjunction of the sacred and the secular, as all of our existence is brought into captivity to Christ) becomes a paradigm not just for becoming a Christian, but also for the life-long process of sanctification. Here the opposition of secular and sacred is contradicted by the process of all things coming together under the Lordship of Christ.

By thus giving voice to God's calling in the world *and* to the integrity of humanity, we support Badcock's concerns for human responsibility as well as divine command. Yet we do so by acknowledging the ways in which the worldly and the heavenly, the divine and the human, the secular and the sacred come together in Jesus Christ. It is this conjunction of heaven and earth that allows social-scientific and historical analyses into the very heart of theology. Because God speaks in and through the world, social-scientific analyses can take their part in uncovering God's will. This is implicit in Hardy who speaks about God giving us talents and abilities along with interests and concerns — a conjunction of heredity and environment which is identifiable and analyzable through scientific and social-scientific analyses. It also corresponds with Hardy's affirmation that "I was placed here for a purpose, and that purpose is one which I am, in part, to discover, not invent."[40] We neither construct nor invent a calling which can only come from God. But coming from God doesn't mean that it overpowers us. We still need to discover our callings, using all the resources available in the world that God has created, is redeeming, and will bring to its fulfillment, as the realm of God grows to encompass "all in all." At which point — but not before then — the conversation may end.

---

40. Hardy, *The Fabric of This World*, 93.

Theological Identity: A Dance of Loyalty

Kathleen D. Billman

What a gift to be invited to contribute to a project whose purpose is to honor Daniel Migliore by gathering essays that will, in tone and purpose, "stress the need for conversation that is marked by rigor, commitment, mutual trust, and civility — all hallmarks of Dan's theological existence for the last four decades."[1] On the other hand, what a challenge to write such an essay! Gratitude for Dan's fruitful ministry as a theologian, teacher, and church leader motivated my saying yes to the challenge.

In the preface to the second edition of *Faith Seeking Understanding*, Dan writes, "I have no desire to do 'denominational theology.' Like every Christian theologian, I stand within a particular stream of Christian theological tradition. But Christian theology is necessarily 'catholic' in scope and 'evangelical' in substance or it is not Christian theology at all."[2] This is the point of departure as well as the "coming home" place for the conversation I offer, inspired by the playful yet serious dialogues found in the appendices of *Faith Seeking Understanding*.

The conversation begins with the recognition that for increasing num-

1. From the letter of invitation sent by Bruce McCormack and Kimlyn Bender.

2. Daniel L. Migliore, *Faith Seeking Understanding*, 2nd ed. (Grand Rapids: Eerdmans, 2004), xii.

I have borrowed part of the title of my Ph.D. dissertation, in which loyalty conflict was also an important theme. See Kathleen D. Billman, "The Dance of Loyalty: Loyalty Issues in Cross-Cultural Research and Pastoral Care with Liberian Immigrants," unpublished Ph.D. dissertation, Princeton Theological Seminary, 1992.

bers of Christians in the United States, no single "stream of Christian theological tradition"[3] shapes their theological identity. It is not unusual to hear seminary students reflect on different faith heritages they are seeking to integrate or candidates for faculty positions explain how their theological identities are not reducible to one heritage. Many parish pastors wonder to what degree denominational identity should influence evangelism and worship endeavors. Theological faculties may wrestle with how important denominational identity is in the hiring of new faculty colleagues, even as they strive to honor other important criteria for building a faculty. Adding to the challenge, ecumenical leaders and "emerging church" proponents labor for new theological alliances.

There are many reminders that the shaping, nurturing, and articulating of Christian theological identity is often a complex process. For church leaders in/of former "*main*stream" denominations in the U.S., these identity questions take place amidst a context of struggle, as so many congregations, judicatories, seminaries, and other church agencies attempt to navigate powerful currents that threaten the very survival of their institutions. They do so while also being painfully aware that Christianity in the United States is seen by many as "toothless and compliant, if not downright supportive" of U.S. imperialism — and so hardly recognizable as the community of the crucified and risen Christ who came to preach good news to the poor.[4]

Because the complexity of forming and articulating theological identity is an important dimension of my own faith and because so much of my life has been invested within/in denominational institutions (two struggling United Methodist urban congregations and one Lutheran seminary), the conversation is no mere academic matter for me. It occurs within myself.

Even as a child, I vaguely understood that there were significant differences between the cross-centered piety of my German Lutheran paternal

---

3. The image of the "stream" is a very rich one. I especially appreciate the following definition from Thomas A. Langford, *Practical Divinity: Theology in the Wesleyan Tradition* (Nashville: Abingdon Press, 1983), 11: "A tradition is a stream through history. A stream may have neat clear banks, or it may flow across boundaries and be difficult to trace. Some streams seem to remain pure and carry their original water from source to estuary; others continually acquire new content and become mixtures from many springs. . . . A historical stream is a tradition insofar as it possesses dominant characteristics and conveys an enduring sense of meaning. Tradition releases an inner pulsation that is felt, known by, and shapes those related to it, even if the basic awareness is not fully explicable."

4. Mark Lewis Taylor, "Spirit and Liberation: Achieving Postcolonial Theology in the United States," in *Postcolonial Theologies: Divinity and Empire,* ed. Catherine Keller, Michael Nausner, and Mayra Rivera (St. Louis: Chalice Press, 2004), 41.

family and the exuberant faith of my socially engaged Methodist maternal family — and that the interplay between the two traditions formed me theologically. My wrestling with contrasting theological accents and pieties began long before I had theological language to verbalize this inchoate "conversation." The older I become, however, the more deeply I appreciate the internal conversation that was my first experience of recognizing that there is richness as well as conflict when identities intersect and loyalties are tested. Like the familiar image of two overlapping circles, there is a space that represents the distinctiveness of each unique conversation partner as well as a space of intersection — a "third space" where something new can occur. That "something new" *requires* difference to sustain its vitality while at the same time evoking new loyalties and possibilities for theological construction and purposeful action.

The identity issues that bubble up in the currents of the conversation below are not limited to a Methodist-Lutheran interface. Other influences are present in the conversation, particularly the influence of those who are exploring the implications of postcolonial studies for theology and whose work on how identity is constructed is both illuminating and challenging. That theological "voice," deeply indebted to liberation theology's emphasis on the God who labors to overcome every oppression that wounds and divides God's people, cries out for a way to carry on the struggle for justice in a manner that takes into account the fact that "[o]ur colors and cultures, our sexualities and nationalities, crisscross each of our identities, forming complex mazes of power. Whatever our bloodlines or our religious backgrounds, we find ourselves within these mazes. We find these mazes within us."[5]

The way these issues are articulated in the conversation below is limited and messy. I approach them not as a systematic theologian but simply as a believer who has chosen to live within and to invest in ecclesial institutions. I approach them as a white, middle-class, U.S. heterosexual woman who has received the privileges that my race, access to higher education, sexual orientation, and (as of this writing) relative physical health and access to health care have bestowed. I approach them as a pastoral theologian who is concerned about how theology fosters liberating practices of ministry in a polarized, broken, and unjust society. Finally, I approach them as someone who fears that the dean's office and the seminary classrooms where I spend so many hours are far too removed from the travail and delight of congregations struggling to be faithful in a confusing, fragmented world — and even

---

5. Keller et al., *Postcolonial Theologies*, 3.

more removed from the daily cries and courageous dances of those who daily struggle for life and breath in the midst of terrible hunger, disease, poverty, and unremitting violence.

Three conversation partners ruminate on these concerns: the voice of the Lutheran theological influence (Marty), the voice of the Methodist theological influence (Wesla), and an agitating voice that goads them both (Aggie), voicing the suspicion that their conversation is a waste of time and energy, when there are other more important sources of theological identity and greater challenges to Christian witness than what absorbs their attention. The feminizing of the names of the debaters acknowledges not only my gender but the influence of feminist/liberationist critical and constructive work on these expressions of Christianity that "streams" its way through this internal conversation.

New Testament scholar Barbara Rossing has employed the geological metaphor of the "braided stream" to speak of how traditions and voices interact. Braided streams are "rivers of many branches, criss-crossing, weaving together, and then dividing again." Up close they are rocky and tumultuous, but an aerial view reveals that it is the impact of water on rocks that gives sparkle and that the criss-crossing and up-close messiness looks, from a distance, like beautiful strands of French-braided hair.[6]

Conversation about important issues is sometimes rocky, tumultuous, and messy. But when characterized by civility and a humble recognition of the limits of any human viewpoint, the conversation is also not without laughter and beauty. Dan Migliore's theological dialogues in the appendices of *Faith Seeking Understanding* reveal both the messiness and the beauty of the "braided stream" of theological conversation.[7] If the conversation to follow reflects even a fraction of that vitality, the tribute I intend will be accomplished.

A Conversation

Aggie: I see you two are huddled together again. It looks like you are commiserating at the moment rather than arguing. I consider that a step forward.

6. See Barbara R. Rossing, "(Re)Claiming *Oikoumene?* Empire, Ecumenism, and the Discipleship of Equals," in *Walk in the Ways of Wisdom: Essays in Honor of Elisabeth Schüssler Fiorenza,* ed. Shelly Matthews, Cynthia Briggs Kittredge, and Melanie Johnson-DeBaufre (Harrisburg: Trinity Press International, 2003), 74-87.

7. See Daniel L. Migliore, *Faith Seeking Understanding: An Introduction to Christian Theology,* 2nd ed. (Grand Rapids: Wm. B. Eerdmans, 2004), 354-401.

Wesla: You of all people know that there are some fundamental theological agreements that we both hold: *sola gratia,* acknowledgement of the tragic flaw in humanity called "original sin," dependence on the classical creeds of the Christian faith with some fresh interpretations by feminist and liberationist theologians —

Marty (interrupting): Wesla, there are many distinctions to be made even concerning the points of agreement you have mentioned thus far. Since you tend toward theological sloppiness in your efforts to emphasize agreements over disagreements, please curb your tendency to smooth everything out —

Wesla: For heaven's sake, I distinctly remember an agreement I *thought* we shared just a moment ago —

Aggie (laughing): Doesn't take much to get you two going, does it? Just the smallest hint of doctrinal mushiness will set you off, Marty, and you, Wesla, are heartbroken every time you think a consensus will not hold so that you can launch your next crusade to improve something or other. Do you need a handkerchief?

Marty: You may want to rethink your "divide and conquer" strategy, Aggie, and your stereotypes. ELCA Lutheranism is on the forefront of ecumenical dialogue, or haven't you noticed? What other denomination has forged full communion agreements with *both* Episcopalian *and* Reformed brothers and sisters, and you-know-who is next.[8] Stop characterizing me as being so intent on doctrinal purity that I lack an ecumenical spirit — nothing could be further from the truth!

Aggie: Oh, and that's going smoothly in the rank and file of ELCA Lutherans, is it?

Wesla: Stop it, Aggie! What we were in the process of discussing, before you so rudely interrupted us, was not an example of theological mushiness on *either* of our parts. We were talking about how theological debate and distinctiveness is not just between different ecclesial groups but is constitutive of the lives of more and more individual Christians these days. We were noting the impact of this situation on theological education, parish leadership, worship, evangelism —

Marty: Pardon my interruption, Wesla. Before we leap into practical implications, let me just say that we both cherish the influence of our respective traditions and agree that they live at times in some uneasiness with each

8. ELCA Lutherans and United Methodists are in the midst of an ecumenical dialogue that may lead to a full communion agreement.

other. But to the degree that we can welcome and investigate this dis-ease, we can both be more theologically reflective and purposeful about how we articulate our convictions. If one who knows only one culture knows no culture,[9] it is arguable that one who knows only one theological heritage knows none. I find the dissonance compelling.

Aggie: Oh, good grief. Anyone who studies theology with any degree of seriousness is challenged to engage in *that* process; no serious theologian ever simply repeats what they memorized in Sunday School or encountered in handbooks on "Why I Am a Methodist" or "Why I Am a Lutheran." I wonder why either of you make so much of this theological quibbling with each other, which often seems like "much ado about nothing." No, I take that back — I do understand it. For one thing, you each represent a family loyalty. Remember that family therapist who said you two would spend a lifetime trying to reconcile the Lutheran and Methodist sides of your maternal and paternal families?

Marty: Did anyone say "reconcile"? Why must everything be reconciled? And why do you reduce the issue under consideration to something idiosyncratic and personal, as if there is not something more significant at stake?

Wesla: Heaven forbid we get too personal, Marty! When we forget the personal experience dimension of theological identity, we lose — not gain — theological insight! When what "counts" theologically is only what is intellectualized and verbalized, with no attention paid to the life that is *lived* in the *practices* of faith — well, we don't have the full theological picture, do we? Theology and practice should never be separated. And I can give you a very personal for-instance: you talk all the time about what a pessimistic view you have of human nature. Fine! You came by that honestly. But if that is the case, why are you so disappointed in yourself and others whenever you experience afresh how mired you are in our "tragic flaw"? Isn't it partly because you were influenced by the unquenchable optimism not only of our Methodist grandfather but our middle-class U.S. mainstream Protestant identity? Doesn't that gap between intellect and piety sometimes create confusion for you and others? Can we ever glimpse the whole theological picture without factoring in the gap between what is expressed intellectually and what is "believed" emotionally? And —

Marty: Oh, so you represent "piety" and I represent "intellect"?

9. This axiom is explored in David Augsburger's *Pastoral Counseling across Cultures* (Philadelphia: Westminster Press, 1986), 16-19.

Aggie (looks back and forth between Wesla and Marty and dissolves into uncontrollable laughter)

Wesla: I'm so glad we amuse you, Aggie. Okay, I'll try to get back to my point, if I can remember what it was. Here goes: Theological conviction animates the pieties and practices that characterize Christian life in the world (and our *practices* shape theology, too — but that is a different conversation!),[10] but so do many other variables, and part of what we were discussing with one another is that very complexity, even if we view it from unique vantage points. Both of us have a stake in promoting our theological heritages, especially when both our denominations are attempting to survive and flourish amidst extremely challenging social conditions, and the larger social trend seems to be in the direction of "spiritual but not religious."[11]

Marty: Wesla is being a bit imprecise. "Theological heritage" is itself a many-splendored thing, since there are great divergences on matters of theological accent, piety, and worship practice *within* each of our respective denominations, as you so lovingly reminded us a few seconds ago, Aggie. On the matter of disunity you goaded *me* about, for example, there are significant historical reasons why the descendents of many European Lutheran immigrants to the U.S. are quite comfortable with bishops and do not get all exercised about the matter of apostolic succession, while others have good historical reason to be fearful of bishops' authority. The latter strongly oppose aspects of the full communion agreement with the Episcopalians that concern apostolic succession and are much more interested in conversations with our Reformed colleagues. Martin Marty (nice name, "Marty") has described how differences regarding church polity among Lutherans arise from diverse histories, if you're interested.[12] Of course, there is more to say concerning the fierce theological debates that have occurred regarding the

10. See chapter 3 of *Rachel's Cry: Prayer of Lament and Rebirth of Hope* (Cleveland: United Church Press, 1999) for a reflection on the relationship between several major theologians' reflections on the psalms of lament and on their experiences of personal suffering that gave rise to different views they expressed about the place of lament in the life of the Christian.

11. In his book *Spiritual but Not Religious: Understanding Unchurched America* (Oxford: Oxford University Press, 2001), Robert C. Fuller argues that this phrase, which increasing numbers of (U.S.) Americans employ as a self-descriptor, has a long history in the U.S. dating back to the colonial period. He offers a very positive view of the spirituality of the unchurched, predicting that it "will likely continue to be the only viable option for a growing sector of the American population" (173).

12. Martin E. Marty, *Lutheran Questions, Lutheran Answers* (Minneapolis: Augsburg Books, 2007), 150-152.

Kathleen D. Billman

interpretation of the Augsburg Confession on these matters, but I fear we would digress too much to get into them.

Wesla: I've already read that book, Marty, and am trying to read through a plethora of new books that have to do with reclaiming Lutheran identity since, after all, we serve in a Lutheran seminary.[13] What you call "imprecision" on my part is simply my (apparently futile) effort to avoid unnecessary digression. Do you think for one moment I am ignorant of the many different historical and social realities that contribute to differences *within* our denominations? Good heavens, how many times have I tried to present Methodism in more complex and nuanced terms than how I hear it stereotypically portrayed by some Lutherans! And how many times have I listened to African-American Lutheran students describe how fellow students have simply assumed that they were originally Baptists or Methodists who converted to Lutheranism somewhere along the line rather than being life-long Lutherans! Judging an entire tradition by one's own limited cultural expression of it is something we both resist, and you know it! Please do not lecture me on the very point where we had established agreement right from the beginning of this conversation: A great number of U.S. Christians (of whatever "stream" or "streams" of Christian tradition) are shaped by such a variety of different influences in this pluralistic society that theological identity (other than a generic "Christian" identity) is a very difficult thing to articulate. That's *one* of the things we were talking about before Aggie arrived on the scene — remember? And I thought we were both agreed that, despite some difficulties we each have with the limits and problems of denominationalism, we both want some of the distinctive theological emphases of our respective ecclesial traditions to be preserved.

Aggie: So it's theological *distinctiveness* you want to preserve? Funny, I thought you were getting ready to mount an argument for how people can be both Lutheran and Methodist at the same time!

Marty: Let me try to help with this confusion, since in listening to the

13. Augsburg Fortress's "Lutheran Voices" series currently includes over twenty small volumes of reflection on various aspects of Lutheran identity and its implications for worship, witness, biblical interpretation, and other aspects of Christian faith and practice, written especially with lay audiences in mind. This series exemplifies how much current effort is directed to revitalizing and clarifying Lutheran theological identity. See also *The Gift of Grace: The Future of Lutheran Theology*, ed. Niels Henrik Gregersen, Bo Holm, Ted Peters, and Peter Widmann (Minneapolis: Fortress Press, 2005), which brings together in one anthology perspectives of several global leaders in the worldwide Lutheran communion on key dimensions of Lutheran theology.

266

two of you I am getting confused myself. First, I think we are all in agreement that theological difference manifests itself right in the very heart of different streams of Christian tradition. For example, it has become something of a truism that there are greater theological differences between so-called "liberals" and "conservatives" *within* denominations, for example, than between liberals of different communions and conservatives of different communions. We are also aware that there are many Christians working to resist the fractured nature of institutional and civic life, and to articulate sound theological — *gospel* — reasons to bring together those willing to cross certain theological boundaries and resist theological polarization to make a real difference in public life.[14] So let us take that as a given. I am completely *for* engaging in certain kinds of collaborative endeavors in our limited human efforts to join God's mission of justice and peace in the world (even though I am not as hopeful as Wesla sometimes seems to be about how much positive difference can be made by any of these efforts). When we do not come together across denominational and theological lines in solidarity with those experiencing the greatest impact of the evils of poverty, institutionalized oppression of many kinds, disease, and war, everything Niebuhr said about the scandal of denominationalism is, in my view (and, I think, in Wesla's view, too), correct.[15]

Wesla: Amen to that last point, but this speech is getting a bit long, Marty.

Marty: Look who's talking! As I was saying, there are many commitments that blur the theological boundaries between Wesla and me and it is very important to acknowledge that. But rather than creating a theological mush, we would like to embrace mutual affirmation and admonition as a creative internal dynamic rather than resolve the tensions.

Aggie: Well, well. I am reminded of a term utilized in one of Dan Migliore's theological dialogues: *Horsegeschichte*.[16] Look, you are talking out of both sides of your mouth. How can you argue, on the one hand, for respecting and preserving the uniqueness of each stream of your respective theological traditions yet, on the other, wail that you are not fully understood if people do not recognize your theological "hybridity" (or whatever it

---

14. See Jim Wallis, *God's Politics* (HarperSanFrancisco, 2005) for a provocative argument about possible places of faith convergence that might unite those often separated into "right" and "left" religious camps into a more effective political force in U.S. politics.

15. H. Richard Niebuhr, *The Social Sources of Denominationalism* (New York: Meridian Books, World Publishing Company, 12th printing, 1972).

16. Migliore, *Faith Seeking Understanding*, 374-375.

Kathleen D. Billman

is you are arguing for)? Who really cares, anyway? If you want to be everything to all people, why don't you think in grander terms? Join the "emerging church," and you can make a case for why you are liberal/conservative, charismatic/contemplative, Anabaptist/Anglican, depressed-yet-hopeful, plus several other things![17]

Marty: As a matter of fact, both of us were talking about hybridity when you entered the conversation — but not in the sense you infer. You seem to be talking out of both sides of your mouth, too. On the one hand, you insinuate that when we discuss our Lutheran/Methodist interface we are traveling down an inconsequential road that makes no real difference in today's world. On the other hand, you seem to be accusing us of falling prey to thinking of theological traditions as a kind of smorgasbord, from which we can pick and choose what we like, whether there is theological coherence in the platter we are creating or not. That probably isn't even fair to some of the leaders of the emerging church movement, and it certainly is not fair to us.

Aggie: Just trying to have a little fun . . .

Wesla: Aggie, you might try to make more of an effort to understand what is at stake here! What I think both of us have been recognizing is that this conversation between us — one that was not even very self-conscious for a long time — was our first means of experiencing that there is a "third space" in human conversation that is, paradoxically, nourished by difference but in which new possibilities may emerge that transcend but do not obliterate those differences. This creative dynamic we are wrestling with is not limited to the denominational differences we have been discussing these past few minutes. Neither of us can forget that the playing field of human conversation is not a level field (even in the church), and both of us are concerned to foster theological conversation and *action* that assists struggles for human dignity, equality, and freedom. We have both become interested in postcolonial theology for just these reasons. We see the conversations about postcolonial theology to be deeply indebted to liberation theology, yet at the same time wrestling with some difficulties we experienced with liberation theology, particularly in the area of how "identities" are described, for example, "oppressed" and "oppressor." Our conversation about hybridity takes place in that context.

Marty: We were recalling the years we participated in a Women of

---

17. In *A Generous Orthodoxy* (Grand Rapids: Zondervan, 2004), Brian D. McLaren, a strong voice in the emerging church movement, explicates how all these descriptors fit with his Christian self-understanding.

Color/White Women's Dialogue group. We were remembering how messy it was, but also how promising it was at the same time. In general, the white women focused on unity — emphasizing elements of women's experience (sexual violence, the struggles of lesbian women, experiences of the pain associated with social class) that cut across the color line. In a sense, we were trying to say that our identities are thicker than our whiteness. In general, the African-American women in the group tried to get us white women to seriously examine the ways that racial privilege distorts our relationships with one another and to make real changes in some of our behaviors in order to resist racism's influence on our community. We have never forgotten the power of those conversations, and of experiencing how easy it was for us to hurry over the very real differences in our situations and the situations of women of color. Both Wesla and I are opposed to thinking about hybrid identities in ways that mute the need to resist the dynamics of domination-subordination. But we are equally opposed to un-nuanced conversations that conceive power and difference in too-simplistic terms. Anyway —

Aggie: Could I just get a word in here —

Marty: Just another minute, please. The Dialogue Group had very tumultuous, often painful conversations. But what some of us said came out of that dialogue was an experience of that "third space" Wesla and I have been talking about — that place where the deepest encounter with difference (not a shallow one!) engenders something new for all who participate in it. A new language and awareness may come into being that is not unrelated to where we have come from but helps us to engage it, reform it, even transcend it at times. An example of re-engaging my own tradition came when, in the midst of a very painful conversation, I *experientially* was grasped by what it means to be *simul justus et peccator*. It happened when I realized that so much of what we were doing as white women was trying to justify ourselves as being somehow different from other white people — more trustworthy . . . more *innocent,* somehow. But in the very realization that there was no innocent place to stand, it became breathtakingly clear that it was *Christ* who made the conversation possible and called us to engage in it precisely where brokenness was most acute and we were at our most helpless. There was a moment — fleeting but unforgettable — when this realization found *mutual* expression and celebration. And in that moment, *communion* came, not as an achievement but as a gift. Sometimes I think that justification by grace through faith has become little more than a slogan in my tradition. Amidst the *experience* of our utter lack of innocence and/or our total entrapment in systems of injustice, it became so much more than that — it gave me the

hope to carry on, trusting in something more than human ability or innocence, something "Other" that made it possible to encounter "otherness"
without fear and even without self-focused guilt.

Wesla: Yes, and in both the wonder and transitory nature of those experiences I wonder if we did not meet the God that Mayra Rivera describes —
the God of the crossroads.[18]

Aggie: It is all very well to have a sparkling theological moment, but let's
be realistic. Do you see any evidence that the theological enterprises in
which you are engaged make a real difference in the world? The sweep of
your social ministries is at times very impressive, but both your denominations have failed to confront in a meaningful way the ideology that has resulted in a destructive war, the curtailing of civil liberties, and the gap between the rich and the poor that is widening right in your own backyard, not
to mention the horrors occurring in the rest of the world. You both are so
obsessed with keeping your institutions intact in this easily fragmented society that you are fearful of risk-taking for the sake of changes you both believe are important to make, even within your respective communions. Both
your "streams" have gone the way of all reform movements in the history of
the church. It remains to be seen whether the new forms Christianity is taking will have anything like the social impact of either of the movements your
traditions initiated at two very different periods of history. Yet both of you,
despite your different levels of confidence in the human capacity to grow
deeper in Christian love in this life, long for your institutions to better embody the grace and freedom of the gospel. You have both longed for changes
that have been slow in coming, and you both realize that the young see
things from such a different view and life experience. If you were even
twenty years younger, would this conversation that so preoccupies you today
matter? If you had not invested so many years in shoring up struggling par-
ishes and other institutional structures, would you be more open to the
promise that perhaps there are theological horizons and practices that neither of you can even imagine today? Would you be willing to admit that part
of what you want to retain is your medical benefits and pension plans?

Wesla: Do you think that is not part of what we recognize is at stake in
our conversations with each other, Aggie? Do you think we are not cognizant
of the critique that has been made of U.S. Christian communities' "widespread failure to resist U.S. imperial practice" and "accommodating of em-

---

18. See Mayra Rivera, "God at the Crossroads: A Postcolonial Reading of Sophia," in
Keller et al., *Postcolonial Theologies*, 186-203.

pire"?[19] It was to John Wesley that Niebuhr attributed one recognition of which you speak: "Whenever riches have increased, the essence of religion has decreased in the same proportion. Therefore I do not see how it is possible in the nature of things for any revival of religion to continue long. . . . So, although the form of religion remains, the spirit is swiftly vanishing away. Is there no way to prevent this?"[20] Wesley attempted to answer his own question by advocating that the faithful need to give away much of that increasing abundance — and, of course, Marty will be the first to step in to say that such a view of human growth in grace was far too hopeful. But if all endeavors, however much launched in hope and fervor, ultimately falter, then does not the recognition that "we are no better than our parents" (to borrow from Elijah's lament) make us leery of grand schemes?

Marty: Why, Wesla, if you are truly leaning toward more pessimism about the human capacity to grow in grace, I see that I have influenced you more than I ever thought possible. And in return for such an admission, I will admit that your conviction that faith is nourished by the *practices* and *spiritual disciplines* of faith has influenced me. Now everywhere you look, it seems that Lutherans are getting into the conversation about faith practices and spirituality, bringing their own theological passion to the conversations. But I digress.

Wesla: Yes, you are digressing, but the point you just made about *practices* is very important, especially because it's a slippery slope from pessimism about the human capacity to change situations of injustice to lack of willingness to take action at all. It is difficult, in the U.S. context, not to over-spiritualize and over-individualize faith practices, and one has only to look at the bookshelves in Barnes & Noble and Borders Books to see how many voices are trying to influence individual seekers. It is hard to sell *tentatio* as a crucial dimension of the Christian life, isn't it, Marty? Aggie, what I want to say to *you* is that people need communities in which they *practice* their faith and do not merely intellectualize about it. Praising God, mutually bearing burdens, hearing the Word preached, and celebrating the sacraments are intimately related to prophetic witness — we both still believe that these are all essential aspects of the Christian life. And these practices always take place in broken communities.

19. Mark Lewis Taylor, "Spirit and Liberation: Achieving Postcolonial Theology in the United States," in Keller et al., *Postcolonial Theologies*, 40.

20. John Wesley original quote from Southey, *Life of Wesley*, vol. II, 305-306, quoted in H. Richard Niebuhr, *The Social Sources of Denominationalism*, 70-71.

Aggie: Well, I see we've come full circle. This is where I came in — the two of you getting all cuddly. And perhaps we've come full circle to what you said launched the conversation — the conviction, expressed by Dan Migliore, that "Christian theology is necessarily 'catholic' in scope and 'evangelical' in substance or it is not Christian theology at all." Perhaps out of the interplay between you will come something a little less defensive on both your parts. Since you both seem to be fated to cast your lot with mainstream institutions, the least you can do is try to push each other to think a little more out of the box. Perhaps there are places — we might call them "estuaries" — where streams of theological heritage meet the tide that flows in from the sea, and there, in that place, something new will be birthed. You seem to be looking for those places, as your streams converge and diverge like that "braided stream" metaphor you seem to like so well.

Marty: Aggie, you old curmudgeon, I never knew you had a penchant for tidy little endings, or that you had such a capacity for optimism. Was that your best effort to leave us on an inspirational note? You're beginning to sound like Wesla.

Wesla: I resent that, Marty.

Aggie (turning away, rolling her eyes as she turns): See you later.

Luther's Ghost — Ein gluehender Backofen voller Liebe

George Newlands

I

In the decade of student revolution, Dan Migliore, Darrell Guder, and I were studying theology in Germany, the land of Martin Luther. We did not know each other. We were, of course, and obviously remain, archetypal revolutionaries. We have since had long association with Reformed theology. But what of Luther, whom I guess we all read surreptitiously from time to time? In this essay I want to look briefly at the role of Luther — or rather, a kaleidoscopic variety of Luthers — in Reformed theology. The reason lies in a simple truth: Luther is often excoriated but ever present as a sort of "hidden hand" in Reformed thought from Calvin to Barth and beyond.

It might seem that this is an odd topic for a Scottish theologian. After all, Luther did not get off to a particularly promising start in the Scottish Reformation. On the morning of February 29, 1528, a meeting of top Scottish theologians decided — it being too damp for golf — to condemn Patrick Hamilton, our first genuinely Lutheran theologian, to be burned that afternoon. Sadly, they had overlooked the fact that no suitable store of combustible material had been arranged. Still, they were able to burn him a little at noon before taking lunch, a little more before adjourning to a Starbucks in the afternoon, and finished the day with a celebratory fellowship barbecue just after six o'clock in the evening.[1]

---

1. Iain Torrance notes that "he was roasted rather than simply burned alive." See the

Deus vivifacit occidendo, as Luther puts it. As is well known, Hamilton's fate inspired others to take an interest in Luther: "Patrick's Places" has generated a vast scholarly literature on justification from Hamilton to McCormack, not to mention Contarini to Küng. Not least of these eminent Luther scholars in Scotland was the impressively learned Alexander Alesius, who was happily to escape both the fire and the local climate to end his days in a chair of theology in Leipzig.[2] England too had its martyrs. In my old college, Trinity Hall, Cambridge, Thomas Bilney demanded "to go up to Jerusalem" so importunately that the local bishop eventually burned him in 1531 on grounds of pastoral necessity.

In those days all decent theologians, like Professor Migliore himself, came from a solid Catholic background. We might illustrate the complexity of the Reformation debate on justification, to which we shall have to return again and again, by noting that Gerhard Ebeling — well-known straw man of modern Reformed polemic as a Lutheran, neo-Kantian, modernist, Enlightenment liberal — once suggested that a crucial difference between Lutheran and Catholic thought was that the former stressed Word and faith, where the latter stressed sacrament and love.[3] Yet Luther, too, stressed the centrality of the divine love — God as *a glowing oven full of love.*[4] He could be heard when provoked to utter comments to the effect that *hoc est corpus meum. Fides, spes,* and *caritas* have been central to all respectable theology from St. Paul to Luther to Barth — "Gott ist der Liebender in der Freiheit." I shall suggest here that a concentration on one aspect of the gospel as the essence of the faith is always suspect, but that an all-embracing conceptual benevolence can become too diffuse to be illuminating.

But what of Luther as the ghost, constant guest, ghostis/hostis, at the Reformed feast? It was after all a ghost of sorts, a Teufel's Gespenst, that first brought Luther into the monastery. "Überall hat hier 'Gespenst' den ganz allgemeinen Sinn von 'Tauschung, Vorspieglung,' ohne das dabei an etwas Bildhaftes gedacht wird," said Karl Holl — another ghost haunting Re-

---

Dictionary of Scottish Church History and Theology, ed. Nigel M. de S. Cameron (Downers Grove, IL: InterVarsity Press, 1993), 390-391.

2. See Gotthelf Wiedermann, "Alexander Alesius," in *New Dictionary of National Bibliography,* vol. 2 (Oxford: Oxford University Press, 2004), 640-644.

3. It is a pity that Ebeling's magisterial three-volume *Dogmatik des christlichen Glaubens,* which focuses on experience, the experience of the presence of God in prayer, has never appeared in English. I have tried to summarize the main elements in *God in Christian Perspective* (Edinburgh: T&T Clark, 1994), 21-23, 229-231, 342-343, 392.

4. Sermon of 15 March 1522.

formed corridors.[5] It is this mysterious, diaphanous — dare I say ubiquitous — aspect of the Lutheran legacy which sails through the Reformed tradition, always to be treated warily and not to be trifled with.

Surely without Luther there is no Calvin. And there were, of course, many precursors to the Reformation. Luther was himself faintly scandalized to think of himself bracketed with Huss. Most figures, however, were victims of the doctrine of the unripe time. Reform movements require scholarship and time for "reception." They also need a prophetic figure — and that figure for the Reformation was Luther, who combined public witness with profound theology. "Er hat von Grund aus d.h. vom Gottesbegriff aus neu gebaut."[6]

Calvin's turn to reform did not begin with Luther, but his reading of Luther gave depth and urgency to his theological development. From Luther's exegesis of the Bible, Calvin developed his own understanding of the heart of the gospel, especially as expressed by Paul. He learned that the Christian life is a life of participation in God through union with Christ. Repentance happens through participation in Christ, through which the laws of God and nature are interpreted. "With repentance and justification we participate in the 'perfect gentleness' which is God's most complete accommodation to our humanity."[7] We shall return to the nature of participation below.

Embodiment has become a catchword of much postmodern theology. Luther was clear that faith had to be incarnated in the ordinariness of life and in flesh and blood. We all know that Calvin, on the other hand, laid a distinctive stress on the role of the Spirit. Yet Calvin was always concerned to avoid the spiritualization of the gospel. God's presence is a hidden presence, but it is always a *true* presence. The word as preached and the right administration of the sacraments brings Christ as presence into the community. As with Luther, worship is central to Christian life.

We should acknowledge here that, as in all else, there is always a possibility in embodiment of turning the gospel into its opposite. The death of Hamilton, Luther on the widest assortment of marginalized groups, Calvin on Servetus, the embodiment of the divine law in theocracy each testify to this fact. Equally, the appeal to the Spirit as justification, such as in John Knox's "We have the Spirit and you do not," and to the Trinity (see Thomas

---

5. Karl Holl, *Gesammelte Aufsätze* I (Darmstadt: Wissenschaftliche Buchgesellschaft, 1948), 15n.1.

6. Ibid., 2.

7. M. S. Johnson, in *The Legacy of Calvin,* ed. D. Foxgrover (Grand Rapids: Calvin Studies Society, 2000).

Aikenhead, executed in Scotland, who serves a salutary reminder to all M.Div. students) will not guarantee discipleship. But the abuse does not take away the proper use. Or, as Luther put it: *Nulla enim heresies unquam fuit, quae non etiam vera aliqua dixerit. Ideo vera non sunt neganda propter falsa.*[8] And indeed despite the evident *falsa,* Luther could understand the *humilitas fidei* and envisage Christian freedom as being Christ to one another.

Among the Reformed, Brian Gerrish has reflected over the years on Calvin's relationship to Luther. In "John Calvin on Luther," he notes that "The casual reader of the *Institutes,* who is not skilled in identifying unacknowledged debts or anonymous opponents, could certainly be pardoned for concluding that Calvin had never heard of Luther."[9] He also notes that, "On the other hand, a glance at the first edition of Calvin's *Institutes,* already published in 1536, is sufficient to prove that he was deeply indebted to Luther, and this, no doubt, promised better things."[10] The most important sources are his correspondence and the "minor theological treatises." "We may say, then, that Calvin's churchmanship and evangelicalism prevented him from being narrowly confessional. Nevertheless, the plain fact is that his affection for Luther was occasioned by the generosity of Luther himself."[11] "In the treatise against Pighius Calvin sums up his opinion of Luther in a single sentence. 'We regard him as a remarkable apostle of Christ, through whose work and ministry, most of all, the purity of the gospel has been restored in our time.'"[12]

In "The Pathfinder — Calvin's Image of Luther," Gerrish noted that Luther and Calvin never met, and that Calvin's understanding of Luther may have been hampered by his lack of German, concluding that "For all his devotion to Luther, Calvin never appeals to his ideas as though they were final and definite. Luther for him was not an oracle but a pathfinder — a pioneer, in whose footsteps we follow and whose trail has to be pushed on further."[13] Later, he mentions Calvin's own distinction, concerning his relation to Lu-

8. Martin Luther, *Martin Luthers Kritische Gesamtausgabe* (Weimar: Akademische Druck, 1883), 694:30; originally cited by Holl, *Gesammelte Aufsätze,* 415n.2.

9. Brian Gerrish, "John Calvin on Luther," in *Interpreters of Luther,* ed. Jaroslav Pelikan (Philadelphia: Fortress Press, 1968), 67.

10. Ibid., 71.

11. Ibid., 69.

12. Ibid., 79.

13. B. Gerrish, "The Pathfinder: Calvin's Image of Luther," in *The Old Protestantism and the New: Essays on the Reformation Heritage* (Chicago: University of Chicago Press, 1982), 27-48.

ther — that is, the distinction between being an ape and being a disciple — and suggests that there is an important distinction between continuity as repetition and continuity as development as a "Reformed habit of mind."[14]

It would take too long and involve a descent into a catalogue of often tedious cases for us to explore the long historical dialogue between Luther and the Reformed tradition, although some mention, however, is allowable. It is, of course, true that much seventeenth-century theological literature is preoccupied with confessional polemic between Lutherans and Reformed. Every area of doctrine could be and was to be exhausted to provide ammunition for a triumphalist celebration of the virtues of one confession over against the other. We need only recall the complex dances of the theologians over theories of *kenosis* from the sixteenth to the nineteenth century and beyond: my *krypsis* is better than your *kenosis* and my *genus apotelesmaticum* simply encapsulates the truth of the universe. Nothing here was to be less sophisticated than medieval arguments over varieties of the doctrine of impanation and the like. But at the same time, the Reformed Confessions — notably the Heidelberg Catechism — are built up in dialogue with Lutheran documents, and the *Confessio Augustana* is respected in Reformed communities. Communities living side by side inevitably influenced one another in subtle ways, and there were to be a series of church unions from the nineteenth century on. These were perhaps more influenced by Enlightenment notions of tolerance than by Reformation principle, although tolerance is also a theological virtue. Church music influenced by Luther's hymns, quintessentially in the magnificent work of Johann Sebastian Bach, has kept Luther fresh in cultural memory.

The reading of Luther himself was a seminal part of theological education, at least on the European continent, and it continues to be so. The presence of Lutheran faculties and Lutheran churches from Finland to Germany ensures a constant flow of new interpretations of Luther, both as historical studies and as systematic theology. Reception of Luther through different cultural frameworks continues to generate both creativity and controversy. Schleiermacher was more influenced perhaps by Calvin than by Luther, but Luther was of course important to him. Looking at more modern German interpretation, we see the Luther of Theodosius Harnack transformed through the influence of Albrecht Ritschl, and transformed again into the strongly community-orientated Luther of Karl Holl. For Holl, Luther is the key to the gift of the German spirit to humanity, an anti-

14. Brian Gerrish, in Foxgrover, *The Legacy of Calvin*, 158ff.

dote to American and Anglo-Saxon empiricism. For Hirsch, Luther is the stepping stone to a National socialist polity. For Althaus, he is key to a revitalising of the church as church. For Ebeling, Luther was the source of an existential interpretation of the gospel in a hermeneutical framework appropriate for a theology of religionless Christianity. For Ernst Wolf, Luther could be read in conjunction with Barth as the basis for a theology of resistance against the cultural imperialism of National Socialism. For many, Luther provided in the end of the day a kind of ultimate spiritual refuge from and a bastion of resistance to the complexities, dangers, and uncertainties of the contemporary intellectual flux. With this appreciation there was at least sometimes awareness there were many Luthers, and that the master himself was *simul justus et peccator,* by no means the source of an infallible organic unity of truth.

In the Scandinavian countries, in America, and to a lesser extent in other parts of the world, interpretation continues as an ever-evolving area of scholarship. It would be misleading to see Reformed interaction to Luther as a reaction to a fixed corpus of thinking. There is a good discussion of this wide legacy in the *Cambridge Companion to Luther,*[15] including a fine survey of Luther's ecumenical significance from Günther Gassmann, who highlights Thomas Carlyle's view of Luther as a prophet of intellectual freedom.

In England, it seems that Luther was very little read till Coleridge and others brought a kind of brief mini-Renaissance at the beginning of the nineteenth century. Luther was important to Hooker, arguably the keeper of the theological title deeds of the Church of England, but interest in the twentieth century was largely stimulated by the Methodist Gordon Rupp and the Reformed Brian Gerrish. The situation in Scotland was perhaps slightly better — certainly from 1880 the work of T. M. Lindsay, James Mackinnon, and others brought Luther to light in new ways. More recently the rise of Barth scholarship has again placed Luther in the margins, and he is seen perhaps more as a stormy figure of European church history than as a source of theological renewal.

In America the influence and dynamism of immigrant Lutheran communities in the nineteenth century was reflected in the new Lutheran scholarship led by Walther, Schaff, and Krauth, and in twentieth-century scholars from Wilhelm Pauck to Robert Jenson. Luther has been of interest, too, to American Catholic theologians — one of the best recent essays on the

15. Donald McKim, ed., *Cambridge Companion to Luther* (Cambridge: Cambridge University Press, 2003).

hiddenness of God in Luther is David Tracy's lecture, "Form and Fragment: The Recovery of the Hidden and Incomprehensible God."[16]

II

What of the great Reformed icon of modern theology, Karl Barth himself? Barth is famously on record as having said that Luther is an inspiring figure, but Calvin is a far better teacher. A mythology has grown up of Lutheran gloom, of the pessimism of the North German plain. The contrast between the law and the gospel smacks of dualism, practically Gnosticism, political quietism, Scotist dualism, and potentially the whole raft of Old Testament plagues. Calmer reflection, however, seems to suggest something rather different. I want to examine the Luther legacy in some more detail.

When does Barth first mention the name of Luther? Enthusiasts for numbers might note that in *Romans,* and even in *Church Dogmatics* I/1 and I/2, there are more mentions of Luther than of Calvin. Indeed, Luther played an important role in the great Barthian revolution. Barth is often seen as the great Christocentric theologian, but Luther, too, was always Christocentric: *Wo nit Christus ist, da ist finsterniss, es scheyene wie gross und hell es ymer mag.*[17]

In *The Theology of the Reformed Confessions* Barth tells us that he was not in *Romans* a consciously confessional theologian. "It was not for me a matter of significance that I was Reformed. I was not a confessional Reformed Christian."[18] Only with the move to a Reformed chair did he begin to develop a more Reformed stance. In the lectures, he notes the dangers of a creeping Lutheranization of Reformed communities. As it happens, he sees other dangers too. We come now to the Scots Confession of 1560. Here another spirit, which is radical and aggressive, is blowing. It closes with the words, "Arise, O Lord, and let thine enemies be confounded." Bristly John Knox and his friends are speaking here.[19]

As the lectures develop, Barth settles in to the task of creating a consciously Reformed theology. His strictures remain more of Lutheranism than of Luther.

---

16. David Tracy, "Form and Fragment: The Recovery of the Hidden and Incomprehensible God," in *Reflections: Journal of the Center of Theological Inquiry* 3 (2000): 62-88.

17. Martin Luther, *Martin Luthers Kritische Gesamtausgabe,* 528:21; originally cited in Ernst Wolf, *Peregrinatio* (Munich: Kaiser Verlag, 1962), 68n.160.

18. Karl Barth, in *Theology of the Reformed Confessions,* trans. Darrell and Judith Guder (Louisville: Westminster John Knox Press, 2002), viii.

19. *Theology of the Reformed Confessions,* 127.

George Newlands

(There is an excellent comprehensive account of Barth's Reformed development in John Webster's essay "Barth and the Reformed Confessions.")[20] But in the *Göttingen Dogmatics,* we hear very little of Luther himself.

In the *Church Dogmatics,* Luther returns much more frequently — the index to *CD* I/1, for example, offers sixty-one citations. Luther can be quoted appreciatively when appropriate, but he can also be firmly criticized. Barth is now much more sure of his own Reformed position, and consequently much less inhibited about Luther. If Luther is to be criticized, it is to be for real and not imaginary mistakes. Typical is this comment found in *CD* I/2:

> It would be a sorry delusion to think that in this matter, because of his well-known and pointed doctrine about the law and the gospel, and because of the tone of belittlement with which in this connection the name of Moses in particular is incidentally mentioned by him, Luther is bound to look in a different direction from Calvin.[21]

There is to be no scoring of cheap points.

When we turn to Barth's correspondence, we find that in 1967 he can quote Luther approvingly to a Japanese scholar in Göttingen, criticize him firmly a month or two later in a letter to a Zurich pastor, Max Schoch, and then compare Hans Küng to him as a good example of courage in a letter to Küng. In his later years, deeply interested in Vatican II, Barth seemed to have more interest in Catholic than in Lutheran theology.

Barth's relationships with Luther, Lutherans, and even Liberals were of course complex. He saw good theology and bad theology in Luther. He was suspicious of "the Lutherans," but many of his close friends were Lutheran: Ernst Wolf, Helmut Gollwitzer, Eberhard Jüngel. He broke with the Liberals, but kept up an affectionate correspondence with Martin Rade until Rade's death in 1940.[22] Rade was dismissed for criticizing National Socialism in November 1933. In a letter to Pastor Max Schoch on June 9, 1967, Barth wrote:

> Luther's *Romans* was one of the books I read and had ready to hand at Safenwil in 1916-1918. But even then I had some mistrust of the man which became stronger during my fifteen years at German universities — the German soul is by nature Lutheran — and here at Basel when I held a

20. See John Webster, *Barth's Early Theology* (New York: T&T Clark, 2005), 41-65.

21. Barth, *Church Dogmatics* I/2 (Edinburgh: T&T Clark, 1956), 76.

22. Christoph Schwöbel, ed., *Karl Barth–Martin Rade. Ein Briefwechsel* (Gütersloh: Gütersloher Verlagshaus Gerd Mohn, 1981).

seminar on Luther and the fanatics. Calvin is not my man at every point, but he was and is the superior teacher.[23]

One of the central issues in Christian systematic theology (indeed for some theologians *the* central issue) is of course the doctrine of justification by faith. This *locus classicus* continues to be the subject of impassioned debate in the twenty-first century. How does the Reformed tradition relate to the tradition of Luther in this area? Once again we note at the outset that there are many different Lutheran interpretations, and many different Reformed interpretations, of justification.

The doctrine of justification by faith can be related to many different areas of the biblical narrative, but it derives most immediately from Paul, whose sources stretch back into the Hebrew Bible and beyond. It is decidedly inconvenient for contemporary dogmatics that the interpretation of Paul among biblical scholars has undergone seismic shifts in recent years. Indeed, some scholars believe that Paul would have found "the 'received' doctrine of justification by faith unrecognizable."[24]

In Protestant doctrine, sinners are saved by the atoning death of Christ, through which God is enabled (roughly!) to impute to us the righteousness which belonged to Christ alone, thereby achieving our salvation. Instead, in the more recent formulations, God is enacting the new creation by transforming all created relationships, encompassing the Gentiles and conquering the powers of the universe.

How is justification to be construed today? This issue remains as keenly debated today as it ever was. For example, Bruce McCormack sees justification as an attempt to say what is essentially human as part of a "covenant ontology."[25] Through justification we are granted participation in true human-

---

23. Karl Barth, *Letters, 1961-1968*, trans. Geoffrey W. Bromiley (Edinburgh: T&T Clark, 1981), 255.

24. See Douglas Harink, *Paul Among the Postliberals* (Grand Rapids: Brazos Press, 2003).

25. In the standard Reformed account of justification, as Bruce McCormack puts it, "The just judge acts justly in that he forgives those whom he 'clothes' with Christ's righteousness. Clothed with Christ's righteousness, they are already in him what they are only gradually being made in themselves, the 'new humanity.'" See Bruce McCormack, "*Justitia aliena*: Karl Barth in Conversation with the Evangelical Doctrine of Imputed Righteousness," in *Justification in Perspective* (Grand Rapids: Baker Academic Press, 2006), 171. Indeed, justification must always be for us a *justitia aliena*. In the seminar in the winter semester of 1966 on *de divina revelatione* Barth asked whether we should choose Christ or his benefits. Ever seeking the *via media*, I diffidently suggested *Christus cum beneficiis suis indutus*. The

ity which is at the same time true participation in God. This is a regenerative process, a judicial act with transformative consequences. "The faith and obedience by means of which my humanity conforms to the humanity of Jesus Christ is the effect of the divine transformation given in justification of the ungodly. . . . At its heart, forensicism is deeply ontological."[26]

As such, justification has consequences beyond the individual; it has consequences for the individual in *community*. McCormack preserves the link with judgment while opening up the social dimensions of the act. This move approaches the wider significance given to justification by Paul Lehmann — another Princeton theologian — for whom "the reality of justification transfigures the nature of the boundary between the Christian community and the world." Thus justification becomes a gateway to liberation theology, the kind of liberation theology which Dan Migliore has himself envisaged, without losing the theological heart of the matter.[27] In justification, we participate truly in the person and work of Jesus Christ, as Christ is really present in us and to us. Yet, as McCormack stresses, we remain fully human, utterly dependent on the grace of God. We are not deified.

Eberhard Jüngel has written an impressively precise study of justification. This stresses against Tuomo Mannermaa, the distinguished Finnish theologian who has daringly connected justification and participation to orthodox understandings of *theosis*, the forensic dimension of justification. Jüngel shares with Ebeling an existential understanding of personal righteousness through grace alone, defends a highly traditional and ultra-conservative doctrine of total depravity, and combines this with a strictly exclusive Christology.[28] Little is said here about issues of sin and evil, exploitation and discrimination and the connection between justification and justice in the real world, apart from making a sensible distinction between God's justice and ours. Jüngel's approach reminds us of the importance of Migliore's concern for engagement.

Dan Migliore has highlighted the nature of Christian participation in

---

great man would have none of it. Nevertheless, he still welcomed my wife and me to his sadly incomplete Schleiermacher seminar in the spring semester of 1968.

26. See Bruce McCormack, "What's at Stake in Current Debates Over Justification? The Crisis of Protestantism in the West," in *Justification: What's at Stake in the Current Debate*, ed. Mark Husbands and Daniel J. Treier (Downers Grove: InterVarsity Press, 2004), 81-117, esp. 115.

27. Daniel Migliore, *Called to Freedom* (Louisville: Westminster John Knox Press, 1981).

28. Eberhard Jüngel, "Rechtfertigung: Dogmatisch," in *Religion in Geschichte und Gegenwort* 4:7, 111-118; cf. Tuomo Mannermaa, *Christ Present in Faith* (Minneapolis: Fortress Press, 2005).

Christ in his seminal article, "*Participatio Christi:* The Central Theme of Barth's Doctrine of Sanctification," where he notes that "Christian life is a *participatio Christi* in the active, agential, ethical sense of free and glad participation in the service of Jesus Christ and his work of reconciliation."[29] The idea of participation is meticulously unfolded in relation to Barth by Paul Nimmo in his book *Being in Action,*[30] from which I have learned much on this issue. In a reflection on being as action, Nimmo detects an ontic dimension in Barth's view of participation. All individuals participate in Jesus Christ through divine election, but there is also for the Christian a response in action to the passive participation in Jesus Christ. This ethical participation occurs only as a gift of the grace of God, being realized only as an event, and always related to Christian community. Here is participation without divinization, but with genuine humanization. Such an interpretation is essentially consonant with the thought expressed in Karl Barth's essay in the Ernst Wolf Festschrift, "Extra nos — pros nobis — in nobis," in which he addresses the question, "Wie kann was er extra nos war und tat, in nobis Ereignis warden?"[31]

The understanding of the center of Lutheran-Reformed discussion is not unconnected to the urgent need for effective delivery of doctrinal affirmations within public theology. Despite often voiced reservations about modernization of the pure essence of the doctrine in Luther, justification is related to grace and simultaneously to justice. Whatever else, the luxury of permanent suites in a dogmatic Wartburg was not what Luther intended. Justification has consequences for this world as well as the next. "The churches need to understand that human rights work is an expression of the churches' public theology."[32]

III

Justification is related to justice, but justice distinctively related to transcendence and to reconciliation. How can we find new points of entry to transcendence in the twenty-first century? Here we must turn to modern focal

29. Daniel Migliore, "*Participatio Christi:* The Central Theme of Barth's Doctrine of Sanctification," in *Zeitschrift für Dialektische Theologie* 18:3 (2002): 286-307.

30. Paul Nimmo, *Being in Action: The Theological Shape of Barth's Ethical Vision* (Edinburgh: T&T Clark, 2007).

31. Karl Barth, "*Extra nos–pro nobis–in nobis*," in *Hoeren und Handeln: Festschrift für Ernst Wolf,* ed. H. Gollwitzer (Munich: Kaiser Verlag, 1962), 15.

32. Lutheran World Federation documentation 51 (2004), 51.

points in Christian doctrines of God — existence and being, relationality and the image of God, otherness and gift, divine action and human response, universality and particularity, grace and history — and make a provisional assessment of the new directions which might be taken.

We have noted a potential tension between one Lutheran interpretation (in this case Mannermaa's Finnish interpretation) and one Reformed interpretation (Jüngel), as tension between the forensic and the theotic. Since Mannermaa there have been interesting attempts to re-imagine grace as gift from a number of quarters, including the Finnish Lutheran tradition. Gifts have many dimensions, from expressing deep affection to facilitating defense contracts. I want to suggest briefly here a construal of justification as the gift of the divine hospitality.

Hospitality in talking about God suggests a language of being and sharing. We can trace notions of the hospitable God in the pre-modern era, in the modernism of Schleiermacher, and in postmodernity. Much has been said of hospitality in relation to God in the tradition of French philosophy arising largely out of the work of Jacques Derrida, who reflected famously on the theme of "impossible hospitality." To be hospitable, it is first necessary that one must have the *power* to host. One also must have some control, for otherwise, one cannot be host. There is a need to abandon all claims to property or ownership; if one does not, then one cannot be a host. Christian theology might reflect that only God can do this. Derrida in *De l'Hospitalitié* considers hospitality and hostility, the other and the stranger, from Plato and Herodotus to Oedipus and Antigone and the issue of fratricide. He invokes Klossowski and Kant on the law of hospitality. There is an inevitable hostility/ hospitality dialectic. One must be prepared to accept the truly strange and uncomfortable. So, this remains always an impossible possibility.

> Hospitality is culture itself and not simply one ethic among others. Insofar as it has to do with the *ethos,* that is, the residence, one's at home, the familiar place of dwelling, as much as the manner of being there, the manner in which we relate to ourselves and to others, to others as our own or as foreigners, *ethics is hospitality;* ethics is entirely coextensive with the experience of hospitality, whichever way one expands or limits that.[33]

In a seminar at the University of Sussex, Derrida discussed friendship, democracy, and hospitality. Hospitality involves unconditionality.

33. Jacques Derrida, *On Cosmopolitanism and Forgiveness* (London: Routledge, 2001), 16-17.

But of course this unconditionality is a frightening thing, it's scary. When I speak of hospitality I have in mind the necessity not to simply assimilate the Other, but that's an *aporia.* Hospitality, and hospitality is a very general name for all our relations to the Other, has to be re-invented at every second, it is something without a pre-given rule. We have to negotiate also, that's a complicated unconscious operation, to negotiate the hospitality within ourselves. . . . If you are at war with yourself you may be allergic to the Other, that's what complicates the issue.[34]

Kant's idea of hospitality, described by Derrida as "cosmopolitics," has laws and limits. For Derrida, unconditional hospitality asks no question of the stranger, there is no legal, political, or moral obligation, it is "rendered," "given prior to all knowledge of the subject.[35] Unconditional hospitality "produces itself as impossible" and can "only be possible on condition of its impossibility."[36] There is an aporia between the law of hospitality and the laws of hospitality, between a law or a politics of hospitality and an ethics of hospitality necessary to do the impossible. If there is hospitality, the impossible must be done.[37]

Christian theology might reflect that hospitality is not only a feature of God's eternal dance of love, but is radiantly manifested in the out-working of that life in the creation, redemption, and completion of humanity and the entire cosmos. It is often a judgment on our inhospitality. We might reflect that this is somewhat akin to Niebuhr's notion of the relevance of an impossible ideal, or the vision of eschatological hope.

The consciously postmodern theologian Jim Olthuis, asking "What of Derrida?" comments that "Derrida remains on the threshold." Derrida points illuminatingly to relationality. Olthuis's response is this: "I am loved, therefore I am. . . . The gift of love is also the gift *for* love. The gift is simultaneously a call."[38] He also notes that "[t]he *Gelassenheit* of love eschews control. I want to suggest an ethics of mutuality in which self-sacrifice is seen not as the heart of ethics, but as an emergency compromise ethic because of

34. See www.hydry.umn.edu/derrida/pol+fr.html.
35. Jacques Derrida and A. Dufourmantelle, *On Hospitality* (Stanford: Stanford University Press, 2000), 27; originally cited by Paula Keating, "The Conditioning of the Unconditioned," *Borderlands* 3:1 (2004).
36. Jacques Derrida, *Adieu to Emmanuel Levinas* (Stanford: Stanford University Press, 1999), 19-20.
37. Derrida, *On Hospitality,* 14.
38. Jim Olthuis, in *The Hermeneutics of Charity,* ed. James K. A. Smith and Henry Isaac Venema (Grand Rapids: Brazos Press, 2004), 34.

the breakdown of mutuality."³⁹ Caputo adds that: "Creation must be a risk for God, a venture into the outside in which God makes Godself vulnerable. Otherwise creation is simply a divine display of power, a laser show of lights and explosive cosmic events."⁴⁰ Richard Kearney in the same volume adds this gloss:

> Everyone makes their choice, but the God of love and justice is the only God I'm interested in. I'm not interested in the God of evil and sadism. I'm just not interested in these Gnostic (or neo-Gnostic) notions that see the dark side of God — destruction and holocaust — as an indispensable counterpart of the good side. Such theories or theodicies can justify *any-thing.*⁴¹

How far can we go with postmodernity? David Klemm in a Glasgow paper raises some sharp questions about the "posts" and searches for a new Christian theological humanism.

> Deconstructive theology thinks not the transcendent other but traces of the other — infinitely deferring that of which the trace is a trace. Consequently, in much postmodern theology, theological language loses its subject matter and is indistinguishable from any other utterance. It becomes the theological equivalent of Duchamp's readymades.
>
> For postmodern theology, nothing is — or, I should say, not even nothing is holy. Post-liberal theology, by contrast, denies the experience of the holy as a universal human capacity in order to protect the special status of its own particular position. . . . For different reasons, neither form of post-theology can affirm authentic humanism. [In post-liberalism,] [t]heology once again inscribes exclusivism on to its own body of thought.
>
> Theological humanism is both an outlook on being in the world and a practical orientation to life's problems. . . . Theological humanism wants to affirm and appropriate the positive contributions of both postmodern and post-liberal theologies, while negating and transcending their deficiencies. On the one hand, it has the task of reconstructing religious traditions in order to challenge them to realise their own most humane expressions. On the other hand, theological humanism has the task of de-

39. Ibid., 36.
40. Ibid., 50.
41. Richard Kearney, in ibid., 68.

veloping theological interpretations of significant expressions in any domain of culture.[42]

Jim Olthuis voices similar theological reservations about aspects of postmodernism in his "Is the Postmodern Not Postmodern Enough?", but moves in a more conservative direction.

> In the world of being-as-power, suffering has no legitimate place.[43]

> Indeed, I suspect the postmodern self will be shown to be as mythical as its predecessor, another adapted, false self. There is still room for an agent self that is not absolute, with no claims to self-authorization and full presence, but a gifted/called self, gifted with agency and called to co-agency by an *Other*.[44]

There are, however, constructive construals of the postmodern which are germane to this enquiry. Outstanding is Calvin Schrag's *God as Otherwise than Being*: "The grammar of 'gift' has become virtually a household topic in certain contemporary philosophical and theological circles."[45] In seeking precision in talk of being he discusses "superessential essence" and hyperessentiality.

> The not-being of this and that is not the assertion of an absence. It is rather a serendipitous effort to point to the superabundance or surplus of the divine majesty. . . . Whereas the denials within deconstruction "defer" all determinations of being in its positivity as presence, negative theology continues to reside in the hollow of a metaphysics of theism.[46]

He adduces another Princeton theologian, Wentzel Van Huyssteen, who speaks of coming "to the point where we can celebrate the truth behind truth, the God behind God, and the religious behind religion."[47] Schrag widens the discussion to consider the work of Marion, who reflects Derrida and

---

42. David Klemm, in a Glasgow paper, "Theology and the End of Art," November 2005.

43. Olthuis, in Smith and Venema, *The Hermeneutics of Charity*, 26.

44. Olthuis, in Smith and Venema, *The Hermeneutics of Charity*, 28.

45. Calvin Schrag, *God as Otherwise Than Being* (Evanston, IL: Northwestern University Press, 2002), xv.

46. Ibid., 11, 12.

47. J. Wentzel Van Huyssteen, *Essays in Postfoundational Theology* (Grand Rapids: Wm. B. Eerdmans, 1997), 43.

George Newlands

the much earlier work of Marcel Mauss. Marion exemplifies the danger of ecclesiastical idolatry[48] in Catholicism and in Protestantism.

> The truth of the sacraments and its tenuous connection with an elusive presence remains one of the more enigmatic truths of institutionalized religion. . . . And it is here we have much to learn from Levinas, specifically from his accentuation of the disclosure of the Deity in the face and call of the neighbor and the stranger, the afflicted and the suffering, in which there is a beckoning to a responsibility that points beyond the multiple responsibilities in the economy of civil society.[49]

In his book *Given Time*,[50] Derrida's principal point is that the insertion of a gift into a network of exchange relations means that one cannot dispossess without first possessing.

> With the instantiation of the gift as love, external to the economies of distribution and exchange, reward and recompense, we have an occasion to refigure and revise the metaphysical concept of transcendence, which has been such a bane for classical theism. . . . Insofar as the gift exceeds even the domain of the ethical, the transcendence at issue cannot be construed as a moment within the ethical itself, a move that was made in certain expressions of nineteenth- and early-twentieth-century liberal theology, which sought to reduce religion to morality. . . . An infinite God who is found in the depths of the finite soul is no longer God, and the self that seeks to constitute itself as infinite loses itself as finite self. . . . The gift is transcendent.[51]

Schrag speaks of the asymmetry that always travels with the gift, "the grammar of asymmetrical reciprocity," and goes on to explore the ethics of charity in the (very Reformed) village of Le Chambon in World War II. Justice and democracy also become asymmetrical.[52]

In the context of hospitality, it is worth reflecting on the very similar preoccupation with gift in Marion and others. In *The Idol and the Distance*, Marion explores the saturated phenomenon. This becomes a mysterious and undefined cipher, somewhat perhaps like *Moby Dick*, or Barth's Word of

48. Schrag, *God as Otherwise Than Being*, 92.
49. Ibid., 92, 99.
50. Jacques Derrida, *Given Time* (Chicago: University of Chicago Press, 1992).
51. Ibid., 111-113.
52. Schrag, *God as Otherwise Than Being*, 142.

288

God? The icon can become an idol for theologians, and nothing is exempt. Biblical metaphors appear to be normative for Marion and the relation of all this to engagement remains unclear.

Marion, in answer to Mauss, suggests that "[g]ift can be just pure givenness."[53] For Marion, there is the actuality of pure givenness (contra Derrida). Robyn Horner stresses that "For the Marion of *God Without Being,* God gives Godself in a gift of love that can be recognised but not appropriated."[54]

The question, however, remains: how to unpack the gift and use it? Parcels are useless as such. Is this only a form of Neoplatonism repackaged? we might speculate. For Marion, no historical criticism of the New Testament is needed. All is achieved by intuition. Here there seems to be theology without a cross. Where is this world? *Gelassenheit* may be too comfortable. In Christian theology, we might reflect, Christomorphic action happens through history and politics and not just through vision. One might recall Jürgen Moltmann's early criticism of the epiphany of the eternal present. Rather, hospitality concretizes a specific gift, unpacking the package. There would appear not to be much instantiated incarnation in Marion — or priority for the marginalized. One might reflect that we may not be able to give without self-interest. But God *qua* God can — this is part of the divine/human asymmetry.

Does the icon of gift obscure as much as it reveals? Paul Lakeland has said of Marion:

> His fundamental theology is only a natural theology, in other words, and he must retire into revelation to spell out the austere phenomenological concept of contentless giving. . . . Christ the icon of God is *not* transparent at all, but deeply and ineradicably colored by historical circumstance and profoundly reflective of the tragedy of being human in a nonanthropocentric universe.[55]

To return to the Reformed tradition of Luther and Calvin, the gift is examined in a rather different dimension by the Finnish Lutheran theologian, Risto Saarinen, who has also written on Luther and justification.[56] Here is an

---

53. Jean Luc Marion, *The Idol and the Distance* (New York: Fordham University Press, 2001), 115.

54. See Robyn Horner, *Jean Luc Marion: An Introduction* (Aldershot: Ashgate, 2005), 101.

55. Paul Lakeland, *Postmodernity* (Minneapolis: Fortress Press, 1997), 95, 109.

56. Risto Saarinen, *God and the Gift* (Collegeville, MN: Liturgical Press, 2005).

George Newlands

ecumenical theology of giving. Ecumenism is often explained in terms of an "exchange of gifts" (cf. the notion of Reception in *Lumen gentium*). That there are problems with gifts, from Mauss to Bourdieu, is abundantly clear. "No free gifts" is a slogan of anthropologists, but at the same time it is a challenge to theology.[57] Saarinen, too, quotes Derrida. One should make the effort of thinking "the transcendent illusion of the gift" and Marion on givenness in these terms: "somewhat like Karl Barth or Hans Urs von Balthasar, Marion is opting for a consistent theology of revelation, in which revelation gives God without the alienating Cartesian category of objective being."[58] He finds some help in the work of John Milbank. For Milbank, a gift without being cannot be a gift of anything.[59] What is needed is "precisely an ontology of the gift." Is there here real reciprocity? There are clues in Luther on God's gift in Christ. This leads to reflection on forgiveness and negative giving, forgetting (Milbank) sacrifice and thanksgiving (Girard) and Luther on spiritual sacrifice.[60] Ecumenical giving means sharing reciprocity.

What does this postmodern talk of gift amount to? Not necessarily a great deal. As we have already suggested, much depends on whether the gift can be unwrapped and used, in practice, old and new. Hospitality means unwrapping and distributing the gift. Being and other than being — all have metaphorical elements and have value — but none is a magic formula. Unwrapping the gift: faith, engagement, and human rights. In thinking of a hospitable God, all the basic structuring elements of the Christian understanding of God should be represented fully. But this need not be a comprehensive study of all aspects of the classical doctrine of God. It is a focused meditation on hospitality and God. Hospitality in recent thinking can be seen especially though not exclusively through the emancipatory theologies. The hospitable Christ in twentieth-century hospitality has been seen notably through the friendship motif. The hospitality and friendship motif can be seen though the contemporary novel in its emancipatory themes. The hospitable God is the source and goal of emancipatory theology — expressed through being/active love/creation/redemption. Hospitable faith attempts to express faith afresh in reviewing our image of God. Belief in God usually derives as much from the Christian tradition, the events concerning Jesus, as from contemplating the question of what it is for there to be a God.

57. Ibid., 18.
58. Ibid., 27.
59. Ibid., 30.
60. Ibid., 89.

The inhospitable God should be rejected firmly; this is a lesson from emancipatory theology's critique of traditional church views. We may find it best to begin from the tradition of human faith in force, presence, absence, rather than from God as being. Faith arises from grace through the Word of God. Beginning from God as hospitable may have a practical cost — hiding enemies of the state poses risks. It may be desirable to begin from community rather than confession. What holds the Christian community together is not a common theology but a common faith.

Above all, with the hospitable God it is the tone which determines the music. Desmond Tutu says this:

> Ubuntu. A person with ubuntu is welcoming, hospitable, warm and generous, willing to share. Such people are open and available to others, willing to be vulnerable, affirming of others, do not feel threatened that others are able and good, for they have a proper self-assurance that comes from knowing that they belong in a greater whole.[61]

God only has us.

IV

Not every sort of hospitality will express the distinctiveness of the Christian gospel. What would it mean to think of Jesus Christ as the incarnate hospitality of God? I return to Luther. In March 1522, Luther left the security of the Wartburg and returned to Wittenberg, where he delivered his eight famous "Invokavit" sermons. This is from the seventh.

> We shall now speak of the fruit of this sacrament, which is love; that is, that we should treat our neighbor even as God has treated us. Now we have received from God naught but love and favor, for Christ has pledged and given us His righteousness and everything that He has, has poured out upon us all His treasures, which no man can measure and no angel can understand or fathom, for God is a glowing furnace of love, reaching even from the earth to the heavens.
>
> Love, I say, is a fruit of this sacrament. But I do not yet perceive it among you here in Wittenberg, although there is much preaching of love and you ought to practice it above all other things. This is the principal

61. Desmond Tutu, *God Has a Dream* (New York: Doubleday, 2004), 26.

thing, and alone is seemly in a Christian. But no one shows eagerness for this, and you want to do all sorts of unnecessary things, which are of no account. If you do not want to show yourselves Christians by your love, then leave the other things undone, too, for St. Paul says in 1 Corinthians, "If I speak with the tongues of men and of angels, and have not love, I am as sounding brass or a tinkling cymbal." (1 Cor 13:1) This is a terrible saying of Paul. And further: "And though I have the gift of prophecy, and understand all mysteries of God, and all knowledge; and though I have all faith, so that I could remove mountains, and have not love, I am nothing.

The Lutheran tradition, like the Reformed tradition, has been and doubtless will be developed in all sorts of directions, in conservative and in progressive frameworks. I want to suggest that what matters is not the genetic pedigree — theologies are not quite like racehorses — but the service to the gospel today which the huge variety in the tradition can still encourage. We do not have to go back quite as far as 1522 to find a comprehensive vision of the unconditional love of God and the Christian response in love.

God *is* self-expending, other-affirming, community-building love. The exchange of love that constitutes the eternal life of God is expressed outwardly in the history of costly love that liberates and reconciles.[62]

That God's life can be described in the light of the gospel with the beautiful metaphors of Trinitarian hospitality and the dance of Trinitarian love has far reaching implications. . . . If the triune God is understood as a continuing history of victorious and compassionate love, it follows that we must not, like so much of the tradition, think of the Trinity primarily in retrospect. . . . We must also think of the Trinity prospectively, looking forward to the glorious completion of the history of divine love. . . . Like faith, Christian love is an act of freedom. It is the free practice of self-limitation and regard for the other. It is the willingness to assist others, especially those others called enemies, and to take the first step in promoting justice, mutuality and friendship.[63]

This profound and irenic vision recalls the tradition of Alesius, whom we met at the beginning of this paper, rather than Knox. One of the most learned of the early Reformers, Alesius devoted considerable effort to identi-

62. Daniel Migliore, *Faith Seeking Understanding* (Grand Rapids: Wm. B. Eerdmans, 1991), 63.
63. Ibid., 70-71, 137.

fying the best in Protestant and Catholic traditions and to seeking reconciliation rather than polemic. It is not always the most strident theologians who are the wisest, and who contribute most to a mature and thoughtful Christianity.

Dan Migliore calls on us not to look backward but to look forward. I have taken a brief look at the Lutheran ghost in the Reformed tradition and suggested there may be scope for more reciprocal appreciation in the future, not uncritical but not unmindful. In 2006 the executive committees of the World Alliance of Reformed Churches and the World Lutheran Federation met together for the first time. In 2013, they hope to have a joint ecumenical Assembly. *Quid Athenis cum Jerusalem? Quid Wittenberg cum Geneva?* However that may be, it is a pleasure and an honor to write an essay for a distinguished, wise, and faithful servant of the Reformed tradition, the Reverend Professor Daniel Migliore.

Theology in Dialogue with Society and Culture

Which Forms and Themes Should Christian Theology Uphold in Dialogue with Secular Culture?

Michael Welker

Translated by Stephen Lakkis

My experiences with Daniel Migliore are not only of those unforgettable theology courses which we presented together in Princeton, or of him as a charming dialogue partner in many of our personal discussions. His writings — which aim at the content of theological teaching and concentrate on its most important aspects — have also left a strong impression on me, especially his major work *Faith Seeking Understanding*.[1] The *Expository Times* is certainly justified when it writes: "This is theology with a sure and sharp pastoral touch . . . an ideal primer of doctrine for students." Without Dan's example, I would never have offered an introductory course into theology in Germany and would never have taken this approach to thinking about the essentials of Christian theology in discussion with today's secular culture in the West — as I wish to do here.

The need today consciously to acknowledge the existence of a cultural ecology (in addition to a natural ecology) is one many observers of Western societies had already recognized some time ago. If this culture is to be both stable and creative, then a religiosity cultured in its forms and contents is vital. Yet many people (with the media industry leading the way) still see the content of religion as something which can be culturally manipulated in order to produce either entertainment or dismay at will, a mass for manipulation which can be used and abused to our hearts' content. They do not see that religious contents deteriorate when subjected to reductionistic or dis-

---

1. Daniel L. Migliore, *Faith Seeking Understanding: An Introduction to Christian Theology* (Grand Rapids: Wm. B. Eerdmans, 1991).

torting public presentation, and that they can lose their orienting power despite their strong opposition to such abuse. Indeed, a presentation which constantly empties them of meaning, trivializes, and distorts them can even transform them into destructive entities. Paul grasped this fact with his (at first) puzzling warning that "the good and holy law of God" can be transformed into a power which no longer allows us to recognize or curb sin, but instead aggressively strengthens it. Distorted religion can surface as a driving force behind the processes of stultification and increasing fanaticism. This does not only arise with extreme occurrences. When religion is regularly presented as banal, embarrassing, and ridiculous, or as inhuman and crassly irrational, then it becomes a culturally destructive entity.

Yet these processes of banalization and the systematic evacuation of meaning not only threaten religion from without, but also from within. Indeed, the self-secularization and self-banalization of religion is the greatest challenge facing all who work in theological and religious education. To combat this process, one must patiently and steadfastly uncover and convey the deep, enduring (but still thoroughly fragile) rationalities and consistencies of the knowledge of faith and the knowledge of humanity which are contained in the religious traditions. It is our task to help ensure that the orienting power of that knowledge of humanity in the religious traditions can also bear fruit today. In the following paper, I wish to name some central themes in the Judeo-Christian traditions which require such cultural-ecological care. But first, I will precede this with a few remarks touching upon some very elementary *forms of thought*, the ways in which they are made plausible, practiced, and cared for publicly. While these forms of thought play an important role today under the headings of "modernity and post-modernity," they are rarely explained clearly.

I. Monism, Dualism, Pluralism

Not only in a general education, but also in a religious education, it is important to be able to deal with the differences between (a) monistic, (b) dual or dualistic, and (c) pluralistic forms of thought and orientation.

The monistic world-view still remains the paradigm of typical modern thought. It speaks of *one* reason, *one* rationality, it assumes *one universal* morality, and the final unproblematic unity of all reality. The modern, monistic world-view likes to see religion as yokelish, obsolete, as belonging to a past world. According to this position, religion does not belong to *the* rational world-view — the only one which is right and true. Over against such a world-view, religious education must reawaken a sense for the importance of *differing* rationalities and symbol-systems in our cultures, social spheres and sciences.

One religious educator has reported good experiences using comparative art appreciation exercises with 10- to 12-year-olds. For example, he showed them an image of one of Salvador Dali's famous melting clocks and a picture of a round, functioning wall-clock and then asked them to formulate and comment upon their impressions. But we have a wide range of other possibilities for reflecting upon different rationalities and symbol-systems. For example, one could use analogies between the different life journeys taken by those in biblical and current contexts: for example, reflections about modern careers in consultancy and management paralleled with Joseph's career in Egypt. Such carefully chosen double-perspectives can help to break up and correct a naïve, but also historically developed, monism.

However, the danger of correcting a monistic view "of reality" is that it may produce a dualizing or even dualistic world-view, together with all its corresponding clichés: faith versus reason, the invisible versus the visible, the objective versus the subjective. Time and again, religious thought has happily sought to reinforce itself with such dualistic clichés, or has allowed others to push it in this direction. Of course, we cannot avoid living and working with dual orientations. However, ensuring that these dual orientations do not "freeze" into fixed dualisms is a great challenge which also needs to be faced, especially by religious education. A populist so-called "popular opinion," different forms of fundamentalism, religious and ideological narrow-mindedness, and fanaticism all happily avail themselves of dualisms and often use mutual negations to stabilize themselves: "I am not what you are, and you are not what I am!"

Over against this orientation, religious education should help people to see the provisional aspects of all dual schemas, the partiality of interests, the advantages and disadvantages, the orientational achievements and dangerous reductions. "God and Man," I and Thou, faith and reason, church and society, church and state — we are familiar with a multitude of (mostly harmless) orientational dualities which we encounter in religious and theological texts and which we must be able to engage reflectively. We should see them as perspectival limitations and not as finalized, ultimate representations of "reality." Yet there are also potentially dangerous dualisms (friend/enemy, believer/unbeliever, heaven/hell, etc.) which we encounter, and which might be sensible and understandable in times of persecution and struggle, but which also bring with them obstacles to our understanding, moral callousness, and aggressive attitudes. It is one of the great cultural challenges of our time not only to acquaint but intimately to familiarize ourselves with pluralistic configurations over against monistic, dual and dualistic orientations.

Pluralistic configurations are not to be equated with a diffuse "plurality": an indeterminate and endless multitude of views and perspectives. One of today's greatest cultural scourges is the equation, indeed, confusion of pluralism with a diffuse plurality of views, attitudes, opinions, lifestyles, etc. This type of indifferent arbitrariness, this type of relativism, is beyond opportunities for clear academic observation and our ethical capacities for control. Though it continues to occur, vague conceptions of "plurality" and "relationality" must not be confused with social, scientific, cultural, and economic pluralism. Pluralism refers to a particular *formal constellation* of differing spheres: a structured "community of communities."[2]

The Judeo-Christian traditions offer a multitude of pluralistic structures, beginning with the pluralism of the canonical writings. As the Heidelberg Egyptologist, Jan Assmann, has shown,[3] canonical traditions developed under the influence of traumatic experiences of discontinuity. In Israel, this was the experience of exile, of deportation; in the New Testament it was the event of the cross and resurrection. These radical experiences of discontinuity led to the need for interpretation, a need which could not be satisfied by just a single interpretation. What is required here is a limited number of perspectives, a "pluralistic library" (as Heinz Schürmann once stated) which repeatedly concentrates these memories and in doing so constantly resolves these concentrations in a multi-perspectival way. In this alternating process of problematization and re-concentration, the pluralistically structured canonical texts purposefully promote the quest for truth and the pursuit of new insights which orient us toward that truth.

---

2. Cf. M. Welker, "Was ist Pluralismus?" in *Wertepluralismus. Sammelband der Vorträge des Studium Generale der Ruprecht-Karls-Universität Heidelberg im Wintersemester 1998/99* (Heidelberg: C. Winter, 1999), 9-23; idem, *Kirche im Pluralismus*, 2nd ed. (Gütersloh: Kaiser, 2000); idem, "'. . . And Also Upon the Menservants and the Maidservants in Those Days Will I Pour Out My Spirit': On Pluralism and the Promise of the Spirit," in *Soundings* 78 (1995): 49-67.

3. Jan Assmann, *Fünf Schritte auf dem Weg zum Kanon* (Münster: Lit, 2000).

II. The Significance of the Canonical, Biblical Traditions and the Importance of a Culturally Formative Communal Memory

One of the great blessings which can guide "truth-seeking communities" is a form of memory, conditioned by the biblical canon, which I have termed "canonical memory." It is important that this great achievement is made comprehensible, which in turn allows for the development of a sense for correctly understood, cultivated pluralism. Just as modern pluralistic societies seek to cultivate a balance between differing social "sub-systems" — such as law, politics, economics, education, the media, and religion — without placing them into a simplistic hierarchical order, so too in theology and in the church we hold fast to the pluralistic balance of the canonical traditions, even though we may privilege certain biblical texts and authors at particular times and in certain contexts.[4]

The great *historical weight* of the Bible and its impressive growth over more than a millennia also need explicit communication in our religious and secular environments. Again, it must be expressed more clearly in religious education that the Bible takes up and reflects upon a millennia of religious experience, worldly wisdom, vastly differing experiences of crisis and liberation, of threshold experiences, and above all of experiences of the breakdown of law, morality, and political conditions. Due to this basis, the Bible bears incredibly immense *cultural weight:* for better or worse, it has played a long and powerful role in the formation of both cultural and world history. It is a shame that for many, this is something which only first becomes apparent when visiting a museum. The cultural significance of the biblical traditions can also be differentiated into *existential, moral, and symbolic significance.*[5]

Yet above these aspects, the Bible also bears a great *canonical weight,* since in a wide range of ways the biblical traditions mutually refer to one another, stand in discussion with one another, and learn from each other. It is doubtful that they could ever be brought into a system or reduced to a single idea — nor should they. Yet they are in fact joined to one another in many ways, which is why we can speak of the "growth of the canon." However, this great historical, cultural, and canonical weight is grounded in a *theological*

---

4. Cf. M. Welker, "Kommunikatives, kollektives, kulturelles und kanonisches Gedächtnis," *Jahrbuch für Biblische Theologie,* vol. 22: *Die Macht der Erinnerung* (Neukirchen-Vluyn: Neukirchener, 2008), 321-331.

5. Cf. M. Welker, "Sola Scriptura? The Authority of Scripture in Pluralistic Environments," in *A God So Near: A Festschrift in Honor of Patrick D. Miller,* ed. B. Strawn et al. (Winona Lake: Eisenbrauns, 2002), 375-391.

weight, in the contents of those biblical traditions, in their manifold witnesses to God and to God's work among humanity. It is God himself, God's revelation in the history of Israel and in Jesus Christ, God in his creative, salvific, and uplifting actions, which gives the Bible its incredible force of presence.

If we wish to make the significance of the canonical biblical traditions and the importance of caring for and maintaining canonical memory clear to others today, then we should help them to become sensitized to the importance of communal memory and mutually shared expectations. Jan Assmann distinguishes between several forms of communal memory, especially between *communicative* and *cultural memory.* Communicative memory comes to us of its own accord whenever we move and live in human societies. Not only is our memory continually fed and shaped by the flux of our own experience, but it also occurs deliberately at home and school, through relatives and friends, yet also through the media and many forms of memorial culture. Thus while we differentiate our memories as individuals, we are also constantly bringing them into tune with those of others. This liquid, communicative memory is always being reconstructed. Great catastrophes and outstanding events can change it from one day to the next. Yet within communicative memory we also maintain what Assmann calls "cultural memory," a memory which upholds particular contents and particular forms, maintains their stability, and keeps special watch over them purposefully in order to steer communal orientation to the present and future. Cultural memory is a great good, a great achievement; it can adopt static and dynamic forms; it can be ideologized, and it can keep a living culture alive.

A third form of memory should also be pointed out in addition to communicative and cultural memory: that is, what I have called *"canonical memory."* This form of memory is directed by a *structured* pluralism of canonical texts (in other words, precisely the opposite of a diffuse and arbitrarily expandable "plurality" of texts!). It is exactly this structured, pluralistic composition of the (Jewish, Christian, and possibly also Confucian) canon together with that canonical memory which is oriented toward it which lend themselves both to concentration *and* creative self-critique. They simultaneously serve to maintain both communal orientation *as well as* difference of perspective. Canonical memory rejects the alternatives of stability or dynamism, preservation or renewal. It erects normative structures and transforms them. Conveying the great good of canonical memory is one of the main tasks of religious education today. This major task is addressed best when the power of the biblical orientations are displayed with regard to the central contents of faith. But what are these "essentials," faith's truly indispensable contents? While I certainly do not claim to offer a definitive list of *all* the fruitful and central aspects of the doctrines of faith, I would like to suggest the following ten themes.

III. Top Topics in Theology

1. The first complex of most important themes lies in the area of the *doctrine of creation*. One of our central tasks here is to use the subtlety of the creation narratives (for example, in the Priestly texts) to correct abstract theism as well as the deism of the "first second" and other simplistic metaphysical images of God. Important here is the discovery that the creation narrative refers to two temporal systems: first *the days of God*, with the initial differentiation of light from darkness, and then on the fourth day (with the help of the heavenly bodies) the establishment of *days under the heavens*. This key insight allows us to shake that prejudice which sees the biblical texts as naïve and obsolete. "God's days" (which, while analogous to "days under the heavens," represent incredibly immense periods of time) are linked first to cosmic, then biological, cultural, and finally religious processes. In doing so, thoroughly evolutionary developments are included in creation, for it is not only God who acts but also the creatures. The creatures are expected to cooperate in the process of creation, though on a graduated scale. In a variety of ways, these insights, among others, can address and alter that prejudice which sees us dealing here with a naïve world-view. In this context, the analogies and differences to the cosmologies of the natural sciences can then be discussed in a fruitful way. Analogies and differences to the world-views of the ancient Near East can illustrate the millennia-spanning period of "human knowledge." Even the critique of widespread dualistic clichés (e.g., nature versus culture) or entrenched and unimaginative religious models (such as abstract religious models of dependence) can then be problematized in a fruitful way.[6]

2. Still in the area of doctrines of creation, a second "essential" complex of themes deals with the relationship between the *imago Dei and the divine call to human dominion*. In the course of unending ecological brutalism, we were told well into the 1970s that the biblical texts and the Judeo-Christian

---

6. Cf. M. Welker, "Was ist Schöpfung? Zur Subtilität antiken Weltordnungsdenkens," in *Jahrbuch der Heidelberger Akademie der Wissenschaften für 2006* (Heidelberg: Universitätsverlag, Winter 2007), 84-88.

traditions wanted nothing other than to transform nature into "an object" which the human being (responsibly) has at his or her disposal. In opposition to this stance a critical countermovement arose led by Lynn White and others who proclaimed the biblical commission to human dominion to be the root of modern Cartesianism and the fundamental evil of modern cultural development. It is the Bible which must bear the blame for the modern, ecologically brutal "maître et possesseur de la nature" (Descartes)![7]

This prompted the development of an unsatisfactory evasive maneuver which, with its focus on the Yahwistic creation narrative, attempted either to stress the "cultivation and preservation of creation" or interpret away those elements dealing with the use of violent force in the commission to dominion. These efforts were largely misdirected. On the one hand, we have a long Jewish and Christian history of interpretation which clearly illustrates how the *call to dominion* explicitly speaks the language of slaveholders and conquerors. The human being is expressly set above other creatures. On the other hand, this prioritization is balanced by the destiny of the human being in the *imago Dei*, in the image of God. Yet it is ancient Near Eastern, royal ideology which is expressed in this image: despite all their privileges, and while safeguarding their own interests, the human beings are still to seek justice and the protection of the weak. Thus we have here the construction of a complex ethos which spans a divide, a tension. Self-preservation, justice, and the protection of the weak need not (and must not) be mutually exclusive. The insight that human beings do not live up to their great destiny — that a renewal of the *imago* is needed — leads then into important connecting themes, such as Christology and pneumatology, both of which equally influence anthropology and ethics.

3. A third indispensable complex of themes in the context of the doctrine of creation is *the symbol of the fall and the doctrine of sin*. Here too, it is important that we first persevere under apparent inconsistencies, especially the one which arises in Genesis 3:22, when it is said of Adam that he "has become like God, knowing good and evil." The Reformers could think of no other solution than to describe this as "divine irony." Hegel and left-wing Hegelianism saw "the fall" as a "return to God's image" and as confirmation of human autonomy: What could the human being want more than to know

7. See here Daniel Migliore, *Faith Seeking Understanding*, 80-98; Christian Link, *Schöpfung. Schöpfungstheologie angesichts der Herausforderungen des 20. Jahrhunderts* (Gütersloh: Gütersloher Verlag, 1991), 358ff., 455ff.; M. Welker, *Creation and Reality: Theological and Biblical Perspectives* (Philadelphia: Fortress Press, 1999), chapter 5.

the difference between good and evil? Dietrich Bonhoeffer was one of the few who clearly saw this as a certification that, after the fall, the human being could then distinguish that which is detrimental to life and that which promotes life, but *only from his or her own perspective* — a task in which they constantly fail. The Hebrew text characterizes the man as *'aHad,* as a "loner"; he has not "become the likes of us" (as Luther translates, seeing this as an ironic remark), but has rather become only "like *one* of us." The early church speculated whether this meant isolation from the Trinity or from the heavenly hosts. But whatever the case, isolation was pronounced and then executed in their expulsion from paradise.

We have here a recognition of moral perspectivism, the relativity of our own world-views, and the deep need for orientation in our value systems — all of these points find a fruitful point of contact here. Yet a range of theologically, religiously, and morally explosive insights is also based here: that sin cannot be reduced merely to guilt but rather represents a fundamentally and systemically false orientation, and that the differentiation of sin and guilt allows us to correct a naïve moralism.[8] The biblical traditions confront us with the fragility and fragmentary nature of our morality and our world-views, and confront us with the systemic distortions which go hand in hand with them — and thus with the need for continual reorientation. This reorientation occurs through the guidance of God's law and God's gospel.

4. The systemic distortion which accompanies the power of sin becomes clear in an especially dramatic way on the *cross of Christ.* With a view focused on the crucifixion, recent theologies of the cross have placed a primary stress on God's suffering, compassion, and benevolence as well as God's confrontation of death. While this is not false, it is one-sided and fails sufficiently to express the revelatory character of the cross. As Jürgen Moltmann displayed in his book *The Crucified God,* Jesus not only dies forsaken by God, but dies as an insurgent and blasphemer.[9] He also dies in confrontation with the political and religious powers. The cross reveals a conspiracy between the world's good powers: two forms of law (Jewish and Roman), imperial politics, the ruling religion, and public opinion immunize each other, indeed even mutually strengthen one another, in their opposition both to the gift of God's goodness and to the very presence of God!

---

8. Cf. Sigrid Brandt, Marjorie Suchocki, and Michael Welker, eds., *Sünde. Ein unverständlich gewordenes Thema,* 2nd ed. (Neukirchen-Vluyn: Neukirchener Verlag, 2005).

9. Jürgen Moltmann, *Der gekreuzigte Gott. Das Kreuz Christi als Grund und Kritik christlicher Theologie* (Gütersloh: Kaiser, 2002), chapter 4.

A theology which focuses on the cross is central for theologically exposing the endangerment of the world and the self-endangerment of human beings, phenomena which we are repeatedly forced to suffer in our times in the form of fascism, racism, ecological brutalism, or in many other latent forms.

5. Yet by itself, the theology of the cross is hopeless and groundless if it is not perceived under the light of the *resurrection*. Here we find ourselves before a very sensitive issue, a place where the meaning and soundness of the religious world-view is repeatedly called into question. The main problem facing the theology of resurrection is the constant confusion of resurrection with physical resuscitation. Normally, when dealing with this confusion, physical resuscitation is simply dismissed as implausible. Yet this distorts the fact that the biblical texts do not actually speak of a physical resuscitation but of something quite different. It is only if we take particular texts in isolation — such as Luke's account of Jesus eating fish (Luke 24:43) — that we could pass off the resurrection as a physical resuscitation. However, any examination of the resurrection texts in their broader context simply excludes this type of confusion. At no point does anyone say: "Nice that you're back, Jesus!" Instead we see *proskynesis,* an awareness of God and worship, individuals testifying to a theophany, to a revelation of God! Yet, as the texts stress, there is also doubt.

The Emmaus Road narrative is particularly telling. The eyes of the disciples are closed. They do not recognize Jesus, which would be particularly unusual if we were dealing with a physical resuscitation. At the breaking of bread their eyes are opened, yet immediately "he vanished from their sight" (Luke 24:31). This disappearance does not prompt in them a feeling that they had witnessed a ghostly event, but rather reminds them of a second *evidential experience.* "Were not our hearts burning within us while he was talking to us on the road, while he was opening the scriptures to us?" (Luke 24:32). Certainty — that the Risen One is among us, with us, and that he lives! — grows from *various evidential experiences.* Yet he does not live with and among us as the pre-Easter Jesus did but rather, as the biblical texts state, "in spirit and in faith," as the resurrected and exalted Christ in a new "body of Christ."

Today, it is very hard to make this presence in spirit and in faith intelligible, but I believe that cultural memory and canonical memory can be helpful for a secularized "common sense." First and foremost: we must explain clearly that the resurrection is not a natural event, but rather something more comparable to a cultural event. Particularly helpful here is the sobering insight that when the biblical texts speak of the reality of the resurrection, they repeatedly (and quite consciously) hold tight to the agonizing tension between manifest presence (which could be mistaken for mere resuscitation) and appearance. The appearance of the Resurrected One is, and remains, connected with the testimony of witnesses. This does not make it a construction or reduce it to wishful thinking; rather, these testimonies refer back to the pre-Easter Jesus. The Resurrected One brings with him *the fullness of his person and of his entire pre-Easter life.*[10] Presence "in the spirit and in faith" brings the wholeness and fullness of existence, which then sets free a wealth of connections with this life, and entwines people into this life in a variety of ways in the testimonies of the "disciples."

6. In their use of the image of the many-membered *"body of Christ"* as *the form of the Christian church,* the New Testament traditions both purposefully present and emphasize pluralistic orientations. Differing gifts and differing ways of life are called into service by the Resurrected One. Not only are differing connections to the life of Jesus Christ possible and tolerated, they are precisely the point of the post-Easter "body" in which Christ testifies to his presence. For some people, it is the attention given to children or table fellowship which is particularly important; for others, it is diaconal activity; still for others, the expounding of the scriptures; for others again, the confrontation of political and religious powers. A multitude of gifts are activated here and set into many fruitful relationships with each other. Many differing ecumenical models (hierarchical and democratic forms of church), differing forms of the imitation of Christ and their interaction can be conceived upon the basis of this church structure — yet also powerful forms of decay in proclamation, preaching, and mission. On this basis we can not only describe and critically differentiate liberating missionary and diaconal developments, but also culturally imperialistic manifestations of the church and Christian religiosity.[11]

7. Even more difficult than the topic of the resurrection, yet no less important, is that of *Christ's parousia,* often called Christ's "second coming." As with other eschatological topics, it offers the possibility for illustrating a culture of communal expectation in addition to a culture of remembrance. The

10. Cf. M. Welker, "Theological Realism and Eschatological Symbol Systems: Resurrection, the Reign of God, and the Presence in Faith and in the Spirit," in *Resurrection: Theological and Scientific Assessments,* ed. T. Peters, R. Russell, and M. Welker (Grand Rapids: Wm. B. Eerdmans, 2002), 31-42; Hans-Joachim Eckstein and Michael Welker, eds., *Die Wirklichkeit der Auferstehung,* 3rd ed. (Neukirchen-Vluyn: Neukirchener Verlag, 2007).

11. Cf. Andreas Feldtkeller and Theo Sundermeier, eds., *Mission in pluralistischer Gesellschaft* (Frankfurt: Lembeck, 1999).

educational task here is to explain how the eschatological visions of a community also strongly determine its real culture and morals, and that our eschatological moods are subject to astounding fluctuations. One need only think back to the 1960s, to those feelings of the dawn of a new messianic era, or to the apocalyptic mood of extermination which arose during the 1980s. These changes in eschatological mood have been examined in finer detail as part of a large-scale discussion with the natural sciences and published under the title: *The End of the World and the Ends of God: Science and Theology on Eschatology.*[12]

Characteristic of Judeo-Christian eschatology is a double structure: an *eschatological complementarity.* On the one hand, we find an orientation toward progress, even if such progress is not linear or predictable but rather occurs through diverse developments. The Kingdom of God is "coming," yet it comes in such a way that it remains hidden to many. It shows itself in many actions of love and forgiveness, in many small steps so that one is unable to say definitively "it is here, or it is there." Eschatological progress mostly occurs in *emergent* developments of perfection ("Many small people in many small places, taking very small steps can change the face of the world"), in the careful, constant growth of a seed.[13] Yet we see here only one side to eschatology.

At the same time, we look to an event which will be a definitive final state, an event which does not occur in this time. The parousia of Christ comes in all times! This denies all cultures and all views of history the possibility of declaring themselves absolute, of ideologizing their own values and their own achievements. It is the language of parousia which brings about this achievement of the "coming of the Son of Man with his angels, from one end of the earth to the end of heaven" (Mark 13:27; Matt. 16:27 and 24:31 par).

To a type of rationality which focuses on the "natural," this all sounds utterly fanciful. And indeed, the "theophany of the end times" is of necessity fanciful for a life lived in time. For the Son of Man will not come in one time or in one place but rather in all times and in all the world's places. For this reason, the images and visions of this event are necessarily pushed into the realm of the supernatural. From a clear eschatological rationality, these im-

12. John Polkinghorne and Michael Welker, eds., *The End of the World and the Ends of God: Science and Theology on Eschatology* (Harrisburg: Trinity, 2000).

13. Cf. Daniel Migliore, *Faith Seeking Understanding,* 231-251; Michael Welker, "The 'Reign' of God," *Theology Today* 49 (1992): 500-515; Michael Welker and Michael Wolter, "Die Unscheinbarkeit des Reiches Gottes," in *Reich Gottes, Marburger Jahrbuch Theologie XI,* ed. W. Härle and R. Preul (Marburg: Elwert, 1999), 103-116.

ages and visions push all views of history and the world to their limits. "The earth and the heaven fled from his presence" (Rev. 20:11). Creation is replaced by a "new creation." These types of statements are what we find in the powerful eschatological images. This correction and limitation by end-times eschatology of ideas of progress (be they historical, moral, etc.) is indispensable if we wish to think of a reality which is not totally assimilated into an earthly context. Yet the correction of an abstract end-times eschatology is also indispensable. Those who doggedly demand only the "Day of Judgment," the Last Judgment of the world, and other such events in an ominous end-time have missed the religious message. It is for this reason that a complementary eschatology is indispensable. Present and (simultaneously!) future eschatology — the Kingdom of God is both present and "coming" — as well as the eschatology of end-times and eternity must always be understood in their difficult and demanding relationship to one another.

The continuity of eschatology with the actions of the pre-Easter Jesus and his presence as the Risen One are decisive here. The coming Christ stands in a line of continuity with the pre-Easter, the resurrected, and the present Jesus Christ! Those who — through faith, love, and acts of forgiveness — already share in Christ's life, also have a share in his eternal life which possesses a validity beyond the aspects of our earthy lives, and which is not lost with this life's end. While this is very difficult to convey, good, theologically oriented teaching should at least introduce us to these ideas.

8. The eighth large thematic complex lies in the field of *pneumatology: the doctrine of the Holy Spirit*. Here too, the biblical traditions offer good material for illustrating the defeat of monistic and dualistic forms of thought to the benefit of pluralistic structures. The key symbol here is the "pouring out of the Spirit." This symbol is thoroughly anti-hierarchical. The prophet Joel had already stressed how "women and men, old and young, menservants and maidservants" would testify to God with each other and for each other when the Spirit is poured out (Joel 2:28f.). We forget that this is sensational in a patriarchal society where men have the say; this is sensational in societies which compel the young into obedience; this is sensational in slave-holder societies (a given in the ancient world).

The Pentecost report in Acts 2 expressly picks up Joel's promise and radicalizes the pluralistic differentiation, establishing connections in this revelatory experience between differing nations and cultures and languages. The pouring out of the Spirit does not abolish the differences between these varying nations and cultures and languages, but rather allows those who are separated by these aspects together to hear of "God's great deeds." To appre-

Michael Welker

ciate the great importance of this figure of the outpouring of the Spirit, one must see it against the background of the self-endangerment of the world under the power of sin. With the outpouring of the Spirit, God repeatedly steers against the world's own self-delusion. Time and again, the outpouring of the Spirit breaks up moral, religious, political, and legal oversimplifications and distortions. There is good reason why the third article of the Creed not only stresses the constitution of the community of saints but also "the forgiveness of sins" — liberation from the power of sin — as the primary work of the Spirit.[14]

9. While one can illustrate the importance of the Spirit and its outpouring quite well by contrasting it with communal self-endangerment and self-destruction ("sin"), its blessing and its importance can also be made clear by contrasting it with the effects of *"the law,"* which (in its own way) seeks to put a stop to sin. "Law and Spirit" — here too we must be sure critically to distance ourselves from simplistic dualisms. Dualisms which simply identify Spirit with "good" and law with "bad" are not "standing firm in the Reformed tradition," but (to put it bluntly) are theologically and ethically crazy. The biblical, legal traditions are truly fascinating. A careful study of the "Book of the Covenant" (Exod. 20:22–23:19) can turn into a first class intellectual and cultural adventure.

At the center of the Book of the Covenant are legal conflicts: the theft of cattle, murder, manslaughter, etc. We can familiarize ourselves here with the basic elements of legal thinking, with its development and its refinement. It's like a beginners' course in law: How are difficult conflicts and legal problems dealt with legally? Surrounding these legal texts (which deal with the law and the administration of justice), we find a second group of legal texts which focus on the protection of the acutely and chronically weak. A law regarding slavery draws our attention to the slaveholder societies of the ancient world but also to Israel's peculiarity: Slaves are to be set free after seven years, so that even slaves are to be protected under the law! We find corresponding forms of laws in favor of widows and orphans, the foreigner, the poor and the oppressed. I have called these regulations "mercy laws" or the "mercy code of the law."[15]

14. Cf. here Daniel Migliore, *Faith Seeking Understanding*, 165-184; Michael Welker, *God the Spirit*, trans. John Hoffmeyer (Philadelphia: Fortress Press, 1994).

15. Michael Welker, "Erbarmen und soziale Identität. Zur Neuformulierung der Lehre von Gesetz und Evangelium II," in *Evangelische Kommentare* 19 (1986): 39-42; idem, "Moral, Recht und Ethos in evangelisch-theologischer Sicht," in *Marburger Jahrbuch Theologie* XIII, ed. W. Härle and R. Preul (Marburg: Elwert, 2002), 67-81.

By making mercy part of the content of the law, by placing the laws of mercy at the same level as laws regulating conflicts among equals, an incredibly normative dynamics proceeded from which our cultural history continues to live today. It is by no means a given that we should be shaped by a morality which is determined by the pursuit of justice and mercy, of justice and the protection of the weak. As is well known, Nietzsche ridiculed this morality and sharply attacked it. The Olympic ethos, which today's media constantly conveys to us (either directly or indirectly) stands in diametric opposition to this biblical ethos. It is one of our great educational responsibilities to ensure that this difference is not simply surrendered to the market game.

A third group of legal texts deals with the cult, the relationship with God or, more precisely, the ordered, public relationship to God and the search for the knowledge of God and knowledge of the truth. One cannot overestimate the importance of recognizing and doing justice to the inner dynamics of the biblical law with its pursuit of such knowledge, and with its pursuit of justice and the protection of the weak. We must deal with this task precisely in a religious culture which writes off the law as a mere "demand," or reduces it to the "ten commandments" with their (truly fruitful and important) community ethos. If religious education wishes to work on the most important interdisciplinary and interreligious issues, on the foundational issues facing our culture and the so-called "discourse of values," then it must discover the topic of the "law" and learn to engage it competently. Yet an intensive examination of the "law" actually takes us much further.

10. The Isaianic traditions which speak of a messianic savior or a "servant of God" upon whom "the Spirit of God rests" (esp. Isa. 11:2; 42:1; and 61:1), repeatedly deal with the triad of justice, protection of the weak, and the knowledge of God and the truth. However, the one upon whom the Spirit rests will usher in this fulfillment of the law not only for Israel but also for the Gentiles. Yet a range of normative conflicts are inevitable here since the Gentiles will neither simply be integrated into Israel nor will they simply adopt Israel's laws; rather they will search for justice, mercy, and the knowledge of God from out of their own traditions. Here we have the place where those important questions facing *the pluralism of norms and the correlation between different moral and legal systems, and even the question of the plurality of religions* are to be addressed. In the field of pneumatology, the relativity as well as the corruptibility of norms can be tackled without descending into relativism or normative arbitrariness.

On the one hand, in this light we see that even this wonderful law and its developmental dynamics can fall under the power of sin. The early textual prophetic tradition (those prophets who "spoke in the Spirit") had already made this more than clear; in the words of Amos, Micah, Hosea, and Proto-Isaiah: "You have a cult, you speak justice in the gate, but you misuse worship, and you pervert the law because you despise mercy for the poor and the weak." Yet there are even worse distortions in which the self-concealment and self-immunization of evil are perfected. Even politics, law, and morality are used to conceal a society's pitilessness and lack of mercy. An entire society completely immunizes itself against the prophetic vision and against the prophetic warning and call to repentance. In this situation, the outpouring of the Spirit becomes an act of God's salvific intervention, renewing interpersonal relations and, in the words of the Reformation, bringing people back on "the path of Christ."

The structural insights into the relations of *the law and the Spirit* are far-reaching. The distortions in this complex normative ethos (developed out of the pursuit of justice, protection of the weak, and the search for truth) are called into question by the renewing power of the pluralistic outpouring of the Spirit, leading both to its renewal and its perfection. This large topic also offers a good starting point for a proper dialogue with Israel as well as with other religions and moral traditions. On this basis, we can genuinely (and fruitfully) bring into contact with each other the differing ways of working on this ethos, the work on cultural and canonical memory, and the differing ways for maintaining communal memory and expectation, as well as the guidance of cultural developments. In such an exchange, not only individual but also communal partners, such as cultures and religions, can mutually challenge and enrich each other.

Faith in the Public Square

David Fergusson

Dan Migliore's theology has been marked by an abiding concern to relate the convictions of Christian theology to our broader social and cultural life. In seeking to be faithful to the distinctives of the church, he has also sought to recognize and accommodate insights from elsewhere. This has resulted in his commitment to a generous orthodoxy, a respect for difference, and a lucidity of expression. By engaging with the secular and other faiths, he establishes conversations that are unfailingly courteous and often illuminating. This must in part explain why *Faith Seeking Understanding* has proved, at least here in Edinburgh, the most useful and enduring of textbooks for over a generation. In what follows, I offer a defense of the public significance of theology and church life which I hope is consistent with his exemplary practice.

Modern hostility to the intrusion of faith commitments in the public sphere is not hard to find. There is an argument that runs along the following lines. The provincial beliefs of one religious group should not be allowed to dominate the lives and social order of the majority who do not share these. To permit this is undemocratic, oppressive, and threatening to civic harmony. Our advocacy of ethical and political views should be on grounds that are in principle accessible and reasonable to all. Even when a religious party commands the allegiance of a majority of citizens, it cannot be allowed to ride roughshod over the commitments of the minority who are entitled to equal and fair treatment. This entails that a policy proposal based on a conviction about the universal lordship of Jesus, such as we find in Barmen 1, is seen as at best parochial and at worst theocratic. In a liberal democracy, it must be judged inappropriate, incomprehensible, in bad form, or even worse. This argument and its leading concepts are of course indebted to the traditions of political liberalism. I shall argue first that despite its intuitive appeal it suffers fatal weaknesses, and second that the presence of theological discourse in the public domain need not be adverse to the conditions of democratic politics.

Is there a common rationality that can be employed in public argument and decision-making within a pluralist society? To an important extent, this question has dominated the shaping of political liberalism since the early modern period. In refusing to privilege the assumptions of a single faith community, the state requires to find a basis for policy that does not repose upon particular religious claims. One of the standard arguments for religious tolerance held that, despite the presence of significant doctrinal disagreement between rival faith groups, there was a strong moral consensus that enabled citizens to live together peaceably. In the 16th century, Sebastian Castellio pointed out that while Jews, Christians, and Muslims may disagree over the doctrine of the Trinity they are quite unanimous on the condemnation of brigands and traitors.[1] But how is this consensus to be articulated?

Alongside the gradual emergence of claims for state neutrality, philosophies that could articulate a basis for political life irrespective of faith-based convictions became more prevalent. John Locke argued for a measure of religious toleration by promoting a political theory in which the natural rights of each citizen to life, liberty, and property were protected. The political life of society could thus be fairly organized even in the absence of a common religious affiliation.[2] A century later, the First Amendment to the Bill of Rights in the USA refused to prioritize any particular expression of religion. The interpretation of this amendment continues to be vigorously contested.

In one important strand of political liberalism, philosophers have sought to offer a set of procedures for the conduct and resolution of public disagreement. John Rawls in his earlier work argued for a set of principles that balanced freedom and equality from an original position in which each citizen is blind to his or her particular status, advantage, and social location. These principles are constitutive of a liberal society and only those arguments that appeal to them can be admitted as legitimate within the public domain. Other considerations must be bracketed as expressing the more private preferences of citizens.[3]

1. Sebastian Castellio, *Concerning Heretics,* ed. Roland Bainton (New York: Columbia University Press, 1935), 131.

2. John Locke, *Second Treatise on Civil Government* (c. 1681), in *Political Writings* (Harmondsworth: Penguin, 1993), 261-387.

3. John Rawls, *A Theory of Justice* (Cambridge, MA: Harvard University Press, 1991).

In similar neo-Kantian vein, Jürgen Habermas has argued for commitment to universal norms that govern procedures of speech and action. A claim or command to act presupposes commitment to norms that are tacitly accepted within the speech community. So Habermas offers the Kantian criterion that a "moral principle is so conceived as to exclude as invalid any norm that could not meet with the qualified assent of all who are or might be affected by it."[4] This establishes a principle of universalization according to which all can accept the consequences of an indiscriminate observance of a norm for the satisfaction of everyone's interests. In turn, this generates social obligations of impartiality, consensus, and compromise that are more fundamental than particular and competing conceptions of the good. These provide the moral basis for a post-metaphysical, secular society. With the disenchantment of our world and the rise of pluralism, modern societies will need these procedural rules for resolving claims and promulgating policy. However, as with the formalism of Rawls's philosophy, such proposals suffer from both an abstractness and circularity. The demand for commitment to principles of action that rationally precede the more particular attachment of citizens misrepresents the actual situation in which we find ourselves. Our moral standards tend to belong to forms of life that give account of examples, practices, and traditions in which these have emerged and make sense. Even when lacking coherence or adequate articulation, they indicate the ways in which our norms of action are derivative. To identify a set of fundamental principles of justice that prescind from the particularities of moral training, tradition, and teaching is to misrepresent the actual condition of citizens in plural societies. According to a range of critics from Hegel onwards, this merely reproduces Kant's error of attempting to derive a system of morals on the basis of a detached and formal principle of universalizability. This problem is reinforced by the failure in Rawls and others to adduce a significant set of moral exemplars whose life and witness can be recast in terms of his theory of justice. Those that are available seem to appeal to more particular traditions of justice, human flourishing, and the dignity of the person.

This last remark illustrates the ways in which a commitment to the "hyper-goods" of liberalism itself seems to require a vision of the good life

---

4. Jürgen Habermas, "Discourse Ethics: Notes on a Program of Philosophical Justification," *Moral Consciousness and Communicative Action* (Cambridge, MA: MIT Press, 1990), 63. For recent discussion of Habermas, see Nicholas Adams, *Habermas and Theology* (Cambridge: Cambridge University Press, 2006).

with an attendant meta-ethical theory.[5] A commitment to freedom, equality, and the service of others requires some account — religious or humanist — of the ends of human life. Yet here there is no agreement within political liberalism as to what this constitutes. Alasdair MacIntyre's story of the recent history of moral philosophy narrates the failure of successive theories to explain key moral concepts in the absence of particular traditions that offer an account of the telos of human life.[6]

In his later writings, Rawls defends his approach in more pragmatic terms. An account of political justice must offer the moral resources for a society comprised of differing commitments, religious and non-religious, to live peaceably. A modern liberal society is one in which there is "an overlapping consensus" of different moral approaches as to fundamental principles of justice and equality.[7] While these may be grounded and articulated quite differently, there is tacit agreement that public debate must appeal to those criteria and principles that are commonly accepted. Reasons for public advocacy must be reasons that can be recognized by all (or almost all) citizens as compelling. This constitutes the framework for moral debate. Alternative appeals to religious premises whether these cite a teaching authority or a sacred text are illegitimate unless these can be phrased in terms of more universal principles expressing a social consensus. As Richard Rorty puts it, the adducing of religious reasons in public is a "conversation stopper" that is in thoroughly bad taste.[8] To introduce them to public debate seems either impolite, irrelevant, or unfairly assertive. In our liberal democracies, citizens have a responsibility to advocate their positions in terms accessible to their fellow-citizens and not merely to their co-religionists. To invoke the will of God in support of an ethical claim is to allude to the state of one's private life rather than to any consideration that is publicly significant. A model of rationality here emerges in which a consensus over salient reasons must be agreed, at least tacitly, for public debate and argument to take place in ways that are intelligible, civil,

5. Cf. Charles Taylor, *Sources of the Self* (Cambridge, MA: Harvard University Press, 1989), 88.

6. See Alasdair MacIntyre, *After Virtue* (London: Duckworth, 1981).

7. See John Rawls, *Political Liberalism* (New York: Columbia University Press, 1996), 133ff. A similar recognition of the contribution of particular traditions to the complexion and vigor of democratic society can increasingly be found in the work of Habermas. See, e.g., *The Future of Human Nature* (London: Polity Press, 2003).

8. Richard Rorty, "Religion as Conversation-stopper," in *Philosophy and Social Hope* (London: Penguin, 1999), 168-174.

and useful. Yet, despite its appeal, this model too has elicited some formidable objections.

As a description of communicative action, it seems flawed. Citizens in our pluralist societies appear to be able to converse, argue, differ, and even agree without prior recourse to a consensual rationality. Political debate takes place across traditions and cultures without any of the participants being aware of a prior agreement about what count as valid reasons. There are relatively few claims made that present as "conversation stoppers." To take an unpromising example, those who advocate the teaching of creation science in our public schools may seem in the grip of egregious presuppositions about scriptural authority that render discussion useless. Yet even here a good deal of conversation does take place regarding the interpretation of Genesis 1–11, the current state of evolutionary science, and the respective boundaries of scientific and religious explanation. This happens without any of the contending parties specifying in advance what exactly count as legitimate reasons and forms of argument in the dispute. Similarly, the protracted debate in Europe about the wearing of headscarves or veils by Muslim women in public contexts reveals the possibility of intelligible disagreement over a range of considerations about individual freedom, Islamic traditions, inter-personal communication, and respect for diversity. The secular criticism that religiously informed claims are no more than self-referential assertions is disconfirmed by the actual conditions of our public disagreements.

A further difficulty with the Rawlsian position concerns the narrowing of possibilities on this model of rationality. In an attempt to identify a *modus operandi* for a society comprised of different commitments and visions of the good life, this philosophy appears to be inclusive of all citizens. Yet in excluding precisely those convictions that are most significant for many citizens, the model is experienced as oppressive and discriminatory. If one cannot allude to God, Jesus, and the Bible in public reasoning, then the sources and norms of many of our most deeply held beliefs and values seem to be bracketed out. This problem appears merely to be deferred by the concession that these concepts can be invoked but only if they prove translatable into a more public discourse. This is a frequent source of complaint in the USA where interpretations of the First Amendment threaten to banish religious convictions from the public sphere altogether, relegating them instead to a private domain of mere preference and taste. Stephen Carter writes of the creation of "a culture of disbelief." While the original intention of the First Amendment was to prevent the state from displaying a preference for any one ecclesial communion, its present effect is to keep religion out of public life. According to Carter this is creating a new establishment "of religion as a hobby, trivial and unimportant for serious people, not to be mentioned in serious discourse. And nothing could be further from the constitutional, historical or philosophical truth."[9]

A third and related difficulty concerns the thinning out of the self that enters the public arena. We are required to come shorn of those commitments and loyalties that will often shape our identity. To function socially, the self must be irrevocably attached to the principles of liberalism while yet remaining free to adopt any one of a range of commitments to particular conceptions of the good life. This is sometimes referred to as the problem of the "unencumbered self," an agent whose moral identity must first be fixed irrespective of any particular lifestyle choices or faith commitments adopted.[10] The autonomous individual of liberalism is largely a fiction that ignores the extent to which we are shaped by social location, roles, attachments, and obligations. These inevitably determine subsequent choices and expressions of identity. Endemic to Rawls's account of the original position is a faulty account of the self. He or she must be understood as a rational agent transcending particular choices. "No role or commitment could define me so completely that I could not understand myself without it. No project could be so essential that turning away from it would call into question the person I am."[11] As most novels attest, the way we understand our selves may develop across time and in face of changing circumstances, but we each come from somewhere and are shaped ineluctably by that social location. Our place and engagement within the public domain will reflect aspects of home, school, interests, aptitudes, faith, and upbringing. "Home is where one starts from. As we grow older the world becomes stranger, the pattern more complicated of dead and living."[12]

---

9. Stephen Carter, *The Culture of Disbelief* (New York: Basic Books, 1993), 115. In criticism of Stephen Carter, Rorty claims that one's private life is far from trivial ("Religion as Conversation-stopper," 170). A rejoinder to this might begin by noting the difficulty in demarcating the public from the private. For example, the state has some responsibility to protect the welfare of children inside the home.

10. See Michael Sandel, *Liberalism and Its Critics* (Oxford: Blackwell, 1984).

11. Michael Sandel, "The Procedural Republic and the Unencumbered Self," in *Communitarianism and Individualism,* ed. Shlomo Avineri and Avner De-Shalit (Oxford: Oxford University Press, 1992), 19.

12. T. S. Eliot, "East Coker," in *Four Quartets,* from *Collected Poems* (London: Faber, 1963), 203.

The actual dynamics of democratic debate appear to challenge the Rawlsian thesis of public rationality. Here almost any consideration that a citizen regards as relevant can be brought into play. It may be criticized, queried, or rejected by others but in most cases it can function within public debate. Arguments about slavery, votes for women, divorce, the treatment of animals, and faith-based holidays can be conducted by a wide range of participants. Their arguments will sometimes appeal to deeply held religious convictions but will often also advert to more secular notions of freedom and rights. At the same time, much advocacy will take the form of pointing to inconsistencies and unforeseen consequences inherent in the position of opponents. Jeffrey Stout describes this form of reasoning as "immanent criticism."[13] The arguments that are rehearsed in democratic societies will appeal in diverse ways to earlier moral examples and texts whether classical, scriptural, ecclesial, or literary. This is part of the cut and thrust of healthy debate and is integral to the ways in which social mores shift and are revised across time.[14]

Amidst much that is controversial in his recent work, Richard Dawkins shows persuasively that judged by our contemporary standards even the most enlightened of our nineteenth-century ancestors would appear quaintly sexist or profoundly racist. We should judge them only by the best standards that existed at that time, not by our own *Zeitgeist*. He offers the following example.

> When the sailors first landed in Mauritius and saw the gentle dodos, it never occurred to them to do anything other than club them to death. They didn't even want to eat them (they were described as unpalatable). Presumably, hitting defenceless, tame, flightless birds over the head with a club was just something to do. Nowadays such behaviour would be unthinkable, and the extinction of a modern equivalent of the dodo, even by accident, let alone by deliberate human killing, is regarded as a tragedy.[15]

Dawkins also notes that shifts in public opinion take place not through any single source of authority or medium of communication. In modern societies, debate is uncontrolled and is spawned by conversations in bars and over

13. Jeffrey Stout, *Democracy and Tradition* (Princeton: Princeton University Press, 2004), 69.

14. Behind this criticism there lurks some serious misgivings around the secularization thesis. Neither the disappearance of religious activity nor its retreat to a private domain now appears to be an inevitable feature of modernity. Cf. Charles Taylor, *A Secular Age* (Cambridge, MA: Harvard University Press, 2007).

15. Richard Dawkins, *The God Delusion* (London: Bantam Press, 2006), 267.

dinner tables, through radio chat shows and TV soap operas, through agony columns, films, newspapers, books, political speeches, and websites. These different outlets for public debate do not suggest an observance of strict Rawlsian rules. Instead, a broad repertoire of considerations is introduced that reflects the amalgam of traditions, communities, discourses, and loyalties comprising modern society.

Yet Dawkins's views seem less plausible in two further claims that he makes. The assertion that moral change is generally for the better is asserted rather than argued. From the perspective of those advocating change this is almost trivially true, yet he fails to acknowledge that earlier forms of wisdom may be abandoned or at least occluded by contemporary civilization.[16] Are we really better than our grandparents?

Moreover, Dawkins's insistence upon the diverse and patchwork nature of modern moral debate sits uneasily with the further claim that the religious nurture of children is the enemy of responsible decision-making and action. The arguments brought by those with faith-based convictions to public debate do not suggest that reasoned conversation is prevented by their standard practices of upbringing. Even papal encyclicals, often regarded by critics as amongst the more authoritarian forms of moral pronouncement, are readily intelligible to a wider ecumenical, secular, and multi-faith audience beyond the Roman Catholic Church. For example, the arguments against the death penalty in *Evangelium Vitae* (1995) work effectively in public debate. These include scriptural and theological claims but also other considerations relating to human dignity and restorative justice that have a broad appeal. If not accepted, these can readily be comprehended; they function not as "conversation stoppers" but as a strong contribution to a subject on which almost everyone has an intelligible opinion. In his exchange with Habermas, Benedict XVI speaks about the dangers of a "pathological reason" that becomes detached from older traditions of law and wisdom. At the same time, he acknowledges that the pathologies of religion need to be checked by reason.[17]

In his recent discussion of democratic culture, Jeffrey Stout points out

---

16. His comments on abortion, for example, would cause unease even amongst many secular supporters of a regime that permits the termination of pregnancy within specified temporal bounds. "The moment of birth provides a natural Rubicon for defining rules, and one could argue that it is hard to find another one earlier in embryonic development. Slippery slope arguments could therefore lead us to give the moment of birth more significance than utilitarianism, narrowly interpreted, would prefer." Ibid., 293.

17. Jürgen Habermas and Joseph Ratzinger, *The Dialectics of Secularization: On Reason and Religion* (San Francisco: Ignatius Press, 2006), 78.

that both the standard characterizations and criticisms of political liberalism fall into the trap of assuming that it amounts to a commitment to a thin set of fundamental principles lacking adherence to any particular moral tradition.[18] However, an array of examples from nineteenth- and twentieth-century writers ranging from the abolitionists to Martin Luther King demonstrate the ways in which social critics frequently drew upon older religious and political traditions to argue their case. In strict Rawlsian terms these look inadmissible, yet they were rhetorically effective and are now seen as landmarks in the development of liberal society.

Stout resists defining the democratic tradition simply in terms of state neutrality, public reason, or procedural processes. It represents a commitment to particular attitudes, a love of specific goods and virtues, an account of political authority, and a holding of one another responsible for our beliefs and actions. Ethical reasoning is central to this tradition. "Protestors rarely just march. They also carry signs that say something. They chant slogans that mean something. They sing songs that convey a message. And they march to or from a place where speeches are given."[19] Democratic habits do not derive from self-evident moral propositions. Like any other tradition, democracy has its own history and context, requiring a particular training and orientation of its participants. To illustrate this, Stout turns his attention to a group of writers who do not often feature in the canons of secular liberalism. These include three public intellectuals — Emerson, Whitman, and Dewey — who, as essayists, contributed to the development of a political culture that was rooted in convictions about character and the formative role of religion, family, and local community. While this tradition came frequently to adopt a critical stance towards earlier pieties, it remained indebted to these. Thus it sought their reform rather than their abolition.

> [O]ur political culture is a nobler thing than its leading theoretical defenders and detractors make it out to be. Judging by how the members of our society behave, they are more deeply committed to freedom, and to a more substantive, positive kind of freedom, than the theorists suspect. For historically they have not restrained themselves in the way contractarians have proposed. That is why Rawls has trouble corralling his historical examples. The Abolitionists did not restrain themselves in this way. Abra-

18. Stout, *Democracy and Tradition*, 75: "The more thoroughly Rawlsian our law schools and ethics centers become, the more radically Hauerwasian the theological schools become."

19. Ibid., 6.

ham Lincoln did not. Martin Luther King, Jr., did not. Dorothy Day did not. Rosemary Radford Ruether does not. Wendell Berry does not. Furthermore, many members of our society would resist with considerable fury any traditionalist attempt to establish an orthodox alternative to freewheeling democratic exchange. More power to them.[20]

In the cross-currents of democratic debate many moral positions are continually challenged, revised, or reinforced. The need to react to new circumstances and fresh problems and challenges requires a scrutiny of arguments and reasons. On occasion this can lead to a re-appropriation of positions previously held or alternatively their revision. For example, we might wish to insist that the traditional *ius in bello* of just war theory now needs to be maintained more vigorously in face of pressures generated by the war against terror. On the other hand, many of our social attitudes towards other faiths, sexual orientation, and animals have undergone adjustment over the past generation. Few of us think and act like our forebears in this respect.

Where does this leave the church and its moral reasoning? When it enters the melting pot of democratic debate, will its traditional sources and norms appear to be compromised? No longer viewed as authoritatively grounded in divine revelation, these might become merely one voice in an interminable conversation. If our collective moral sensibilities are as fluid and open-textured as our recent history suggests, what price a moral code once revealed and forever acknowledged and proclaimed?

A response to this set of issues will facilitate a clearer account of the nature of moral reasoning. Alasdair MacIntyre's recent work is noteworthy for the ways in which it shows the significance of traditions of moral enquiry in understanding our contemporary situation. Our ethical commitments are not merely intuited or derived from an abstract set of principles self-evident to all rational agents. Instead they are situated within recognized social practices with their standards of excellence and authoritative examples. These in turn belong to communities of enquiry with their established traditions comprising stories, texts, rituals, doctrines, and histories of moral development. Democratic culture depends upon the presence of these traditions and their accessibility to a wide range of citizens. Resources are thus offered for moral formation and reflection. While we should acknowledge that living traditions ought never to remain static — if they do so, they rapidly become reactionary — it is at least as important to recognize that our reasoning is

20. Ibid., 84-85.

never divorced from thick traditions of moral discourse. Theologically this is of some significance. For Christian moral reflection, Scripture, church, and tradition — there are in-house disagreements about how these are configured — will have an indispensable place. These shape our understanding of how life is to be lived *coram Deo,* its source and final purpose, our identity as persons created and redeemed in the divine image, the significance of a common life for human flourishing, and a range of practices including forgiveness. Reason thus has an ecclesial location and belongs to a life of faith, hope, and love marked by communal reading and interpreting of Scripture.

A related anxiety that surrounds this account of tradition-centered moral enquiry is whether it leads to a perspectivalism or relativism. This might prevent moral conversation between rival traditions, thus ignoring the extent of agreement within a pluralist society. If my moral reasons are determined by my faith commitment, does this undermine meaningful public debate? It is of course anxieties such as these that motivate the Rawlsian advocacy of a social space in which context-dependent reasons are forbidden. Both Catholic and Protestant theology have historically dealt with this problem by proposing theories of natural law, common grace, or the orders of creation. Broadly speaking, these claim that in nature and history human life will flourish only through being informed socially by the acceptance of certain norms and patterns. These typically include the keeping of promises, truth-telling, recognition of the authority of the state, and provision for marriage, the raising of children, and the regulation of economic life. Their appearance in human societies is taken as a sign of divine providence. As elaborate moral theories such approaches encounter significant problems, and tend towards a somewhat conservative and static account of social life. Nevertheless, they characterize the significant measure of moral agreement and cooperation that can be detected in all societies, even those comprised of a patchwork of different faiths and traditions. And they draw attention to moral platitudes about for example truth-telling, notions of fairness, a concern for the welfare of children, hospitality towards strangers that are neither parochial nor ephemeral.

The presence of the so-called golden rule across the religious traditions of the world is one illustration of this important phenomenon. As an appeal to compassion and fairness, it offers trans-cultural resources for moral insight and agreement on a range of issues, while also extending our native human capacities for empathy and sympathy.[21] Although not amounting to a

---

21. For further articulation of this claim see George Hunsinger, "Torture, Common

universal moral theory or a comprehensive moral code, it does provide within different traditions recognition of an ethical concord. Another sign of this degree of commonality is found in the attempt of the early Christian communities to evince their truthfulness by leading lives that would be recognized as matching the highest standards known in the pagan world. This is a standard apologetic move in the face of suspicion and hostility, and it is repeated despite the simultaneous recognition that there is also something distinctive and quite new in the faith now practiced. Even within the New Testament, moral discourse reveals a selective borrowing from pagan sources and its adaptation to Christian self-understanding.[22]

Although complex, the social vision that tends to be articulated by the Christian writers of the early centuries is one in which the distinctiveness of baptismal commitment is emphasized alongside the need to make a positive contribution to the societies within which they live and work. There is no aspiration toward social control or to the attainment of a uniquely privileged position alongside the secular authorities. Its numerical size must prevent this, yet it does not preclude a socially constructive contribution from these religious bodies. Indeed, this is part of their divine mandate and it takes the form of following Jeremiah's injunction to exiled Jews to seek the welfare of the city in which they have been sent (Jer. 29:7). Even as a minority body, the church has the task of making a distinctive public contribution without aspiring to a position of social control or dominance. To this one might add the hope that in a post-Christian context, the churches may discover a greater freedom for social and political witness, a critical position that may be enabled by a greater distancing of church from state. Grace Davie notes in this context the ways in which after the secularization of the 1960s Anglican bishops discovered the freedom to engage in criticism of government policy.[23]

At the same time, we should register also the ways in which the church can be led into a keener appreciation of its own moral traditions by secular forces and movements. In recent times the churches have often accepted moral arguments and supported changes in practice that have been led at least in part by more secular forces, though also resonant with earlier Chris-

---

Morality and the Golden Rule," *Theology Today* 63 (2006): 375-379; and John Hick, *An Interpretation of Religion* (London: Macmillan, 1989), 313ff.

22. Cf. Wayne Meeks, *The Origins of Christian Morality* (New Haven: Yale University Press, 1993).

23. Grace Davie, *Religion in Britain since 1945: Believing without Belonging* (Oxford: Blackwell, 1994), 149ff.

tian social ideals. These include abolitionism, votes for women, the establishment of the welfare state, and comprehensive education.[24]

A preoccupation with the distinctiveness of moral beliefs may in any case obscure another aspect of the contribution of the churches to contemporary culture. This is less to do with what is morally counter-cultural but more to do with providing people with the resources, motivation, focus, and encouragement to engage ethically with social and political culture. This contribution to our social capital should not be treated lightly. Our contemporary situation is arguably marked as much by moral disengagement as by disagreement. Citizens can too easily become indifferent to or disaffected from public processes. In facilitating moral debate and motivating people, the churches (and other voluntary associations) play an important role in civil society. One hears, for example, of politicians who will gladly welcome invitations to speak at churches since they are assured of a larger and more patient audience than at other public meetings. Within western democracies, the role of the churches in providing safe spaces for conversation across a range of issues, including the state and the economy, is badly needed, particularly at a time of voter apathy and single-issue political movements. Congregations can mobilize people not only to work for the church itself, but to engage with other civic organizations and to increase awareness of international problems that offer few votes for politicians. Research suggests that this is a pervasive effect of institutionalized religion, over against more individualized forms of spirituality.[25]

I began by criticizing the political liberalism of John Rawls. This should not be taken as a dismissal of liberal society *per se*. In many respects, the churches have a stake in the more plural and religiously diverse societies that emerged in Europe from the early modern period onwards. Toleration was demanded by religious dissidents, by those on the underside of social forces, and arguments were advanced on theological grounds for admitting difference. Civil cohabitation was better than violence. Christ did not force his disciples to follow him. The faith is spread by the free action of the Holy Spirit and not by political coercion. People of different faiths can coexist by virtue of their shared moral commitments. These arguments all admit a degree of pluralism into our social order but they were advanced initially on

---

24. Cf. Eberhard Jüngel, "The Gospel and the Protestant Churches of Europe: Christian Responsibility for Europe from a Protestant Perspective," *Religion, State and Society* 21 (1993): 137-149.

25. See the discussion in David Hollenbach, *The Common Good and Christian Ethics* (Cambridge: Cambridge University Press, 2002), 100ff.

specifically theological grounds rather than on self-evident principles of autonomy and equality. Within that social space demanded by religious liberty, the cause of Christ can be proclaimed and pursued.[26]

In terms of moral reasoning, this places a burden on citizens in a religiously pluralist context to articulate themselves in ways that can be understood. At the same time, it creates the further obligation to seek to understand others and to interpret them *in optimem partem*. This can happen without a prior Rawlsian agreement on what constitute valid reasons for everyone in the public domain. Amongst the most effective moral voices have been those who were able to master more than one ethical discourse. Without the fusion of biblical piety and the language of human rights, Martin Luther King would have been less effective in the civil rights struggles of the 1960s. One thinks also of the capacity of papal encyclicals, the writings of Rabbi Jonathan Sacks, and the reflections of the Archbishop of Canterbury to communicate effectively with audiences far beyond the faith communities that they represent. These require a judicious discernment of when to support and when to challenge regnant practices and trends in contemporary society, but they can do so intelligibly through a fluency in different moral languages. This capacity to speak in faithful adherence to one's own tradition, while also remaining patient of other ways of seeing and living in the world, will prove increasingly important to Christian moral discernment in our contemporary social life.

26. In his discussion of the growth of toleration in early modern England, John Coffey notes the inherently theological nature of the arguments advanced. See *Persecution and Toleration in Protestant England 1558-1689* (Harlow: Longman, 2000).

Reading for Preaching: The Preacher in Conversation with Storytellers, Biographers, Poets, and Journalists

Cornelius Plantinga Jr.

Preachers usually learn theology from theologians, and why not? Good theologians think hard about God and the world through all the mysteries of creation, fall, redemption, and consummation. Then they publish the fruit of their thinking, inviting us to gather as much of it as we want. Augustine, Anselm, Aquinas, Calvin, Schleiermacher, Barth, and a host of others offer preachers nourishment that a forty-year ministry will never consume. Who would ever outgrow Augustine on the heart's true home, or Aquinas on the virtues? People praise the breadth and imaginative vision of Karl Barth's theology, but the preacher who merely looked up his weekly text in Barth's Scripture indexes would already be way ahead.

The great theologians, moreover, encourage habits of lifetime learning. For example, they encourage preachers to get into the interrogative mood and stay there a while. Can we hurt God? If not, how can God have compassion? If so, is God's interior life at our disposal? How can a virtue such as patience be both fruit of the Spirit and also our human calling? Why, besides its other victims, is sin a form of self-abuse? What, exactly, does God get out of the atoning sacrifice of Jesus Christ? If Jesus was truly sinless, if he never grieved over his treacheries or mourned his neglect of loved ones, can we still say that in him God was sharing our lot? How does petitionary prayer work, and for whom? Why is grace sometimes more devastating than punishment?

Thoughtful preachers seek theological guidance in their shelves of old books, but also among their new ones. They have Anselm of Canterbury on "faith seeking understanding," but they also have Daniel Migliore of Princeton on it. They mean to keep fresh water flowing in their theology. Like the faithful farmer Robert Frost describes, resourceful preachers are always out to "clean the pasture spring."[1]

Delight and Diction

In this mission theologians help the preacher immeasurably, but so do story-tellers, biographers, poets, and journalists. Apart from its theological advantages, a program of this more general reading appeals to preachers for lots of reasons, one of which is sheer pleasure. There's a peculiar joy in entering an author's world, dwelling in it for a time and coming to love it enough that leaving fills one with longing and a sense of loss.

Another reason to read has to do with the preacher's continuing need to sharpen her language, which is her first tool. Here poetry comes to mind, but not primarily for pulpit quotation. Most audiences aren't trained to listen to poetry from outside the Bible, and won't readily grasp it on a single hearing. And, frankly, some listeners cannot shake a blue-collar suspicion of poetry: isn't it too delicate a perfume?

But the preacher, reading and reciting poetry behind closed doors, has much to gain. Poets may revise thirty or forty times in search of a precise beginning or ending, a staccato rhythm to match the topic, or a perfectly soft or hard word to finish a line. Perhaps above all, the revising poet is trying for economy, wanting to "prune luxuriance" rather than "fan scarcity."[2] Madeleine L'Engle describes the goal here:

> The good writer will always limit herself. The simplest word is almost always the right word. . . . One of my favorite authors, Anon, wrote, centuries ago:
>
> > The written word
> > Should be clean as bone,
> > Clear as light,
> > Firm as stone.
> > Two words are not
> > As good as one.[3]

---

1. Frost, "The Pasture," in *The Poetry of Robert Frost: The Collected Poems,* ed. Edward Connery Lathem (New York: Henry Holt, 1969), 1.

2. I owe this contrast to Ernest Campbell.

3. L'Engle, *A Circle of Quiet* (New York: Seabury, 1972), 148-149.

A preacher who absorbs one poem a day (perhaps from Garrison Keillor's *The Writer's Almanac*)[4] will tune his ear, strengthen his diction, and stock his pond with fresh, fresh images. That's before breakfast: after it, there's a day's worth of rumination on whatever the poet has seen of the human condition.

A program of general reading may delight the preacher and enlarge her command of language. In these respects, children's literature can be a boon. Books written for children are never written only for them. As Tolkien saw, such books are written for the *childlike*. They move us into a world where we can see with young eyes what children fear, whom they trust, why they hope with such heartbreaking conviction. We see that adults do not always respect children's intelligence and sense of fair play, and that children can be indignant at such folly. The preacher making friends with children's literature will remember that children were important to Jesus, prime exemplars of those who receive the loving power of God and simply live off it.[5]

Good children's literature also has a quality of prose that the preacher may want. Perhaps we could call this quality "deep simplicity," or, following Vatican II in its recommendation of the type of vernacular wanted for celebrating the eucharist, "noble simplicity." We have all read or heard it:

> [Mr. Beaver said:] "They say Aslan is on the move — perhaps has already landed." . . .
>
> "If there's anyone who can appear before Aslan without their knees knocking, they're either braver than most or else just silly" [said Mrs. Beaver].
>
> "Then he isn't safe?" said Lucy.
>
> "Safe?" said Mr. Beaver; ". . . 'Course he isn't safe. But he's good. He's the king, I tell you."[6]

Preachers whose language finds deep simplicity will see that their delighted audience includes not just 10-year-olds, but also their parents and grandparents because in the heart of every adult there still lives a child who can be moved by a story.

4. http://writersalmanac.publicradio.org/.

5. Gary D. Schmidt, author of such prizewinning novels as *Lizzie Bright and the Buckminster Boy* (2004) and *The Wednesday Wars* (2007) makes such observations in his regular visits to "Imaginative Reading for Creative Preaching," a summer seminar at Calvin College, underwritten by The Center for Excellence in Preaching of Calvin Theological Seminary.

6. C. S. Lewis, *The Lion, the Witch and the Wardrobe* (New York: Scholastic, 1978), 67, 80.

Starting the Heart and Bridging the Gap

And that is yet another advantage for the preacher who reads general literature. "True religion," said Jonathan Edwards, "consists in great measure in
. . . the fervent exercises of the heart."[7] Edwards meant that, at its core, true
religion has to do not just with kindling our passions, but also with aiming
them in the right direction. The world is full of good. The Godly person will
say Yes to it with all his heart and then act accordingly. The world is also full
of evil. The Godly person will say No to it with all her heart and then act accordingly. The world is full of the mixture of good and evil so that the Godly
person sometimes needs the gift of discernment before he knows what to say
or how to act.

In any event, true religion always begins from the central place in us
where we "hate what is evil" and "hold fast to what is good" (Rom. 12:9). A
sequence of hearty Yes's and No's lies at the center of true religion, said Edwards, and this is why we sing our praise instead of merely saying it. This is
why we preach the word instead of simply reading it. This is why in the
Lord's Supper we "eat and drink our God."[8] The reason is that these are ways
God customarily uses to start human hearts.

So preachers expose themselves to John Steinbeck's *The Grapes of
Wrath* not only for its insights, or illustrations, or structural genius. They
read to get moved by compassion and by a hunger for justice. Preachers follow Ma Joad and her brood to California because they know a simple fact:
their preaching is meant by God to move human hearts, and they have no
hope of success in this mission unless they are vulnerable to being moved
themselves.

As citizens of the Kingdom of God that embraces people of "every nation . . . all tribes and peoples and languages" (Rev. 7:9), preachers will also
want their reading to help close the circumstantial gap between themselves
and people whose lives may otherwise be unfamiliar. As Adrian Piper writes
in a discerning essay, if you say as a man that you can't imagine what it
would be like for a woman to be raped, or that as a white person in a majority white culture you can't imagine what it's like to be racially taunted, then
maybe you are humble and realistic. Maybe you know the presumption expressed by anything in the neighborhood of "I know just how you feel." On

7. Edwards, *The Works of Jonathan Edwards*, vol. 2: *Religious Affections*, ed. John E.
Smith (New Haven: Yale, 1959), 99.
8. Ibid., 115.

the other hand, maybe your ignorance is due only to a cool lack of interest. Maybe you don't care to read literature, view paintings, listen to requiems, or partake of any other "literary and artistic products designed precisely to instruct us" about the exigencies of lives other than our own. Ignorance of the literary and fine arts is thus a serious sin of omission.[9] If so, perhaps purgatory, in a fine blending of judgment and grace, will include massive remedial instruction in the arts. The point is that identification with others may be partly instinctive, but it is also partly deliberate — and thus dependent upon an educated attempt to stretch our sympathies across circumstantial distance.

Think in this connection of a novel like Shusaku Endo's *Silence*,[10] which asks whether, under the pressure of sin, love can take unthinkable forms — ones that look a lot like betrayal. In the course of raising this question, the novel takes us to sixteenth-century Japan, giving us a feel not only for the Christian mission there, and the ingenuity of its persecutors, but also for the Japanese suspicion that Christianity is less a religion than a means of Western cultural imperialism.

Or, consider Khaled Hosseini's *The Kite Runner*,[11] a tightly plotted first-person novel that explores the consequences for children of the sins of their fathers. The theme is universal, but the setting is particular: most of the story transpires in contemporary Kabul. As a result the reader gets not only a cracking good story, but also exposure to Afghan culture — to food and drink, male and female relationships, Mullahs, kite-flying contests, tribal and intra-Muslim struggles between Pashtun Sunnis and Hasara Shi'as, and the daily threat of the Taliban. At one point the narrator, 12 years old at the start, reveals how dazed he was to discover that the movies were dubbed and that John Wayne didn't really speak Farsi and wasn't actually Iranian.

In *Enrique's Journey* Sonia Nazario tells of the thousands of Central American children and teens who migrate north through Mexico each year in hope of reaching the United States and of being reunited with their loved ones. She tells in particular the story of Enrique, a boy from Tegucigalpa, whose father had left the family derelict and whose mother then had to face a cruel dilemma: she could stay with her family and watch her children go hungry or she could migrate to the U.S., get a job, and send money home.

9. Adrian M. S. Piper, "Impartiality, Compassion, and Modal Imagination," *Ethics* 101 (1991): 739.

10. Endo, *Silence*, trans. William Johnson (New York: Taplinger, 1980).

11. Hosseini, *The Kite Runner* (New York: Riverhead, 2003).

She left when Enrique was only five and, across the years, faithfully fulfilled her mission of supporting her children from abroad. After twelve years of this program, Enrique finally decided he couldn't bear to be without his mother, packed up some meager belongings, and began a 1600-mile odyssey in trucks, buses, and especially on the tops of dangerous freight trains. After numerous failed attempts, he finally arrived at Nuevo Laredo, where a "coyote" hired by his mother smuggled him across the Rio Grande into the promised land.

To authenticate her story of Enrique's journey, Nazario duplicated it, riding on swaying boxcars and facing all the same threats as the migrants did — of heat, cold, assault, robbery, rape, and accidental mutilation. She tells, as had Steinbeck in *The Grapes of Wrath,* of the community that forms among migrants who travel and hope together: they share information, clothing, warnings of hazards, and what little food they can beg or buy. She tells of the sexual predators who see migrating girls as their natural prey (What else are they for?) and of kind-hearted local padres and residents who have little themselves, and yet give it to migrant strangers. Nazario offers no easy answers to the immigration challenge that the U.S. faces on its southern border, but her stellar journalism pretty much insures that her readers will never look at migrants the same way again.

Preachers read to delight themselves, to tune their language, to get their hearts going, and to enlarge their sympathies for people whose lives are quite different from their own. Occasionally a work of fiction appears that can even help a minister's sense of vocation and pastoral identity. In 2004 Marilynne Robinson published *Gilead,* an epistolary novel that would win a Pulitzer Prize and a front-page celebratory review by James Wood in *The New York Times* Book Review. Remarkably, such high praise (there was an avalanche of it in big newspapers across the land) came to a novel about a quiet, small-town Christian minister, John Ames, who describes sermon texts and tells how it feels to baptize a baby. It turns out that this 76-year-old man is full of grace and truth, but also of doubt and, for most of his life, painful loneliness. He accepts that Scripture is a complex ancient literature and that, some of the time, it's tough to interpret. He pours himself into his sermons, "trying to say what was true" in them, but he is also serene in the knowledge that one day somebody will probably burn them. Ames celebrates the sacrament of sheer existence in his church members, treating each as unrepeatable. Each, to him, is a unique and incandescent divine thought. His pastoral identity is secure enough to harbor within it a genial self-irony — an especially appealing species of humility. Ames tells us one of his dreams: "I was preaching to Jesus Himself, saying any foolish thing I could think of, and He was sitting there in his white, white robe looking patient and sad and amazed."[12] John Ames is full of Scripture, but his last words in the novel are King Lear's: "I'll pray and then I'll sleep."

Garnishment and the Quest for Wisdom

People often assume that preachers who read widely are, besides all else, on the prowl for illustrations. These people are right. Preachers are hunter-gatherers. By Thursday noon they already have a sermonic theme derived from Scripture; what's now needed is something to dress or garnish it. Uninspired preachers turn to their copy of *One Thousand Lively Sermon Illustrations* by Theophilus Thistle. A better preacher might consult the stored-up harvest of her reading program. Suppose a preacher wants to depict the dawning of doubt in an innocent mind. It's a big biblical theme: you find it in psalms, in Job, in Gideon, in Jeremiah, and in John the Baptist in prison. Ben Haas has it in *Look Away, Look Away.* Houston Whitely, a 10-year-old black boy in the depression-era South is the son of a po' sharecropper who loses his place because of the failure of the white landowner. The Whitely family travels around for three days in the rain in a tattered, porous wagon. Drenched and chilled, Houston and his brothers watch their father apply for work, and for help, at one place after another. Many of the rebuffs are ugly, but even the polite ones begin to raise a strange new feeling in Houston Whitely. He begins to feel vague uneasiness swelling to fear and then to a kind of dull terror: "What if Papa can't find nothing at all for us to eat? It was the first time he had ever realized that his father was vulnerable and not all-powerful."[13] His father — the strong one who always looked out for Houston and provided for him — was "vulnerable and not all-powerful." This gets a preacher to ponder. What happens to disciples who see their Lord at the mercy of Roman thugs? What happens to people in the age of finite-God theology — people who begin to suspect that the universe is full of places where a helpless God is going to be rebuffed?

The preacher who illustrates from his reading may quote or paraphrase or summarize, but in any case will face questions of judgment. How apt is this illustration? How fancy? How tight is the fit between it and what it illus-

---

12. Robinson, *Gilead* (New York: Farrar, Straus, Giroux, 2004), 68.

13. Haas, *Look Away, Look Away* (New York: Simon and Schuster, 1964), 71.

trates? How useful would this illustration be to a general audience? Preachers also need good judgment about the size of illustrations. Big illustrations are big risks: they may overwhelm the rest of the sermon. Little illustrations, if snipped from their context in the literature, may puzzle listeners, and the preacher who attempts to rebuild the context for them will need time and skill.

But no veteran preacher reads general literature just for its ability to illustrate pre-established themes. For one thing, reading merely for illustrations is too much like work. For another, reading with so narrow an aim distracts the preacher from a bigger and more general advantage, namely, that a well-chosen program of reading tends to make the preacher wise. Here the advantages of learning from theologians and learning from other sorts of authors partly converge. After all, general literature abounds in incidents, characters, images, and observations that illumine everything under the sun, including God, sin, grace, the beauty of creation, life, death, pilgrimage, aging, wonder, terror, longing, and going home. Preachers address the same themes in Scripture, and do so from strength if they possess a mind already rich in understanding of them.

Discernment and Human Character

Let's say simply that wisdom is a reality-based phenomenon: the wise are people who have an unusually rich understanding of God's world and of how to fit into it. They know how human life goes — its times and seasons, its patterns and dynamics, its laws and rhythms. The wise are discerning. A discerning person picks up on things. She notices the difference between pleasure and joy, for example, and between sentimentality and compassion. She understands that facts are stubborn things, and doesn't try to finesse them to suit her wishes. She discerns the differences between things but also the connections between them.[14] She knows creation — what God has put together and what God has kept apart — and can therefore spot the fractures and alloys produced by those who violate it. She knows, for example, that it is possible to be "a good person in the worst sense of the word," namely, one who offers help in ways that make others wish he hadn't bothered.

The discerning person, moreover, possesses an eye for the details and oddities of reality — that mercy sometimes coexists with mendacity, for ex-

14. Lewis B. Smedes, *A Pretty Good Person* (San Francisco: Harper & Row, 1990), 123.

ample, and that pro basketball players descending from a thunderous dunk often look not pleased, but angered. She knows that horses belong in her theology of creation and fall as much as people do, and that champion stallions such as Seabiscuit — a popular hero in the U.S. depression — were sometimes more competitive than their owners. Seabiscuit's trademark was a kind of intimidation born of equine pride: "the horse seemed to take sadistic pleasure in . . . humiliating his rivals, slowing down to mock them as he passed, snorting in their faces, and pulling up when in front so other horses could draw alongside, then dashing their hopes with a killing burst of speed."[15]

Finally, the wise understand that people full of shadows may also be full of a light that causes them. In such and other respects, Lewis Smedes remarks, "a discerning person has the makings of a connoisseur."[16]

In his attempt to become wiser about the lights and shadows, the discerning preacher may want to consult biographies, those revelations of human character, of divine providence, and of their intersection in history. Take Lyndon Baines Johnson, for example. He was an immensely complicated man, "a character out of a Russian novel" who contained "a storm of warring human instincts." He was "sinner and saint, buffoon and statesman, cynic and sentimentalist, a man torn between hungers for immortality and self-destruction."[17] As a young school teacher in the hill country of Texas, Johnson showed a generous heart for his students at the "Mexican school" of Catulla. He saw their poverty, their hunger, their pain, and came to their side. He arrived at school early and stayed late. He toted sports equipment after school, visited in his students' hovels, took his students to heart. He was a compassionate teacher.[18]

But his ambition took him to the nation's House of Representatives and then to the Senate. Johnson came to the U.S. Senate in 1949 as the junior senator from Texas. He then rose through the ranks, becoming his party's Assistant Leader, then its Leader. Finally, in 1955, when Democrats took over the Senate, he became Majority Leader — one of the most powerful in the history of the position. According to his major biographer, Robert Caro, power was Johnson's food and drink. He liked to say, "I do understand power, whatever else may be said about me. I know where to look for it, and how to

15. Laura Hillenbrand, *Seabiscuit: An American Legend* (New York: Ballantine Books, 2001), 108-109.

16. Smedes, *A Pretty Good Person*, 128.

17. Russell Baker, *The Good Times* (New York: William Morrow, 1989), 282.

18. Robert Caro, *Master of the Senate*, vol. 3 of *The Years of Lyndon Johnson* (New York: Knopf, 2002), 720-21.

use it."[19] One of the things Johnson understood about power was that it came not only from mastery of timing and parliamentary procedure, but also from mastery of the personal biographies of senators. So Johnson learned his senators. In a visit with Arthur Schlesinger, Johnson

> ran down the list: each man's strengths and weaknesses, who liked liquor too much, and who liked women, and how he had to know when to reach a senator at his own home and when at his mistress's, who was controlled by the big power company in his state, and . . . which senator responded to one argument and which senator to the other argument.[20]

Because much of the Senate's power lay in the bloc of conservative southern Democrats, Johnson had cultivated them for years. Especially in the early 1950s, he flattered them shamelessly, sometimes sitting on the floor so he could physically look up at them. Or he would fulsomely praise his own father and then, ten minutes later, say to a senator, "You've been just like a Daddy to me."[21] Aware that the southern bloc could advance his career, Johnson used all the tricks in his bag to protect the bloc's positions, particularly on "states' rights." Drawing upon his intimate knowledge of senators, he would lie, or flatter, or bully — whatever was necessary to win his way. He would lean his long frame over another senator, grab his lapel, or his shoulder, or his tie with one large paw and jab the senator's chest with the other. He manipulated the Senate's rules and other senators' pride or fear; he threatened and cajoled and beseeched. He called in favors. From 1949 to 1956, using all his powers, Lyndon Johnson blocked every piece of civil rights legislation that came to the floor of the Senate.

But then in August of 1956, at the Democratic nominating convention in Chicago, Johnson came to be whispered about as a possible dark horse nominee for President. Warming to the possibility, Johnson caught presidential fever. He let his imagination take him to the White House, and was then devastated when the convention abandoned him as a "sectional" candidate because of his record on civil rights. He had "the scent of magnolias" on him, and it wrecked his hope of a presidential nomination.[22]

In the fall of 1956 Lyndon Johnson took counsel with himself. And in 1957, he opened his bag of tricks once again. He manipulated and threatened

19. Ibid., epigraph.
20. Ibid., 834.
21. Ibid., 155-156.
22. Ibid., 804-824.

and beseeched and cajoled. He got his southern power base to believe that he was still with them while simultaneously working against them. He got one of the most powerful of them, Richard Russell of Georgia, to believe that only after conceding something to the civil rights movement could Johnson one day become President and protect the South from more vigorous legislation.[23] And then on August 29, Lyndon Johnson rammed through the Senate the Civil Rights Act of 1957, the nation's first major civil rights bill in over eighty years. And, of course, riding his momentum, Johnson would later become the President who did more for civil rights in America than any other president of the twentieth century. His compassion and his ambition were running on parallel tracks at last.[24]

A preacher could learn from a book of theology that God is ever the master of irony, that God hits straight shots with crooked sticks, that God's providence is inscrutable. But he could also learn these kindred truths by reading Caro on Johnson and then pondering the implications of the story.

Middle Wisdom

It may be worth observing at this point that the preacher in quest of wisdom is realistic about what a program of general reading will yield. He doesn't need his reading to yield one desperately deep insight after another that, once ingested, make the preacher more profound than God ever intended anyone to be. To be sure, he would like to draw more from his reading than mere commonplaces (In *Dirty Rotten Scoundrels* Steve Martin's character states that his "Gram-Gram" taught him "it is better to be truthful and good than to not"), but he doesn't expect his soul to be shattered and mended every time he sits to read.

Perhaps the preacher is hoping to acquire "middle wisdom" from her reading. We might say that middle wisdom consists of insights into life that are more profound than commonplaces, but less so than great proverbs. "Pride goes before destruction" (Prov. 16:18), for instance, arises from a depth of centuries and compacts their experience in itself. Middle wisdom is more modest. Still, it's definitely worth acquiring: it can save the preacher from some of the banality, presumption, vagueness, and dogmatism that characterize folly in the pulpit. (Vagueness and dogmatism are especially foolish when combined.)

23. Ibid., 868-870.
24. Ibid., 722-723.

Cornelius Plantinga Jr.

William Maxwell, long-term fiction editor at *The New Yorker,* wrote quiet, luminous stories, including some tiny ones he calls "improvisations." He tells us in the preface that he wrote them to please his wife:

> When we were first married, after we had gone to bed I would tell her a story in the dark. They came from I have no idea where. Sometimes I fell asleep in the middle of a story and she would shake me and say, "What happened next?" and I would struggle up through layers of oblivion and tell her.[25]

Not everything a story has to give us can be stated, let alone aphorized. But sometimes it's possible, and the exercise is clarity-making. In a story titled "The Carpenter," Maxwell gives us a fairy tale with a "turn" in it, a bad one. The village carpenter builds honestly. Everything about him is square. He sawed according to the "even rhythm of his heartbeat," and "used his carpenter's rule and stubby pencil as if he were applying a moral principle." Meanwhile, villagers would come into the shop one at a time, close the door, and watch for a while. But then would come the moment when the visitor would say, "I know I can trust you because you don't repeat anything. . . ." What followed was always a secret that if it got out would ruin life for some other villager.

The carpenter hadn't asked to collect secrets in this way, and there came a season of his life when he began to resent being used as a repository. So he took revenge on the secrets by betraying one of them. Then he betrayed another. Then, one day, he started a damaging rumor that if it got out would get the village fiddler killed. At the end of the story the carpenter still saws and cuts in his shop, but now his plane jams more than it used to and his saw won't follow the pencil line cleanly. Even his tools are no longer honest.

We may think we are honoring someone by telling him our secret. But the knowledge of it may fester in him and turn to poison. Maybe only God can stand to search us and know our hearts.

In *Remembering Denny,*[26] Calvin Trillin tells of a Yale classmate from the '50s. Denny Hansen was handsome, funny, and intelligent. He was a charismatic golden boy from California, who was also a record-breaking swimmer, a genial magnet for admirers, a Rhodes Scholar, and president of everything he joined. All through school days, his friends kept making bets and jokes about the day when Denny Hansen would be elected President of the United

25. Maxwell, *All the Days and Nights: The Collected Stories* (New York: Vintage, 1995), x.
26. Trillin, *Remembering Denny* (New York: Warner, 1993).

338

States. Every time Denny met his friends' parents one of them would predict that Denny would end up on the Supreme Court or become Speaker of the House of Representatives. When Denny Hansen graduated from Yale, poised to begin his Rhodes Scholarship at Oxford, *Life* magazine was there, and later published a splashy story about Denny Hansen, the boy who had it all.

But across the years after college, classmates and friends gradually lost touch with Denny, in part because he did not answer their letters or return their calls. As they later discovered, Denny's career trajectory had flattened out and he had not wanted to say so. After all, he had not become President, or even Speaker of the House. He had never married. His career was a shameful failure: all he had done was to have authored several respected books and occupied a professorship at the Johns Hopkins School of International Relations. And he was homosexual. One day in his middle age the golden boy from California started his car in a closed garage, lay down in it, and ended his life.

We may think we are praising and encouraging the young by predicting great things for them, but the burden of our expectations may shame and crush them.

The preacher learns much about human character from biographies and memoirs. But fiction, too, is famously revealing of it. Here it's interesting to note that goodness is seemingly harder to portray fictionally than evil. Readers find it comparatively boring: a bank deposit is so much less interesting than a bank robbery. The seven deadly sins are the primary colors for literary artists, not the seven deadly virtues. Still, the great writers understand and portray goodness in ways that preachers need both professionally and personally. Dickens's good characters are often too good (e.g., Esther in *Bleak House*), but some are mostly convincing and, anyhow, deeply encouraging — Peggotty, for instance, in *David Copperfield*, Joe Gargery in *Great Expectations*.

But the truly great achievements of fictional goodness are characters like Hardy's Mayor of Casterbridge, or, especially, Hugo's Jean Valjean, whose motives and history make them riven and shadowed figures. The goodness that emerges is all the more believable for being scarred and rough. Can anyone preach the Bible's Peter or Paul without a broad background understanding of what it is to be a man with a past?

But the rare and special moments of goodness portrayal in fiction, so far as the preacher is concerned, are the great moments of grace. Flannery O'Connor's characters, for instance, often have the surprising, offbeat, upside-down features of divine grace. But surely one of the peak moments of grace in contemporary fiction is the end of Steinbeck's *The Grapes of Wrath*. No preacher of compassion can be without it. Rose of Sharon labors in a boxcar, and finally delivers a baby that never draws breath. She and what's left of the Joad family huddle in a barn, needing shelter from the relentless rain and mud.

They discover they are not alone. A man of about fifty and his son are already lying in the barn — the man too weak to take solid food and his son desperately afraid his dad is going to die. The son offers a comforter to Rose of Sharon, who is drenched and shivering. Something then passes between Ma Joad's eyes and Rose of Sharon's. At the very end of the novel, Rose of Sharon makes her way over to the corner where the stranger is lying. She had been a superficial daughter of the gracious and complex Ma Joad. But now, with compassion like that of God, she bares her breast to a dying man who can be saved only by the milk of her kindness.

A program of general reading deepens preaching because it deepens the preacher. It gives the preacher more to be a preacher *with*, and more to be a Christian with. And so, preachers facing those Sundays that keep coming at them attend to their program of reading. They're taking any help they can get.

Charles Hodge as a Public Theologian

John Stewart

Beginning with its founding in 1812 and continuing through several generations, Princeton Theological Seminary housed a thoroughbred line of Reformed theologians usually called the "Old School Presbyterians." During America's antebellum era, Princeton-based Presbyterians such as Archibald Alexander, Samuel Miller, and Charles Hodge were widely read and quoted. Their piety was, of course, deeply personal and unabashedly traditional. They were unimpressed with the avant-garde initiatives that abounded in America's diverse religious communities. Yet, without neglecting a "faith seeking understanding," their Reformed faith was also — and inextricably — social. Over most of the middle decades of the nineteenth century, they endeavored to persuade American churches, especially Presbyterian ones, to engage and influence the societal agendas that preoccupied American citizens. In this sense, it is not inappropriate to refer to them as *public* theologians, and Charles Hodge, as we shall see, was the most outspoken and controversial *public* theologian among these founders.[1] After a disquieting hiatus during the latter decades of the nineteenth century, strands of the ear-

---

1. Throughout this essay I use the terms "public theologian" and "public church" as defined in Martin Marty's *Public Church* (New York: Crossroad, 1981). He writes that "The *public church*, then, is a specifically Christian polity and witness. . . . [It] has little to do with 'saving faith' which refers to the ways in which a person is finally grounded in or reconciled to God. It has to do with 'ordering faith' which helps constitute civil, social and political life from a theological point of view" (16-17). This term receives fuller expression in *New Dimensions in American Religious History*, ed. James P. Dolan and James P. Wind (Grand Rapids: Wm. B. Eerdmans, 1993).

lier *public* theology of the older Princeton Theology re-emerged in the first half of the twentieth century. Led by scholars such as John A. Mackay, James McCord, George Hendry, Paul Lehmann, and Edward A. Dowey, the newer Princeton theologians vigorously engaged most of the controversial public issues in American society, culture, and politics. Many though not all of these scholars' public opinions can be found in the seminary's journal, *Theology Today*. Most were deeply influenced by Karl Barth, himself a public theologian who engaged mid-twentieth-century social and political issues with theological acumen and often at personal risk.

It is not insignificant that Daniel L. Migliore, a contemporary Princeton theologian and an authority on the works of Karl Barth, was promoted in 1998 to the seminary's most prestigious endowed chair in theology, the Charles Hodge Professor of Systematic Theology. In four decades of teaching and writing, Professor Migliore's numerous publications attest not only to his contributions as an advocate of Reformed systematic theology but also as a devoted *public* theologian in service of a publicly engaged Church. His chapter entitled "Christian Hope" in his widely used textbook, *Faith Seeking Understanding*, especially demonstrates his advocacy of a *public* theology. His recent, penetrating book *The Power of God and the Gods of Power* is only one of his many critiques of the political and cultural issues in American society. While striving for clarity and exhibiting an irenic understanding of the Christian faith, he has campaigned for greater justice for the oppressed and a hope-filled *shalom* for all. In this sense, Professor Migliore stands squarely within the lineage of Charles Hodge.[2]

It is not accidental that Princeton Theological Seminary reserves its most honored chair for the successors of Charles Hodge (1797-1878).[3] Hodge set exceedingly high standards for Protestant theological discourse, and, at the same time, he was passionate about social and political issues during the middle decades of America's turbulent nineteenth century. This essay, however, carries a specified and narrower focus. I want only to establish the underappreciated fact that Hodge was a *public* theologian deeply embedded in America's ways of life. More than a systematician of Christian theology, Hodge rarely separated his personal faith, his appropriation of biblical man-

2. Daniel L. Migliore, *Faith Seeking Understanding: An Introduction to Christian Theology*, 2nd ed. (Grand Rapids: Wm. B. Eerdmans, 2004), and idem, *The Power of God and the Gods of Power* (Grand Rapids: Wm. B. Eerdmans, 2008).

3. The indispensable source for the life and thought of Charles Hodge is to be found in Archibald Alexander Hodge, *Life of Charles Hodge* (New York: Charles Scribner, 1880). This sole biography of Hodge was written by his son and is hereafter designated as *LCH*.

dates, the Reformed expressions of the Christian faith, or his critiques of controversial issues in America's antebellum society and culture. Further, Hodge thought the Church exhibited in Presbyterian communities was to be "the provisional expression of the Kingdom of God." Such theological premises inevitably required his wading into the ambiguities and messiness of American society and politics. During a professional lifetime of fifty years, Hodge, contrary to popular estimates, did change his mind and alter opinions he had stoutly defended earlier.

A Necessary Interlude: Charles Hodge and American Historiography[4]

There are reasons why Charles Hodge, until the last decade or so, has been subjected to dour estimates by Protestant theologians and historians of American culture. He has been (and still is) dismissed for multiple reasons: for seeking to repristinate a rigid scholasticism of the seventeenth century; for refusing to adopt a historically driven hermeneutic for biblical interpretation; and for leading a schismatic movement in American Presbyterianism during the antebellum period known as "Old School Presbyterianism." A more serious scholarly opinion has degraded Hodge as the intellectual primogenitor of American fundamentalism of the twentieth century. These tired interpretations can be followed elsewhere.[5] They are, however, inadequate because of their wholesale neglect of Hodge's voluminous essays (some 140 of them!) in the journal he edited for over forty years, known as *The Biblical Repertory and Princeton Review* (hereafter,

---

4. Throughout this essay, I am indebted to a group of scholars who contributed essays in John W. Stewart and James H. Moorhead, eds., *Charles Hodge Revisited: A Critical Appraisal of His Life and Word* (Grand Rapids: Wm. B. Eerdmans, 1997). Hereafter cited as *Hodge Revisited*.

5. For a brief introduction to the literature about Hodge, see John Stewart, *Mediating the Center: Charles Hodge on American Science, Language, Literature and Politics* (Princeton, NJ: Princeton Theological Seminary, 1995), 1-7. For a general survey of American evangelicalism, see Leonard Sweet, ed., *The Evangelical Tradition in America* (Macon, GA: Mercer University Press, 1984). The linkage of Hodge and later fundamentalism was noted in the 1970s in Ernest Sandeen, *The Roots of Fundamentalism* (Chicago: University of Chicago Press, 1970). For a more recent treatment, see George Marsden, *Fundamentalism and American Culture*, 2nd ed. (New York: Oxford University Press, 2006). Even the ubiquitous "Wikipedia" says that "fundamentalism started among the conservative Presbyterian academics at Princeton Theological Seminary. . . ."

BRPR) or, later, as the *Princeton Review*.[6] Scholars get only a truncated Hodge if they only consult his late-in-life, methodologically wooden, three-volume *Systematic Theology* (1871-72) or his famed pamphlet (1874) that reduced Darwinism to atheism.

Hodge was a special kind of an American apologete for a certain kind of Christian faith. His orthodox Presbyterian upbringing (by the age of 16 he had memorized the Westminster Shorter Catechism in Latin) and a life-long theological commitment to an Augustinian-Reformed expression of the Christian faith, made him allergic to Enlightenment rationalities (he called them "neologies") as well as the many formulations of American mysticisms. Wedded to a genre of Scottish common sense philosophy and a fierce opponent of Immanuel Kant, he was no promoter of what William Hutchison has called the "modernist impulse in American Protestantism."[7] His several critiques of American Transcendentalism were severe and uncompromising. However, Hodge's frequent involvements and lucid analyses of American political and social movements are much the equivalents of his better known contributions in biblical, theological, and ecclesiological discourses.[8] To better understand Hodge as a *public* theologian, only one case study will be considered here, namely, his prolific commentaries on the socio-political issues that led up to America's tragic Civil War (1861-1865).[9]

---

6. Hodge's entire journal has been placed online in the University of Michigan's "Making of America" series. It can be accessed through http://moa.umdl.umich.edu and includes a helpful "search engine." It was one of twelve journals selected to demonstrate America's nineteenth-century cultural heritage. The contemporary seminary journal, *Theology Today,* mentioned above, is the successor to the *BRPR*.

7. See William R. Hutchison, *The Modernist Impulse in American Protestantism* (Durham, NC: Duke University Press, 1992), 2-9. On the floor of the Presbyterians' General Assembly in 1865, the New School theologian W. G. T. Shedd remarked that "Dr. Hodge has done more for Calvinism than any other man in this country." A century later, a similar opinion was offered by the distinguished Yale University historian Sydney Ahlstrom.

8. It must not be glossed over that, beginning with his professorial appointment to the seminary in 1822 until his retirement in 1872, Hodge was a productive biblical scholar (four New Testament commentaries), church leader (moderator of two General Assemblies), the author of an immensely popular introduction to the Christian faith (*The Way of Life,* 1935), the major contributor to the journal that he edited for over forty years, and a professor for over 3,000 students.

9. The literature about America's "irrepressible conflict," the Civil War, fills libraries. For a narrative of the events behind Hodge's concerns, see the magisterial book by James McPherson, *The Battle Cry of Freedom* (New York: Oxford University Press, 1988). Excellent explanations of Hodge's theological milieu can be found in Mark Noll, *America's God: From Jonathan Edwards to Abraham Lincoln* (New York: Oxford University Press, 2002), and

Charles Hodge and His Public Theology

After his return from two years of study in Germany in 1828, Hodge reconfigured the journal he had started earlier in 1825 and gave it a new name, the *Biblical Repertory and Princeton Review*. His *initial* purpose was to alert American audiences to the rising tide of biblical and theological scholarship in Germany and England. Intricate works of radical higher or historical biblical criticism were summarized and then countermanded, often with other Continental and British biblical scholars. By the early 1830s, however, Hodge, without abandoning his original purpose, began to include reviews of a wider American political discourse. Ever the advocate of a theology in service of the Church, articles about social and political issues perplexing American denominations appeared more regularly. Among the earliest issues receiving comment were the Temperance movement (1830 and 1831), an essay entitled "The Advancement of Society" (1831), Sabbath keeping as a civil responsibility (1832), and an essay on the history and future of the African Colonization Society (1833).

During the mid 1830s the *BRPR* took a decided turn. The nation's controversies over slavery, that "peculiar institution" in America, began to consume the attention of a wide spectrum of American cultural and political leaders. Earlier efforts to return African-Americans to their African homelands (a movement that captured the attention and money of Hodge's colleagues, Archibald Alexander and Samuel Miller) had petered out. The famed Virginia legislature debates concluded with the notion that slavery was no longer a necessary evil but a positive good, especially for the black slave and American society. At the same time, abolitionists' initiatives, both North and South, demanded immediate emancipation for Americanized slaves. The same decade witnessed a series of governmental compromises and boundary distinctions that tried to limit the extension of slavery westward. In 1832, President Andrew Jackson's decision to send troops to Charleston's harbor to collect federal tariffs intensified the growing chasm between North and South. This incident, known as the "Nullification Controversy," has been called the "Prelude to the Civil War." This provocative intrusion drew Hodge's comment and analysis. Hodge never disguised his dislike for the Democrat Andrew Jackson; nevertheless, he publicly supported Jackson's bold and controversial intervention.

E. Brooks Holifield, *Theology in America: Christian Thought from the Age of the Puritans to the Civil War* (New Haven, CT: Yale University Press, 2003).

By the middle of the decade, Presbyterians in general and the Princeton theologians in particular were irreversibly drawn into the growing dilemma and conflict over slavery and its expansion westward. For Hodge, May of 1835 emerged as a pivotal moment. He was apparently surprised by a politically charged confrontation in that year's General Assembly of Presbyterians meeting in New York City. A group of influential Northern Presbyterian leaders pushed through a resolution that required the Presbyterians not only to go on record as opposing slavery and calling it a "heinous sin," but also to exclude from the Lord's Table all slaveholders and advocates of slavery.[10] Hodge's reaction appeared the following year (1836). His article "Slavery" was published in the April issue of the *BRPR*. It was clearly designed to influence the upcoming debates in the 1836 Assembly in May. This article solidified his place as a Reformed theologian increasingly embedded in American antebellum politics. Nearly fifty pages in length, this article circulated widely in both the North and South and generated heated controversies.[11] Without tracing every intricate argument, three sections are instructive for this essay. First, after assailing the demands of radical or immediate abolitionists and,

10. For Hodge's account of this Assembly, see "General Assembly," *BRPR* 7 (1835): 450-452. This 1835 report of the General Assembly was the first of what would become an annual practice of critiquing the actions of Presbyterian Assemblies. With one exception, Hodge produced his analysis every year through 1867. As Mark Noll notes, one of Hodge's associates wrote later that "there was no inducement to prepare a good article [about a General Assembly] in the July Review, because every one turns at once to that on the General Assembly which absorbs all interests." This quote is from Mark Noll, *The Princeton Theology, 1812-1921* (Grand Rapids: Baker Book House, 1983), 4.

11. Charles Hodge, "Slavery," *BRPR* 8 (1836): 268-305. This essay has been the source of extended and continuous comment and analyses. Shorn of two paragraphs where Hodge called for gradual emancipation of slaves, it was reprinted in 1860 in a famous pro-slavery compendium entitled *Cotton as King*. An analysis of this legendary book and Hodge's contribution to it can be found in Larry Tice, *Proslavery: A History of the Defense of Slavery* (Athens, GA: The University of Georgia Press, 1987). For the evolution of Hodge's views on slavery, see David Murchie, "From Slaveholder to American Abolitionist: Charles Hodge and the Slavery Issue," in *Christian Freedom: Essays in Honor of Vernon G. Grounds*, ed. K. W. M. Wozniak and S. J. Grentz (Lanham, MD: University Press of America, 1986), 127-152. Another and different appraisal of Hodge and slavery can be found in Allen Guelzo, "Charles Hodge's Antislavery Moment," in *Hodge Revisited*, pp. 299-326. A more recent and balanced appraisal of Hodge's views on slavery can be found in David Torbett, *Theology and Slavery: Charles Hodge and Horace Bushnell* (Macon, GA: Mercer University Press, 2006). As many have noted, Hodge himself held slaves in his own household. To the best of my information, Hodge never offered a public explanation about this Princeton practice. Torbett's book offers one analysis based on very limited extant sources.

apparently, advocating a gradual emancipation, Hodge squarely acknowledged that "The subject of slavery is no longer one on which men are allowed to be of one mind. The question is brought up before our public bodies, civil and religious. Almost every ecclesiastical society has been in some way called to express an opinion of this subject. . . ." Second, with the earlier Assembly in mind and after a review of historical and biblical precedents, Hodge wrote that "slaveholding is not necessarily sinful." The implication *and* context are clear: Presbyterians could not excommunicate members over an issue where the Bible is ambiguous. Third, "the opinion that slaveholding is itself a crime, must [will] operate to produce the disunion of the states, and the division of all ecclesiastical societies in this country."[12] During the next four decades, these 1836 pronouncements stalked and haunted him.[13] By the late 1840s, he was revising each of them.

Hodge wrote several more articles about slavery, each of which gradually liberalized his 1836 views. In his 1849 article "Emancipation" he maintained that his Old School Presbyterians "have been the truest friends of slaves and the most effectual advocation of emancipation."[14] One can trace the evolution of Hodge's views elsewhere, and further exegeting is beyond the primary intent of this essay. What is beyond denial, however, is this: Charles Hodge, a stout defender of biblical infallibility and God's sovereignty in all human affairs, was, by the mid 1830s, deeply embroiled in the nation's most pressing social and political controversy, slavery.

In succeeding volumes of the *BRPR*, Hodge and colleagues addressed — as theologians — a widening range of America's political issues and social controversies. Richard J. Carwardine, in a carefully crafted book, *Evangelicals and Politics in Antebellum America,* has traced Hodge's affinity with American Whiggery, his views on Southern aggression in Kansas, his defense of Unionism, and his rebukes of Southern discontents. Carwardine's work provides an indispensable background for Hodge's public endorsement of Abraham Lincoln's political platform, candidacy, and presidency.[15] As a po-

12. Hodge, "Slavery," 273, 277, 301.

13. His article seems to have carried weight especially among the conservative Presbyterians from the Northern states. The 1836 General Assembly, after debating the resolutions of the previous year, voted (150 to 94) "that this whole subject [slavery] be indefinitely postponed."

14. Hodge, "Emancipation," *BRPR* 21 (1849): 585.

15. Richard J. Carwardine, *Evangelicals and Politics in Antebellum America* (New Haven: Yale University Press, 1993). I am indebted to Professor Carwardine's nuanced appraisal of Hodge's political views.

litical commentator and critic, Hodge reached his zenith in the 1860s. On April 12, 1861, "this mighty scourge," as Lincoln described the Civil War, came upon Hodge's nation and Church.

Charles Hodge on America's Civil War[16]

American historians write continually about the "war that never goes away." That war, and the issues leading to it in the late 1850s, never went away in Hodge's mind and heart either. He authored a series of controversial articles that agonized over the "irrepressible conflict," as the war would be called.[17]

In the spring of 1859, after attending the General Assembly in Rochester, New York, Hodge wrote to his brother, Hugh Hodge (a professor of women's medicine at the University of Pennsylvania), that "North and South [Presbyterians] mingled without a jar."[18] Within a year's time, that presumed amiability disintegrated. In the January 1861 issue of the *BRPR*, Hodge penned an uncharacteristically harsh appraisal of the "Thanksgiving Sermon" preached earlier by the Rev. Benjamin M. Palmer of New Orleans. Palmer, who had been offered in 1860 the chair of Pastoral Theology and Rhetoric at Princeton Seminary, eventually became the first moderator of the Presbyterian Church of the Confederate States of America. Palmer's sermon spelled out the Southern case for secession: abolitionism in the North was equated with the excesses of the French Revolution and a growing atheism in American society required the South to preserve divine truth. More importantly, Palmer claimed the South had a moral obligation to preserve its way of life.[19] Palmer had argued that all governments possess stewardship — "a providential trust" — to preserve a people's culture and societal norms. Hodge was appalled. He reprinted Palmer's words at some length, including

16. In this section I have relied on a much longer interpretation of Hodge's views about the Civil War that can be found in my monograph, *Mediating the Center: Charles Hodge on American Science, Language, Literature and Politics* (Princeton, NJ: Princeton Theological Seminary, 1995). I have quoted very liberally from the book in this essay.

17. For a survey on these articles, and their attending controversies, see *LCH*, 333-336.

18. *LCH*, 445. Later, his biographer provides background details of how Hodge became embroiled in three irrepressible issues facing the Presbyterian church in the 1860s. The second issue was "The relation of the Church to political questions." See *LCH*, 460.

19. This sermon was printed in pamphlet form and widely circulated. A contemporary historian claimed that Palmer had done more than "any other non-combatant in the South to promote rebellion." For further comment about Palmer, see E. T. Thompson, *Presbyterians in the South*, 3 vols. (Richmond, VA: John Knox Press, 1963, 1973), 1:556-558.

these: "what, at this juncture, [asks Palmer] is their [the South's] providential trust? I answer, that it is *to conserve and perpetuate the institution of domestic slavery as now existing.*" That fiduciary responsibility, Palmer concluded, was a "duty *to ourselves, to our slaves, to our world, and to Almighty God.*" Hodge found Palmer's sense of duty odious.

> It propounds a theory suited to an emergency. It proposes a doctrine which reconciles men's wishes with their conscience. It teaches a privileged class that it is their high duty to be lords and masters. . . . It is a monstrous perversion of the nature of the trust confided to them. [The] great and noble trust committed to Southern slaveholders is not to perpetuate slavery, but to promote the intellectual, moral, religious and social culture and the elevation of four millions of Africans entrusted to them. [The sermon] is a fearful shock to the public mind. It has alarmed the North, as though a gulf which neither civil nor religious institutions can span.[20]

Equally abrasive was Hodge's widely circulated article, "The State of the Country."[21] Composed *before* South Carolina's secession (December 20, 1860), it was published in the January 1861 issue of the *BRPR after* that secession.[22] Nothing Charles Hodge ever wrote provoked such volatile responses. Hodge insisted that he intended his article to be moderate and conciliatory, an intention he later remarked was unrealistic. In it, he argued that the concept of "nation" was historically valid and perpetually inviolate;[23] that the concept of "state sovereignty" was at odds with the idea of the framers of the Constitution; that the South misinterpreted the North's endorsement of radical abolitionists; that many in the North, like himself, acknowledged that the South had legitimate grievances; that secession was unwise as well as immoral; and that the nation's role as a "city on the hill," as well as the witness of the Christian Church, was jeopardized by the threat of secession.

20. Hodge, "Short Notices," *BRPR* 33 (1861): 169-171.

21. Hodge, "State of the Country," *BRPR* 33 (1861): 1-36. This article was quickly published as a pamphlet and sold in the thousands according to Hodge's biographer.

22. The literature about the causes and circumstances of the South's secession is vast. I have relied on James M. McPherson's magisterial narrative, *The Battle Cry of Freedom* (New York: Oxford University Press, 1988). His research provides a useful and necessary background for Hodge's essays in the 1860s. See especially chapter 8, "The Counterrevolution of 1861."

23. To contextualize Hodge's concerns about the "perpetuity" of the Union, see Kenneth Stampp, *The Imperiled Union* (New York: Oxford University Press, 1980), especially the opening essay, "The Concept of a Perpetual Union," 3-36.

"The destruction of the life of a nation is a thousand times worse than suicide; for it is not merely self-destruction, but the destruction of posterity. Our national life we have received from fathers, we hold in trust, and are bound to transmit it to future generations." As an afterthought, he quickly added that the government should compensate Southerners for all fugitive slaves and that the Missouri Compromise should be reestablished as the dividing line between slave and free states.

Hodge, by temperament a mediator, was not prepared for the acrimonious, *ad hominem* fury that his article generated.[24] In March, the Atlanta newspaper *Constitutionist* (March 1861) called Hodge a traitor to the American tradition, a "mouthpiece of the Republicans," and a naïve theologian out of touch with political realities. The *Southern Presbyterian* (April 1861) called the article "unfair, one-sided and a lamentable attack upon the South." The most notable Southern Reformed theologian and friend of Hodge, James H. Thornwell, wrote scornfully in the *Southern Presbyterian Review,* "What rational man ever thought that it is immoral to hold in involuntary servitude anyone who is, by his own mental state, unfit for freedom."[25]

With war declared (April 12, 1861), Hodge's *BRPR* published in that same year three more politicized articles: "The Church and Country," "The Kingdom of Christ," and "American Nationality." Stunned by the enormity of the South's secession, a writer (presumably Hodge) lamented in the July 1861 issue, "And oh, what was it [the war] but a ghastly hallucination which could lead them [i.e., the Southerners] to commit wholesale robbery, perjury, and treason verily thinking they were doing God's service?"

In the history of American Presbyterianism, no General Assembly can equal the one that met in Philadelphia in May of 1861. For drama and long-range consequences, it is without peer. By the time the Assembly adjourned, all the Southern states had withdrawn from the Union except Tennessee and

24. As late as 1871, Hodge wrote that this 1861 article "was received in the South, to our surprise, with universal condemnation, expressed in terms of unmeasured severity. In the North, it was pronounced as moderate, fair and reasonable, except by the Abolitionists, who rivaled their Southern brethren in their denunciations." Hodge, "Retrospect of the History of the Princeton Review," in *Index Volume of the Biblical Repertory and Princeton Review* (Philadelphia: Peter Walker, 1871), 32.

25. This Hodge-Thornwell exchange can be found in Hodge's article, "Church and Country," *BRPR* 33 (1861): 343-344. The distinguished historian of American slavery E. Genovese commented that "Hodge and his compatriots looked like ultra-conservatives in Princeton in the North but looked like liberal temporizers in Columbia, South Carolina and the South." See his *The Southern Front: History and Politics in the Cultural War* (Columbia: University of Missouri, 1995), 87.

North Carolina. Hodge, as a past moderator (1842 and 1846), lobbied all spring long, his biographer says, to head off a North and South split in the Old School Presbyterian Church. Hodge's mediatory efforts, however, were derailed by the volatile resolutions proposed by the Rev. Gardner Spring, pastor of the Brick Presbyterian Church in New York City and a friend of Hodge. The Spring Resolutions required all Presbyterians nationwide to declare allegiance to the Constitution and to the Federal government. The contentious Assembly voted to remand the Resolutions to a committee on which Hodge served. With the Resolutions considerably softened and undercut, the majority of the committee reported out its revised recommendations. However, a minority report endorsed the original wording and intent of the Spring Resolutions and won by a narrow margin. In such an atmosphere, most, if not all, Southern Presbyterians, long suspicious of the Northern churchmen's intentions, vowed to leave the denomination. Disheartened and rejected, Hodge later wrote that he had refused "at the command of an excited multitude to sing the 'Star Spangled Banner' at the Lord's table." In deference to "our Southern brethren," Hodge filed a formal "protest" that went unsupported. In the July issue of the *BRPR* (1861), Hodge wrote a long, but futile, rebuttal. His summary of the 1861 General Assembly reads like a lament.

> Presbyterians were in arms against Presbyterians. . . . The General Assembly was called upon to take sides. . . . Our church was as much divided as the country. It was the case of a mother who was called upon to take part for one child against another. It was in vain she urged that both were her children. . . . God had not made her a judge or divider in such matters. This plea availed nothing. She was in the hands of the more powerful of the two, and speak she must. . . . Those who resisted the action of the Assembly were denounced in the streets as secessionists, as pro-slavery, as trucklers to the South, as traitors to their country. The scourge of public indignation was lifted over their heads.[26]

A year later, the disappointment had not gone away. Hodge analyzed in 1862 the nation's and his church's partition in more caustic language.

> The South has always been as a spoilt child, to which the other members of the family gave up for the sake of peace. . . . If she [the South] loved slavery; she might take what measures she saw fit to cherish and perpetu-

---

26. Hodge, "The General Assembly," *BRPR* 32 (1861): 542-544.

ate it. But when she demanded, as a condition of her continuance in the Union, that the nation, as a nation, should love it, should legalize it, and extend it; that every territory . . . should be a slave territory . . . then the reason, heart and consciences of the North said, No![27]

Hodge, the theologian, took keen interest in the progress and stalemates of the war. According to his biographer, Hodge was admitted each spring of the war into the North's military headquarters in Washington, DC, and he summarized his observations and critiques in frequent letters to his physician brother in Philadelphia.[28]

Three essays between 1862 and 1865 are too noteworthy to bypass. The first of these was an essay entitled "The War" that appeared in the January 1863 issue of the *BRPR*. In this article, more than any other, Hodge reflected theologically about America's political condition and the unprecedented suffering by citizens North and South. With the nation hemorrhaging and with the unprecedented carnage of the Battle of Antietam (September 1862) in mind, Hodge ventured into theological minefields. Why is such enormous human suffering generated by fellow citizens? Which wars are just and which are not? How do "means and ends" function in political decisions? It is a model of Hodge's reasoning powers, ethical foundations, and political commentary, all of which were couched in the womb of American Reformed theology. This essay in particular has received more recent attention from the Yale University historian Harry S. Stout. In his seminal work, whose subtitle reads "A Moral History of the American Civil War," Stout maintains that Hodge was one of the few, if not the lone, American theologian, North or South, who interpreted the justification of the war in the classical Christian ethical categories of "just cause" *(jus ad bellum)* and "just conduct" *(jus in bellum)*.[29] Only a few of Hodge's arguments are necessary for the purposes of this essay.

Hodge begins the article by observing that "the war which is now desolating our country . . . will modify essentially our political and social institutions. . . . The interests involved in this struggle are so monumental . . . [that] none but the frivolous in this matter be indifferent or neutral. Men must take sides; they must speak out. Silence is impossible." Following this introduction, Hodge, the Reformed theologian, addressed the perplexing issue of

27. Hodge, "England and America," *BRPR* 35 (1863): 19.
28. Many of Hodge's letters written while in Washington are reprinted in *LCH,* 471-481.
29. Harry S. Stout, *Upon the Altar of the Nation: A Moral History of the American Civil War* (New York: Viking Press, 2006).

the sovereignty of God that mingled with the magnitude of human suffering brought on by political turmoil.

Secondly, across the American landscape, preachers, journalists, and politicians sought a more transcendent meaning for the war's tragedy by weighing theological conundrums like divine punishment, unpredictable interventions and battlefield victories, and God's absence or strange blessings. In four pages, Hodge wrestles with those weighty issues and, in the end, finds them mostly insoluble.

> We are not to take for granted that God is against us. We are not to assume, even that should the rebellion be successful, that God approves the cause of the Confederates, that he favours the perpetuity and extension of slavery; or that he condemns the efforts of the [Federal] government to preserve our national life and institutions. . . . Do not the Scriptures and all experiences teach us that God is sovereign, that the orderings of his providence are not determined by justice, but by mysterious wisdom for the accomplishment of higher ends than mere punishment and reward? We are in His hand, and we are to lean on His will and our duty, not from adverse or prosperous dispensations of providence, but from His holy Word.

Next, Hodge argued that, according to "the great principle of the [Christian] moral law, the will of God, however revealed, binds nations as well as individuals." In that light, Hodge deplored the justification of war as a matter of mere political or social expediency. "[A]ccording to the scheme of ethics which for many years has been practiced in Europe and America, there is no higher principle of [their] action than expediency. . . . Expediency, so far as moral questions are concerned, is not only a wrong rule of action, but one which can lead neither to certainty nor unanimity of judgment." Within this more encompassing proposition, Hodge discussed the necessities and limitations of a war's means and ends. "War is a tremendous evil. It is no slight matter for parents to give up their children to death. The government which calls for this great sacrifice must make a case of necessity. There must be a moral obligation to make war, or war itself is a crime. . . . The end that sanctifies the means, is the motto of fanaticism."[30] In the wake of this proposition, Hodge concluded the abolition of slavery was *not ini-*

---

30. While considering this article, this author has pondered more than once how Charles Hodge might have "spoken to power" about the justification of the American invasion of Iraq in this twenty-first century.

tially a "just cause" for going to war. Only the preservation of the Union provided a "just cause" for warring. However, as the awful war progressed, Lincoln determined that the emancipation of slaves (January 1863) was inseparable from the initial reason for going to war. In the end, Hodge endorsed Lincoln's reasoning: going to war was justified to save the Union and the emancipation of slaves was necessary and justified for the greater end of preserving the Union.

Finally, in keeping with classical "just war" theory, Hodge argued that only combatants were morally authorized to wage war. "[It] is one of the humane regulations of modern warfare that private property is entitled to protection. . . . What we hold, however, to be immoral and demoralizing is the doctrine that private property is a lawful prize of war. Indiscriminate plunder, or wholesale confiscation . . . we believe to be contrary to the law of God and the usages of civilized society. . . . Here, again, we think that federal authorities are entitled to great condemnation." Hodge, apparently, had already by 1863 come to the sober judgment of later historians who have called America's Civil War Western civilization's first "total war."[31] No article of Hodge's better clarifies his commitment to a theology in service of the public than this lengthy essay "War," but one other essay in the *BRPR* requires mentioning.

Hodge had voted twice for Lincoln and had been an admirer of Lincoln and an advocate for his war policies.[32] When the news reached Princeton of Lincoln's assassination on April 14, 1865 (a Good Friday), Hodge, according to the student who brought the news, was "convulsed in his entire nature when I told him the facts of the case. With quivering lips, a face as paled as death, he said 'O it cannot be, it cannot be!' When I read him Secretary Stanton's dispatch, Dr. Hodge burst in a flood of tears." Later that day, when the seminary community assembled in Miller Chapel, Hodge was asked to pray. "The petitions began with a sob, and ended with a sob, the great heart seemed to break with the weight that was upon it."[33]

In July of 1865, Hodge published his last formal comments about the war in an article entitled "President Lincoln."[34] It was a carefully crafted

31. For whatever reasons, Hodge never publicly acknowledged that General David Hunter, his brother-in-law by a second marriage, was severely reprimanded by Lincoln for Hunter's "scorch the earth" campaign in Virginia's Shenandoah Valley in the spring of 1863.

32. A modest glimpse of Hodge's involvement in Princeton's local politics is followed in William Gillette, *Jersey Blue: Civil War Politics in New Jersey, 1854-1865* (New Brunswick, NJ: Rutgers University Press, 1994), 121, 184, 327

33. For further details of Hodge's reactions to the assassination, see *LCH*, 482-485.

34. Hodge, "President Lincoln," *BRPR* 37 (1865): 435-458.

summary of Hodge's thoughts about the war, its causes, and its perpetrators. Part theology, part politics, and part eulogy, he addressed three issues: his final appraisal of American slavery, his chastisement of Southern church leaders, and his tribute to Lincoln.

In this 1865 Lincoln article, Charles Hodge distanced himself from his earlier 1836 article on slavery. After briefly tracing the history of the role slavery played in a terrible war, Hodge wrote plainly: "It cannot be reasonably doubted that the great design of the authors of the rebellion was the extension and preservation of African Slavery." Each word in this sentence was carefully nuanced: the war was intentionally begun by leaders; it was constitutionally a rebellion, not a "war between states"; it was fueled by economic goals requiring the extension and protection of slavery; and it was a slavery confined to a particular race. In moral tones harsher than Hodge had ever written before, Hodge denounced American slavery as sinful and those Southern slave laws that "perpetuated slavery [as] unscriptural, immoral and, in the highest degree, cruel and unjust." He censured those slave laws that required "the perpetual degradation of a class of our fellow-men." He then turned up the heat on Southern slaveholders and church leaders.

> There is not one man in a thousand who will not be more or less corrupted by the possession of absolute power, even when that power is legitimate. But when it is illegitimate, and requires for its security the constant exercise of injustice, no community and no human being can escape its demoralizing influence. . . . The moral sense becomes perverted by the necessity of justifying what is wrong, so that we see even good men, men who we must regard as children of God, vindicating what every unprejudiced mind instinctively perceives to be wrong. It is enough to humble the whole Christian world to hear our Presbyterian brethren in the South declaring that the great mission of the Southern church was to conserve the system of African slavery. Since the death of Christ, no such dogma stains the record of an ecclesiastical body.[35]

Finally, Hodge reflected poignantly on Lincoln's presidency. "When Mr. Lincoln died, the nation felt herself widowed," he wrote. "She rent her garments, she sat in the dust, put ashes on her head, and refused to be comforted." Calling the assassination "a most mysterious event," Hodge tried to salvage some meaning or deeper purpose. But he could not. "What are we, that we should pretend to understand the Almighty unto perfection, or that

35. Hodge, "Lincoln," 438-439.

we should assume to trace the ways of him whose footsteps are in the great deep . . . ? It makes us feel our own ignorance and impotency."[36] By Hodge's estimate, Lincoln excelled in several ways. Hodge admired the quality of Lincoln's character and, with some eloquence, said why.

> None but pedants can look on Mr. Lincoln as an uneducated man. He had a culture a thousand times more effective than that usually effected in the schools of learning. He was remarkably sagacious; perceiving intuitively the truth, presenting it clearly. . . . Some of his state papers and public letters are masterly. . . . [But] the crowning trait of his character was tenderness of heart; it was this more than his talents, position or services that endeared him to the people. . . . It was made a complaint against him by sterner men, that he often stood in the way of justice. . . . God poured on his head the excellent oil of mercy, and its fragrance fills the land.[37]

Such comments reveal as much about Hodge's values as they do about Lincoln.

Again, Hodge tried to analyze the source of Lincoln's "public service," noting that few statesmen anywhere had such a "Herculean task" of governing during a national crisis. Hodge suggested that Lincoln's leadership rested on two characteristics: he exhibited a political style that kept him from being "wedded to one idea, or to any abstract principle. If one plan would not do, he would try another . . . but what was *best* he did not attempt to decide beforehand." The other characteristic that Hodge admired was Lincoln's "spirit of conciliation."[38] Compared to contemporary analyses of Lincoln's pragmatic political theory, Hodge's analysis was not far off the mark.[39]

36. Hodge, "Lincoln," 444-445.
37. Hodge, "Lincoln," 446-447.
38. Hodge, "Lincoln," 449. In the same essay Hodge wrote: "Another prominent feature of Mr. Lincoln's administration was a spirit of conciliation. From first to last, he endeavored to persuade the revolted States to return to their allegiance, in order to save them from the miseries of war. And in the process of reconstruction, his ruling idea was to disturb as little as possible existing relations, to inflict as few penalties as possible, and to restore all rights and privileges as fully and as rapidly as was consistent with public safety" (ibid., 450). Hodge was making reference here to Lincoln's early (December 1863) plans for post-war "amnesty and reconstruction." Lincoln's veto of the Wade-Davis Bill (July 1864) that demanded an "iron-clad" oath of allegiance prior to reconciliation was, according to Lincoln, vindictive and unworkable.
39. Several essays in John L. Thomas, ed., *Abraham Lincoln and the American Political Tradition* (Amherst, MA: University of Massachusetts Press, 1986) suggest that Hodge was not far off the mark when compared to later opinions.

Finally, Hodge commented admiringly on Lincoln's handling of the slavery issue. Hodge's citation of Lincoln's views about the "unity of mankind" must have resonated with Hodge's earlier skirmishes with those American scientists who accounted for human diversities by theories of polygenesis or multiple origins. "It was," Hodge insisted, "the great scriptural truth of the unity of the human race as to origin and species, which lay the foundation for all President Lincoln's opinions and policy in regard to slavery." Hodge pressed on. Since all persons are the children of Adam and made of one blood and possessing the same nature,

> therefore are all entitled to be regarded and treated as men. No symptom of permanent slavery can be justified, except on the assumption that the enslaved class are a different and inferior race. . . . He [Lincoln] held that every man fit to be free was entitled to be free; that every man able to manage property had the right to hold property; that every man capable of discharging the duties of a father is entitled to the custody of his children. From this it would follow, by parity of reason, that every man who has the intelligence and moral character to the proper exercise of the elective franchise [i.e. the right to vote] is entitled to enjoy it, if compatible with the public good. In other words, these rights and privileges cannot justly be made dependent on the colour of the skin or any other adventitious difference.[40]

Hodge concluded this sustained commentary of the Civil War era with a prayer that "the Spirit which was on him [Lincoln] who led us through the wilderness, may be given in double measure to him [President Andrew Johnson] whose office it is to give the nation rest."

In the years following his tribute to Lincoln in 1865, Hodge's public theology went into hibernation. He resigned, after forty years, as editor of the *BRPR* and turned to intramural theological topics that included: a revision of his commentary on the book of Romans; an unsuccessful effort to prevent the reunion of Old and New School Presbyterians; and an increased involvement with ecumenical efforts in the Reconstruction era. He also began gathering past and new material for his upcoming summary of a Reformed systematic theology, a project that would require three thick volumes. In contrast to his earlier public concerns in the *BRPR*, Hodge wrote but one piece as a public theologian after 1865. In an article in 1871 entitled "Preach-

---

40. Hodge, "Lincoln," 456-457. These estimates of Lincoln by Hodge can be put in perspective if read in conjunction with Merrill D. Peterson's *Lincoln in American Memory* (New York: Oxford University Press, 1994).

ing the Gospel to the Poor," Hodge lamented, "It is with great reluctance that we are constrained to acknowledge that the Presbyterian Church in this country is not the church for the poor."[41] Finally, beginning in 1871, his *magnum opus, Systematic Theology,* appeared. With one small exception, there is not one paragraph on slavery, the Civil War, or political institutions. By the 1870s, this public theologian had apparently given up on a Reformed theologian's obligation to enter the public domain of politics and societal practices.

So the question remains: Why did Hodge abandon his earlier eagerness to engage public issues? One possible clue is that Hodge was too wearied and too rejected to continue to "speak to power." According to his son and biographer, Hodge suffered deeply as the war waged on. "As he grew older, his general nerve force grew less and less capable of resisting depressing influence. He wept easily, and often against his will. He was exhausted by the effort involved in public speaking and by all draughts upon his emotions." He openly wept in his seminary classes and wrote to his brother about his inability to sleep. Recounting the emotional toll the war and polemical confrontations had taken, he concluded in a letter to his physician brother, "All this is, I suppose, what you would call nervous." For therapy, he retired more frequently to his farm on the nearby Millstone River. Added together, these symptoms are the tell-tale signs of exhaustion and depression.[42]

Quite plausibly, another answer lies beneath Hodge's retreat as a public theologian. Recently, antebellum theologians, including Hodge, have come under closer scrutiny. Mark Noll, a distinguished historian of American Protestantism and recognized authority on the Princeton theology of the nineteenth century, has examined the theologizing about war in his *The Civil War as a Theological Crisis.*[43] Noll sought to clarify two questions: first, how was the Civil War interpreted as a theological event? And, secondly, what did the American experience of the Civil War contribute to American theology more generally? Noll proposes two interlocking answers. One was the deepening rigidity of antebellum theologians: "Despite the conflict's horrific character and the way it [the Civil War] touched personally many of America's greatest religious thinkers, the conflict seems to have pushed theologians down the roads on which they were already traveling rather than

41. Hodge, "Preaching the Gospel to the Poor," *BRPR* 43 (1871): 87.

42. See *LCH,* chapter 11.

43. Mark A. Noll, *The Civil War as a Theological Crisis* (Chapel Hill, NC: University of North Carolina Press, 2006).

compelling them to go in new, creative directions."[44] With fixed habits of mind and solid state convictions, Presbyterian theologians in both North and South had become as polarized as their nation's political leaders and devoid of any outside authority to reconcile their disparities. Elite theologians as well as pastors, North and South, regularly assured their populations that their providential God could be counted on to bless their partisan efforts. As the horrors of the war became more and more public, that assurance of divine providence wore thin. Hodge admits as much in his 1863 essay "War."

A second answer to Noll's inquiry revolves around theologians' use of the Bible. It was generally assumed in the antebellum era that the Bible was the unimpeachable resource for determining right and wrong even in social and political arenas. As Lincoln said in his Second Inaugural Address, "Both read the same Bible and pray to the same God; and each invokes His aid against the other." Decades before the war, differing views and debates over the Bible's mandates about slavery as well as God's providential direction over socio-cultural agendas, came to irresolvable impasse. The Bible itself was at the center of this haunting stalemate.

> The country had a problem because its most trusted religious authority, the Bible, was sounding an uncertain note. . . . [Trust] in the Bible was not solving disagreements about what the Bible taught concerning slavery. . . . The supreme crisis over the Bible was that there existed no apparent biblical resolution to the crisis. . . . It was left to those consummate theologians, the Reverend Doctors Ulysses S. Grant and William Tecumseh Sherman, to decide what in fact the Bible actually meant.[45]

To exacerbate political impasses, appeals to the Bible were not sufficient to keep Protestant denominations from splitting along North and South lines.[46] Protestants in general, and the Presbyterians in particular, were as disoriented and divisive as the nation. Northern and Southern ecclesiologies, in a service to regional socio-political views, bypassed or cancelled out each other. The net result of these theological crises, Noll suggests, was that ordinary American citizens and, especially their political leaders, were left with the impression that Protestant theology was of little help in the *realpolitik* of America's most crippling issues. By the last third of the nine-

44. Ibid., 16.
45. Ibid., 30.
46. See especially C. C. Goen, *Broken Churches, Broken Nation* (Macon, GA: Mercer University Press, 1997).

teenth century, Presbyterian-styled Protestantism became increasingly relegated to personal and private domains.[47] William James and other American pragmatists, in the aftermath of the war, proposed another solution to the theological crises the war generated: all religious truth claims were to be measured only by their practicality.[48]

In short, by the time of the publication of his *Systematic Theology* in 1871, Hodge, the *public* theologian, was publicly engaged no longer. He had other issues, less messy ones, to explain.

47. Southern Presbyterians reaffirmed their earlier defended "passivity doctrine" by which their church was to remain aloof from social and political entanglements. Northern Presbyterians turned their attention to sundry Reconstruction voluntary associations, and, generally, remained out of the loop of politics and policies until the turn of the century when the influence of the Social Gospel took hold with many, though not all, denominational leaders.

48. See John P. Diggins, *The Promise of Pragmatism: Modernism and the Crisis of Knowledge and Authority* (Chicago: University of Chicago Press, 1994), esp. 1-21.

Contributors

Kɪᴍʟʏɴ J. Bᴇɴᴅᴇʀ, University of Sioux Falls

Kᴀᴛʜʟᴇᴇɴ D. Bɪʟʟᴍᴀɴ, Lutheran School of Theology at Chicago

Dᴀᴠɪᴅ J. Bʀʏᴀɴᴛ, Eckerd College

Dᴀᴡɴ DᴇVʀɪᴇs, Union Theological Seminary and Presbyterian School of
Christian Education

Dᴀᴠɪᴅ Fᴇʀɢᴜssᴏɴ, University of Edinburgh

Gᴇᴏʀɢᴇ Hᴜɴsɪɴɢᴇʀ, Princeton Theological Seminary

Gʀᴇɢᴏʀʏ Aɴᴅᴇʀsᴏɴ Lᴏᴠᴇ, San Francisco Theological Seminary

Mᴀᴛᴛʜᴇᴡ D. Lᴜɴᴅʙᴇʀɢ, Calvin College

Bʀᴜᴄᴇ L. McCᴏʀᴍᴀᴄᴋ, Princeton Theological Seminary

Jüʀɢᴇɴ Mᴏʟᴛᴍᴀɴɴ, University of Tübingen

Gᴇʀʀɪᴛ Nᴇᴠᴇɴ, Protestant Theological University, Kampen

Gᴇᴏʀɢᴇ Nᴇᴡʟᴀɴᴅs, University of Glasgow

Cᴏʀɴᴇʟɪᴜs Pʟᴀɴᴛɪɴɢᴀ Jʀ., Calvin Theological Seminary

Cʏɴᴛʜɪᴀ L. Rɪɢʙʏ, Austin Presbyterian Theological Seminary

Gᴇʀʜᴀʀᴅ Sᴀᴜᴛᴇʀ, University of Bonn

Contributors

KATHERINE SONDEREGGER, Virginia Theological Seminary

STEPHEN L. STELL, Austin College

JOHN STEWART, Princeton Theological Seminary

THOMAS R. THOMPSON, Calvin College

MICHAEL WELKER, University of Heidelberg